C000170912

Modern
JAPANESE
Grammar

Modern Japanese Grammar: A Practical Guide is an innovative reference guide to Japanese, combining traditional and function-based grammar in a single volume.

The *Grammar* is divided into two parts. Part A covers traditional grammatical categories such as nouns, verbs, adjectives, particles, topics, honorifics, etc. Part B is carefully organized around language functions, covering all major communication situations such as:

- Initiating and ending a conversation
- Seeking and giving factual information
- Expressing gratitude, likes and dislikes
- Making requests and asking for permission and advice.

With a strong emphasis on contemporary usage, all grammar points and functions are richly illustrated throughout with examples written both in romanization and Japanese script (a mixture of **hiragana**, **katakana**, and **kanji**).

Main features of the *Grammar* include:

- Clear, succinct and jargon-free explanations
- Extensive cross-referencing between the different sections
- Emphasis on areas of particular difficulty for learners of Japanese.

Both as a reference grammar and a practical usage manual, *Modern Japanese Grammar: A Practical Guide* is the ideal resource for learners of Japanese at all levels, from beginner to advanced. No prior knowledge of grammatical terminology or Japanese script is required and a glossary of grammatical terms is provided.

This *Grammar* is accompanied by the *Modern Japanese Grammar Workbook* (ISBN 978-0-415-27093-9), which features related exercises and activities.

Naomi H. McGloin is Professor of Japanese Language and Linguistics at the University of Wisconsin-Madison, USA.

Mutsuko Endo Hudson is Professor of Japanese Language and Linguistics at Michigan State University, USA.

Fumiko Nazikian is Senior Lecturer and Director of the Japanese Language Program at Columbia University, USA.

Tomomi Kakegawa is Associate Professor of Japanese at the University of Wisconsin-Eau Claire, USA.

Routledge Modern Grammars

Series concept and development – Sarah Butler

Other books in the series

Modern Mandarin Chinese Grammar
Modern Mandarin Chinese Grammar Workbook

Modern French Grammar, Second Edition
Modern French Grammar Workbook, Second Edition

Modern German Grammar, Second Edition
Modern German Grammar Workbook, Second Edition

Modern Italian Grammar, Third Edition
Modern Italian Grammar Workbook, Second Edition

Modern Brazilian Portuguese Grammar
Modern Brazilian Portuguese Grammar Workbook

Modern Russian Grammar
Modern Russian Grammar Workbook

Modern Spanish Grammar, Third Edition
Modern Spanish Grammar Workbook, Third Edition

Modern JAPANESE Grammar

A Practical Guide

Naomi H. McGloin
Mutsuko Endo Hudson
Fumiko Nazikian
Tomomi Kakegawa

Routledge
Taylor & Francis Group

LONDON AND NEW YORK

First published 2014
by Routledge
2 Park Square, Milton Park, Abingdon, Oxon OX14 4RN

and by Routledge
711 Third Avenue, New York, NY 10017

Routledge is an imprint of the Taylor & Francis Group, an informa business

© 2014 Naomi H. McGloin, Mutsuko Endo Hudson, Fumiko Nazikian and Tomomi Kakegawa

The right of Naomi H. McGloin, Mutsuko Endo Hudson, Fumiko Nazikian and Tomomi Kakegawa to
be identified as authors of this work has been asserted by them in accordance with sections 77 and 78
of the Copyright, Designs and Patents Act 1988.

All rights reserved. No part of this book may be reprinted or reproduced or utilised in any form or
by any electronic, mechanical, or other means, now known or hereafter invented, including photocopying
and recording, or in any information storage or retrieval system, without permission in writing from the
publishers.

Trademark notice: Product or corporate names may be trademarks or registered trademarks, and are
used only for identification and explanation without intent to infringe.

British Library Cataloguing in Publication Data
A catalogue record for this book is available from the British Library

Library of Congress Cataloging in Publication Data
McGloin, Naomi Hanaoka.
    Modern Japanese grammar : a practical guide / Naomi H. McGloin, Mutsuko Endo Hudson,
Fumiko Nazikian, Tomomi Kakegawa.
        pages cm. – (Routledge Modern Grammars)
    Includes bibliographical references and index.
    1. Japanese language–Grammar.   2. Japanese language–Textbooks for foreign speakers–English.
I. Title.
    PL533.M34 2013
    495.682′421–dc23
                                                                                2013009912

ISBN: 978-0-415-57199-9 (hbk)
ISBN: 978-0-415-57201-9 (pbk)
ISBN: 978-0-203-85662-8 (ebk)

Typeset in Times New Roman
by Graphicraft Limited, Hong Kong

MIX
Paper from
responsible sources
FSC® C013604

Printed and bound by CPI Group (UK) Ltd, Croydon, CR0 4YY

Contents

Part A Structures

CONTENTS

CONTENTS

CONTENTS

CONTENTS

ix

Part B   Functions

CONTENTS

CONTENTS

CONTENTS

CONTENTS

CONTENTS

CONTENTS

Introduction

This book is a reference guide which provides an overview of Japanese grammar and its functions. The book is divided into two major parts: *Structures* and *Functions*.

Part A – Structures is a concise grammar of Japanese organized in the familiar and traditional way, describing the forms and major constructions of the language. This section should be used for quick reference when you want to know about or review a form or structure. For example, if you want to review the verbal conjugation patterns, the use of particles **wa** and **ga**, or the structure of the passive form, you should consult this section.

Part B – Functions is the larger of the two. It is organized around language functions, and it will present *situationally appropriate* expressions, not merely what is *grammatically accurate*. This section will cover four major areas: social interaction and communication strategies, giving and seeking information, expressing emotions and sensations, and speaking as performing acts (e.g. requests, permission, advice.) If you want to know, for example, how to address someone, how to apologize, how to invite someone, how to compliment others, etc., you should consult this section.

Often, the same ground is covered in both parts of this book, although the emphasis is different. Extensive cross-references between sections are provided and indicated by arrows in the margin. It is important to refer back and forth between the two parts of the book, so you can get a good grasp of both the structures and the way they are used. There is also an index of words and topics so that readers can find information quickly and easily.

All Japanese utterances can be either in formal (polite) style or informal (casual) style. We have tried to include examples in both styles for each situation as much as possible. Where needed, moreover, sentences are marked 'F' for formal style, 'I' for informal style, and 'VF' for very formal style that contains honorifics.

We hope readers will find this book informative and helpful. We will be delighted to learn how the book has been used and to receive any comments you might have.

Acknowledgments

We would like to express our appreciation to the three reviewers of the manuscript for providing us detailed and very helpful feedback. We believe their comments greatly helped improve the quality of the manuscript. We also thank our Routledge editors Andrea Hartill and Samantha Vale Noya, and senior editorial assistant Isabelle Cheng for their encouragement and patience. We are grateful to Tessa Carroll for her careful editing of the manuscript, and to Hironori Nishi for his help with preparing an index. Our appreciation also goes to Jim McGloin, Grover Hudson, Manuel Fernandez, Helaine Minkus, and Keiko Kawabata for proofreading our English and/or giving feedback on various parts of the manuscript.

Naomi Hanaoka McGloin
Mutsuko Endo Hudson
Fumiko Nazikian
Tomomi Kakegawa
March 10, 2013

Glossary of grammatical terms

Adjectives (see **13**)

Adjectives are words that describe nouns and pronouns. There are two types of adjectives in Japanese – **i** adjectives and **na** adjectives. Each type has its own conjugation patterns.

> 東京は<u>大きい</u>町だ。 (**i**-adjective)
> **Tookyoo wa <u>ookii</u> machi da.**
> Tokyo is a big city.

> 東京は<u>にぎやかな</u>町だ。 (**na**-adjective)
> **Tookyoo wa <u>nigiyaka na</u> machi da.**
> Tokyo is a bustling city.

Adverbs (see **14**)

Adverbs are words that precede and modify verbs, adjectives, other adverbs, and even whole clauses.

> 田中さんはいつも<u>とてもゆっくり</u>話します。
> **Tanaka-san wa itsumo <u>totemo yukkuri</u> hanashimasu.**
> Tanaka-san always talks very slowly.

> <u>確かに</u>そう言いました。
> **<u>Tashika ni</u> soo iimashita.**
> (He) definitely said so.

Agent

The agent is the performer of an action. In a passive sentence, the agent, if present, is followed by the particle **ni** 'by.'

> <u>花子が</u>メリーを呼んだ。
> **<u>Hanako ga</u> Merii o yonda.**
> Hanako invited Mary.

> メリーが<u>花子に</u>呼ばれた。
> **Merii ga <u>Hanako ni</u> yobareta.**
> Mary was invited by Hanako.

Aspect (see **27.1**)

Aspect refers to the manner in which an action or state is viewed with respect to its beginning, duration, completion, or repetition. In Japanese, **-te iru**, **-te aru**, **-te shimau** are some of the most common aspectual markers.

> 今勉強し<u>ています</u>。
> **Ima benkyoo <u>shite imasu</u>.**
> I am studying right now.

スミスさんは結婚し<u>ています</u>。
Sumisu-san wa kekkon <u>shite imasu</u>.
Mr/Ms Smith is married.

窓が開け<u>てあります</u>。
Mado ga <u>akete arimasu</u>.
The window has been opened.

もう食べて<u>しまいました</u>。
Moo tabete <u>shimaimashita</u>.
I've already eaten.

Case particles (see 10.1)

Case particles are short functional words that are attached to nouns and indicate the grammatical role the nouns play with respect to the verb. They are **ga** (subject), **o** (direct object), **ni** (indirect object), and **no** (possessive).

ジョン<u>が</u>リサ<u>に</u>自分<u>の</u>犬の写真<u>を</u>見せた。
Jon <u>ga</u> Risa <u>ni</u> jibun <u>no</u> inu no shashin <u>o</u> miseta.
John showed Lisa a picture of his dog.

ジョン<u>が</u>テニス<u>を</u>やっています。
Jon <u>ga</u> tenisu <u>o</u> yatte imasu.
John is playing tennis.

Classifiers (see 16)

Classifiers are suffixes that are used with numbers in counting objects, including people and animals. Different classifiers are used depending on the characteristics of these objects (e.g. **-mai** for flat objects, **-hon/-ppon/-bon** for long cylindrical objects, **-hiki/-piki/-biki** for small animals, etc.)

ワインを<u>二本</u>もらった。
Wain o <u>ni-hon</u> moratta.
I received two bottles of wine.

犬が<u>二匹</u>います。
Inu ga <u>ni-hiki</u> imasu.
There are two (classifier) dogs.

紙を<u>一枚</u>とってください。
Kami o <u>ichi-mai</u> totte kudasai.
Please hand me one sheet of paper.

Clauses

A clause is a grammatical unit that contains at least a predicate (e.g. verb). A clause can be either a dependent clause or a main clause.

<u>日本語は難しい</u>と思いません。
<u>Nihongo wa muzukashii</u> to omoimasen.
I don't think Japanese is difficult.

<u>日本のドラマをたくさん見た</u>から、耳が良くなりました。
<u>Nihon no dorama o takusan mita</u> kara, mimi ga yoku narimashita.
Because I watched many Japanese TV dramas, my listening comprehension improved.

In the above sentences, **omoimasen** and **mimi ga yoku narimashita** are the main clauses, while the parts followed by **to** and **kara** are the subordinate clauses.

Complement (clause) (see **26**)

A complement is a clause which functions as the subject or the object of a verb. A complement clause is indicated by **koto**, **no**, or **to**.

娘がピアノをひく<u>の</u>を聞いた。
<u>Musume ga piano o hiku no</u> o kiita.
I listened to my daughter play the piano.

話を説明する<u>の</u>が難しいことがわかった。
<u>Hanashi o setsumee suru no</u> ga muzukashii koto ga wakatta.
I realized that explaining the story was difficult.

友達はパーティーに来る<u>と</u>言いました。
Tomodachi wa <u>paatii ni kuru to</u> iimashita.
My friend said that he/she will come to the party.

Compounds (see **17**)

A compound is a single word formed by combining two (or more) words. The meaning of a compound is not always the sum of the two.

巻き寿司は人気がある。
<u>Maki-zushi</u> wa ninki ga aru.
Rolled sushi is popular.

かねがなり始めた。
Kane ga nari-hajimeta.
The bell started to ring.

Conjunctions (see **22**)

Conjunctions connect two or more clauses into one sentence. Some examples are **kara** 'because,' **noni** 'although,' **keredo(mo)** 'but.'

日本語は面白い<u>から</u>勉強しています。
Nihongo wa omoshiroi <u>kara</u> benkyoo shite imasu.
(I) am studying Japanese because it is interesting.

誰もいない<u>のに</u>、声が聞こえます。
Dare mo inai <u>noni</u>, koe ga kikoemasu.
Although there is no one, there is a voice.

ドイツに住んでいた<u>けれど</u>、ドイツ語が話せません。
Doitsu ni sunde ita <u>keredo</u>, Doitsugo ga hanasemasen.
Although (I) lived in Germany, (I) cannot speak German.

Connectives (see **22**)

Connectives appear at the beginning of an independent sentence and indicate how that sentence relates to the previous sentence. Examples include **sorede** 'and so,' **sorekara** 'and then,' **dakara** 'therefore,' and **demo** 'but.'

お金がありません。<u>だから</u>、アルバイトをしなければなりません。
Okane ga arimasen. <u>Dakara</u>, arubaito o shinakereba narimasen.
(I) don't have money. So, (I) have to work part-time.

バスがなかなか来ませんでした。<u>それで</u>クラスに遅れてしまいました。
Basu ga nakanaka kimasen deshita. <u>Sorede</u> kurasu ni okurete shimaimashita.
The bus was late. And so, I was late for class.

毎日忙しいです。<u>でも</u>、楽しいです。
Mainichi isogashii desu. <u>Demo</u>, tanoshii desu.
I am busy every day. But, I am happy.

レストランで食事をしました。<u>それから</u>公園を散歩しました。
Resutoran de shokuji o shimashita. <u>Sorekara</u> kooen o sanpo shimashita.
(We) ate at a restaurant. Then, (we) took a walk in the park.

Copulas

Da (plain form)/**desu** (polite form) are called copulas in Japanese. They are attached to a noun and a **na**-type adjective and function like the **be**-verb in English. Another copula form, **de aru**, is mainly used in formal writing.

あの人は先生<u>だ</u>。／あの人は先生<u>です</u>。
Ano hito wa sensee <u>da</u>. / Ano hito wa sensee <u>desu</u>.
That person is a teacher.

桜の花はきれい<u>だ</u>。／桜の花はきれい<u>です</u>。
Sakura no hana wa kiree <u>da</u>. / Sakura no hana wa kiree <u>desu</u>.
Cherry blossoms are pretty.

桜は日本の象徴<u>である</u>。
Sakura wa Nihon no shoochoo <u>de aru</u>.
Cherry blossom is the symbol of Japan.

Demonstratives (see **9**)

Demonstratives are words that indicate entities to which a speaker is referring, such as 'this' and 'that' in English.

<u>あの</u>建物は何ですか。
<u>Ano</u> tatemono wa nan desu ka.
What is <u>that</u> building?

<u>これ</u>は面白いですね。
<u>Kore</u> wa omoshiroi desu ne.
<u>This</u> is interesting.

Desiderative

The desiderative is a form expressing the meaning 'want to do.' It is a suffix **tai**, that is attached to a verb (stem). When the subject is the third person, the suffix **tagaru** is used.

私はおすしが食べ<u>たい</u>（です）。
Watashi wa osushi ga tabe-<u>tai</u> (desu).
I want to eat sushi.

子供はおかしを食べ<u>たがって</u>います。
Kodomo wa okashi o tabe-<u>tagatte</u> imasu.
The children want to eat sweets.

Evidentials (see **28**)

Evidentials are sentence-final expressions such as **mitai**, **soo**, **yoo**, and **rashii** which are used to express the speaker's impressions, inferences, degrees of certainty, and information sources, etc.

ルームメイトはゆうべは帰りが遅かった<u>みたい</u>です。
Ruumumeeto wa yuube wa kaeri ga osokatta <u>mitai</u> desu.
It seems that my roommate came home late last night.

ちょっと風邪をひいた<u>よう</u>です。
Chotto kaze o hiita <u>yoo</u> desu.
It seems that I have caught a cold.

このケーキはおいし<u>そう</u>ですね。
Kono keeki wa oishi <u>soo</u> desu ne.
This cake looks delicious, doesn't it?

Formal Style

Formal style is the style of speech used in situations where one feels formality is appropriate or required (e.g. meeting a person for the first time, addressing strangers, speaking in business/public meetings, making public presentations, etc.) or when talking to someone for whom one feels respect is due, such as one's social superiors. In formal style, the predicate is in the polite form.

私は学生です。
Watashi wa gakusee desu.
I am a student.

あした行きます。
Ashita ikimasu.
I will go tomorrow.

Generic nouns

Generic nouns are nouns that refer to classes such as the Japanese (Japanese people in general), or a member of the class as a representative of its class.

日本人は温泉が好きだ。
Nihonjin wa onsen ga suki da.
Japanese people like hot springs.

くじらは哺乳動物だ。
Kujira wa honyuu doobutsu da.
A whale is a mammal.

Honorifics (see 29)

Honorifics is the use of language to show respect to someone who is considered to be socially superior in terms of social rank, age, and other factors such as social distance. There are three types of honorifics: **teeneego** 'polite form' (e.g. **o-/go-**, **desu**, **masu**), **sonkeego** 'exalting form' and **kenjoogo** 'humbling form.' The use of **sonkeego** directly exalts the person/people referred to, and by using **kenjoogo**, the speaker humbles his/her own actions, and thereby shows respect to the individual to whom respect is due.

先生、何時ごろまで研究室に<u>いらっしゃいますか</u>。(尊敬語)
Sensee, nanji goro made kenkyuushitsu ni <u>irasshaimasu</u> ka. (sonkeego)
Professor, how late are you going to be in your office? (exalting form)

社長はもう<u>お帰りになりました</u>。(尊敬語)
Shachoo wa moo <u>o-kaeri ni narimashita</u>. (sonkeego)
President (of company) has already gone home. (exalting form)

社長、おかばん、<u>お持ちします</u>。(謙譲語)
Shachoo, okaban, <u>o-mochi shimasu</u>. (kenjoogo)
President (of company) (X), I will carry your briefcase. (humbling form)

先日田中先生に<u>お目にかかりました</u>。(謙譲語)
Senjitsu Tanaka-sensee ni <u>o-me-ni kakarimashita</u>. (kenjoogo)
I met Prof./Dr. Tanaka the other day. (humbling form)

Informal style

Informal style is the style used in casual situations, such as when talking with one's close friends or family members. In this style, the predicate is in plain form.

行く。　　　　　タクシーだ。
Iku.　　　　　**Takushii da.**
I will go.　　　　It's a taxi.

In-group/out-group

In-group consists of the speaker and those whom the speaker considers to be close and to share a sense of 'we-ness,' such as family members and close friends. Out-group consists of people who are outside of one's in-group. The membership, however, shifts depending on the interactional situation. One's superior at one's workplace, for example, might belong to an out-group when one is talking to someone in the same work place. However, the same individual will be part of one's in-group if one is talking to someone outside of one's work place.

社長は今オフィスにいらっしゃいません。 (talking to an in-group member.)
Shachoo wa ima ofisu ni irasshaimasen.
(Company) President (X) is not in the office right now. (exalting form)

社長は今出かけておりますが。 (talking to an out-group member.)
Shachoo wa ima dekakete orimasu ga.
(Company) President (X) is not here right now. (humble form)

Nouns/noun phrases

Nouns are words which denote people, animals, places, things, or concepts. A noun phrase is a noun with a modifier.

Objects

There are two kinds of object – direct object (DO) and indirect object (IO). Direct objects are nouns and pronouns that are directly affected by the action of the verb. In Japanese, direct objects are usually marked by the particle **o**. Indirect objects are nouns and pronouns to which/ whom an action is directed. They are generally marked by **ni**.

私は友達に (IO) ワインを (DO) あげた。
Watashi wa tomodachi ni wain o ageta.
I gave my friend a bottle of wine.

Out-group (see In-group)

Plain form

Plain form ends in **-i** (i-adjectives), **-ru/-u** (verbs), and **da** ('be' verb), and their past tense variants. This form is used in casual conversation and in formal writing (e.g. newspaper articles, science books, novels), as well as in most subordinate clauses.

元気だ。
Genki da.
I'm fine.

東京はおもしろい。
Tookyoo wa omoshiroi.
Tokyo is interesting.

あした行く。
Ashita iku.
(I) will go tomorrow.

あとで食べる。
Ato de taberu.
(I) will eat later.

Polite form

Polite form is the predicate form with **desu** or **masu** and their past tense and negative variants. This form is used in speaking in a formal (polite) style.

元気<u>です</u>。
Genki <u>desu</u>.
I'm fine.

東京はおもしろい<u>です</u>。
Tookyoo wa omoshiroi <u>desu</u>.
Tokyo is interesting.

あした行き<u>ます</u>。
Ashita iki<u>masu</u>.
(I) will go tomorrow.

あとで食べ<u>ます</u>。
Ato de tabe<u>masu</u>.
(I) will eat later.

Postpositions (see **10.2**)

A postposition is a short word that follows a noun/pronoun expressing concepts such as time, manner, and location.

毎朝7時<u>に</u>おきます。
Maiasa shichiji <u>ni</u> okimasu.
I get up <u>at</u> seven every morning.

箸<u>で</u>食べました。
Hashi <u>de</u> tabemashita.
I ate <u>with</u> chopsticks.

Predicate (see **1.1**)

A predicate is the part of the sentence that expresses what the subject does or is and how it is. Verbs, **i**-type adjectives, and the copula can be predicates in Japanese.

父は仕事に<u>行きました</u>。
Chichi wa shigoto ni <u>ikimashita</u>.
My father <u>went</u> to work.

今日は寒いです。
Kyoo wa <u>samui desu</u>.
It <u>is cold</u> today.

Prefix (see **15.6.2**)

A prefix is a short element that is attached to the beginning of a word to add an additional meaning to or to change the meaning of the word.

<u>不</u>完全   <u>元</u>首相
<u>fu</u>-kanzen   <u>moto</u> shushoo
<u>in</u>complete   <u>former</u> prime minister

Pre-nominal form

The pre-nominal form is the form used in modifying a noun. It is N + **no** for nouns, **na**-adj. + **na** for **na**-adjectives, and plain forms for **i**-adjectives and verbs.

私の出身の町は静かな町です。
Watashi no shusshin no machi wa shizuka-na machi desu.
My hometown is a quiet town.

きのう会った人は面白い人でした。
Kinoo atta hito wa omoshiroi hito deshita.
The person I met yesterday was an interesting person.

Pronoun (see 8)

A pronoun is a word that is used to replace a noun or noun phrase.

> スーパーでりんごを買った。<u>それ</u>はあまりおいしくなかった。
> **Suupaa de ringo o katta. <u>Sore</u> wa amari oishiku nakatta.**
> I bought an apple at the supermarket. <u>It</u> was not very tasty.

> <u>私</u>はもう帰ります。
> **<u>Watashi</u> wa moo kaerimasu.**
> <u>I</u>'m going home now.

Resultant state (see 19.2.1)

A resultant state is a state that is brought about as the result of an action or event expressed by the verb.

> 窓が開いています。
> **Mado ga aite imasu.**
> The window is open.

The window opened or was opened at some point in the past and the result remains: it is open.

Sentence (see 5)

A sentence is commonly made up of a subject and a predicate and expresses a complete idea. The subject can be omitted in Japanese, so a sentence minimally consists of a predicate.

> 田中さんは親切です。
> **Tanaka-san wa shinsetsu desu.**
> Mr/Ms Tanaka is kind.

> 行く？
> **Iku?**
> Are (you) going?

A sentence may contain more than one clause.

> 昨日は雨が降ったから、出かけなかった。
> **Kinoo wa ame ga futta kara, dekakenakatta.**
> Because it rained yesterday, I didn't go outside.

Sentence-final particles (see 10.4)

Sentence-final (interactional) particles are short functional words generally attached to the end of an utterance and convey various speaker sentiments and attitudes. The most common final particles are **ne**, **yo**, and **ka**.

> いい天気ですね。
> **Ii tenki desu <u>ne</u>.**
> It's beautiful weather, isn't it.

> おいしいよ。
> **Oishii <u>yo</u>.**
> It is delicious, I tell you.

> おいしいですか。
> **Oishii desu <u>ka</u>.**
> Does it taste good?

Subject (see 1.4)

The subject of a sentence is the animate or inanimate entity that performs the action or undergoes the process denoted by the verb. If the sentence denotes a state rather than an action, the subject is what the predicate (verb, adjective or copula phrase) describes.

今夜は<u>月</u>がきれいですね。
Kon'ya wa <u>tsuki</u> ga kiree desu ne.
<u>The moon</u> is beautiful tonight.

さっき<u>田中さん</u>が来ましたよ。
Sakki <u>Tanaka-san</u> ga kimashita yo.
<u>Mr/Ms Tanaka</u> came just a little while ago.

Suffix

A suffix is a short element that is attached to the end of a word to change the meaning of or to add an additional meaning to the word.

寒<u>い</u>	→	寒<u>さ</u>	子供	→	子供<u>っぽい</u>
samu-<u>i</u>		**samu-<u>sa</u>**	**kodomo**		**kodomo-ppoi**
cold		cold<u>ness</u>	child		childish

Tense (see 27)

A tense indicates the time at which the event expressed by the predicate takes place or the time frame when the state described by the predicate is true. The tense is expressed by a suffix, which attaches to the predicate. There are two tenses in Japanese: nonpast and past.

映画を見る。(nonpast)
Eega o miru.
(I) watch movies.

映画を見た。(past)
Eega o mita.
(I) watched movies.

Topic (see 1.4, 11)

The topic of a sentence is what the whole sentence is about. The topic often overlaps with the subject of a sentence, but it can be other parts of speech as well. Topics are marked by the particle **wa** in Japanese.

わたしは出かけます。
<u>Watashi</u> wa dekakemasu.
<u>I</u>'m going out.

<u>週末</u>は買い物に行きます。
<u>Shuumatsu</u> wa kaimono ni ikimasu.
On <u>weekends</u>, I go shopping.

晩ご飯は、たいていうちで食べます。
<u>Bangohan</u> wa, taitee uchi de tabemasu.
As for <u>dinner</u>, I usually eat at home.

Verb (see 12)

A verb is a word that expresses the physical or mental activities carried out by the subject of a sentence.

私はよく映画を<u>見ます</u>。
Watashi wa yoku eega o <u>mimasu</u>.
I often <u>watch</u> movies.

英語が<u>わかります</u>か。
Eego ga <u>wakarimasu</u> ka.
Do you <u>understand</u> English?

GLOSSARY OF GRAMMATICAL TERMS

– Action verbs (see **12.3**)

Action verbs are verbs that express actions that a person, animal, organization, etc. performs.

> 私は晩ご飯を<u>食べました</u>。
> **Watashi wa bangohan o <u>tabemashita</u>.**
> I <u>ate</u> dinner.

> 犬が<u>吠えました</u>。
> **Inu ga <u>hoemashita</u>.**
> A dog <u>barked</u>.

– Stative verbs (see **12.3**)

Stative verbs describe the state of a person, animal or thing. For example, **aru** '(for animate things) to exist, to have' and **iru** '(for inanimate things) to exist, to have' are stative verbs.

> 公園にブランコが<u>あります</u>。
> **Kooen ni buranko ga <u>arimasu</u>.**
> <u>There are</u> swings in the park.

> 私は妹が<u>います</u>。
> **Watashi wa imooto ga <u>imasu</u>.**
> I <u>have</u> a younger sister.

– Intransitive verbs (see **12.2**)

Intransitive verbs are verbs that do not take a direct object. They express events, movements or the spontaneous changes undergone by the subject.

> 昨日から新学期が<u>始まりました</u>。
> **Kinoo kara shingakki ga <u>hajimarimashita</u>.**
> The new semester <u>started</u> yesterday.

> 台風で木が<u>倒れた</u>。
> **Taifuu de ki ga <u>taoreta</u>.**
> Trees <u>fell</u> because of the typhoon.

– Transitive verbs (see **12.2**)

Transitive verbs are verbs that take a direct object. They express what an agent does.

> 私はよく本を<u>借ります</u>。
> **Watashi wa yoku hon o <u>karimasu</u>.**
> I often <u>borrow</u> books.

> 父は新しい車を<u>買った</u>。
> **Chichi wa atarashii kuruma o <u>katta</u>.**
> My father <u>bought</u> a new car.

Verb phrase

A verb phrase is a verb plus another word within a sentence that is closely connected with the verb such as a direct object, a complement, or an adverb.

> 昨日は<u>レストランで友達に会いました</u>。
> **Kinoo wa <u>resutoran de tomodachi ni aimashita</u>.**
> Yesterday, I <u>met with my friend at a restaurant</u>.

> 明日は<u>ゆっくり休みたいです</u>。
> **Ashita wa <u>yukkuri yasumitai desu</u>.**
> Tomorrow, I <u>want to relax</u>.

Abbreviations and symbols

The following abbreviations and symbols have been used.

adj.	adjective
aff.	affirmative
dict. form	dictionary form
DO	direct object
F	formal (polite) style
I	informal style
IO	indirect object
Lit.	literally
N	noun
neg.	negative
Ø	means that the expected words (e.g. subject, object) are not overtly mentioned
S	sentence
V	verb
VF	very formal (polite) style
*	indicates that the sentence is ungrammatical
(·)	indicates micro pause
?	indicates rising/questioning intonation

Notes on romanization

The romanization used in the *Modern Japanese Grammar: A Practical Guide* basically follows the Hepburn system. Hence, kana syllables such as し, つ, ち, じ, and ふ are romanized as **shi**, **tsu**, **chi**, **ji**, and **fu**, respectively. Several modifications, however, have been made, and they are:

1. Long vowels are represented by double letters, as in **aa**, **ii**, **uu**, **ee**, **oo**.
2. The verb 言う(いう) 'to say' is romanized as **yuu** even though it is spelled with **i** and **u** in hiragana.
3. ん is always romanized as **n**.

Apostrophe ['] is used after **n** (ん) when it is followed by a vowel or a glide sound (e.g. げんいん **gen'in** 'cause,' ほんや **hon'ya** 'bookstore,' and きんようび **kin'yoobi** 'Friday').

Part A

Structures

1

Introduction: major features of Japanese grammar

Basic word order

The basic word order of a Japanese sentence is *subject–predicate*. Japanese is therefore classified as a *verb-final language*. The 'subject' can be, and often is, absent, especially when its identity is clear from the context. The *predicate* may be a verb, an **i**-type adjective, or a *copula*. The copula is attached to a noun or a **na**-type adjective, and functions like the 'be' verb in English (e.g. 'is,' 'are'). The main predicates are underlined in the examples in this section.

花子さんが<u>来た</u>。(verb)
Hanako-san ga <u>kita</u>.
Hanako <u>came</u>.

空が<u>青い</u>。(**i**-type adjective)
Sora ga <u>aoi</u>.
The sky <u>is blue</u>.

これが問題<u>だ</u>。(noun + copula)
Kore ga mondai <u>da</u>.
This <u>is</u> the problem.

地下鉄が便利<u>だ</u>。(**na**-type adj. + copula)
Chikatetsu ga benri <u>da</u>.
The subway <u>is</u> convenient.

When the predicate is a verb, the associated noun phrases, such as those representing time, location, partner, direct object (DO) and indirect object (IO), usually *precede* the verb. Some typical word orders are provided in (1)–(4). Any of the phrases appearing in parentheses need not be overtly expressed. A rule of thumb is that when a pronoun is used in English, nothing is used in Japanese.

■ (1) (subject) (time) (location) verb ← 'exist, be there, etc.'

学生が教室に<u>いる</u>。
Gakusee ga kyooshitsu ni <u>iru</u>.
There <u>are</u> students in the classroom.

■ (2) (topic = subject) (time) (location) verb ← 'come, go, return, etc.'

私は来年ロンドンに<u>行く</u>。
Watashi wa rainen Rondon ni <u>iku</u>.
I'll <u>go</u> to London next year.

■ (3) (topic = subject) (time) (partner) (location) (do) verb ← 'do something'

マリはケンと銀座ですしを<u>食べた</u>。
Mari wa Ken to Ginza de sushi o <u>tabeta</u>.
Mari <u>ate</u> sushi with Ken in Ginza.

- (4) (topic = subject) (time) (IO) (do) verb ← 'do something to someone'

ジョンは昨日リサにメールを<u>送った</u>。
Jon wa kinoo Risa ni meeru o <u>okutta</u>.
John <u>sent</u> an e-mail to Lisa yesterday.

The short words following the nouns in the above examples (**ga**, **wa**, **to**, **ni**, **de**, **o**) are called *particles*, and they indicate the grammatical relation of each noun to the verb. Noun phrases followed by these particles can be switched without affecting the meaning of the sentence, although the focus will likely be different. The example immediately above basically means the same as does the following, with the position of the time word and the indirect object switched.

ジョンはリサに昨日メールを<u>送った</u>。
Jon wa Risa ni kinoo meeru o <u>okutta</u>.
John <u>sent</u> an e-mail to Lisa yesterday.

To summarize, although the predicate usually appears at the end of a sentence, the order among noun phrases is relatively free.

▶ 5; 10

1.2 Modification pattern

The term *modify* means to 'limit, qualify, give additional information,' etc. in grammar. The 'modifier' always <u>precedes</u> the word it modifies in Japanese. Below, the words surrounded by brackets [ ] indicate a modifier. When a word modifies a noun, there are four patterns.

- (1) [noun] noun

［日本の］ 山
[Nihon no] yama
[Japanese] mountain, mountain [in Japan]

- (2) [**i**-adjective] noun

［高い］ 山
[takai] yama
[high] mountain

- (3) [**na**-adjective] noun

［きれいな］ 山
[kiree na] yama
[beautiful] mountain

- (4) [clause] noun (A *clause* is a sentence within a sentence.)

［私が昨日見た］ 山
[watashi ga kinoo mita] yama
mountain [that I saw yesterday]

The following are more examples of type (4).

［このアニメを作った］ 人はだれですか。
[Kono anime o tsukutta] hito wa dare desu ka.
Who is the person [who made this *anime*]?

あれは ［弟がよくやる］ ゲームです。
Are wa [otooto ga yoku yaru] geemu desu.
That's a game [that my younger brother often plays].

昨日は ［駅前にある］ 喫茶店で友達に会いました。
Kinoo wa [ekimae ni aru] kissaten de tomodachi ni aimashita.
Yesterday I met with my friend in the coffee shop [which is in front of the station].

▶ 7.2; 25

When a word modifies a verb, too, the modifier (an adverb) always precedes the verb.

▶ 14

あの人は ［いつも］ ［ゆっくり］ 話す。
Ano hito wa itsumo yukkuri hanasu.
He/she [always] speaks [slowly].

Sometimes, an adverb modifies a whole sentence, expressing the speaker's judgment of the event. In such cases, the adverb appears at the very beginning of the sentence.

［さいわい、］ 雨は降らないでしょう。
[Saiwai,] ame wa furanai deshoo.
[Luckily,] it probably won't rain.

［おどろいたことに、］ 答えを知っている人はいませんでした。
[Odoroita koto ni,] kotae o shitte iru hito wa imasen deshita.
[Surprisingly,] no one knew the answer.

Subordinate (adverbial) clauses expressing manner, time ('when, while'), condition ('if'), reason ('because'), concession ('although'), etc. <u>precede</u> the main clause.

▶ 22; 23; 24; 45

［立ったまま or 立って］ そばを食べています。 ← manner
[Tatta mama or Tatte] soba o tabete imasu.
They are eating *soba* (buckwheat noodles) [while standing].

［ボーナスが出たら］ 新しいスーツを買いたいんです。 ← condition
[Boonasu ga de-tara] atarashii suutsu o kaitai n desu.
[If there is a bonus,] I'd like to buy a new suit.

1.3 Particles

Particles are short functional words attached to an element within a sentence. Those that are attached to nouns are similar to *prepositions* in English (e.g. 'at,' 'in,' 'to,' 'by', 'with') expressing such functions as time, location, direction, means, and partner. Unlike English prepositions, Japanese particles (also called *postpositions*) <u>follow</u>, instead of precede, the element with which they are associated. For example, **Nihon de** (Lit. Japan in) means 'in Japan.' Particles are classified into five types in this book. Some examples appear below.

Case particles: **ga** (subject), **o** (DO), **ni** (IO) 'to,' **no** (X's Y)
Postpositions: **de** 'at, in, by, with,' **ni** 'at, to, for,' **to** 'with,' **e** 'to,' **kara** 'from,' **made** 'until'
Adverbial particles: **wa** 'topic,' **mo** 'also,' **shika** 'only,' **dake** 'only,' **sae** 'even'
Conjunctive particles: **to** 'and,' **ba** 'if,' **to** 'if, when(ever),' **kara** 'because,' **ga** 'but,' **keredo(mo)** 'but,' **noni** 'although'
Sentence-final particles: **ne, yo, ka, wa, zo, ze, sa**

Case particles, postpositions, adverbial particles follow nouns and noun phrases. While case particles indicate the grammatical roles of nouns, such as subject (**ga**), direct object (**o**), and indirect object (**ni**), postpositions bear specific meanings. Conjunctive particles connect either nouns or clauses. Sentence-final particles appear at the end of a sentence and indicate the function of a sentence (e.g. question) and speaker attitudes (e.g. emphasis).

▶ 10; 22

1.4 Subject and topic

Subject and *topic* are quite different, and the distinction is made overtly in Japanese – by the use of the particles **ga** (subject) and **wa** (topic), respectively. The difference between **ga** and **wa** can sometimes be likened to that between an indefinite noun (e.g. 'a man') and a definite one (e.g. 'the man') in English.

> A man came to see me yesterday. The man was wearing a black shirt.

In the first sentence, 'a man' is the subject, but not the topic of the sentence, since this person is being introduced into the discourse for the first time. 'The man' in the second sentence is both the subject and the topic of the sentence. Both the speaker and the hearer know who 'the man' refers to, and the sentence is about him. The following is the Japanese version of the same sentences.

> きのう男の人が会いにきました。その人は黒いシャツを着ていました。
> **Kinoo otoko no hito ga ai ni kimashita. Sono hito wa kuroi shatsu o kite imashita.**

Broadly speaking, **ga** introduces new information and **wa** introduces shared (or 'old') information or an entity which is familiar to both the speaker and the hearer.

> (a) 田中 :　あの人は何をしている人ですか。
> **Tanaka:**　**Ano hito wa nani o shite iru hito desu ka.**
> What does he (= that person) do?
>
> 山田 :　あの人は医者です。
> **Yamada:**　**Ano hito wa isha desu.**
> He (= that person) is a doctor.
>
> (b) 田中 :　どの人が医者ですか。
> **Tanaka:**　**Dono hito ga isha desu ka.**
> Which one is the doctor?
>
> 山田 :　あの人が医者です。
> **Ano hito ga isha desu.**
> <u>That person</u> is the doctor.

The noun marked by **ga** is the subject of the sentence, while that marked by **wa** is the topic of the sentence. In (a), Tanaka and Yamada are talking about a certain person (i.e. 'that person,' who is perhaps in the same room). Tanaka asks what he does, and Yamada answers that he is a doctor, using **wa**. In (b), on the other hand, Tanaka might be at the hospital, looking for a doctor. Seeing there are several people around, he asks which one is the doctor. Yamada then points to one person and says that 'that person is <u>the</u> doctor.' Here, **ga** is used.

A topic most often expresses the subject at the same time, but it can have any number of functions; e.g. direct object, indirect object, time, location, partner. For a detailed description of 'topic', see **11**.

▶ **10.1; 11**

1.5 'Agglutinative' morphology

To express tenses (nonpast and past), moods and voices, such as negative ('not'), potential ('can do'), desiderative ('want to do'), causative ('make someone do'), and passive (e.g. 'was done something to'), the verbal root is followed by a suffix, which in turn is followed by another. The order of these suffixes is generally fixed, with the tense morpheme appearing at or near the end of the sentence.

> Verbal root – potential – negative – tense
> Verbal root – causative – passive – desiderative – negative – tense

> 読ませた
> **yom-ase-ta** (V-causative-past)
> made (someone) read

食べられる
tabe-rare-ru (V-potential-nonpast OR V-passive-nonpast)
can eat OR be eaten

行かせられたくない
ik-ase-rare-taku-na-i (V-causative-passive-desiderative-negative-nonpast)
don't want to be made to go

The negative **-na-i** and desiderative **-ta-i** are conjugated in the same manner as **i**-type adjectives, while the potential **-(rar)e-ru**, causative **-(s)ase-ru**, and passive **-(r)are-ru** morphemes are conjugated like a verb.

▶ 12.6; 15; 20; 21; 27; 63.1

1.6 Ellipsis

The general rule in Japanese is that, other than the main predicate (verb, **i**-adjective, copula[1]), whatever element the speaker assumes is 'obvious' in the context can be absent (or omitted). This phenomenon is called 'ellipsis,' and is widespread. The absent phrases may be the subject, direct and indirect object, time, location, means, partner, and the like. The particle associated with an absent noun must also be absent. In the examples below, the phrases in parentheses in the English equivalents are absent in Japanese.

NOTE | [1]The copula can be omitted in casual speech.

> A: 宿題は Ø したの？
> **Shukudai wa Ø shita no?**
> Did (you) do the homework?

> B: Ø Ø もうやったよ。
> **Ø Ø Moo yatta yo.**
> (I) did (it) already.

It is clear from the context that the identity of the missing subject in A's question is 'you,' while it is 'I' in B's response, and that the missing direct object is 'it,' that is, 'homework.'

Particles such as **wa** and **o** are often omitted in conversation, especially of a casual type. **Ga** and **ni**, too, are sometimes omitted. This is because these particles express *functions*, such as topic, direct object, subject, and indirect object, respectively, rather than *meanings*. On the other hand, the particles classified as 'postpositions,' such as **de** 'at, in (place),' **ni** 'at, in (time),' **to** 'with,' and **kara** 'from,' do express meanings and, therefore, cannot be omitted.

Formal speech:

> これ Ø (← は) お気に召すかどうか分かりませんが . . .
> **Kore Ø (← wa) o-ki ni mesu ka doo ka wakarimasen ga . . .**
> I hope you'll like this. (Lit. I don't know whether you'll like this or not, but . . .)

> 私 Ø (← は) 鈴木と申します。本日はお電話 Ø (← を) 戴きましてありがとうございました。
> **Watakushi Ø (← wa) Suzuki to mooshimasu. Honjitsu wa o-denwa Ø (← o) itadakimashite arigatoo gozaimashita.**
> My name is Suzuki (Lit. I humbly call myself Suzuki). Thank you very much for your telephone call today.

Casual speech:

> お兄さん Ø (← は) もう帰ってきた？
> **Oniisan Ø (← wa) moo kaette kita?**
> Did/Has your brother come back yet?

今雨 Ø（← が）降ってる？
Ima ame Ø (← ga) futte ru?
Is it raining right now?

私 Ø（← は）きのうアパートで友達と晩ご飯 Ø（← を）食べてたんだけどー。
Atashi Ø (← wa) kinoo apaato de tomodachi to bangohan Ø (← o) tabete ta n da kedoo.
I was having dinner with my friend in my apartment yesterday, and . . .

▶ 31.14

2

Pronunciation

Inventory of basic sounds

The basic sounds of Japanese are provided below, followed by some rules.

Vowels: /a/ /i/ /u/ /e/ /o/

Consonants:

stops: /p/ /t/ /k/ /b/ /d/ /g/
fricatives: /s/ /z/ /h/
liquid: /r/
glides: /w/ /y/
nasals: /m/ /n/

(1) Vowels may be short or long. Long vowels are transcribed with double letters herein; e.g. **oka̲a̲san** 'mother,' **gakus̲e̲e** 'student,' **yu̲u̲ki** 'courage.'

(2) The vowel /u/ is not pronounced as far back as the English /u/, and the lips are not as rounded; e.g. **u̲ta** 'song,' **ku̲ki** 'stem.'

(3) High vowels /i/ and /u/ are often voiceless when they occur between voiceless consonants or word finally when preceded by a voiceless consonant; e.g. **hi̲to** 'person,' **su̲ki** 'like,' **ikimasu̲** 'I'll go.'

(4) The /r/ sound is a flap and is pronounced with the tip of the tongue making a quick tap at the alveolar ridge, right behind the teeth; e.g. **re̲e** 'zero,' **ryokoo** 'trip.'

(5) The pronunciation of some of the consonants depends on the vowel that immediately follows.

/s/: [s] before /a, u, e, o/; [sh] before /i/; e.g. **s̲a̲ru** 'monkey,' **s̲h̲igoto** 'job.'
/z/: [z] before /a, u, e, o/; [dj] before /i/; e.g. **z̲o̲ori** 'sandals,' **a̲j̲i** 'taste.'
/t/: [t] before /a, e, o/; [ch] before /i/; [ts] before /u/; e.g. **te** 'hand,' **mi̲ch̲i** 'road,' **ts̲u̲no** 'horn.'
/d/: [d] before /a, e, o/; [dj] before /i/; [dz] before /u/; e.g. **ka̲d̲o** 'corner,' **mi̲j̲ika** 'close,' **tsuz̲u̲ki** 'continuation.'
/h/: [h] before /a, e, o/; [ç] before /i/; [ɸ] before /u/; e.g. **h̲a̲to** 'dove,' **h̲i̲mo** 'string,' **fu̲ta** 'lid.'

Syllable and mora

As a timing unit, *syllable* and *mora* are both important in Japanese. A mora may consist of a single vowel (e.g. **e** 'painting'), a consonant + vowel (**ka** 'mosquito'), a consonant + y + vowel (**kyuu** 'nine'), the second element of a long vowel (**kyuu** 'nine'), syllabic nasal (more accurately, 'moraic' nasal) [N] (e.g. **hon** 'book'), or the first element of a (non-nasal) double consonant (e.g. **sakka** 'writer'). Each mora is pronounced with roughly an equal length of time, or one beat. **Hokkaidoo** (place name), for example, contains three syllables (**Hok-kai-doo**) and six moras (**Ho-k-ka-i-do-o**), while **kyandii** (candy) contains two syllables (**kyan-dii**) and four moras (**kya-n-di-i**).

9

The two sets of phonetic symbols in Japanese, **hiragana** and **katakana**, are based on mora so that there is a unique symbol for each vowel, a consonant + vowel combination, the moraic nasal (ん or ン), the first element of a double consonant (っ or ッ), and the second element of a long vowel. Children's sound games are generally based on mora. The word **tomato** 'tomato' トマト, for example, is a palindrome in Japanese.

The mora is useful in poetry such as *haiku*, which consists of 5+7+5 moras, or 17 in total. When longer words are shortened or new words are created by combining two words, they often have three or four moras; e.g. **su-ma-ho** (from **sumaato** + **hon** 'smart phone'), **pa-so-ko-n** (from **paasonaru** + **konpyuuta(a)** 'personal computer'), **Ma-ku-do** (from **Makudonarudo** 'McDonald's'), **ho-t-to** (from **hotto koohii** 'hot coffee'), **depa-chika** (from **depaato** + **chika** 'department store basement floor').

Sequential voicing (*rendaku*)

When two words (morphemes) are compounded, the initial voiceless consonant of the second element is voiced; /t/→/d/, /k/→/g/, /s/→/z/, /h/→/b/. This is called *sequential voicing*. (Modern Japanese /h/ was pronounced [p] in Old Japanese, which explains the change /h/→/b/.)

> **maki** 'roll' + **sushi** 'sushi' → **maki-zushi** 'sushi roll'
> **hito** 'person' + **hito** 'person' → **hito-bito** 'people'
> **ori** 'folding' + **kami** 'paper' → **ori-gami** 'paper folding'
> **senba** '1000 birds' + **tsuru** 'crane' → **senba-zuru** '1,000 (paper) cranes'

The rules for sequential voicing are not simple, nor are they uniformly applied. Loan words from the West do not generally undergo sequential voicing. It also does not apply if the second element contains a voiced sound, such as /b, d, g, z/. For example, **oo-** (big) + **koe** (voice) becomes **oo-goe** (loud voice), but the combination of **oo-** (big) + **kaze** (wind) is **oo-kaze** (big wind), and not *oo-gaze. Sometimes even the same word behaves differently depending on the word it is combined with; e.g. **inochi** 'life' + **hiroi** 'picking' → **inochi-biroi** 'narrow escape' (**rendaku** applies), **ochiba** 'fallen leaves' + **hiroi** → **ochiba-hiroi** 'fallen leaf picking' (**rendaku** does not apply). Additional examples follow.

> **yude** 'boil' + **tamago** 'egg' → **yude-tamago** 'hard-boiled egg'
> **hi** 'sun' + **kage** 'shade' → **hi-kage** 'shade'
> **kami** 'paper' + **koppu** 'cup' (loan word) → **kami-koppu**

Accent

Japanese is a pitch-accent language, as opposed to stress accent. Each mora carries a high (higher) or low (lower) pitch. Unlike a tone language such as Chinese, once we know where the pitch falls for each word, the accent pattern is predictable in Japanese, although the location of where the pitch falls (i.e. the accented mora) has to be learned for each word. Pitch patterns vary greatly according to geographic regions. The discussions in this section concern **kyootsuugo** 'Common Japanese,' which is based on the Tokyo dialect. In Tokyo Japanese, the pitch of the first two moras is always different; high (H)–low (L) or low (L)–high (H).

Japanese words are either 'accented' or 'unaccented.' With unaccented words, the pitch of the initial mora is low, but that of the second mora is high and stays high for the rest of the word.

> Unaccented: **gakusee** (L–H–H–H) 'student'; **keezai-teki** (L–H–H–H–H–H) 'economical'
> Accented: **sensée** (L–H–H–L) 'teacher'; **keezái-gaku** (L–H–H–L–L–L) 'economics'

Once the location of accented mora is known, the accentuation pattern is predictable following the rules below.

(1) The pitch falls after the accented mora.
(2) Once the pitch falls, it stays low.

(3) The initial mora of a word is always low unless it is accented.

(4) The moraic nasal (e.g. **n** in **ho.n** 'book,' **ka.n.ke.e** 'relation'), the moraic consonant (the first element of a double consonant; e.g. **ga.k.ko.o** 'school,' **i.s.sa.tsu** 'one book,'and the second element of a long vowel (e.g. **ga.ku.se.e** 'student'), are never accented.

With accented words, there are *n*+1 pitch patterns for *n*-syllable words; i.e. two pitch patterns for one-syllable words, three for two-syllable words, four for three-syllable words, and so on.

> Initial mora accented: **námida** (H–L–L) 'tear'; **háshi** (H–L) 'chopsticks'
> Second mora accented: **anáta** (L–H–L) 'you'; **hashí** (L–H) 'bridge'
> Third mora accented: **atamá** (L–H–H) 'head'
> Unaccented: **sakura** (L–H–H) 'cherry blossoms'; **hashi** (L–H) 'edge'

When the accent falls on the word-final mora, its pitch pattern may seem identical to that of an unaccented word. Accented and unaccented words, however, can easily be distinguished by attaching a particle like **ga**; e.g. **hashí** 'bridge'+**ga** (L–H–L) vs. unaccented **hashi** 'edge'+**ga** (L–H–H); **atamá** 'head'+**ga** (L–H–H–L) vs. unaccented **sakura** 'cherry blossoms'+**ga** (L–H–H–H).

Near homophonous words may be distinguished by accent patterns, as in the following examples.

> **áme** (H–L) 'rain' vs. **ame** (L–H) 'candy'
> **áki** (H–L) 'autumn' vs. **aki** (L–H) 'vacancy'

3

Writing system

Four types of writing system are used in Japanese: **hiragana**, **katakana**, **kanji** and, to a lesser degree, **roomaji**. A very general description of each type follows the example sentence below.

妻はフランス語の通訳としてUNで働いています。
Tsuma wa Furansugo no tsuuyaku toshite UN de hataraite imasu.
wife *topic* France-language 's interpreter as UN at work-ing is
 Kj H Kt   Kj   H   Kj   H R H Kj H H
(H: **hiragana**; Kt: **katakana**; Kj: **kanji**; R: **roomaji**)
(My) wife works (Lit. is working) for the UN as a French interpreter.

3.1 *Hiragana*

Hiragana are a set of 46 phonetic symbols, plus a couple of diacritic devices for voiced and *p* sounds; e.g. あ (a), か (ka), が (ga), ぬ (nu), ほ (ho), ぼ (bo), ぽ (po). They were created from the cursive style of **kanji** (Chinese characters) with similar sounds; e.g. 安→あ (a), 加→か (ka), 奴→ぬ (nu), 保→ほ (ho). They are chiefly used for particles (e.g. で **de** for location), inflected parts (e.g. 行った **itta** 'go-<u>past</u>,' 若い **aoi** 'young-nonpast'), adverbs (e.g. ゆっくり **yukkuri** 'slowly'), and auxiliaries (見ている **mite iru** '<u>is</u> seeing'). Train station names also appear in **hiragana**, as well as in **kanji**, on signs.

The sound and the symbol do not match for the particles **wa** (topic), **e** ('to'), and **o** (direct object). The symbols は (ha), へ (he), and を (originally **wo**) are used respectively. Palatal sounds are written with normal size *i*-row symbols of the **hiragana** chart, followed by small や (**ya**), ゆ (**yu**), or よ (**yo**).

きや	**kya (ki**+small **ya)**	しゅ	**shu (shi**+small **yu)**
りょ	**ryo (ri**+small **yo)**	ぴょ	**pyo (pi**+small **yo)**

▶ Appendix I

3.2 *Katakana*

Katakana are a set of 46 phonetic symbols, a vowel elongation symbol (ー), and a couple of diacritic devices for voiced and *p* sounds; e.g. ア (a), カ (ka), ガ (ga), ヌ (nu), ホ (ho), ボ (bo), ポ (po). They were created by taking a fragment of **kanji** (Chinese characters) with similar sounds; e.g. 阿→ア (a), 加→カ (ka), 奴→ヌ (nu), 保→ホ (ho). Some **katakana** symbols are based on the same **kanji** as those on which the corresponding **hiragana** symbols are based, but not all of them. **Katakana** symbols look angular, compared to the curvy hiragana.

Katakana is used mainly for loan words (especially those from countries other than China), to represent sounds (onomatopoeia), to express special nuances of words, including slang expressions, and to make a sound or word stand out from the rest.

アメリカ **Amerika** 'America'   コンピュータ（一） **konpyuuta(a)** 'computer'
ゴツン **gotsun** 'thump!'   ワンワン **wanwan** 'bowwow'

ヒロシマ **Hiroshima** 'Hiroshima' (as the internationally recognized city)
キツイ **kitsui** 'difficult, harsh' (special meaning; originally 'tight')
モノとコトは使い方が違う。 **'Mono' to 'koto' wa tsukai kata ga chigau.**
　　　　　　　　　　 Mono ('thing') and **koto** ('thing') are used differently.

Palatal sounds are written with normal size **i**-row symbols of the **katakana** chart, followed by small ヤ (**ya**), ユ (**yu**), or ヨ (**yo**).

キャ　　**kya** (**ki**+small **ya**)　　　シュ　　**shu** (**shi**+small **yu**)
リョ　　**ryo** (**ri**+small **yo**)　　　ピョ　　**pyo** (**pi**+small **yo**)

To accommodate foreign sounds, some combinations of **katakana** have been devised that do not exist in **hiragana**.

ウォ **wo** (**u**+small **o**): ウォーター **wootaa** 'water' (or ウオーター **uootaa**)
ティ **ti** (**te**+small **i**): ティーバッグ **tii baggu** 'tea bag'
デュ **dyu** (**de**+small **yu**): デュース **dyuusu** 'deuce' (or ジュース **juusu**)
トゥ **tu** (**to**+small **u**): トゥー **tuu** 'two' (or ツー **tsuu**)
ファ **fa** (**fu**+small **a**): ファイト **faito** 'fighting spirit'

▶ Appendix II

3.3　*Kanji* (Chinese characters)

Kanji are logographic (word-representing) characters borrowed from Chinese since the fifth or sixth century. They are used for nouns and substantive parts of verbs and adjectives; e.g. 'wife,' 'language,' 'interpreter,' 'work' (in 'working') in the first example in this section, '(My) wife works (Lit. is working) for the UN as a French (language) interpreter.' To be literate in Japanese, one needs to know a little over 2,000 characters (called **jooyoo kanji** 'Chinese characters for daily use'), which children learn during their nine years of compulsory education. Young children's books are written in **hiragana**, and it is common for children to use **hiragana** to write words for which they do not yet know the **kanji**. Among adults, there are individual preferences even for the same words. Some people like to use **kanji**, while others do not.

3.4　*Roomaji* (Roman alphabet)

Roomaji is used mainly for acronyms (e.g. BBC, CD, OL 'office lady'), station names (for foreigners' benefit), and some brand names. Recently, it is becoming more and more common to write the names of pop artists (JUJU, Superfly), bands (e.g. GReeeeN, HY, SMAP), and songs (e.g. Love) in romaji (or English).

4

Words

4.1 Types of words according to their origin

Japanese words can be classified into three types according to their origin: those of native origin (**wago**), Chinese origin (**kango**), and Western and other origin (**gairaigo**).

> **Wago:** ie 'house,' te 'hand,' **kumo** 'cloud,' **kami** 'god'
> **Kango:** gakkoo 'school,' **kikai** 'machine,' **kee-ee** 'management,' **chuushoo** 'abstract'
> **Gairaigo:** booru 'ball' (English), **noruma** 'norma' (Russian), **kimuchi** 'kimchi' (Korean), **janbo** 'big' (Swahili meaning 'hello')

Wago (Japanese native words) largely consist of basic words relating to nature, body parts, daily routines, and traditional foods, art crafts, events, and ways of thinking. Most of them have simple sounds composed of consonant+vowel (or just vowel) sequences. As in other languages, words that are important to the speakers often have fine distinctions; e.g. **ine** 'rice (plant),' **kome** 'rice (grain),' **meshi** '(cooked) rice, meal.'

Kango (Sino-Japanese words) are words from Chinese, especially those imported before the fourteenth century. They occupy more than half the modern Japanese vocabulary. Many express abstract, scholarly and complicated concepts (e.g. **genshiryoku** 'nuclear power,' **hukuzatsu** 'complicated'), as well as those relating to one's daily life (e.g. **uma** 'horse,' **isu** 'chair') Many words come in *wago* and *kango* pairs; e.g. **owaru** vs. **shuuryoo suru** 'to end,' **muzukashii** vs. **konnan na** 'difficult.' In such cases, the *kango* represents concepts and matters of more formal nature.

Gairaigo (loan words) have come from various sources and at different times. In the sixteenth century Portuguese words (e.g. **pan** 'bread') were borrowed, and later Dutch words (e.g. **garasu** 'glass'). Since the nineteenth century, there has been an influx of words from German (e.g. **karute** 'patient's medical record'), French (e.g. **dessan** 'sketch'), Italian (**sonata** 'sonata') and, especially, English (**konpyuuta(a)** 'computer'). As new inventions and concepts are imported, so are the words along with them; e.g. **robotto** 'robot,' **konbini** 'convenience store.' Some words have triplets of *wago*, *kango* and *gairaigo*; e.g. **meshi** 'rice (sounds rough)', **gohan** 'rice (polite),' **raisu** (served with a Western meal),' and **kokoro** 'heart, spirit', **shinzoo** 'heart (organ),' **haato** 'heart (shape).' Words borrowed from certain languages are not considered *gairaigo*; e.g. **tonakai** 'reindeer' from Ainu.

4.2 Mimetic words

The Japanese language makes an extensive use of mimetic words, which can be classified into **giongo**, which mimics sounds (*onomatopoeia*, or *phonomimes*) and **gitaigo**, which expresses phenomena (*phenomimes*) and psychological states (*psychomimes*). These words are not only used in comic books and small talk, but in literature and intellectual conversations.

> **Giongo** (sounds): gaan 'pow,' **chirin** 'ting,' **tonton** 'light knock,' **dondon** 'loud knock,' **gatagata** 'loud rattle,' **buubuu** 'oink oink,' **zaazaa** 'pouring rain'

Gitaigo (phenomena and psychological states):

sarasara 'smooth,' **nyokinyoki** '(grow) quickly,' **karakara** 'dry,'
futo 'suddenly,' **gunto** 'remarkably,' **jitto** '(sit) still,' **gyotto** 'startled'

雷がゴロゴロ鳴っています。
Kaminari ga gorogoro natte imasu.
Thunder is rumbling.

課長の靴はいつもピカピカです。
Kachoo no kutsu wa itsumo pikapika desu.
The section chief's shoes are always shiny.

ふと見上げると、星がきれいだった。
Futo miageru to, hoshi ga kiree datta.
I looked up at the sky without thinking, and saw beautiful stars.

It is sometimes difficult to distinguish **giongo** from **gitaigo**; e.g. **perapera** 'fluent,' **shikushiku** 'sobbing.' Mimetic words with repeated elements express a repeated action or a prolonged state; e.g. **dokidoki** 'pounding heart,' **nebaneba** 'sticky.' Though of native origin, mimetics form a class of their own phonetically. For example, voiced consonants (e.g. b, d, z), /r/, and /p/ rarely occur in initial position of **wago** (native words), but are common in mimetics (and in **gairaigo**); e.g. **riinriin** 'ring-ring,' **pekopeko** 'hungry.'

▶ 70.2

Interrogatives

Interrogatives (also called *question words*) are words that are used to ask for information; e.g. 'who,' 'what,' 'when,' 'where,' 'why,' and 'how.' Most Japanese interrogatives start with **do-, iku-** or **nan(i)-**. **Do-**words are part of the demonstrative series **ko-so-a-do**; e.g. **koko** 'this place, here,' **soko** 'that place, there,' **asoko** 'that place far away, (way) over there,' and **doko** 'which place, where' (See **9**). **Iku-**words are few in number in modern Japanese, but **ikutsu** 'how many (objects), how old (age)' and **ikura** 'how much (price)' are used frequently. With another noun or a suffix attached to it, **nani** means 'what . . .'; e.g. **nani-go** 'what language.' **Nan** can be attached to any *counters* (*classifiers*) (see **16**) of Chinese origin, and mean 'how many . . .'; e.g. **nan-ko** 'how many (objects).'

do-	どれ	**dore**	which thing (out of three or more)
	どちら	**dochira**	which thing (out of two)
	どこ	**doko**	which place, where
	どう	**doo**	how
	どうして	**doo shite**	why (Lit. how + doing)
	どの	**dono** (+ noun)	which . . .
	どのぐらい	**dono gurai**	how much (amount), how long (time)
	どんな	**donna** (+ noun)	what type of . . .
iku-	いくつ	**ikutsu**	how many, how old
	いくら	**ikura**	how much (price)
nan(i)	何（なに or なん）	**nan(i)**	what
nani-	何人（なにじん）	**nani-jin**	what nationality
	何色	**nani-iro**	what color
nan-	何人（なんにん）	**nan-nin**	how many (people)
	何匹	**nan-biki**	how many (small animals)
	何歳	**nan-sai**	how old
	何度	**nan-do**	how many times, what degree (temperature)
	何時間	**nan-jikan**	how many hours
Other	誰	**dare**	who
	いつ	**itsu**	when

Nani 'what' is often shortened to **nan** when preceding /t/, /d/, /n/, (and /r/).

何がありますか。	**Nani ga arimasu ka.**	What is there?
何を買いますか。	**Nani o kaimasu ka.**	What are you going to buy?
何で行きましたか。	**Nan(i) de ikimashita ka.**	By what means did you go?
それは何ですか。	**Sore wa nan desu ka.**	What is that?
今何と言いましたか。	**Ima nan to iimashita ka.**	What did s/he just say?
何の本ですか。	**Nan no hon desu ka.**	What is the book about?

The above Japanese words can only be used in questions, unlike 'what,' 'which,' etc. in English, which can appear in declarative sentences; e.g. '<u>What</u> I want to say is this: the book <u>which</u> I read yesterday was interesting.'

4.4 Indefinites

Indefinite words refer to a person, thing, place, etc. in a vague way; e.g. 'something,' 'someone,' 'somewhere.' Japanese indefinites are formed by attaching the particle **ka** to an interrogative word; e.g. **nani** 'what,' **nani ka** 'something'; **dare** 'who,' **dare ka** 'someone.' In negative sentences the particle **mo** is attached to interrogatives; e.g. **nani mo** '(not) anything, nothing'; **dare mo** '(not) anyone, no one.' With indefinites, the particles **ga** (for subject) and **o** (for direct object) are usually omitted.

何か（が）ありますか。
Nani ka (ga) arimasu ka.
Is there something/anything?

何もありません。
Nani mo arimasen.
There isn't anything / There's nothing.

何か（を）見ましたか。
Nani ka (o) mimashita ka.
Did you see something/anything?

何も見ませんでした。
Nani mo mimasen deshita.
I didn't see anything; I saw nothing.

誰か（が）来ますか。
Dare ka (ga) kimasu ka.
Is someone/anyone coming?

誰も来ません。
Dare mo kimasen.
No one is coming.

When other particles are attached to interrogatives (e.g. **doko ka <u>ni</u>** 'to/in some place,' **dare ka <u>to</u>** 'with someone'), **mo** appears <u>after</u> those particles in negative sentences.

Q: ねこはどこ<u>に</u>いましたか。
Neko wa doko ka ni imashita ka.
Did you find your cat somewhere/anywhere?

A: どこ<u>に</u>もいませんでした。
Doko ni mo imasen deshita.
She was nowhere; I didn't find her anywhere.

Q: 誰か<u>と</u>話しましたか。
Dare ka to hanashimashita ka.
Did you talk with someone/anyone?

A: 誰とも話しませんでした。
Dare to mo hanashimasen deshita.
I didn't talk with anyone.

English and Japanese indefinites are quite different. In English, for example, the speaker can use words like *someone* and *something* even when he/she actually knows the person's identity (e.g. *I was busy because someone came to see me*), but this is not possible in Japanese. Also, Japanese indefinites cannot be modified as can English counterparts; e.g. *something nice*. A noun is required, in addition to the modifier such as adjectives and relative clauses.

[なにか冷たい物] を飲みたいんですが。
[Nani ka tsumetai mono] o nomitai n desu ga.
I'd like to drink something cold.

[どこか静かな所] に行きましょう。
[Doko ka shizuka na tokoro] ni ikimashoo.
Let's go somewhere quiet.

[だれか答えを知っている人] はいませんか。
[Dare ka kotae o shitte iru hito] wa imasen ka.
Is there anyone who knows the answer?

To express the meaning 'anything,' 'anyone,' etc. in the sense of 'whatever, no matter what,' and 'whoever, no matter who,' the particle combination **demo** is attached to interrogatives; e.g. **nan** 'what,' **nan demo** 'anything'; **dare** 'who,' **dare demo** 'anyone.'

Q: 何がいいですか。
Nani ga ii desu ka.
What would be good?

A: 何でもいいです。
Nan demo ii desu.
Anything would be fine.

Q: いつ行きましょうか。
Itsu ikimashoo ka.
When shall we go?

A: 私にはいつでも同じです。
Watashi ni wa itsu demo onaji desu.
Anytime would be the same for me.

誰でもいいから、呼んで下さい。
Dare demo ii kara, yonde kudasai.
It doesn't matter who, please call (someone).

Words like **nan demo** 'anything, whatever' and **dare demo** 'anyone, whoever' can also be used to mean 'everything' and 'everyone,' respectively.

こんな簡単な事、誰でもできます。
Konna kantan na koto, dare demo dekimasu.
Anyone/Everyone can do such a simple thing.

うちの犬は何でも食べます。
Uchi no inu wa nan demo tabemasu.
My dog eats anything/everything.

日本はどこでも込んでいます。
Nihon wa doko demo konde imasu.
It's crowded anywhere/everywhere in Japan.

To express an indefinite amount, **nan-/iku-** + counter + **ka** 'some, several' and **nan-/iku-** + counter + **mo** 'many' can be used. The latter expression indicates an amount or number surprisingly large to the speaker, and/or an exaggeration 'many, many . . .'

何時間か寝ました。
Nan-jikan ka nemashita.
He/she slept several hours.

何時間も寝ました。
Nan-jikan mo nemashita.
He/she slept many, many hours.

問題がいくつかあります。
Mondai ga ikutsu ka arimasu.
There are some problems.

問題がいくつもあります。
Mondai ga ikutsu mo arimasu.
There are many, many problems.

5

Sentences and sentence patterns

5.1 Sentences

5.1.1 Formal and informal style sentences

Informal style sentences end with the main predicate in plain form, while in formal style sentences, the main predicate is in polite form. All predicates in Japanese have both a plain form and a polite form. (See **6.2** regarding how they are used.) The following illustrates sentences with predicates in plain and polite nonpast affirmative forms.

	Nonpast plain form	*Nonpast polite form*
Verb:	**-u** or **-ru**	**-(i)masu**
	ik-u 'go'; **tabe-ru** 'eat'	**ik-imasu; tabe-masu**
i-Adjective:	**-i**	**-i desu**
	yasu-i 'is cheap'	**yasu-i desu**
Copula:	**da**	**desu**
	shizuka da 'is quiet'	**shizuka desu**

► 6.2; 12.1; 13

5.1.2 Affirmative and negative sentences

A negative sentence is formed by changing the main predicate into a negative form, typically represented by **-na-** or **-n**.

► **15.1** on conjugation patterns.

	Nonpast plain affirmative	*Nonpast plain negative*
Verb	**-u** or **-ru**	**-anai** or **-nai**
	ik-u 'go'; **tabe-ru** 'eat'	**ik-anai; tabe-nai**
i-Adjective:	**-i**	**-ku nai**
	yasu-i 'is cheap'	**yasu-ku nai**
Copula:	**da**	**ja nai** or **de wa nai**
	shizuka da 'is quiet'	**shizuka ja**[1] **nai**

	Nonpast polite affirmative	*Nonpast polite negative*
Verb	**-(i)masu**	**-(i)masen**
	ik-imasu 'go'; **tabe-masu** 'eat'	**ik-imasen; tabe-masen**
i-Adjective:	**-i desu**	**-ku nai desu/-ku arimasen**
	yasui desu 'is cheap'	**yasuku nai desu/yasuku arimasen**
Copula:	**desu**	**ja nai desu** or **ja arimasen**
	shizuka desu 'is quiet'	**shizuka ja nai desu/shizuka ja arimasen**

[1] **ja** can be replaced by **de wa** in a more formal style.

5.1.3 **Past and nonpast tense sentences**

A past tense sentence is marked by the past tense morpheme **-ta** appearing at the end of the main predicate.

▶ **12.1; 13.1.1; 13.2.1** on conjugation patterns.

	Past affirmative plain form	*Past affirmative polite form*
Verb:	**-ta**	**-(i)mashita**
	it-ta 'went'; **tabe-ta** 'ate'	**ik-imashita; tabe-mashita**
i-Adjective:	**-katta**	**-katta desu**
	yasu-katta 'was cheap'	**yasu-katta desu**
Copula:	**datta**	**deshita**
	shizuka datta 'was quiet'	**shizuka deshita**

	Past negative plain form	*Past negative polite form*
Verb:	**-(a)na katta**	**-masen deshita**
	ik-anakatta	**ik-imasen deshita**
	tabe-nakatta	**tabe-masen deshita**
i-Adjective:	**-ku nakatta**	**-ku nakatta desu** or **-ku arimasen deshita**
	yasuku nakatta	**yasuku nakatta desu** or
		yasuku arimasen deshita
Copula:	**ja nakatta**	**ja nakatta desu** or
		ja arimasen deshita
	shizuka ja nakatta	**shizuka ja nakatta desu** or
		shizuka ja arimasen deshita

5.2 Sentence patterns

5.2.1 Nominal (copulative) sentences

The idea of X is Y, where both X and Y are noun phrases, is expressed by X **wa** (or **ga**) Y **da** in Japanese. **Da** (informal style), **desu** (formal style), and **de aru** (literary form) are called *copulas*. This structure is generally used to describe the identity or attributes of the subject.

> 花子は学生だ。
> **Hanako wa gakusee da.** (informal style)
> Hanako is a student.

> 花子は学生です。
> **Hanako wa gakusee desu.** (formal style)
> Hanako is a student.

> 我が輩は猫である。(literary)
> **Wagahai wa neko de aru.**
> I am a cat.

▶ Appendices (conjugation tables)

Given a specific context, a nominal predicate sentence can express a wide variety of meanings beyond the identity or attribute of the subject. For example, this construction can be used as an answer to a question such as the following.

> Q: 明日は何をしますか。
> **Ashita wa nani o shimasu ka.**
> What are you going to do tomorrow?

A: 子供はサッカーです。私は買い物です。
Kodomo wa sakkaa desu. Watashi wa kaimono desu.
The kids (will play) soccer. I (will go) shopping.

Taken out of context, **Kodomo wa sakkaa desu** would mean 'the kids are soccer,' which does not make sense. However, in this context, the meaning 'what the kids will do is play soccer' is clear, and therefore, the X **wa** Y **da/desu** structure can be used.

Similarly, a sentence such as **watashi/boku wa** Y **da/desu** 'As for me, it is Y' is often used in a restaurant to express that what the speaker is ordering is Y.

In informal style speech, the copula **da** is often omitted.

Q: 何にする？
Nani ni suru?
What are you going to have?

A: 私はてんぷら。   僕はカツどん（だ）。
Watashi wa tenpura.   **Boku wa katsudon (da).**
I will have the tempura.   I will have the breaded pork cutlet on rice.

5.2.2   Adjectival sentences

In X is Y, Y can be an adjective. There are two types of adjectives, **i**-type and **na**-type. The **desu** used with **i**-adjectives indicates *politeness*, while that used with **na**-adjectives is a copula.

東京は大きい。 (**i**-adjective)
Tookyoo wa ookii.
Tokyo is big.

東京はにぎやかだ。 (**na**-adjective)
Tookyoo wa nigiyaka da.
Tokyo is lively.

▶ 13

5.2.3   Existential sentences

The structure [place **ni** X **ga aru/iru**] expresses the existence of a thing or a person. The verb **aru** is used to state the existence of an inanimate object, while **iru** is used for an animate object such as a person or an animal. **Ga** markes the subject, a thing or a person that exists.

ここに本がある。
Koko ni hon ga aru.
There is a book here.

あそこに子供がいる。
Asoko ni kodomo ga iru.
There is a child over there.

This should be distinguished from the pattern [X **wa** place **ni aru/iru**], which identifies the location where something/somebody exists. In this structure, X **wa** is the topic of the sentence and the speaker is pointing out where X is.

学校はあそこにある。
Gakkoo wa asoko ni aru.
The school is over there.

子供は家にいる。
Kodomo wa uchi ni iru.
The child is at home.

5.2.4 Verbal sentences

A verb can be intransitive (taking no object), transitive (taking one object), or ditransitive (taking two objects). In general, the subject is marked by **ga** or **wa**, the direct object by **o**, and the indirect object by **ni**. When the context makes it clear, all elements except the verb can be omitted.

> 花子が来た。
> **Hanako ga kita.** (intransitive verb)
> Hanako came.

> 花子が本を読んだ。
> **Hanako ga hon o yonda.** (transitive verb)
> Hanako read a book.

> 花子が太郎にメールを書いた。
> **Hanako ga Taroo ni meeru o kaita.** (ditransitive verb)
> Hanako wrote an email to Taro.

▶ 12

5.2.5 Topic–comment sentences

One of the most common structures in Japanese is the so-called *topic–comment* structure [X **wa** Y]. X represents the topic of the sentence, and Y is a comment on X. In many cases, X corresponds to a constituent of Y, such as the subject, object, or possessor.

Almost any noun, with its associated particle, can be made into a topic of the sentence. In **Hanako ga Ginza de hon o katta** 'Hanako bought a book in Ginza,' for example, the subject **Hanako ga**, the direct object **hon o**, or the location **Ginza de** can be topicalized. The topic particle **wa** replaces **ga** and **o**, but follows other particles like **de** (location) and **to** (partner); X **de wa** (in place X, . . .), X **to wa** (with X, . . .). It normally appears at the beginning of a sentence.

> 花子は　本を買った。
> **Hanako wa hon o katta.**
> Speaking of Hanako, (she) bought a book. (Hanako bought a book.)

Here, the topic **Hanako** is the subject of the verb **katta** 'bought' in the comment part Y.

> この本は　花子が買った。
> **Kono hon wa Hanako ga katta.**
> As for this book, Hanako bought (it).

In the above sentence, the topic **kono hon** is the direct object of the verb in the comment part Y.

In many cases, Y is simply a statement which is relevant to the topic X. There is no constituent of Y that corresponds to X. The following sentences, for example, have both a topic and a subject.

> 象は鼻が長い。
> **Zoo wa hana ga nagai.**
> As for elephants, trunks are long. (Elephants have long trunks.)

> 日本は春と秋がいい。
> **Nihon wa haru to aki ga ii.**
> As for Japan, spring and fall are good (seasons).

▶ 1.4; 11

6

Register and style

6.1 Spoken and written languages

Typically, spoken discourse is spontaneous, fragmented and relatively unplanned, while written discourse is planned. Spoken discourse is characterized by frequent occurrences of ①fillers (**nanka, anoo, eeto**, 'like', 'um', 'er' etc.), ②sentence-/clause- final particles (**ne, yo, sa**, etc.), ③repetitions, ④repairs, ⑤omission of particles like **wa** (for topic) and **o** (for direct object), ⑥sentence fragments, ⑦postposing, etc.

N: なんか最初はさ〜　Eメールの使い方　Ø　知らなくてさ〜お母さん
<u>Nanka</u> saisho wa <u>saa</u> ii-meeru no tsukaikata Ø shiranakute <u>saa</u> okaasan
　　①　　　　　　　　②　　　　　　　　　　　　⑤　　　　　　　　②　　　　⑦
At first (she) didn't know how to use email so, my mother

O: あ〜
Aa

N: んで〜なんかここに来る前に教えて（・）来たみたいな
N dee <u>nanka</u> koko ni kuru mae ni oshiete (.) kita mitaina
　　　　①
and so it's like I taught (her how to do it) before (I) came here.

The same content will appear very different, as shown below:

母は最初はEメールの使い方を知らなくて、ここに来る前に教えてきました。
Haha wa saisho wa ii-meeru no tsukaikata o shiranakute, koko ni kuru mae ni oshiete kimashita.
My mother did not know how to use email at first, and so I taught (her how to do it) before I came here.

6.2 Informal and formal styles

Informal (casual) and formal (polite) styles are distinguished first and foremost by the predicate forms. In informal style, the predicate is in plain form, and in formal style it is in polite form.

▶ 5.1

病院はあの建物ですよ。(F)
Byooin wa ano tatemono desu yo.
The hospital is that building.

病院はあの建物だよ。(I)
Byooin wa ano tatemono da yo.
The hospital is that building.

あした行きますか。(F)
Ashita ikimasu ka.
Will you go tomorrow?

あした行く？ (I)
Ashita iku?
Will you go tomorrow?

In the formal style, the verbs are often in honorific forms (exalting or humbling), as below. **Irasshaimasu** is an honorific (exalting) form of **iku** 'to go' in polite style, and **ukagaimasu** a humbling form of **iku** 'to go' in polite style.

あしたいらっしゃいますか。   あした伺います。
Ashita irasshaimasu ka.   **Ashita ukagaimasu.**
Are you coming tomorrow?   I will come tomorrow.

▶ 29

The formal (**desu/masu**) style is generally used in situations where one feels formality is appropriate or required (meeting a person for the first time, addressing strangers, in business/ public meetings, making public presentations, etc.) or when talking to someone to whom one feels respect is due, such as one's social superiors. Informal (**da/-ru**) style, on the other hand, is used in informal situations, such as when talking with one's close friends or family members. A social superior may also use plain style when talking to his/her subordinates in less formal settings, but this is generally not reciprocated. Adults often use informal style in talking to children.

In face-to-face conversation, the speakers often mix formal and informal styles. A student may shift between the two styles when talking with a professor, and vice versa. Colleagues talking with each other may do the same. How and when the speaker mixes styles is governed by complex factors, but the speaker can project various social identities and relationships through the style mixing. The speaker can also adjust the social distance between him/her and the interlocutor.

Informal (**da/-ru**) style is normally used in formal writing such as newspapers, novels, scholarly articles and essays. Personal letters are usually written in formal style.

Informal speech style has the following characteristics.

(1) The plain (**da/-(r)u**) forms of predicates are used.
(2) Particles, especially **wa** and **o**, are often dropped in informal style.
(3) In informal questions, the copula **da** and the question particle **ka** are dropped.
(4) In informal style, certain vowels are dropped. Also certain types of contraction occur.

Some frequent sound changes include the following.

> **no** 'that' → **n** (**no** → **n** preceding **desu** 'is,' **da** 'is,' **nara** 'if' **mono** 'thing' → **mon**; **node** 'because' → **nde**)
> V-**te/de iru** 'be V-ing' → V-**teru/deru** (**tabete iru** 'is eating' → **tabete ru**; **yonde iru** 'is reading' → **yonde ru**)
> V-**te/de shimau** 'finish V-ing' → V-**chau/jau** (**tabete shimau** 'finish eating' → **tabechau**; **yonde shimau** 'finish reading' → **yonjau**)
> V-**te wa** 'if you do V' → V-**cha** (**tabenakute wa ikenai** 'have to eat' → **tabenakucha ikenai**; **tabete wa ikenai** 'should not eat' → **tabecha ikenai**)
> V-**nakereba** 'have to V' → **nakya** (**tabenakereba ikenai** 'have to eat' → **tabenakya ikenai**)
> V-**te/de oku** 'do V in advance' → **toku/doku** (**tabete oku** 'eat in advance' → **tabetoku**; **yonde oku** 'read in advance' → **yondoku**)
> **to** (**yuu**) → **tte** (**yuu**) 'say that . . .'
> -**ra**, -**ru** → **n** (**suru no** 'do' → **sun no**; **shiteru no** 'be doing' → **shiten no**; **wakaranai** 'don't understand' → **wakannai**; **tsumaranai** 'not interesting' → **tsumannai**)

ジョンはさっき食堂でご飯を食べていましたよ。 (F)
Jon wa sakki shokudoo de gohan o tabete imashita yo.
John was eating in the dining hall a while ago.

ジョンはさっき食堂でご飯食べてたよ。(I)
Jon wa sakki shokudoo de gohan tabeteta yo.
John was eating in the dining hall a while ago.

それは何ですか。(F)
Sore wa nan desu ka.
What is that?

それ何？(I)
Sore nani?
What is that?

何か持って行かなければいけないんですか。(F)
Nani ka motte ikanakereba ikenai n desu ka.
Do we have to bring something?

何か持ってかなきゃいけないの？(I)
Nani ka mottekanakya ikenai no?
Do we have to bring something?

NOTE Every utterance has both formal and informal versions. In the rest of the book, both versions are not always given. In cases where several degrees of politeness/formality are indicated, sentences are marked by VF (very formal/polite), F (formal/polite) and I (informal/casual.)

▶ 30.1

6.3 Feminine (gentle) and masculine (rough) styles

The distinction between male and female speech styles is an important aspect of the Japanese language. Note, however, that the use of strongly feminine (gentle) style and strongly masculine (rough) style has declined in recent decades. The distinction can be most readily seen in (1) specific lexical items, (2) personal pronouns, (3) sentence-final particles, and (4) the use of the copula **da**.

Some specific lexical items include masculine **meshi** 'rice/meal' vs. feminine/neutral **gohan**, masculine **hara** 'stomach' vs. feminine/neutral **onaka**, masculine **kuu** 'to eat' vs. feminine/neutral **taberu**. With respect to personal pronouns, **boku** 'I,' **ore** 'I (rough),' **kimi** 'you,' **omae** 'you (rough),' and **kisama** 'you (rough)' are generally restricted to men, while women might use **atakushi** 'I,' **atashi** 'I,' and **anata** 'you.' (Note, however, that the use of second person pronouns is quite limited.)

▶ 8.1

The use of sentence-final forms can be grouped into four types. The following are some examples.

Strongly masculine:

ぞ	行くぞ
zo	**Iku zo.**
	I am going!

ぜ	行くぜ
ze	**Iku ze.**
	I am going.

〜ないか	行かないか。
nai ka	**Ikanai ka.**
	Won't you go?

V(imperative)よ	行けよ、食べろよ
yo	**Ike yo.** **Tabero yo.**
	Go! Eat!

Moderately masculine:

Plain form よ	行くよ
yo	**Iku yo.**
	I am going, I tell you.

だ＋よ/ね/よね	きれいだよ。 きれいだね。
da+yo, ne, yo ne	**Kiree da yo. Kiree da ne.**
	It's pretty. It's pretty, don't you think?
	きれいだよね。
	Kiree da yo ne.
	It's pretty, right?

Moderately feminine:

Plain form の	行くの↘。
no	**Iku no.**
	I am going, you know.

Strongly feminine:

わ↗	行くわ。
wa	**Iku wa.**
	I am going.

わよ/わね/わよね	行くわよ、行くわね。
wa yo/wa ne/wa yo ne	**Iku wa yo. Iku wa ne.**
	I am going, you know. I am going OK?
	行くわよね。
	Iku wa yo ne.
	(You) are going, right?

N/**na**-adj.＋なの	本なの。 いやなの。
na no	**Hon na no. Iya na no.**
	It's a book. I don't like it.

かしら	行くかしら。
kashira	**Iku kashira.**
	I wonder if (X) is going.

Men and women these days do not use strongly gendered language in their daily conversation. Both men and women tend to speak in a moderately masculine style, and thus there is not much gender difference with respect to sentence-final forms. However, strongly gendered styles are employed in comic books, *anime*, movie subtitles and translations of foreign novels, and also by individuals who want to create certain gendered identities.

7

Nouns and noun phrases

7.1 Types of nouns

7.1.1 Common and proper nouns

In Japanese a noun is not accompanied by articles such as 'a' and 'the,' and generally there is no distinction between a singular and a plural form. **Hon**, for example, can be 'a book,' 'the book,' 'books,' or 'the books.' Japanese nouns, moreover, are not marked for gender as are in many European languages.

Some specific nouns denoting people and personal pronouns can take the plural suffix **-tachi**; **kono hito** 'this person,' **kono hito-tachi** 'these people,' **watashi** 'I,' **watashi-tachi** 'we.' The use of **-tachi** has expanded greatly in recent years so that even animals and objects may take the suffix if the speaker/writer strongly empathizes with them; e.g. **hana-tachi** '(the/my important) flowers.'

▶ 8.1

子供たち	**kodomo-tachi**	the children
男たち	**otoko-tachi**	the men
田中さんたち	**Tanakasan-tachi**	Tanaka and others

There is also no orthographic distinction between common and proper nouns since Japanese scripts do not have capitalization.

7.1.2 Verbal nouns

Verbal nouns are nouns that can also function as a verb when combined with the verb **suru** 'to do.' In the following sentence, **benkyoo** 'study' is a noun.

日本語の勉強は楽しい。
Nihongo no benkyoo wa tanoshii.
The study of Japanese is fun.

In the following, **benkyoo suru** is a verb.

みんな来年も日本語を勉強するでしょう。
Minna rainen mo Nihongo o benkyoo suru deshoo.
Everyone will probably study Japanese next year.

As a noun, **benkyoo** can take a particle and it can be modified just like any other nouns. As a verb, it can take an object noun phrase. It is ungrammatical to have two noun phrases marked with **o** (direct object) in the same clause. One cannot therefore say *__Nihongo o benkyoo o suru__. Instead, one must say **Nihongo no benkyoo o suru** or **Nihongo o benkyoo suru**.

Many of the verbal nouns are of Sino-Japanese origin, such as **kenkyuu** 'research,' **ryokoo** 'trip,' and **kekkon** 'marriage.' Verbs borrowed from English and other languages are used as verbal nouns with the verb **suru** 'to do'; e.g. **deeto suru** 'to date,' **kisu suru** 'to kiss,' **chekku suru** 'to check.'

7.1.3 Formal nouns

Formal nouns are nouns that are used not for their lexical meanings but to serve various grammatical and pragmatic functions. They are always modified by a clause. For example, **tokoro** as a regular noun means 'place,' but as a formal noun, it is used to indicate temporal relations. Other frequently used formal nouns include **koto**, **no**, **mono**, and **wake**.

▶ 18; 23.3; 26.1

> 今食べた<u>ところ</u>です。
> **Ima tabeta <u>tokoro</u> desu.**
> I just ate / I've just eaten.

> スミスさんが日本へ行った<u>こと</u>を知っていますか。
> **Sumisu-san ga Nihon e itta <u>koto</u> o shitte imasu ka.**
> Do you know that Mr/Ms Smith went to Japan?

> 子供の時はよく外で遊んだ<u>もの</u>です。
> **Kodomo no toki wa yoku soto de asonda <u>mono</u> desu.**
> I used to play outside a lot when I was a child.

> 日本に住んでいたから、日本語が上手な<u>わけ</u>です。
> **Nihon ni sunde ita kara, Nihongo ga joozu na <u>wake</u> desu.**
> (He) lived in Japan, so it is natural that his Japanese is good.

7.2 Noun modification

7.2.1 Noun *no* noun

When a noun is used to modify another noun, **no** is used.

> 先生の本
> **sensee no hon**
> teacher's book

In **sensee no hon**, the relationship between the two nouns is that of possessor–possessed. Another common relationship between the two nouns is apposition – that is, the first noun describes an attribute of the second noun.

> 大学生のむすこ
> **daigakusee no musuko**
> (my) son, who is a college student

Any number of nouns can be connected by **no** as long as it makes sense.

> 大学生のむすこのアメリカ人の友達
> **Daigakusee no musuko no Amerikajin no tomodachi**
> an American friend of (my) son, who is a college student

> 大学の近くの喫茶店のコーヒーの味
> **daigaku no chikaku no kissaten no koohii no aji**
> the taste of the coffee of the coffee shop that is near the university

▶ 1.2; 10.1.4

7.2.2 Adjective + noun

Nouns can be modified by adjectives in their pre-nominal forms. For details, see **13.1.2**, **13.2.2**, and **13.4**.

7.2.3 Clause (relative clause) + noun

A noun can be modified by a clause, which comes before the noun. The predicate is in the plain form. The particle **wa** expressing topic cannot appear in a noun-modifying clause, though it can appear to express contrast. The subject within the clause is therefore marked by **ga**. (See 25 for details)

［田中さんが読んだ］本
[Tanaka-san ga yonda] hon
the book [Mr/Ms Tanaka read]

［この本を書いた］人
[kono hon o kaita] hito
the person [who wrote this book]

7.2.4 Pre-nouns + noun

There are a limited number of words called 'pre-nouns.' They only appear as a modifier of a noun and do not conjugate. The examples include **kono/sono/ano/dono** 'this/that/that over there/which,' **konna/sonna/anna/donna** 'this kind of/that kind of/what kind of,' **aru** 'a certain,' **ironna** 'various,' **iwayuru** 'so-called,' **ookina** 'big,' and **chiisana** 'small.'

▶ 9

この人
kono hito
this person

ある人
aru hito
a certain person

大きな家
ookina ie
a big house

いろんな所
ironna tokoro
various places

7.2.5 *to yuu* noun

To yuu modifies a noun and provides information which identifies or explains the noun that follows. N **to yuu** N, for example, is used to identify the name of a person, place or thing.

「たんぽぽ」という映画
'Tanpopo' to yuu eega
a movie called Tampopo

黒沢明という映画監督
Kurosawa Akira to yuu eega kantoku
a movie director called Akira Kurosawa

To yuu can also follow a clause. In [clause **to yuu** N], the clause introduces the content of the following noun, which tends to be related to communications (e.g. **hanashi** 'story,' **uwasa** 'rumor,' **hookoku** 'report,' **shirase** 'notification,' **nyuusu** 'news,' **denwa** 'telephone (call),' and **tegami** 'letter') and human emotions (**ki** 'feeling,' **kimochi** 'feeling,' **kanji** 'feeling,' **osore** 'fear,' and **yorokobi** 'joy').

みんな無事だという知らせがあった。
Minna buji da to yuu shirase ga atta.
We got notification that everyone was safe.

桜が満開だというニュースを聞いた。
Sakura ga mankai da to yuu nyuusu o kiita.
I heard the news that the cherry blossoms were in full bloom.

やっと全てが終わったという気がする。
Yatto subete ga owatta to yuu ki ga suru.
Finally I have the feeling that everything is over.

いつかまた会えるという感じがした。
Itsu ka mata aeru to yuu kanji ga shita.
I had the feeling that I would be able to see (him/her) again.

7.3 Noun and/or noun

Two or more nouns can be listed by the conjunctive particles **to** 'and,' **ya** 'and,' **ni** 'and,' **toka** 'things like,' and **nari** 'things like.'

(1) デパチカでお弁当とケーキを買いました。
    Depachika de obentoo <u>to</u> keeki o kaimashita.
    In the basement of the department store, I bought a boxed lunch and a cake.

(2) テレビでドラマやアニメを見ます。
    Terebi de dorama <u>ya</u> anime o mimasu.
    I watch drama and anime (and other things) on TV.

While **to** is used to list items exhaustively, **ya** gives only a partial list. In (1), for example, what I bought were two things – a boxed lunch and a cake. In (2), on the other hand, drama and anime are just two of the things (I) watch on TV.

手みやげには、食べ物とか飲み物がいいでしょう。
Temiyage ni wa, tabemono <u>toka</u> nomimono ga ii deshoo.
It's good to take things like food and drink as a gift.

Disjunction of nouns can be expressed by N **ka** N or N **nari** N.

食事はビーフかチキンを選んでください。
Shokuji wa biifu <u>ka</u> chikin o erande kudasai.
Please choose either beef or chicken for your meal.

困った時は、両親なり先生に相談したらどうですか。
Komatta toki wa, ryooshin nari sensee ni soodan shitara doo desu ka.
When you are in trouble, you should talk to people like your parents or your teacher.

8

Pronouns

Personal pronouns

Japanese has a variety of personal pronouns for first, second, and third persons. The choice of personal pronouns depends on the degree of formality, the gender, age, rank and status of the speaker and the listener, and other pragmatic factors such as the social and psychological distance between the speakers.

	Formal	*Informal*
First person singular 'I'	**watakushi** (VF) **watashi** (formal for men, neutral for women)	**boku** (male) **ore** (male, rough) **atashi** (female)
Second person singular 'you'	**anata**	**kimi** (male), **omae** (male, rough) **anta** (inelegant)
Third person singular 'he/she'	**kare/kanojo**	**aitsu** (male, rough)

The most common first person pronoun is **watashi**. **Watakushi** is more formal than **watashi**. **Boku** 'I' is predominantly used by male speakers in informal situations, while **atashi** is usually used by female speakers. For the second person pronouns, **anata** is the most neutral form, used mainly by women (and sometimes by older men). Addressing someone older and/or higher in rank with **anata** is considered rude, however. **Kimi** and **omae** are informal second person pronouns, which are predominantly used by male speakers when talking among equals or to someone socially subordinate to the speaker.

The third person pronouns **kare** 'he' or **kanojo** 'she' are not very common. They are inappropriate referring to people higher in rank, babies and small children, historical figures, etc. **Kare** and **kanojo** often mean 'boyfriend' and 'girlfriend', respectively.

Although there are a variety of personal pronouns, their usage is restricted.

1) Pronouns tend to be avoided when the speaker believes that the identity of the referent is obvious to both the speaker and the listener.

> （私は）山田です。
> **(Watashi wa) Yamada desu.**
> (I) am Yamada.

In this example, Yamada is introducing himself/herself. The subject **watashi** 'I' is omitted, because the context makes it obvious.

2) The use of **anata** 'you' should be avoided, especially when talking with your superior, someone you don't know well or someone to whom you don't feel close. When there is a need to address the listener, it is often done by name or title.

> 田中さんは学生ですか。
> **Tanaka-san wa gakusee desu ka.**
> Are (you, Mr/Ms Tanaka) a student?

3) For plural forms of pronouns, one of the suffixes **-tachi**, **-domo**, **-gata** or **-ra** may be added:

	Formal	*Informal*
First person plural 'we'	wata(ku)shi-tachi wata(ku)shi-domo	boku-tachi, boku-ra, atashi-tachi, atashi-ra
Second person plural 'you'	anata-tachi, anata-gata	kimi-tachi, omae-tachi, kimi-ra, omae-ra
Third person plural 'they'	kare-tachi/kanojo-tachi kare-ra/kanojo-ra	

The suffix **-domo** is primarily used with the formal first person pronouns **watashi** and **watakushi** 'I' to form a humble 'we.' Hence **watashi-domo** is more polite than **watashi-tachi**. **-Gata**, used with second person pronouns, is an honorific plural suffix and is more polite than **-tachi**. Hence **anata-gata** 'you (plural)' is more polite than **anata-tachi**. The suffix **-ra** can be attached to first, second and third person pronouns (e.g. **watashi-ra** 'we,' **kimi-ra** 'you (plural),' **anta-ra** 'you (plural),' **kare-ra** 'they'), and is used in informal contexts.

8.2 Reflexive and reciprocal pronouns

The reflexive pronoun in Japanse is **jibun** 'self,' and it refers to only a human referent. Unlike English, which has multiple forms of reflexive pronouns (e.g. 'myself,' 'herself'), Japanese has just one form **jibun** for first, second, and third persons. The plural form is marked by the suffix **-tachi**. **Jibun** or **jibun-tachi** can serve various grammatical functions such as the possessor (with the particle **no**), subject (with **ga**), and instrument/means (with **de**).

(a) 太郎は自分の車で出かけた。
Taroo wa jibun no kuruma de dekaketa.
Taro went out in his own car.

(b) 道子は自分が一番きれいだと思っている。
Michiko wa jibun ga ichiban kiree da to omotte iru.
Michiko considers herself to be the prettiest. (Speaking of Michiko, she thinks she is the prettiest.)

(c) これは学生が自分たちで考えた案です。
Kore wa gakusee ga jibun-tachi de kangaeta an desu.
This is an idea that the students came up with by themselves.

In (a) **jibun** refers to 'Taro' and modifies **kuruma** 'car.' In (b) **jibun** refers to Michiko and functions as the subject of the embedded sentence. In (c) **jibun-tachi** refers to the students.

Otagai 'each other' is a reciprocal pronoun and refers to human referents.

(a) 道子と健はお互いに尊敬しあっている。
Michiko to Ken wa otagai ni sonkee shiatte iru.
Michiko and Ken respect each other.

(b) お互いの気持ちを理解する事が大切だ。
Otagai no kimochi o rikai suru koto ga taisetsu da.
It is important to understand each other's feelings.

In (a) **otagai** refers to Michiko and Ken, and is used to indicate the reciprocal nature of their feelings. Here **otagai ni** 'mutually' acts as an adverb and modifies the verb **sonkee shiau** 'respect each other.' In (b), the referent of **otagai** is people in general. **Otagai**, with the possessive particle **no** 'of,' forms a phrase to modify the following noun, **otagai no kimochi** 'mutual feeling.'

Pronoun modification

In Japanese, pronouns can be modified by nouns, adjectives or clauses.

(a) Modified by nouns

学生の私には高すぎる。
Gakusee no watashi ni wa taka sugiru.
It is too expensive for me, a student.

(b) Modified by adjectives

かわいそうな私
kawaisoo na watashi
poor me

すばらしいあなた
subarashii anata
wonderful you

幸せな彼／彼女
shiawase na kare/kanojo
happy he (him)/she (her)

(c) Modified by clauses

一人では何もできない私
hitori dewa nani mo dekinai watashi
I, who cannot do anything alone

何でもできるあなた
nan demo dekiru anata
You, who can do anything

In (a) the pronoun **watashi** 'I' and the modifying noun **gakusee** are in appositive relationship. In (b), the adjectives provide characterizing information about each of the pronouns **watashi** 'I', **anata** 'you' and **kare/kanojo** 'he/she.' In (c) the pronouns **watashi** 'I' and **anata** 'you' are modified by the preceding clauses.

▶ 7.2

9

Demonstratives (*ko-so-a(-do)* words)

Concept of *ko-so-a(-do)*

Basic usage

There is a series of demonstrative words in Japanese, whose initial sounds are **ko-**, **so-**, **a-** and **do-**; e.g. **kore** 'this thing,' **sore** 'that thing,' **are** 'that thing far away,' **dore** 'which one of the three or more things?'. **Do-**words are interrogatives (question words). The choice of **ko-**, **so-** and **a-** depends on the distance between the speakers and thing(s) referred to by the demonstrative. **Ko-**words are used when the speaker is talking about something close to him-/herself, **so-**words for something close to the listener, and **a-**words for something away from both the speaker and the listener.

> これをください。
> **Kore o kudasai.**
> Please give me this / I will have this.

> それはいくらですか。
> **Sore wa ikura desu ka.**
> How much is that?

> あれは銀行です。
> **Are wa ginkoo desu.**
> That over there is a bank.

> 田中さんの傘はどれですか。
> **Tanaka-san no kasa wa dore desu ka.**
> Which one is Mr/Ms Tanaka's umbrella?

Anaphoric usage

The **ko-so-a(-do)** words are also used to refer to an element mentioned in the preceding discourse. In this case, the **so-**series is used when either the speaker or the listener (i.e. just one party) is familiar with the referent, while **a-**series is used when both the speaker and the listener are (or are assumed to be) familiar with it.

In the following exchange, B is not familiar with the person in question (i.e. Tanaka's friend), and thus **sono** is used.

> A: きのう 田中さんが友達を紹介してくれたよ。
> **Kinoo Tanaka-san ga tomodachi o shookai shite kureta yo.**
> Yesterday Mr Tanaka introduced me to his friend.

> B: その人、どんな人？
> <u>**Sono**</u> **hito, donna hito?**
> What is/was the person like?

In the following exchange, on the other hand, the speaker assumes that the listener knows the person being talking about, and hence uses **ano**.

去年パーティーで会った女の人、覚えてるでしょ。<u>あの人</u>、今どうしてるかな。

Kyonen paatii de atta onna no hito, oboete ru desho? <u>Ano</u> hito ima doo shite ru ka na.

You remember the lady we met at the party last year, right? I wonder what she (Lit. that person) is doing now.

9.2 Types of demonstratives

Ko-so-a(-do) words can refer to things, locations, directions, etc. The words indicating direction have neutral and polite forms.

thing	これ **kore** this thing	それ **sore** that thing	あれ **are** that thing over there	どれ **dore** which one
Location	ここ **koko** here	そこ **soko** there	あそこ **asoko** over there	どこ **doko** where
Direction (neutral)	こっち **kotchi** this way	そっち **sotchi** that way	あっち **atchi** that way over there	どっち **dotchi** which way
Direction (polite)	こちら **kochira** this way	そちら **sochira** that way	あちら **achira** that way over there	どちら **dochira** which way

Some **ko-so-a(-do)** words modify nouns (e.g. **kono** 'this,' **konna** 'this kind of'), and others modify verbs (e.g. **koo** 'this way').

Demonstrative adjective 1	この **kono** this N	その **sono** this N	あの **ano** that N	どの **dono** which N
Demonstrative adjective 2 (kind of)	こんな **konna** this kind of	そんな **sonna** that kind of	あんな **anna** that kind of	どんな **donna** what kind of
Manner	こう **koo** like this	そう **soo** like that (as I or you just mentioned)	ああ **aa** like that (as we know in common)	どう **doo** how

The polite versions of the direction words, **kochira**, **sochira**, **achira**, and **dochira**, can also be used to refer to a person:

こちらは山田さんです。
Kochira wa Yamada-san desu.
This is Mr/Ms Yamada.

そちらは田中さんです。
Sochira wa Tanaka-san desu.
That person is Mr/Ms Tanaka.

あちらはどなたですか。
Achira wa donata desu ka.
Who is that person over there?

鈴木さんはどちらですか。
Suzuki san wa dochira desu ka.
Which person is Mr/Ms Suzuki?

10

Particles

10.1 Case particles

A case particle immediately follows a noun phrase indicating its grammatical function in relation to the verb. There are four such particles; **ga** (nominative case), **o** (accusative case), **ni** (dative case), and **no** (genitive case).

10.1.1 *ga*

Ga marks the subject of the sentence. In a sentence that describes someone's action, 'subject' refers to the *performer* of the action and, when a sentence describes a state, it refers to the person or thing being described.

> 今日友達が来ます。
> **Kyoo tomodachi ga kimasu.**
> A friend of mine is coming today.

> 秋になると、紅葉がきれいです。
> **Aki ni naru to, kooyoo ga kiree desu.**
> When fall comes, the colors of the leaves are beautiful.

Ga expressing subject is used in two types of situations. In one, the speaker assumes that the *subject* part represents a 'new' (unexpected) piece of information to the hearer. In another, the information contained in the *whole sentence* is new to the hearer or something that the speaker has just discovered (e.g. 'Oh, the bus is coming!').

> レディーガガさん<u>が</u>その歌を作りました。
> **Redii Gaga-san <u>ga</u> sono uta o tsukurimashita.**

---

(1) [In response to 'Who wrote that song?']

   <u>Lady Gaga</u> wrote that song / It's <u>Lady Gaga</u> who wrote that song.
   (That someone wrote that song is already known to the speaker and the hearer. What is new is that <u>Lady Gaga</u> did it.)

(2) [In response to 'What happened?' or 'Nice song, isn't it!']

   You know what? Lady Gaga wrote that song.
   (The whole sentence is presented as new information.)

桜<u>が</u>とてもきれいです。
Sakura <u>ga</u> totemo kiree desu.

(1) [In response to 'What is pretty?']

Cherry blossoms are very pretty / It's cherry blossoms that are very pretty. (That something is pretty is already known. What is new is the cherry blossoms part.)

(2) [In response to 'What is the park like?' or to express the speaker's surprise]

The cherry blossoms are very pretty / Oh, the cherry blossoms are very pretty!

▶ **11.5** for more on the differences between **wa** and **ga**

With certain predicates that express states (e.g. liking, desire, ability), the direct object is marked by **ga**, somewhat akin to the object of adjectives in English such as 'to be fond of' and 'to be tired of.' The verbs and adjectives that usually mark the direct object by **ga** include the following.

(1) Likes and dislikes: *suki da* 'like,' *kirai da* 'dislike'

私は甘いものが好きです。
Watashi wa amai mono ga suki desu.
I like sweet things.

(2) Desire: V-*tai* 'want to,' *hoshii* 'want (something)'

ビールが飲みたいなあ！
Biiru ga nomi-tai naa!
I want to drink beer!

新しい車がほしいです。
Atarashii kuruma ga hoshii desu.
I want a new car.

(3) Ability: V-*rareru/-eru* 'can,' *dekiru* 'can do,' *joozu da* 'good at,' *heta da* 'poor at'

何かスポーツができますか。
Nani ka supootsu ga dekimasu ka.
Can you do any sports?

漢字が書けます。
Kanji ga kakemasu.
I can write kanji.

(4) Understanding: *wakaru* 'understand'

「フェミニスト」という言葉の意味がわかりません。
'Feminisuto' to yuu kotoba no imi ga wakarimasen.
I don't understand the meaning of the word 'feminisuto.'

(5) Need: *iru* 'need'

日本に行くには、お金がいります。
Nihon ni iku ni wa, okane ga irimasu.
To go to Japan, one needs money.

10.1.2 *o*

The particle **o** marks the direct object of the verb.

もっと野菜を食べなさい。
Motto yasai o tabenasai.
Eat more vegetables.

母に毎日メールを書いています。
Haha ni mainichi meeru o kaite imasu.
I write an e-mail to my mother every day.

The particle **o** also marks other functions, such as space that one passes through or crosses.

> この道をまっすぐ行ってください。
> **Kono michi o massugu itte kudasai.**
> Please go straight along this street.

> ３つ目の角を右にまがってください。
> **Mittsume no kado o migi ni magatte kudasai.**
> Turn right at the third corner.

> それから、橋を渡ってください。
> **Sorekara, hashi o watatte kudasai.**
> After that, cross the bridge.

> 公園を通っていきましょうか。
> **Kooen o tootte ikimashoo ka.**
> Shall we go through the park?

> ７時頃会社を出ました。
> **Shichiji-goro kaisha o demashita.**
> I left the office around seven o'clock.

> 電車を降りて、バスに乗り換えた。
> **Densha o orite basu ni norikaeta.**
> I got off the train and transferred to the bus.

Some verbs that express emotion (e.g. grieve, rejoice) are intransitive. In such cases, the particle **o** marks cause (of the grief, joy, etc.).

> 父は母の死を悲しんだ。
> **Chichi wa haha no shi o kanashinda.**
> My father grieved at the death of my mother.

There is a constraint that only one use of **o** is allowed in the same clause. To say **benkyoo o suru** 'study' with an object, for example, **X o benkyoo o suru** is not possible. Instead, it is expressed in one of two ways.

> 大学で英語<u>を</u>勉強した。
> **Daigaku de [Eego] <u>o</u> benkyoo shita.**
> I studied [English] in college.

> 大学で英語<u>の</u>勉強<u>を</u>した。
> **Daigaku de [Eego <u>no</u> benkyoo] <u>o</u> shita.**
> I studied English in college. (Lit. I did the [study of English] in college.)

10.1.3 *ni*

The particle **ni** marks indirect object, meaning 'to' or 'for.'

> 私は日本にいる友達にワインを送った。
> **Watashi wa Nihon ni iru tomodachi ni wain o okutta.**
> I sent a bottle of wine to my friend in Japan.

> （私は）友達に電話をかけた。
> **(Watashi wa) tomodachi ni denwa o kaketa.**
> I made a telephone call to my friend.

10.1.4 *no*

The particle **no** links two nouns into a noun phrase, in which the preceding noun modifies the following noun. The meaning varies depending on the relationship between the two nouns, such as the possessor, content, location, or source.

これは私のコンピュータです。
Kore wa watashi no konpyuuta desu.
This is my computer.

これはコンピュータの本です。
Kore wa konpyuuta no hon desu.
This is a book on computers.

あの人は日本語の先生です。
Ano hito wa Nihongo no sensee desu.
He/She is a Japanese teacher (a teacher of Japanese).

日本のデパートはおもしろいと思う。
Nihon no depaato wa omoshiroi to omou.
I think the department stores in Japan are interesting.

私のオフィスの窓からの眺めは素晴らしいです。
Watashi no ofisu no mado kara no nagame wa subarashii desu.
The view from my office window is wonderful.

10.2 Postpositions

Postpositions are particles that follow nouns and indicate various meanings such as location (**ni**, **de**), direction (**ni**, **e**), point in time (**ni**), partner (**to**), means (**de**), starting point (**kara**), ending point (**made**), target (**ni**), and source (**ni**).

10.2.1 *ni*

Two of the most common uses of **ni** are to indicate the location where someone or something exists and the specific point in time (e.g. at two o'clock) when something happens. **Ni** is not used for a time span (e.g. two hours) or non-specific time (e.g. every day). Some typical uses of **ni** are illustrated below.

(1) Location where someone or something exists: 'at, in, on'

めがねはここにありますよ。
Megane wa koko ni arimasu yo.
Here are (your) glasses.

(2) Time when something happens: 'at, in, on'

私は毎朝7時に家を出ます。
Watashi wa maiasa shichi-ji ni ie o demasu.
I leave my house at seven o'clock every morning.

土曜日にやりましょう。
Doyoobi ni yarimashoo.
Let's do it on Saturday.

(3) Direction: 'to'

きのう横浜に行きました。
Kinoo Yokohama ni ikimashita.
I went to Yokohama yesterday.

(4) Place where the result of an action remains: 'on(to),' 'in(to)'

いすに座ってください。
Isu ni suwatte kudasai.
Please sit on the chair.

壁に絵をかけた。
Kabe ni e o kaketa.
I hung a picture on the wall.

駅の前でタクシーに乗りました。
Eki no mae de takushii ni norimashita.
I caught a taxi in front of the (train) station.

どこの大学に入りましたか。
Doko no daigaku ni hairimashita ka.
Which university did you get into?

(5) Source: 'from,' 'by'

それは田中さんに聞いたんですけど...
Sore wa Tanaka-san ni kiita n desu kedo ...
I heard that from Mr/Ms Tanaka.

10.2.2 *de*

The most common use of **de** is to indicate the location where an action or event takes place.

どこで会いましょうか。
Doko de aimashoo ka.
Where shall we meet?

レセプションは東京のホテルでありました。
Resepushon wa Tookyoo no hoteru de arimashita.
The reception was held at a hotel in Tokyo.

Another use of **de** is to indicate the means by which one carries out an action.

時間がないから、タクシーで行きましょう。
Jikan ga nai kara, takushii de ikimashoo.
Since we don't have much time, let's go by taxi.

フォークではなく箸で食べてください。
Fooku dewa naku hashi de tabete kudasai.
Please eat with chopsticks, not a fork.

De also indicates 'scope,' or the time or amount required for the verb (or other predicate) to be realized.

後1時間で映画が始まります。
Ato ichijikan de eega ga hajimarimasu.
The movie starts in one hour.

このリンゴは５つで６００円でした。
Kono ringo wa itsutsu de roppyakuen deshita.
These apples were five for 600 yen. (Lit. 600 yen with five).

二人でどこかに行きませんか。
Futari de doko ka ni ikimasen ka.
Shall we go somewhere, the two of us (Lit. in a group of two)?

世界で一番長い川はアマゾン川でしょう？
Sekai de ichiban nagai kawa wa Amazon-gawa deshoo?
Isn't the Amazon the longest river in the world?

10.2.3 *de* vs. *ni*

De marks the location of an action while **ni** marks the location of an existing person, animal or thing. Generally, the verb **aru** 'be, to exist' takes **ni** when the subject is an object (thing). When the subject represents an event such as a party, lecture and movie, however, the particle **de** is used.

> 林先生の家でパーティーがあるそうです。
> **Hayashi-sensee no ie de paatii ga aru soo desu.**
> I hear there will be a party at Professor Hayashi's house.

Sometimes there is a choice between **de** and **ni** with a location phrase, but the meanings will be different. In (1) below, **shigoto beya** 'the workroom' refers to the place where the shelf making took place. The shelf may have been built for any room, while in (2), it is specifically for the workroom, where the shelf remains.

> (1) 仕事部屋でたなを作った。
> **Shigoto-beya de tana o tsukutta.**
> I made a shelf in the workroom.

> (2) 仕事部屋にたなを作った。
> **Shigoto-beya ni tana o tsukutta.**
> I made a shelf for the workroom.

Likewise, the location **koko** 'here' in (3) indicates where the action (of writing) takes place, whereas it indicates the location where the result of the action remains in (4).

> (3) ここで書いてください。
> **Koko de kaite kudasai.**
> Please write here (in this room).

> (4) ここに書いてください。
> **Koko ni kaite kudasai.**
> Please write here (on this paper).

10.2.4 *to*

The basic meaning of **to** is 'with,' to indicate the partner with whom someone does something.

> 週末は友達と勉強します。
> **Shuumatsu wa tomodachi to benkyoo shimasu.**
> I am going to study with my friends on the weekend.

> 山田さんと結婚することにしました。
> **Yamada-san to kekkon suru koto ni shimashita.**
> I have decided to marry Mr/Ms Yamada.

> 友達と別れてから，一人で喫茶店へ行きました。
> **Tomodochi to wakarete kara, hitori de kissaten e ikimashita.**
> After parting from my friends, I went to a coffee shop alone.

The particle **to** is also used with the object of comparison; e.g. (same) as, (similar) to, and (different) from.

> 韓国語は日本語と似ていると言われています。
> **Kankokugo wa Nihongo to nite iru to iwarete imasu.**
> It is said that the Korean language is similar to the Japanese language.

> 日本語は英語と随分違います。
> **Nihongo wa Eego to zuibun chigaimasu.**
> The Japanese language is quite different from English.

Certain verbs can take either **to** or **ni** to indicate the person with whom one carries out an action. In the following sentences, **to** indicates that the speaker and the friend were equal partners of the action; i.e. the meeting took place with mutual agreement, while **ni** indicates that the meeting was not mutually agreed upon and that the speaker 'ran into' the teacher.

図書館で友達と会いました。
Toshokan de tomodachi to aimashita.
I met with my friend at the library.

図書館で先生に会いました。
Toshokan de sensee ni aimashita.
I saw (or ran into) my teacher at the library.

In the examples below, too, when **to** is used, the friend was an equal partner in the discussion, whereas **ni** indicates that the speaker went to the friend to consult.

友達に相談した。
Tomodachi ni soodan shita.
I consulted my friend.

友達と相談した。
Tomodachi to soodan shita.
I discussed (the matter) with my friend.

10.2.5 *e*

The particle **e** indicates the direction toward which something or someone moves. In speech, the particle **ni** is frequently used instead of **e**.

明日大阪へ行きます。
Ashita Oosaka e ikimasu.
I am going to Osaka tomorrow.

田中さんはもう家へ帰りましたよ。
Tanaka-san wa moo uchi e kaerimashita yo.
Mr/Ms Tanaka has already gone home.

10.2.6 *kara, made*

kara 'from, since' expresses a starting point, both in terms of time and space, and **made** 'until, to' expresses an ending point.

３時まで待ちましょう。
Sanji made machimashoo.
Let's wait until three o'clock.

日本の大学では二月から三月の終わりまで休みのところが多い。
Nihon no daigaku de wa nigatsu kara sangatsu no owari made yasumi no tokoro ga ooi.
Many universities in Japan don't have classes from February through (until) the end of March.

九州から北海道まで日本全国を旅行した。
Kyuushuu kara Hokkaidoo made Nihon zenkoku o ryokoo shita.
I traveled throughout Japan, from Kyushu to Hokkaido.

ここから富士山がきれいに見えます。
Koko kara Fujisan ga kiree ni miemasu.
You can see Mt. Fuji clearly from here.

To indicate a deadline or the point by which something is done, **made ni** 'by' is used.

明日の１時までに連絡してください。
Ashita no ichiji made ni renraku shite kudasai.
Please contact me by one o'clock tomorrow.

10.3 **Adverbial (semantic) particles**

Among the adverbial (or semantic) particles, **wa** (for topic and contrast), **mo** 'also (for similarity),' **shika** 'only,' and **dake** 'just, only' are frequently used. When these particles are added to a noun (or noun + particle), the original function of the noun, such as subject, direct object, loation, and partner, does not change, but additional meanings are expressed. In **Ken ga sushi o tabeta** 'Ken ate sushi,' for example, **Ken** functions as the subject, and **sushi** as the direct object. With the particle **mo** 'also, too' attached to it, **sushi** is still the direct object; **Ken ga sushi mo tabeta** 'Ken ate sushi, too.' Likewise, **Ken** remains the subject in **Ken mo sushi o tabeta** 'Ken, too, ate sushi.'

▶ See **11** for detailed discussion of the particle **wa**

(a) **Ken dake sushi o tabeta.**
Only Ken (subject) ate sushi (direct object).

(b) **Ken wa sushi dake tabeta.**
Ken (subject and topic) ate only sushi (direct object).

(c) **Ken wa gakkoo de benkyoo suru.**
Ken (subject and topic) studies at school (location).

(d) **Ken wa gakkoo de shika benkyoo shinai.**
Ken (subject and topic) studies only at school (location).

When these particles are added to **ga** (subject) and **o** (direct object), they replace **ga** and **o**. Otherwise, they follow other particles. The following are examples with **mo** 'also.'

ga + **mo** → **mo**
o + **mo** → **mo**
ni / de / to / e / made / kara + **mo**
→ **ni mo / de mo / to mo / e mo / made mo / kara mo**

ジョンが来た。メリーも来た。
Jon ga kita. Merii mo kita.
John came. Mary also came.

ジョンは日本語を話す。そして中国語も話す。
John wa Nihongo o hanasu. Soshite Chuugokugo mo hanasu.
John speaks Japanese. And he also speaks Chinese.

マクドナルドはアメリカにある。日本にもある。
Makudonarudo wa Amerika ni aru. Nihon ni mo aru.
McDonald's is in America. It is also in Japan.

Shika and **dake** meaning 'only,' are very different. First, **shika** can only be used in a negative sentence or with a predicate with negative meaning (e.g. **dame** 'no good, bad'), while **dake** can be used in both affirmative and negative sentences. Second, **shika** implies that the speaker views the amount or action expressed in the sentence to be less than expected, while **dake** has no such implication. As such, **dake** sounds objective, meaning 'no more, no less, just that much,' but **shika** sounds subjective, often expressing the speaker's regret (though not always).

五千円しかありません。
Gosen en shika arimasen.
I only have 5,000 yen (and that's too bad).

(ちょうど) 五千円だけあります。
(Choodo) gosen en dake arimasu.
I have exactly 5,000 yen.

昨日は田中さんしか来ませんでした。
Kinoo wa Tanaka-san shika kimasen deshita.
Only Mr/Ms Tanaka came yesterday (I expected more people to show up.)

時間がなかったから、コーヒーだけ飲みました。
Jikan ga nakatta kara, koohii dake nomimashita.
Since I did not have time, I just (only) had coffee.

In response to a question with **takusan** 'many,' for example, **shika** is appropriate, but not **dake**.

Q:　ビールはたくさん飲みましたか。
　　Biiru wa takusan nomimashita ka.
　　Did you drink lots of beer?

A:　いいえ、1本しか飲んでいません。
　　(<u>not</u> *いいえ、1本だけ飲みました。)
　　Iie, ippon shika nonde imasen.
　　(<u>not</u> *Iie, ippon dake nomimashita.)
　　No, I only drank one bottle of beer.

10.4　Sentence-final (or interactive) particles

Among the sentence-final (or interactive) particles, **ka**, **ne(e)**, **yo**, and **yo ne** are the most frequently used.

10.4.1　*ka*

ka is attached to the end of a sentence to form a question.

▶ 32

いつ日本に行きますか。
Itsu Nihon ni ikimasu ka.
When are you going to Japan?

10.4.2　*ne, nee*

ne and **nee** are attached to the end of a sentence to form a tag question and ask for agreement; 'right?' 'eh?'. They are also frequently used to express rapport. In the example below, speaker A comments on the weather and asks for agreement with **ne**. Speaker B answers 'yes, it is,' with another **ne**. The two instances of **ne** are obligatory. Without them, the sentences would be declarative, with the speaker announcing something the other party does not know about, which would be odd in this situation. Such an exchange about weather is often used in place of sentences like 'How are you?' in English, and functions as part of the greetings.

A:　いい天気ですね。
　　Ii tenki desu ne.
　　Nice weather, isn't it.

B:　そうですね。
　　Soo desu ne.
　　Yes, it is.

ne is also used to ask for confirmation.

映画は7時からですね。
Eega wa shichiji kara desu ne.
The movie starts at seven, right?

> A: あのう、山田花子ですけど。
> **Anoo, Yamada Hanako desu kedo.**
> Um, my name is Hanako Yamada.

> B: 山田花子さんですね？
> **Yamada Hanako-san desu ne?**
> Ms Hanako Yamada?

Ne, usually elongated as **nee**, often expresses exclamation.

> きれいですねぇ。
> **Kiree desu nee.**
> (Wow!) It's beautiful, isn't it.

> それは大変だったねぇ。
> **Sore wa taihen datta nee.**
> That must have been tough.

Another function of **ne** is to soften the tone of a request (e.g. V-**te kudasai** 'please do . . .') made by someone higher in rank to his/her social subordinates. When a social subordinate makes a request, it is more appropriately expressed as a question (e.g. V-**te kudasaimasen ka** 'will you please do . . . ?').

> この書類、見ておいて下さいね？
> **Kono shorui, mite oite kudasai ne?**
> Please have a look at this document, OK?

Some instances of **ne(e)** are optional. In such cases, the sentence sounds as though the speaker is consulting his/her memory. The second instance of **ne** in speaker B's sentence below is such an example.

> A: このみかん、いくらですか。
> **Kono mikan, ikura desu ka.**
> How much are these tangerines?

> B: そうですねぇ . . .、500円ですね。
> **Soo desu nee . . . , gohyaku en desu ne.**
> Let's see . . . , they're 500 yen, I'd say.

The particles **ne** and **nee** (as well as **ka, yo**, etc.) are highly interactive and are mainly used in spoken language. In written language such as e-mail messages and personal letters, they may appear when the speaker is writing as if he/she were speaking to the addressee directly.

Ne(e) is used not only after sentences, but also after phrases. With each instance of **ne(e)**, the speaker makes sure that the hearer understands him/her up to that point. The hearer is expected to respond with **hai** or **ee** (in formal conversation) or **un** (in informal conversation) to each to assure the speaker that he/she is following. This kind of **ne** is especially common in telephone conversations.

> あのですね、昨日ですね、お宅にうかがったんですけど。
> **Ano desu ne, kinoo desu ne, o-taku ni ukagatta n desu kedo.**
> Um, yesterday, I visited your place.

10.4.3 *yo*

Yo is used when the speaker provides a piece of new information and asserts it. Not only is it emphatic, but it can also carry such meanings as 'I'm telling you' and 'I bet you didn't know that.' It can therefore sound rude if used to someone higher in rank, such as a student to his/her teacher (e.g. **Wakarimasu yo** 'Of course I understand!').

来月で会社を辞めることにしたよ。
Raigetsu de kaisha o yameru koto ni shita yo.
I have decided to leave the company next month, (I tell you).

それは違いますよ。
Sore wa chigaimasu yo.
I'm telling you, that is wrong.

10.4.4 *yo ne*

Yo ne expresses the combined meaning of asserting and confirming. Three types of usage can be identified.

(1) Confirming that the addressee shares the information:

あそこに青い建物が見えますよね。
Asoko ni aoi tatemono ga miemasu yo ne.
You see a blue building there, right?

(2) Confirming information of which the speaker is not completely certain

私、きのう、寝る時、薬飲んだよね。
Watashi, kinoo, neru toki, kusuri nonda yo ne.
I took medicine when I went to bed yesterday, didn't I?

(3) Asserting + expressing rapport:

あの時は死ぬかと思ったよねえ。
Ano toki wa shinu ka to omotta yo nee.
I thought I was going to die, you know.

▶ 77.2

10.5 **Complex particles**

Ni totte means 'as for' 'for' or 'to' and expresses that some evaluation holds true for someone or from someone's viewpoint.

私にとって外国語の勉強はそんなに難しくない。
Watashi ni totte gaikokugo no benkyoo wa sonna ni muzukashiku nai.
Studying a foreign language is not so difficult for me.

あなたにとって幸せとは何ですか。
Anata ni totte shiawase to wa nan desu ka.
What does happiness mean to you?

Both **ni tsuite** and **ni kanshite** 'about, regarding, concerning' follow a noun phrase and modify the verb, which usually relates to communication; e.g. talk, write, read, think. To modify another noun phrase, the particle **no** is added after the complex particle.

地球温暖化に関して（or について）書きました。
Chikyuu ondanka ni kanshite (or ni tsuite) kakimashita.
I wrote about global warming.

［地球温暖化に関しての（or についての）レポート］を書きました。
[Chikyuu ondanka ni kanshite no (or ni tsuite no) repooto] o kakimashita.
I wrote [a report on global warming].

この問題に関して（or について）どう考えますか。
Kono mondai ni kanshite (or ni tsuite) doo kangaemasu ka.
What do you think about this issue?

11

Topic marker *wa*

The particle **wa** introduces the topic of a sentence. The topic is a word or a group of words that indicates what the sentence is about. When the speaker can assume that the hearer knows what he/she is talking about, the speaker can introduce that item as a topic with the particle **wa**.

▶ 1.4; 5.2.5

11.1 How *wa*-phrases are formed

Any noun phrases, postpositional phrases or nominalized phrases can become a topic of the sentence. **Wa** replaces particle **ga** (subject marker) and **o** (object marker), while it attaches to other particles (**ni, de, to, e, kara, made**, etc.)

田中さんが → 田中さんは
Tanaka-san ga → Tanaka-san wa

本を → 本は
hon o → hon wa

田中さんに → 田中さんには
Tanaka-san ni → Tanaka-san ni wa

日本で → 日本では
Nihon de → Nihon de wa

The topic phrase generally appears at the beginning of a sentence. Compare the sentences with and without a topic.

ジョンがこの本を書きました。
Jon ga kono hon o kakimashita. (no topic)
John wrote this book.

この本はジョンが書きました。
Kono hon wa Jon ga kakimashita. (kono hon wa is the topic.)
Speaking of this book, John wrote it.

京都でお寺を見ました。
Kyooto de otera o mimashita. (no topic)
(I) saw temples in Kyoto.

京都ではお寺を見ました。
Kyooto de wa otera o mimashita. (Kyoto de wa is the topic.)
In Kyoto, (I) saw temples.

11.2 Topic noun phrases

An item which has been mentioned in a previous sentence often becomes the topic in the following sentence(s). In the example below, Smith is introduced as a non-topic first and then becomes the topic of the following sentence.

> 私の友達にスミスという人がいるんですが、<u>スミスさんは</u>日本語がペラペラです。
> **Watashi no tomodachi ni Sumisu to yuu hito ga iru n desu ga, <u>Sumisu-san wa</u>**
> **Nihongo ga perapera desu.**
> I have a friend named Smith, and he/she is fluent in Japanese.

Generic nouns (e.g. 'the Japanese,' 'dogs') and nouns which can be assumed to be publicly known to most people, such as well-known figures, can become a topic without being mentioned previously.

> 日本人はよく働く。
> **Nihonjin wa yoku hataraku.**
> Japanese people work a lot.

> リンカーン大統領はイリノイで生まれた。
> **Rinkaan daitooryoo wa Irinoi de umareta.**
> President Lincoln was born in Illinois.

There are other ways a noun can be a topic without being previously mentioned. The important thing is that the hearer can identify what the speaker is talking about from the context. The sentence type also contributes to whether a noun can be a topic or not. In an [X is Y] type of sentence, where Y characterizes X, X tends to be a topic marked by **wa**.

(a) お金が落ちている。
     Okane ga ochite iru.
     Look! There is money on the ground!

(b) お金は大切だ。
     Okane wa taisetsu da.
     Money is important.

The same noun **okane** appears both in (a) and (b). In (a), money refers to specific money that is on the ground, while in (b), it refers to money in the generic sense. Also, while sentence (a) describes a specific situation that exists at the time of speaking, sentence (b) is a generic statement. Hence, the use of **X wa** in (b).

11.3 *wa* marking contrast

Wa is also used to contrast two or more things, people, etc., whether they are all overtly mentioned or not. The contrastive **wa** is stressed with high pitch. When there is another particle directly preceding it, that particle is pronounced with high pitch.

> 田中さん<u>は</u>来ましたが、山田さん<u>は</u>来ませんでした。
> **Tanaka-san <u>wa</u> kimashita ga, Yamada-san <u>wa</u> kimasen deshita.**
> Mr/Ms Tanaka came, but Mr/Ms Yamada did not come.

> 子供はうち<u>では</u>日本語を話しますが、学校<u>では</u>英語です。
> **Kodomo wa uchi <u>de</u> wa Nihongo o hanashimasu ga, gakkoo de wa Eego desu.**
> My child speaks Japanese at <u>home</u>, but English at <u>school</u>.

In a negative sentence, one **wa** usually indicates contrast. In the example below, the first **wa** (**watashi wa**) indicates topic, but the second **wa** (**osushi wa**) indicates contrast. The sentence states that the speaker does not eat sushi, but implies that he/she eats other Japanese food.

私は日本料理が好きですが、おすしは食べません。
Watashi wa nihonryoori ga suki desu ga, osushi <u>wa</u> tabemasen.
I like Japanese food, but I don't eat sushi.

The following sentence implies that the speaker went to other places, but not London.

夏休みはヨーロッパへ行きました。ロンドンへは行きませんでしたが、
とても楽しかったです。
Natsuyasumi wa Yooroppa e ikimashita. Rondon e <u>wa</u> ikimasen deshita ga, totemo tanoshikatta desu.
I went to Europe for the summer vacation. I did not go to London, but it was a lot of fun.

When there are more than two **wa** phrases in a sentence, the **wa** that immediately precedes the predicate is usually interpreted as contrastive.

私はきのうはコーヒーは飲みませんでした。
Watashi wa kinoo wa koohii <u>wa</u> nomimasen deshita.
I didn't drink coffee yesterday. (The sentence implies that the speaker drank something else.)

11.4 *wa* with adverbs and verbs

The particle **wa** also occurs with adverbs and verbs. When it does, **wa** is invariably interpreted as contrastive. The following sentence means that the speaker can speak a little but not <u>very well</u>.

大学でフランス語を習いましたが、上手には話せません。
Daigaku de Furansugo o naraimashita ga, joozu ni wa hanasemasen.
I took French in college, but I can't speak well.

When **wa** is used with verbs, it follows the stem of the **-masu** form and is followed by an auxiliary verb **suru** 'to do.' The sentence below implies that there are other problems with the person (for example, he is always late for classes.)

休みはしないんですが . . .。
Yasumi wa shinai n desu ga . . .
(He) does not <u>skip classes</u>, but . . .

11.5 *wa* vs. *ga* (summary)

The following principles are useful to keep in mind for the use of the particles **wa** and **ga**, when they both refer to the subject of the sentence.

1. In [X **wa** Y], Y is the comment on X, and the new information one wants to convey in uttering this sentence is the Y part. In [X **ga** Y], X represents the new information. This structure is generally used to identify which X fits Y, such as in answering the question, 'who did Y?' or 'which one is Y?'. When you are looking at a building and the hearer wants to know what that building is, (a) is appropriate. Sentence (b) is appropriate when the hearer wants to know which building is the school.

(a) あれは学校です。
Are wa gakkoo desu.
That's a school.

(b) あれが学校です。
Are ga gakkoo desu.
That's the school.

Sentence (c) is appropriate when you are talking about whether Tanaka came or not, while (d) is appropriate when you are trying to identify who did not come.

(c) 田中さんは来ませんでした。
Tanaka-san wa kimasendeshita.
Mr/Ms Tanaka did not come.

(d) 田中さんが来ませんでした。
Tanaka-san ga kimasendeshita.
It's Mr/Ms Tanaka who did not come.

2. **Ga** is used when one is describing a scene that one can observe.

(You look outside and see a cat.)

あ！庭に猫がいる。
A! Niwa ni neko ga iru.
Look! There is a cat in the yard/garden.

(Looking outside, you notice that it is raining.)

雨が降っている！
Ame ga futte iru!
It's raining!

3. The subject of the subordinate clause is generally marked by **ga**.

In (e), most likely **kodomo** 'child' is the subject of the subordinate predicate (**byooki da** 'be sick'). The main subject of (e) is the speaker. In (f), on the other hand, since **wa** is used, the main subject as well as the subject of the subordinate clause is **kodomo**.

(e) ［子供が病気だから］学校に行けません。
[Kodomo ga byooki da kara] gakkoo ni ikemasen.
Because my child is sick, (I) cannot go to school.

(f) 子供は［病気だから学校に行けません］。
Kodomo wa [byooki da kara gakkoo ni ikemasen].
My child cannot go to school because he/she is sick.

12

Verbs

12.1   Conjugation of verbs

Japanese verbs are grouped into three types, the **-ru**, **-u**, and irregular types depending on the conjugational patterns. The plain nonpast form of **-ru** verbs ends with **-iru** or **-eru**. The plain nonpast form of **-u** verbs ends with **-u**, **-tsu**, **-ru** (**. . . aru**, **. . . uru**, **. . . oru**), **-mu**, **-bu**, **-nu**, **-su**, **-ku**, or **-gu**. However, there are u-verbs such as **kaeru** 'to return home,' **hairu** 'to enter,' **hashiru** 'to run,' and **kiru** 'to cut,' which end with **-iru** or **-eru**.

(1) *-ru* verbs
The basic conjugations of the **-ru** type are as follows.

Dict. form[1]	食べる **taberu** 'eat'	寝る **neru** 'sleep'	起きる **okiru** 'get up'	着る **kiru** 'wear'	教える **oshieru** 'teach'
Plain, neg., nonpast	食べない **tabenai**	寝ない **nenai**	起きない **okinai**	着ない **kinai**	教えない **oshienai**
Polite/nonpast	食べます **tabemasu**	寝ます **nemasu**	起きます **okimasu**	着ます **kimasu**	教えます **oshiemasu**
Plain, aff., nonpast	食べる **taberu**	寝る **neru**	起きる **okiru**	着る **kiru**	教える **oshieru**
Conditional	食べれば **tabereba**	寝れば **nereba**	起きれば **okireba**	着れば **kireba**	教えれば **oshiereba**
Volitional	食べよう **tabeyoo**	寝よう **neyoo**	起きよう **okiyoo**	着よう **kiyoo**	教えよう **oshieyoo**

[1] Dictionary form is the same as the plain affirmative nonpast form.

The plain past form of **-ru** verbs is formed by replacing **-ru** with **-ta**. **-Ta** indicates past tense.

Plain, aff. past	食べた **tabeta** 'ate'	寝た **neta** 'slept'	起きた **okita** 'got up'	着た **kita** 'wore'	教えた **oshieta** 'taught'

(2) -u verbs

The basic conjugations of the **-u** type verbs are as follows.

Dict. form	書く **ka<u>ku</u>** 'write'	読む **yo<u>mu</u>** 'read'	話す **hana<u>su</u>** 'speak'	死ぬ **shi<u>nu</u>** 'die'	待つ **ma<u>tsu</u>** 'wait'
Plain, neg., nonpast	書<u>か</u>ない **ka<u>ka</u>nai**	読<u>ま</u>ない **yo<u>ma</u>nai**	話<u>さ</u>ない **hana<u>sa</u>nai**	死<u>な</u>ない **shi<u>na</u>nai**	待<u>た</u>ない **ma<u>ta</u>nai**
Polite, nonpast	書<u>き</u>ます **ka<u>ki</u>masu**	読<u>み</u>ます **yo<u>mi</u>masu**	話<u>し</u>ます **hana<u>shi</u>masu**	死<u>に</u>ます **shi<u>ni</u>masu**	待<u>ち</u>ます **ma<u>chi</u>masu**
Plain, aff., nonpast	書<u>く</u> **ka<u>ku</u>**	読<u>む</u> **yo<u>mu</u>**	話<u>す</u> **hana<u>su</u>**	死<u>ぬ</u> **shi<u>nu</u>**	待<u>つ</u> **ma<u>tsu</u>**
Conditional	書<u>け</u>ば **ka<u>ke</u>ba**	読<u>め</u>ば **yo<u>me</u>ba**	話<u>せ</u>ば **hana<u>se</u>ba**	死<u>ね</u>ば **shi<u>ne</u>ba**	待<u>て</u>ば **ma<u>te</u>ba**
Volitional	書<u>こ</u>う **ka<u>ko</u>o**	読<u>も</u>う **yo<u>mo</u>o**	話<u>そ</u>う **hana<u>so</u>o**	死<u>の</u>う **shi<u>no</u>o**	待<u>と</u>う **ma<u>to</u>o**

The plain past form of **-u** verbs varies depending on the last syllable of the dictionary form of the verb.

- **(i) -u, -tsu and -ru endings → -tta**

Dict. form	買う **kau**	待つ **matsu**	走る **hashiru**
Plain past	買った **katta** 'bought'	待った **matta** 'waited'	走った **hashitta** 'ran'

- **(ii) -mu, -bu and -nu endings → -nda**

Dict. form	読む **yomu**	呼ぶ **yobu**	死ぬ **shinu**
Plain past	読んだ **yonda** 'read'	呼んだ **yonda** 'called'	死んだ **shinda** 'died'

- **(iii) -su ending → -shita**

Dict. form	話す **hanasu**	のばす **nobasu**
Plain past	話した **hanashita** 'talked'	のばした **nobashita** 'extended'

- **(iv) -ku ending → -ita**

Dict. form	書く **kaku**	歩く **aruku**
Plain past	書いた **kaita** 'wrote'	歩いた **aruita** 'walked'

One exception for this group is **iku** 'to go.' The plain past form of **iku** is **itta** (行く → 行った).

■ (v) **-gu** ending → **-ida**

Dict. form	泳ぐ **oyogu**	ぬぐ **nugu**
Plain past	泳いだ **oyoida** 'swam'	ぬいだ **nuida** 'took (e.g. a coat) off'

(3) Irregular verbs

There are two irregular verbs, **kuru** 'to come' and **suru** 'to do.'

Dict. form	くる **kuru** 'come'	する **suru** 'do'
Plain, neg., nonpast	こない **konai**	しない **shinai**
Polite, nonpast	きます **kimasu**	します **shimasu**
Plain, aff., nonpast	くる **kuru**	する **suru**
Conditional	くれば **kureba**	すれば **sureba**
Volitional	こよう **koyoo**	しよう **shiyoo**

The plain past forms of the irregular verbs are as follows.

Dict. form	くる **kuru**	する **suru**
Plain, past	きた **kita** 'came'	した **shita** 'did'

(4) *te*-forms

V-**te** forms can be obtained by changing the past tense morpheme **ta** to **te**. When the past tense morpheme has a voiced sound /d/, **da** changes to **de**. Te-forms are used to link clauses and also in many constructions with auxiliary verbs.

▶ 19.2; 22.1

NOTE Many Japanese verbs end with the sound **-ru**. Obviously, all the **ru**-verbs and irregular verbs do, and many of the **u**-verbs as well. In fact, **-ru** is the 'default' ending so that it is attached to newly coined verbs, other than those that take **suru** 'to do'; e.g. **sabo-ru** 'to play hooky (from "sabotage" in French),' **guugu-ru** 'to search using Google,' **nabi-ru** 'to navigate,' **sutanba-ru** 'to stand by.'

Transitive and intransitive verbs

Intransitive verbs do not require a direct object. They only require the subject of the sentence. Intransitive verbs represent movements, events or spontaneous changes.

> 今朝私は１０キロ歩いた。
> **Kesa watashi wa juk-kiro aruita.**
> I walked 10 km this morning.

> 台風で木が倒れた。
> **Taifuu de ki ga taoreta.**
> Because of a typhoon, trees fell down.

> 花が咲いた。
> **Hana ga saita.**
> Flowers bloomed.

Intransitive verbs expressing motion take the particle **o** to express traversed space; e.g. **kawa o oyogu** 'swim the river' vs. **kawa de oyogu** 'swim in the river'.

> この道をまっすぐ行ってください。
> **Kono michi o massugu itte kudasai.**
> Please go straight ahead on/along this street.

> 公園を通って行ってください。
> **Kooen o tootte itte kudasai.**
> Please go passing through/via the park.

Transitive verbs require a direct object in addition to the subject of the sentence. Transitive verbs typically express actions with someone acting upon something or someone else; i.e. the direct object.

Many verbs come in intransitive and transitive pairs. There are ten major types of pairs depending on the suffixes. The verbs ending in **-su** are all transitive, and their intransitive counterparts end in **-ru**. One cannot say that all the verbs ending in **-ru** are intransitive, however.

Type	*Intransitive verbs*	*Transitive verbs*
-u/-eru	開く **aku** 'open'	開ける **akeru** 'open'
-aru/-eru	閉まる **shimaru** 'close'	閉める **shimeru** 'close'
-waru/-eru	変わる **kawaru** 'change'	変える **kaeru** 'change'
-ru/-su	直る **naoru** 'be fixed'	直す **naosu** 'fix'
-eru/-asu	出る **deru** 'go out'	出す **dasu** 'take out'
-eru/-yasu	冷える **hieru** 'get chilled'	冷やす **hiyasu** 'chill'
-reru/-su	壊れる **kowareru** 'break'	壊す **kowasu** 'break'
-eru/-u	割れる **wareru** 'break'	割る **waru** 'break'
-ru/-seru	乗る **noru** 'get on'	乗せる **noseru** 'put on'
-iru/-osu	起きる **okiru** 'get up'	起こす **okosu** 'wake up'

Action and stative verbs

Action verbs describe volitional actions such as 'to eat,' 'to walk,' and 'to study.' Stative verbs describe the state of someone or something such as 'to exist,' 'to possess,' or 'to be able to do.'

The following are examples of stative verbs.

> あそこに大きい犬がいる。
> **Asoko ni ookii inu ga iru.** (existence – animate)
> There is a big dog over there.

病院は駅のそばにある。
Byooin wa eki no soba ni aru. (existence – inanimate)
The hospital is near the station.

田中さんは運転ができる。
Tanaka-san wa unten ga dekiru. (ability)
Mr/Ms Tanaka can drive (a car).

▶ 40; 41

12.4 **Punctual and durative verbs**

Punctual verbs express an event or an action, which takes place instantaneously. They include **korobu** 'to fall down,' **kekkon suru** 'to marry,' **kuru** 'to come,' and **iku** 'to go.' With these verbs, there is a clear difference in the state before and after the action or event takes place; therefore, they are also called 'change-of-state verbs.' For example, before **okiru** 'to awake,' one is asleep, but after it, one is awake. Similarly, before **shinu** 'to die,' one is alive, but after it, one is dead.

Durative verbs represent an action or a process, which assumes duration. Some examples are **yomu** 'to read,' **kaku** 'to write,' **taberu** 'to eat,' **utau** 'to sing,' **hashiru** 'to run,' and **benkyoo suru** 'to study.'

▶ 19.2.1

12.5 **Controllable and non-controllable verbs**

Verbs can be categorized into controllable and non-controllable. Controllable verbs describe actions that the agent (doer) is able to control. Non-controllable verbs indicate actions and events that happen beyond the speaker's control or ability. When there is a transitive–intransitive pair of verbs, the transitive verbs express controllable actions while the intransitive counterparts usually express non-controllable, spontaneous happenings.

風で窓が開いた。
Kaze de mado ga aita.
The window opened because of the wind.

暑いから、窓を開けた。
Atsui kara, mado o aketa.
I opened the window because it was hot.

Spontaneous verbs such as **mieru** 'can see,' **kikoeru** 'can hear,' **ureru** 'sell well,' and **kireru** 'cut well' express non-controllable situations.

パワーポイントのスライドがよく見えない。
Pawaapointo no suraido ga yoku mienai.
I cannot see the Powerpoint slides very well (they are not visible).

声が小さくてよく聞こえない。
Koe ga chiisakute yoku kikoenai.
Your/his/her voice is too soft and I can't hear too well (it is not audible).

今年はこのタイプのデザインが売れるでしょう。
Kotoshi wa kono taipu no dezain ga ureru deshoo.
This type of design will sell well this year.

The corresponding transitive verbs such as **miru** 'to look (at), watch, see,' **kiku** 'to listen, hear,' and **uru** 'to sell' can be used to describe controllable situations when they are used in the potential form.

> ニューヨークに行ったら、色々なミュージカルが見られますよ。
> **Nyuu Yooku ni ittara, iroiro na myuujikaru ga miraremasu yo.**
> You can see all kinds of musicals if you go to New York.

> このチャンネルで日本の歌が聴けます。
> **Kono channeru de Nihon no uta ga kikemasu.**
> You can listen to Japanese music on this channel.

12.6 Potential verbs

Potential forms express the meanings of potentiality and ability. The formation depends on the types of verbs; **-ru**, **-u** and irregular verbs. With **-ru** verbs, the final **-ru** is replaced by **-rareru**; with **-u** verbs, the final **-u** is replaced by **-eru**. The potential forms of the irregular verbs **suru** and **kuru** are **dekiru** and **korareru**, respectively. In conversation **-rareru** is often shortened to **-reru** as in **mireru** 'can see,' **tabereru** 'can eat' and **koreru** 'can come.'

Ru-verbs

Dictionary form	Potential plain nonpast
食べる **taberu** 'eat'	食べられる **taberareru**
寝る **neru** 'sleep'	寝られる **nerareru**
教える **oshieru** 'teach'	教えられる **oshierareru**
見る **miru** 'see'	見られる **mirareru**
着る **kiru** 'wear'	着られる **kirareru**

U-verbs

Dictionary form	Potential plain nonpast
読む **yomu** 'read'	読める **yomeru**
買う **kau** 'buy'	買える **kaeru**
書く **kaku** 'write'	書ける **kakeru**
立つ **tatsu** 'stand'	立てる **tateru**
話す **hanasu** 'speak'	話せる **hanaseru**

Irregular verbs

Dictionary form	Potential plain nonpast
する **suru** 'do'	できる **dekiru**
くる **kuru** 'come'	こられる **korareru**

If the verb is transitive, the potential sentence often takes the form [(N1 **wa/ga**) N2 **ga** potential verb]. N2 **ga** represents the object of the verb.

> 田中さんは中国語が話せます。
> **Tanaka-san wa Chuugokugo ga hanasemasu.**
> Mr/Ms Tanaka can speak Chinese.

> さしみがたべられますか。
> **Sashimi ga taberaremasu ka.**
> Can you eat sashimi?

秋葉原に行くと電気製品が安く買えます。
Akihabara ni iku to denkiseehin ga yasuku kaemasu.
If you go to Akihabara, you can buy electronic items cheaply.

私はテニスができます。
Watashi wa tenisu ga dekimasu.
I can play tennis.

The particle **o** is often used to mark N2 in the potential construction.

あなたはこの状況をどう変えられると思いますか。
Anata wa kono jookyoo o doo kaerareru to omoimasu ka.
How do you think you can change the present situation?

今学期の終わりまでに漢字を千読み書きできるようになりたい。
Kongakki no owari made ni kanji o sen yomi-kaki dekiru yoo ni naritai.
I would like to become able to read and write one thousand **kanji** by the end of this semester.

When **o** is used, the focus of the utterance is on the action performed by the verb, and the implication is that one has control over the situation, such as being able to change 'the present situation' or 'being able to learn **kanji**.'

▶ 51

It should be noted that some stative verbs, such as **mieru** 'to be visible,' **kikoeru** 'to be audible,' and **wakaru** 'to understand,' do not have potential forms, as they express non-controllable, spontaneous situations.

12.7 Benefactive (giving and receiving) verbs

There is a category called 'giving and receiving' verbs, e.g. **ageru** 'to give,' **kureru** 'to give (me),' and **morau** 'to receive.' The use of these verbs implies that the speaker views the transaction to be beneficial to the receiver and/or that a favor is being done; hense the label 'benefactive.' There are verbs in Japanese that express the meaning of giving and receiving without such an implication; e.g. **watasu** 'to give, to hand over,' **uketoru** 'to receive.'

The choice of benefactive verb depends on the giver, the receiver, and from whose viewpoint the event is being described. The direct object and the indirect object are marked by the particles **o** and **ni**, respectively. **Ageru** is used when the speaker gives something to someone or when a third party gives something to someone else.

私は田中さんに北海道のおみやげをあげました。
Watashi wa Tanaka-san ni Hokkaidoo no omiyage o agemashita.
I gave Mr/Ms Tanaka a souvenir from Hokkaido.

マリはケンに帽子をあげました。
Mari wa Ken ni booshi o agemashita.
Mari gave Ken a hat.

Kureru is used when someone gives something to the speaker. Since **watashi ni** 'to me' is the default case, it is not usually overtly expressed.

これは友達が結婚祝いに（私に）くれたテレビです。
Kore wa tomodachi ga kekkon iwai ni (watashi ni) kureta terebi desu.
This is a TV set which my friend gave me for my wedding.

クリスマスに両親がアイパッドをくれました。
Kurisumasu ni ryooshin ga aipaddo o kuremashita.
My parents gave me an iPad for Christmas.

The verb **kureru** is also used when someone gives something to the speaker's in-group members, such as his/her family member or close friend.

山田さんは卒業祝いに弟に時計をくれました。
Yamada-san wa sotsugyoo iwai ni otooto ni tokee o kuremashita.
Mr/Ms Yamada gave my brother a watch for his graduation.

Morau is used when the speaker (or his/her in-group member) receives something from someone or when a third party receives something from someone else. In this case, the receiver is the subject of the sentence. As in other types of sentences, **watashi** 'I' is not overtly expressed when it is obvious. The person from whom one receives (i.e. source) is marked by the particle **ni** or **kara** 'from,' and the direct object is marked by the particle **o**.

（私は）いつも叔母に色々な物をもらいます。
(Watashi wa) itsumo oba ni iroiro na mono o moraimasu.
I always receive various things from my aunt.

去年の誕生日に母は父に指輪をもらいました。
Kyonen no tanjoobi ni haha wa chichi ni yubiwa o moraimashita.
On her birthday last year, my mother received a ring from my father.

To indicate the source (i.e. giver), the particle **ni** is preferred when the receiver has a personal relationship with him/her, whereas **kara** is preferred when there is no such relationship (e.g. the source is an institution) or when the speaker puts the person at a distance.

（私は）大学生のとき、国から奨学金をもらった。
(Watashi wa) daigakusee no toki, kuni kara shoogakukin o moratta.
When I was in college, I received a scholarship from the government.

この年になって親からお金をもらうのは気が引ける。
Kono toshi ni natte oya kara o-kane o morau no wa ki ga hikeru.
At my age, it's hard to ask for (receive) money from my parents.

One and the same event can be described with the verb **ageru** 'to give' or **morau** 'to receive,' depending on whose point of view the speaker takes. For example, **Mari wa Ken ni booshi o ageta** 'Mari gave Ken a hat' is a description from the giver Mari's point of view, while **Ken wa Mari ni booshi o moratta** 'Ken received a hat from Mari' is one from the receiver Ken's point of view. Unlike in English, in which the speaker can be the source (e.g. 'Mary received a bouquet of roses from me'), **watashi ni** 'from me' is rare in Japanese. The speaker usually speaks from his/her own point of view. The event therefore would be most likely expressed as 'I gave Mary a bouquet of roses.' Similarly, when an outsider (e.g. acquaintance Ms Tanaka) receives something from an insider (e.g. sister), one would say 'My sister gave Mr/Ms Tanaka a book,' rather than 'Mr/Ms Tanaka received a book from my sister.' It is easier to take the viewpoint of someone with whom the speaker identifies, such as him-/herself and in-group members, than that of someone he/she does not know.

夫は見知らぬ子供にチョコレートをあげた。
Otto wa mishiranu kodomo ni chokoreeto o ageta.
My husband gave chocolate to a child he didn't know.

When the subject functions as the topic (as in the majority of sentences), marked by **wa**, the speaker is taking the viewpoint of the subject noun. With a non-topic subject, marked by **ga**, the subject's viewpoint is not reflected. For example, the first sentence below describes what happened from the viewpoint of the topic ('my wife'), but it is described from the speaker's viewpoint in the second sentence. By using **kureru** 'someone gives me,' the speaker expresses that the receiver ('my wife') has benefited from the event, and that he/she has, too, by extension.

妻は電車で隣に座った人に地下鉄の地図をもらった。
Tsuma wa densha de tonari ni suwatta hito ni chikatetsu no chizu o moratta.
My wife was given a subway map by someone who sat next to her on the train.

電車で隣に座った人が妻に地下鉄の地図をくれた。
Densha de tonari ni suwatta hito ga tsuma ni chikatetsu no chizu o kureta.
Someone who sat next to my wife on the train gave her a subway map.

There are different forms of giving and receiving verbs depending on the relative statuses among the giver, the receiver and the speaker. Although **yaru** 'to give' is traditionally expected to describe giving to someone lower in rank (e.g. one's own child, younger siblings, subordinates at work, animals, flowers), a recent trend, especially among women, is to use the politer verb **ageru** for all of them, as well as for giving to equals.

X > Y: X is socially higher   X = Y: X is socially equal   X < Y: X is socially lower

someone gives me	Giver > Receiver	くださる	**kudasaru**
	Giver = Receiver	くれる	**kureru**
	Giver < Receiver	くれる	**kureru**
I or another gives to someone	Giver < Receiver	さしあげる	**sashiageru**
	Giver = Receiver	あげる	**ageru**
	Giver > Receiver	あげる	**ageru**
	Giver > Receiver	やる	**yaru**
I or another receives from someone	Giver > Receiver	いただく	**itadaku**
	Giver = Receiver	もらう	**morau**
	Giver < Receiver	もらう	**morau**

Here are some examples of each case:

先生がこの辞書をくださいました。   Giver > Receiver
Sensee ga kono jisho o kudasaimashita.
My teacher gave this dictionary to me.

同僚が（私に）この本をくれた。   Giver = Receiver
Dooryoo ga (watashi ni) kono hon o kureta.
My colleague gave me this book.

弟がこの車をくれた。   Giver < Receiver
Otooto ga kono kuruma o kureta.
My little brother gave me this car.

私は先生にギフトカードをさしあげた。   Giver < Receiver
Watashi wa sensee ni gifuto kaado o sashiageta.
I gave a gift card to my teacher.

私は友達に誕生日のプレゼントをあげた。   Giver = Receiver
Watashi wa tomodachi ni tanjoobi no purezento o ageta.
I gave a birthday present to my friend.

毎日花に水をやってね。   Giver > Receiver
Mainichi hana ni mizu o yatte ne.
Please water the flowers every day. (lit. give water to flowers)

（私は）先生にこの本をいただいた。   Giver > Receiver
(Watashi wa) sensee ni kono hon o itadaita.
I got this book from my teacher.

（私は）友達にこのペンをもらった。   Giver = Receiver
(Watashi wa) Tomodachi ni kono pen o moratta.
I got this pen from a friend.

（私は）弟に本をもらった。   Giver < Receiver
(Watashi wa) otooto ni hon o moratta.
(I) got a book from my little brother.

▶ 19.2.8; 42; 43; 73; 78.1.2

12.8 Verbs of wearing

Japanese has several verbs meaning 'to wear, to put on (clothes)' depending on the manner in which one puts things on and where on the body they are worn.

はく	**haku**	(shoes, pants, skirts, socks, etc.)
着る	**kiru**	(shirts, jackets, blouses, sweaters, etc.)
かぶる	**kaburu**	(hats, caps, helmets, etc.)
する	**suru**	(accessories, scarves, neckties, etc.)
かける	**kakeru**	(glasses, sunglasses, etc.)
しめる	**shimeru**	(neckties, belts, seat belts, obi, etc.)

These verbs are used in the form of **-te imasu**, when referring to the current state or a habitual action.

> 田中さんは赤いスカートをはいている人です。
> **Tanaka-san wa akai sukaato o haite iru hito desu.**
> Ms Tanaka is the person who has a red skirt on.

Other examples follow.

> 寒かったら、このセーターを着てください。
> **Samukattara, kono seetaa o kite kudasai.**
> If you are cold, please put on this sweater.

> 今日は寒いから、帽子をかぶった方がいいですよ。
> **Kyoo wa samui kara, booshi o kabutta hoo ga ii desu yo.**
> It's cold today, so you'd better put on a hat.

> 山田さんはいつもすてきなスカーフをしていますね。
> **Yamada-san wa itsumo suteki na sukaafu o shite imasu ne.**
> Ms Yamada always has a nice scarf on.

> スミスさんはあのめがねをかけている人です。
> **Sumisu-san wa ano megane o kakete iru hito desu.**
> Mr/Ms Smith is that person who has glasses on.

13

Adjectives

Japanese adjectives are divided into two groups according to their conjugation pattern: **i**-adjectives and **na**-adjectives.

13.1 *i*-adjectives

All **i**-adjectives end with the vowel **i** in their dictionary form, as in **oishii** 'tasty,' **samui** 'cold,' and **takai** 'high, expensive.' Unlike English adjectives, which require a copula verb 'to be' to function as a predicate, **i**-adjectives can be the predicate of a sentence on their own. They have their own conjugation pattern.

13.1.1 The conjugation pattern

I-adjectives are conjugated (change form) by adding different suffixes to the stem. The stem of an **i**-adjective is the dictionary form (i.e. plain nonpast affirmative form) minus **-i**. Below, hyphens are provided between the stem and suffixes in the conjugation tables only. The adjective **ii** 'good' has a different conjugation pattern; see Appendix IV.

Dictionary Form	**oishi-i**	**samu-i**	**taka-i**
Stem	**oishi-**	**samu-**	**taka-**
	delicious	cold	high

As explained in **6.2**, predicates have plain and polite forms.

Plain form conjugation

- Nonpast affirmative form: stem + **i**

  oishi-i   **samu-i**

- Nonpast negative form: stem + **ku** + **nai**

  oishi-ku nai   **samu-ku nai**

- Past affirmative form: stem + **katta**

  oishi-katta   **samu-katta**

- Past negative form: stem + **ku** + **nakatta**

  oishi-ku nakatta   **samu-ku nakatta**

Polite form conjugation

- Nonpast affirmative form: stem + **i** + politeness marker **desu**

  oishi-i desu   **samu-i desu**

- Nonpast negative form:

  (a) Stem + **ku** + **nai** + politeness marker **desu**

    oishi-ku nai desu   **samu-ku nai desu**

  (b) Stem + **ku** + **arimasen**

    oishi-ku arimasen   **samu-ku arimasen**

- Past affirmative form: stem + **katta** + politeness marker **desu**

  oishi-katta desu   **samu-katta desu**

- Past negative form: stem + **ku nakatta desu** + politeness marker **desu**

  (a) Stem + **ku** + **nakatta** + politeness marker **desu**

    oishi-ku nakatta desu   **samu-ku nakatta desu**

  (b) Stem + **ku** + **arimasen** + **deshita**

    oishi-ku arimasendeshita   **samu-ku arimasendeshita**

▶ See **15.1** for negative forms.

Desu used in the **i**-adjective conjugation in the polite form is not a copula. **Desu** here merely marks politeness. Unlike nouns and na-adjectives, **i**-adjectives can be predicates by themselves and they can form a sentence without **desu** in informal style speech and in writing.

外国の車は高い。
Gaikoku no kuruma wa takai.
Foreign cars are expensive.

映画は面白かった。
Eega wa omoshirokatta.
The movie was interesting.

昨日は寒かったです。
Kinoo wa samukatta desu.
Yesterday was cold.

13.1.2 The pre-nominal form conjugation of *i*-adjectives

When adjectives modify a noun, they take the 'pre-nominal' form. The pre-nominal form of **i**-adjectives is the same as the plain form conjugation shown in **13.1.1**.

▶ See **13.4** for example sentences.

13.2 *na*-adjectives

Na-adjectives are also called 'adjectival nouns' or 'nominal adjectives' because their pattern of conjugation is the same as that for nouns. For example, to be a predicate of a sentence, **na**-adjectives require the copula, like nouns do. Unlike nouns, however, **na**-adjectives cannot serve as the topic, subject or object of a sentence or be modified by adjectives.

▶ **5.1**

13.2.1 The conjugation pattern

The stem of a **na**-adjective is the same as its dictionary form. The **na**-adjective conjugation consists of the stem and the copula **da** in its conjugated form.

Stem: **shizuka** 'quiet'   **kiree** 'pretty, clean'

Plain form conjugation

- Nonpast affirmative form: Stem + **da**

  shizuka da   **kiree da**

- Nonpast negative form: Stem + **ja nai**

  shizuka ja nai   **kiree ja nai**

- Past affirmative form: Stem + **datta**

  shizuka datta   **kiree datta**

- Past negative form: Stem + **ja nakatta**

  shizuka ja nakatta   **kiree ja nakatta**

Polite form conjugation

- Nonpast affirmative form: Stem + **desu**

  shizuka desu   **kiree desu**

- Nonpast negative form: Stem + **ja nai** + Politeness marker **desu**

  shizuka ja nai desu   **kiree ja nai desu**

- Past affirmative form: Stem + **deshita**

  shizuka deshita   **kiree deshita**

- Past negative form: Stem + **ja-nakatta** + Politeness marker **desu**

  shizuka ja nakatta desu   **kiree ja nakatta desu**

▶ See **15.1** for negative forms.

When English adjectives are borrowed into the Japanese lexicon; e.g. **hansamu** 'handsome,' **hotto** 'hot,' and **taito** 'tight,' they are usually conjugated as **na**-adjectives.

13.2.2 The pre-nominal form conjugation of *na*-adjectives

When **na**-adjectives modify a noun, they take the pre-nominal form. The pre-nominal form is the same as its plain form, with one exception: the nonpast affirmative form is the stem + **na**, rather than **da**, e.g. **shizuka na heya** 'quiet room'.

▶ See **13.4** for example sentences.

13.3 *te*-form of adjectives

Dictionary form	samui 'cold'	ii 'good'
	shizuka 'quiet'	kiree 'pretty, clean'
i-adjective stem + **kute**	samukute	yokute (exception)
na-adjective stem + **de**	shizuka de	kiree de

Te-form is used to link an adjective with other predicates, as discussed in **22.1**.

13.4 Attributive and predicative usage

Adjectives are used at the end of a sentence in predicative use and directly preceding a noun they modify in attributive use. To modify nouns, both **i-** and **na**-adjectives appear in their pre-nominal form in nonpast, past, affirmative and negative.

Examples with pre-nominal *i*-adjectives

おもしろい本
omoshiroi hon
an interesting book

おもしろくない本
omoshiroku nai hon
an uninteresting book

おもしろかった本
omoshirokatta hon
a book that was interesting

おもしろくなかった本
omoshiroku nakatta hon
a book that was not interesting

Examples with pre-nominal *na*-adjectives

にぎやかな町
nigiyaka na machi
a lively town

にぎやかじゃない町
nigiyaka ja nai machi
a town which is not lively

にぎやかだった町
nigiyaka datta machi
a town which was lively

にぎやかじゃなかった町
nigiyaka ja nakatta machi
a town which was not lively

Most adjectives can appear in both the sentence final position (predicative use) and pre-nominal position (attributive use).

この鞄は小さい。
Kono kaban wa chiisai.
This bag is small.

小さい鞄
chiisai kaban
a small bag

この建物はりっぱだ。
Kono tatemono wa rippa da.
This building is impressive.

りっぱな建物
rippa na tatemono
an impressive building

There are a few adjectives that cannot modify a noun and can only be used as a predicate; e.g. **ooi** 'many, much,' **sukunai** 'few, little.'

> この辺は木が多いです。
> **Kono hen wa ki ga ooi desu.**
> There are many trees in this area.

> 都会は緑が少ないです。
> **Tokai wa midori ga sukunai desu.**
> There is little greenery in urban areas.

None of the forms of **ooi** 'many, much' (or **sukunai** 'few, little') can be used to modify nouns; e.g. **ooi** (nonpast affirmative), **ooku nakatta** (past negative). As a noun modifier, the form **ooku no** 'many, much' is used instead preceding the noun it modifies (e.g. **ki** 'trees').

> ［多くの木］を植えました。
> **[Ooku no ki] o uemashita.**
> I planted [many trees].

Ooi 'many, much' and **sukunai** 'few, little' may appear directly preceding a noun when they are the predicates of a relative clause. In this case, it is not the adjective by itself, but the whole clause that modifies the noun following it.

► 7.2.3

> ［葉が多い］木を植えた。
> **[Ha ga ooi] ki o ueta.**
> I planted a tree [that has many leaves].

> ［喧嘩が少ない］夫婦は長生きする。
> **[Kenka ga sukunai] fuufu wa nagaiki suru.**
> Couples [who rarely fight] live long.

13.5 Internal state adjectives

Adjectives that express one's internal state (feelings and sensations) require special attention; e.g. **ureshii** 'happy, glad,' **hoshii** 'want,' **kanashii** 'sad,' **kowai** 'scared,' **hazukashii** 'embarrassed,' **itai** 'painful,' **samui** 'cold,' **zannen** 'regrettable.' Using these adjectives, one can state one's own feelings and sensations, but not anyone else's. One can also use these adjectives to ask about the addressee's feelings and sensations, but not a third person's. Hence, **Ureshii** 'I'm happy' and **Ureshii?** 'Are you happy?' are possible, but not **Anata wa ureshii** 'You are happy,' **Hiroshi wa ureshii** 'Hiroshi is happy,' or **Hiroshi wa ureshii?** 'Is Hiroshi happy?'

► 58

> 新しい車がほしい。
> **Atarashii kuruma ga hoshii.**
> I want a new car.

> 新しい車がほしい？
> **Atarashii kuruma ga hoshii?**
> Do you want a new car?

A third person's feelings and sensations can be expressed in one of the following ways.

(1) Add to the adjective an evidential word (e.g. **yoo** 'seem,' **soo** 'I heard, someone said') or a quotation **to itte iru/ita** 'says/said.'

> 同僚は新しい車がほしい<u>ようだ</u>。
> **Dooryoo wa atarashii kuruma ga hoshii <u>yoo da</u>.**
> It seems that my colleague wants a new car.

息子はみんなの前でピアノを弾くのは恥ずかしい<u>そうです</u>。
Musuko wa minna no mae de piano o hiku no wa hazukashii <u>soo desu</u>.
My son says he's too embarrassed to play the piano for everyone.

(2) Use the verbal suffix **-gatte iru**, which indicates that the person is showing signs that he/she is experiencing a certain feeling or sensation. **-gatte iru** needs to be used with caution, however. It is not well regarded in Japanese culture for an adult to display his/her desires and other feelings. It is best to use it only in reference to children, family members, and close friends. A sentence such as **Shachoo wa koojoo o kengaku nasari-tagatte imasu**, 'The company president wants to visit the factory,' even with the honorific expression **nasaru** 'to do (honorific),' sounds rude.

弟は新しい車をほし<u>がっている</u>。
Otooto wa atarashii kuruma o hoshi-<u>gatte iru</u>.
My younger brother wants a new car.
(Lit. He is showing signs that he wants a new car.)

▶ See **28** for an explanation of different evidential markers.

A third person's internal state is expressed without either of the above devices when it is stated in a subordinate clause (that is, not in the main clause) or in a story.

友達の中川さんはドイツに留学<u>したい</u>ので、今ドイツ語学校に通っています。
Tomodachi no Nakagawa-san wa Doitsu ni ryuugaku <u>shitai</u> node, ima Doitsugo gakkoo ni kayotte imasu.
My friend Mr/Ms Nakagawa wants to study abroad in Germany, so he/she is attending a German language school now.

子供は<u>こわい</u>くせに、ジェットコースター が大好きなんです。
Kodomo wa <u>kowai</u> kuse ni, jetto koosutaa ga daisuki na n desu.
Even though he is scared, my child loves roller coasters.

男は金がなかった。しかし、新しい車が<u>ほしかった</u>。そこで、サラ金から金を借りることにした。
Otoko wa kane ga nakatta. Shikashi, atarashii kuruma ga <u>hoshikatta</u>. Sokode, sarakin kara kane o kariru koto ni shita.
The man didn't have money. But he wanted a new car. So he decided to borrow money from a consumer loan company.

14

Adverbs

Meanings expressed by adverbs

Adverbs modify a verb, an adjective, another adverb or an entire sentence. They provide additional information about an action or event, such as manner, time, quantity, degree, and the speaker's judgment about the action or event. They usually precede the word they modify.

In the following examples, **yukkuri** 'slowly' modifies the verb **arukimasu** 'walk,' **itsumo** 'always' the verb **chikoku suru** 'be late,' **tappuri** 'abundantly' the verb **tsuketa** 'put,' **totemo** the adverb phrase **genki yoku** 'energetically,' and **kitto** the whole sentence.

Manner

ゆっくり歩きます。
Yukkuri arukimasu.
I walk slowly.

Time

太郎は学校にいつも遅刻する。
Taroo wa gakkoo ni itsumo chikoku suru.
Taro is always late for school.

Quantity

トーストにバターをたっぷりつけた。
Toosuto ni bataa o tappuri tsuketa.
I put a lot of butter on my toast. (Lit. I put butter on my toast abundantly.)

Degree

子供たちがとても元気よく走っている。
Kodomo-tachi ga totemo genki yoku hashitte iru.
The children are running around very energetically.

Speaker's judgment

きっと明日はいい天気だ。
Kitto ashita wa ii tenki da.
Tomorrow will certainly be a sunny day.

All mimetic words, such as **rinrin** 'ring-ring,' **guruguru** 'round and round,' **kirakira** 'twinkle-twinkle,' and **sassa to** 'quickly,' function as adverbs.

▶ 4.2

星がきらきら輝いている。
Hoshi ga kirakira kagayaite iru.
The stars are shining brightly (lit. twinkle-twinkle).

Derived adverbs

Many adverbs are derived from adjectives and nouns. The adverbial form of **i**-adjectives is obtained by adding **ku** to the stem, i.e. the dictionary form minus **-i**. This is analogous to forming adverbs from adjectives by adding '-ly' in English; e.g. quiet → quietly, beautiful → beautifully. With **na**-adjectives and nouns, the particle **ni** is added to derive adverbial forms.

From *i*-adjectives:

yasashi 'gentle'	+	**ku**	=	**yasashiku** 'gently'
hido 'terrible'	+	**ku**	=	**hidoku** 'terribly'
tadashi 'correct'	+	**ku**	=	**tadashiku** 'correctly'

文字は正しく書いてください。
Moji wa tadashiku kaite kudasai.
Please write the letters correctly.

From *na*-adjectives:

genki 'energetic'	+	**ni**	=	**genki ni** 'energetically'
shizuka 'quiet'	+	**ni**	=	**shizuka ni** 'quietly'
joozu 'skillful'	+	**ni**	=	**joozu ni** 'skillfully'

子供たちは元気に走った。
Kodomo-tachi wa genki ni hashitta.
The children ran energetically.

Some time-related nouns are changed to an adverb by the addition of the particle **ni**.

saisho 'beginning'	+	**ni**	=	**saisho ni** 'at first, firstly'
saigo 'last'	+	**ni**	=	**saigo ni** 'at the end, finally'
tsugi 'next'	+	**ni**	=	**tsugi ni** 'next'
chooki 'long term'	+	**ni**	=	**chooki ni** 'for a long time'

最後にみんなで夕食を食べた。
Saigo ni minna de yuushoku o tabeta.
We all ate dinner together at the end.

Many time-related nouns function as adverbs without the particle **ni**; e.g. **kyoo** 'today,' **kinoo** 'yesterday,' **ashita** 'tomorrow,' **asa** 'morning,' **yoru** 'night,' and **ima** 'now.' In most cases, **ni** is required when the English counterparts are expressed with prepositions such as 'at, on, in' (e.g. at nine o'clock, on Sunday, in August), but not with others (e.g. now, every day). **Asa** '(in the) morning' and **yoru** '(at) night,' neither of which require **ni**, are exceptions.

朝、歯を磨く。
Asa, ha o migaku.
I brush my teeth in the morning.

From verbs:
There is a small group of adverbs that are derived by repetition of a verb.

miru 'see'	→	**mirumiru** 'in a twinkle'
masu 'increase'	→	**masumasu** 'more and more, increasingly'
naku 'cry'	→	**nakunaku** 'in tears'

６月になり、ますます暑くなった。
Rokugatsu ni nari, masumasu atsuku natta.
June came, and it has become increasingly hotter.

Some verbs in **te**-form are interpreted like an adverb.

Dictionary form		*Te-form*
yorokobu 'to be glad'	→	**yorokonde** 'gladly'
isogu 'to hurry'	→	**isoide** 'quickly'
kakureru 'to hide'	→	**kakurete** 'secretly'

いそいで来てください。
Isoide kite kudasai.
Please come quickly.

14.3 Adverbs requiring specific endings

(1) Affirmative

Adverbs such as **mare ni** 'rarely' and **zehi** 'by all means, without fail, definitely' require the associated predicates to be in the affirmative.

そういうことも稀に<u>ある</u>。
Soo yuu koto mo mare ni <u>aru</u>.
That kind of thing happens once in a long while.

(2) Negative

Adverbs such as **amari** 'seldom,' **kesshite** 'never,' **taishite** '(not) very,' and **metta ni** 'rarely' require the associated predicates to be in the negative . . . **nai**.

父はめったにタバコを<u>すわない</u>。
Chichi wa metta ni tabako o <u>suwanai</u>.
My father rarely smokes.

▶ 15.4

(3) Conjecture

Adverbs such as **osoraku** 'probably,' **tabun** 'maybe,' **hyotto suru to** 'by a remote possibility,' and **moshi ka suru to** 'by some chance' are usually used with predicates expressing conjecture, such as **daroo** 'may' and **kamoshirenai** 'might.'

娘はおそらくもう到着した<u>だろう</u>。
Musume wa osoraku moo toochaku shita <u>daroo</u>.
My daughter has <u>probably</u> already arrived.

もしかすると来月休みがとれるかもしれない。
Moshi ka suru to raigetsu yasumi ga toreru kamoshirenai.
I might possibly be able to get a day off next month.

(4) Conditional

Adverbs such as **moshi** 'if', **man ga ichi** 'if by any chance' and **tatoe** 'even if' are always used within a clause ending in a conditional form.

もし何か良い物を見つけ<u>たら</u>、お知らせしますね。
Moshi nani ka ii mono o mitsuke-<u>tara</u> o-shirase shimasu ne.
If I find something nice, I'll let you know.

たとえ優勝するのは無理<u>でも</u>、やってみます。
Tatoe yuushoo suru no wa muri <u>demo</u>, yatte mimasu.
Even if it were impossible to win, I would try.

(5) Resemblance

Adverbs such as **maru de** 'entirely' and **atakamo** 'just as if' co-occur with a predicate expressing resemblance.

> まるで夢の<u>よう</u>です。
> **Marude yume no <u>yoo</u> desu.**
> It is just like a dream.

Some adverbs are interpreted differently depending on whether they are used in affirmative or negative sentences; e.g. **mada** '(not) yet, still,' **moo** '(not) any more, already,' **zenzen** '(not) at all, totally,' **amari** '(not) very, excessively,' **totemo** '(not) possibly, very,' and **nakanaka** '(not) easily, quite.' In the following examples, (a) sentences are in the negative and (b) sentences are in the affirmative.

(1) a. まだ分かりません。
   Mada wakarimasen.
   I don't know yet.

   b. まだ考えています。
   Mada kangaete imasu.
   I'm still thinking.

(2) a. もう要りません。
   Moo irimasen.
   I don't need it any more.

   b. もう分かりました。
   Moo wakarimashita.
   I've figured it out already.

(3) a. 全然眠れなかった。
   Zenzen nemurenakatta.
   I couldn't sleep at all.

   b. 心配していたけど、全然大丈夫だった。
   Shinpai shite ita kedo, zenzen daijoobu datta.
   I was worried, but it was totally fine.

(4) a. 今日はあまり天気がよくない。
   Kyoo wa amari tenki ga yokunai.
   The weather is not very good today.

   b. あまり暑かったのでエアコンをつけた。
   Amari atsukatta node eakon o tsuketa.
   It was excessively hot, so I turned on the air-conditioner.

(5) a. 辛すぎてとてもたべられない。
   Karasugite totemo taberarenai.
   It is too spicy and I cannot possibly eat it.

   b. この夏はとても暑い。
   Kono natsu wa totemo atsui.
   This summer is very hot.

(6) a. 顧客の名前がなかなか覚えられない。
   Kokyaku no namae ga nakanaka oboerarenai.
   I cannot easily remember my clients' names.

   b. この映画はなかなかおもしろい。
   Kono eega wa nakanaka omoshiroi.
   This movie is quite interesting.

15

Negation

Negative verbs, adjectives and nouns

Negative forms are constructed by attaching a suffix **-(a)nai** or **-en**. Examples for nonpast negative forms are given in the table below. For past tense, change **-nai** to **-nakatta** and **(-i)masen** to **(i)masen deshita**. Note that the **-nai** is an **i**-adjective.

▶ 12.1; 13.1.1; 13.2.1

	Plain negative	*Polite negative*
Nouns 'is not Japanese'	日本人じゃない **Nihonjin ja nai**	日本人じゃありません **Nihonjin ja arimasen**
		日本人じゃないです **Nihonjin ja nai desu**
Na adjectives 'is not pretty, clean'	きれいじゃない **kiree ja nai**	きれいじゃありません **kiree ja arimasen**
		きれいじゃないです **kiree ja nai desu**
I-adjectives 'is not tasty'	おいしくない **oishiku nai**	おいしくありません **oishiku arimasen**
		おいしくないです **oishiku nai desu**
Verbs 'not eat'	食べない **tabe-nai**	食べません **tabemasen**
		食べないです **tabe-nai desu**
'not drink'	飲まない **nom-anai**	飲みません **nomimasen**
		飲まないです **nom-anai desu**

There are several patterns for verbal negative forms:

(1) **-ru** verbs: **-ru** → **-nai** (e.g. **tabe-ru** 'to eat' → **tabe-nai**)
(2) **-u** verbs: **-u** → **-anai** (e.g. **yom-u** 'to read' → **yom-anai**, **tats-u** 'to stand' → **tat-anai**)
(3) For **-u** verbs whose dictionary forms end in **u** (う) (e.g. **ka-u** 'to buy,' **su-u** 'to inhale,' **yuu** ← **i-u** 'to say'), insert 'w' as in **kaw-anai**, **suw-anai** and **iw-anai**.

(4) The negative form of **aru** 'to exist' is simply **nai**.

> 庭に木がある。→ 庭に木がない。
> **Niwa ni ki ga aru. → Niwa ni ki ga nai.**
> There is a tree in the yard/garden. → There is no tree / are no trees in the yard/garden.

(5) Irregular verbs: **suru** 'to do' → **shi-nai**; **kuru** 'to come' → **ko-nai**

There are two polite negative forms, **-masen** and **-nai desu**. While **-masen** is a more established form, **-nai desu** is used very often, especially in conversation. The **-nai desu** form tends to occur in answers to questions. By using **-nai desu**, the speaker focuses on and emphasizes the **negative** fact. Hence, when a negative sentence is used for affirmative meanings as in invitations (**Kore tabemasen ka** 'would you like to (Lit. won't you) eat it?'), **-nai desu ka** is unacceptable.

> じゃ、毎日運動するんですか。
> **Ja, mainichi undoo suru n desu ka.**
> Then, you exercise every day?

> いいえ、毎日はしないですよ。
> **Iie, mainichi wa shinai desu yo.**
> No, <u>not</u> every day.

15.2 Limiting the scope of negation

Wa after a word or a phrase functions to specify what is being negated. In the following sentence, for example, the speaker is not saying that he/she does not drink all drinks but that he/she does not drink <u>beer</u>.

▶ 11.3

> ビールは飲みません。
> **Biiru <u>wa</u> nomimasen.**
> I don't drink beer (implying that I drink other things.)

Similarly,

> 家では勉強できません。
> **Uchi de <u>wa</u> benkyoo dekimasen.**
> I can't study at home (implying that I do study elsewhere.)

> 日本人のようには話せません。
> **Nihonjin no yoo ni <u>wa</u> hanasemasen.**
> I can't speak like a Japanese (although I do speak Japanese.)

> このごろは寒くはないです。
> **Konogoro wa samuku <u>wa</u> nai desu.**
> It hasn't been cold recently (though not exactly warm.)

Other ways of limiting the scope of negation involve the use of **to wa kagiranai** 'not necessarily the case,' **wake de wa nai** 'it does not mean' or the like.

> 日本人がみんなすしが好きだとは限らない。
> **Nihonjin ga minna sushi ga suki da to wa kagiranai.**
> It's not necessarily the case that all Japanese like sushi.

> いつもビデオゲームをしているわけではない。
> **Itsumo bideogeemu o shite iru wake de wa nai.**
> (I) am not always playing the video game.

15.3 Negative *-te* forms (-*nakute* vs. -*naide*)

The negative **-te** form for adjectives and the copula is **-nakute**.

> お手洗いじゃなくて、お寺です。
> **O-tearai ja nakute, o-tera desu.**
> It's a temple, not a restroom.

> あまり高くなくて、よかった。
> **Amari takaku nakute yokatta.**
> I am glad that it was not too expensive.

There are two negative **-te** forms for verbs: **-nakute** and **-naide**. There are three principles one can follow in using these forms.

1. If you want to indicate the sense of 'without doing something' or 'instead of doing something,' use **-naide**. **-Nakute** is ungrammatical in this case.

> 宿題をしないで授業に出るのはよくない。
> **Shukudai o shi-naide jugyoo ni deru no wa yoku nai.**
> It's not good to attend class without having done homework.

> きのうはパーティーに行かないで、勉強した。
> **Kinoo wa paatii ni ik-anaide benkyoo shita.**
> Yesterday I studied instead of going to the party.

2. In constructions such as V(neg)-**te kudasai**, V(neg)-**te hoshii**, V(neg)-**te morau**, where V(neg) and the following words form a larger verb phrase, use **-naide**. Again **-nakute** is ungrammatical in these constructions.

> 忘れないでくださいね。
> **Wasure-naide kudasai ne.**
> Please do not forget.

> 見ないでほしい。
> **Mi-naide hoshii.**
> I want you not to look (at it).

> 大きな声で話さないでもらいたい。
> **Ookina koe de hanas-anaide morai-tai.**
> I would like (you) not to talk in a loud voice.

3. When a V(neg) phrase indicates a reason or cause, **-nakute** is preferred.

> 理由が分からなくて困っています。
> **Riyuu ga wakar-anakute komatte imasu.**
> I don't understand the reason, and I am at a loss.

> 日本語でうまく言えなくて、恥ずかしかったです。
> **Nihongo de umaku ie-nakute hazukashikatta desu.**
> I could not say (it) well in Japanese, and I was embarrassed.

15.4 Expressions requiring a negative ending

Some adverbs and other words typically co-occur with negative predicates. Some of these include:

あ（ん）まり[1]	a(n)mari	'not much'
決して	kesshite	'not at all, never'
ちっとも[2]	chittomo	'not at all'
ぜんぜん[3]	zenzen	'not at all'
別に[2]	betsuni	'not particularly'
めったに	mettani	'rarely'
ろくに	rokuni	'hardly'
まさか[2]	masaka	'no way (could it be true)'
一 + counter	ichi + counter	'not even one'
もだれ/何/どこへ/ 　どこに+も	mo dare/nani/doko e/ doko ni + mo	'no one/nothing/nowhere'

NOTE
[1] **A(n)mari** can sometimes co-occur with affirmative predicates, as in **A(n)mari atsukute nemurenakatta** 'it was so hot I could not sleep;' the implication is negative in the sense that it was too hot.
[2] These adverbs indicate that the following predicates are in negative form; therefore, even when they stand alone (without accompanying negative predicates), the remark is interpreted to be in the negative.
[3] **Zenzen** can sometimes be used in affirmative sentences also, as in **zenzen daijoobu** 'it's totally fine.'

▶ **14.3**

最近の映画はあんまり面白くない。
Saikin no eega wa anmari omoshirokunai.
Recent movies are not that interesting.

秘密ですから、決して言わないでください。
Himitsu desu kara, kesshite iwanaide kudasai.
It's a secret, so please don't tell anyone.

ちっともわからない。
Chittomo wakaranai.
I don't understand it at all.

Q: どこかわるいんですか。
   Doko ka warui n desu ka.
   Is something wrong?

A: いえ、別に。
   Ie, betsuni.
   No, not particularly.

まさかスピード違反でつかまるとは思わなかった。
Masaka supiido ihan de tsukamaru to wa omowanakatta.
I did not imagine that I would ever be stopped for speeding.

今日は客が一人も来なかった。
Kyoo wa kyaku ga hitori mo konakatta.
Not one customer came today.

辞書は一冊も持っていない。
Jisho wa issatsu mo motte inai.
I don't have a single dictionary.

一日中何も食べないのはよくない。
Ichinichi-juu nani mo tabenai no wa yokunai.
It's not good not to eat anything all day.

家にはだれもいませんでした。
Uchi ni wa dare mo imasen deshita.
There was nobody at home.

▶ 4.4

Shika 'only' also occurs always with negative predicates (or with words with negative meaning; e.g. **dame** 'no good, bad'). However, the meaning in this case is not negative. In the following sentence, for example, the speaker does not deny 'reading.' Rather, the speaker negates reading other things besides 'comic books.'

▶ 10.3

漫画しか読まない。
Manga shika yomanai.
(I) read only comic books.

スミスさんは日本語でしか話さない。
Sumisu-san wa Nihongo de shika hanasanai.
Mr/Ms Smith speaks only in Japanese.

15.5 Other ways of expressing negation

15.5.1 *mono (desu) ka*

V + **mono desu ka/mon desu ka/mon ka** with falling intonation is used to impart negative meaning rhetorically.

あの人に私の気持ちがわかるもん（です）か。
Ano hito ni watashi no kimochi ga wakaru mon (desu) ka.
He can't possibly understand my feeling.

一日に漢字を百も覚えられるもん（です）か。
Ichinichi ni kanji o hyaku mo oboerareru mon (desu) ka.
There is no way one can memorize a hundred **kanji** in a day.

▶ 18.3

15.5.2 Prefixes *mu, hi, fu,* and *mi*

Sino-Japanese negative prefixes 無 **mu**, 非 **hi**, 不 **fu** and 未 **mi** occur as components of words (nouns or **na**-adjectives.) The following are some of the commonly used words that have these prefixes.

無：無関心	**mukanshin**	uninterested
無意味	**muimi**	meaningless
無免許	**mumenkyo**	no license
無能	**munoo**	incompetence
無意識	**muishiki**	unconscious

政治に無関心な人は多い。
Seeji ni mukanshin na hito wa ooi.
There are many people uninterested in politics.

無免許運転をしてはいけない。
Mumenkyo unten o shite wa ikenai.
You should not drive a car without a license.

不：不公平　　**fukoohee**　　　unfair
　　不便　　　**fuben**　　　　inconvenient
　　不足　　　**fusoku**　　　　lack, insufficiency
　　不景気　　**fukeeki**　　　recession, bad economic condition
　　不幸　　　**fukoo**　　　　unhappiness, misfortune
　　不自然　　**fushizen**　　　unnatural

最近、寝不足だ。
Saikin nebusoku da.
Lately, (I am suffering from) lack of sleep.

携帯電話がないと不便だろう。
Keetai denwa ga nai to fuben daroo.
I think it is inconvenient not to have a cell phone.

非：非常識　　**hijooshiki**　　　lacking in common sense
　　非現実的　**higenjitsuteki**　unrealistic
　　非協力的　**hikyooryokuteki**　uncooperative
　　非社交的　**hishakooteki**　　anti-social
　　非凡　　　**hibon**　　　　　extraordinary

夜中に電話をかけてくるなんて、非常識だ。
Yonaka ni denwa o kakete kuru nante, hijooshiki da.
(He) is lacking in common sense to call (me) in the middle of night.

世界から戦争がなくなることを期待するのは、非現実的なことだろう。
Sekai kara sensoo ga nakunaru koto o kitai suru no wa, higenjitsuteki na koto daroo.
It's probably unrealistic to expect wars to disappear from the world.

未：未完成　　**mikansee**　　　unfinished
　　未解決　　**mikaiketsu**　　unresolved
　　未婚　　　**mikon**　　　　unmarried
　　未成年　　**miseenen**　　　minor, underage
　　未知　　　**michi**　　　　unknown

未婚の女性が増えている。
Mikon no josee ga fuete iru.
Unmarried women are increasing in number.

未解決の問題が多い。
Mikaiketsu no mondai ga ooi.
There are many unsolved problems.

16

Numbers and classifiers

16.1 General remarks about numbers and classifiers

There are two number series in Japanese, those of native (J) origin and those of Chinese (C) origin. The native numbers go only from 1 to 10 (and then skip to 20 in some cases). Interestingly, the multiples in this series start with the same consonant; 1 and 2 with 'h,' 3 and 6 with 'm,' and 4 and 8 with 'y.'

	1	2	3	4	5	6	7	8	9	10
J	hi	fu	mi	yo	itsu	mu	nana	ya	kokono	too
C	ichi	ni	san	shi	go	roku	shichi	hachi	ku/kyuu	juu

Although the native numbers have limited usage, one of the most common is to express the ages 1 to 10 and 20; e.g. **hito-tsu** '1 year old,' **too** '10 years old,' **hatachi** '20 years old.' The suffix **-tsu** attached to the numbers here is a classifier for age, as well as for counting, in general. Other categories that use native numbers include **hito-ri** 'one person,' **futa-tabi** 'two times, again,' **yo-tsubu** 'four grains, pills.' They also appear as part of set phrases; e.g. **hito-kasegi suru** 'to earn money,' **hito-hada nugu** 'to do a favor (Lit. 'to take off one layer of skin'),' and **hito-kawa mukeru** 'to change' (Lit. 'to peel one layer of skin').

There are three ways to say 'zero': **ree**, borrowed from Chinese, **zero** from English, and a native word meaning 'circle,' **maru**. Room number 306, for example, may be pronounced **san ree roku**, **san zero roku**, or **san maru roku**. When a sequence of numbers is given, such as telephone, house, and room numbers and postal code, the Chinese series is used, in which case, the vowel in a one-syllable word is lengthened; **ni** '2' → **nii**, **shi** '4' → **shii**, **go** '5' → **goo**. In the Chinese series, bad luck numbers are 4 and 9, and they are sometimes avoided. This is because there are homophones (words with same pronunciation) with unlucky meanings. **Shi** can mean '4' or 'death,' and **ku** can mean '9' or 'suffering.'

As a default, Chinese series numbers appear with 'classifiers' (see **16.2**) of Chinese origin, and native numbers with native classifiers. The series are sometimes mixed, however. To tell the time, for example, Chinese origin words are used with **ji** 'o'clock'; e.g. **ichi-ji** 'one o'clock.' For 'four o'clock,' however, the native word **yo** 'four' is used, as in **yo-ji**, instead of **shi**. This is probably because the non-existent **shi-ji** sounds too similar to **shichi-ji** 'seven o'clock.' Likewise, many people nowadays say **nana-ji** to mean 'seven o'clock' instead of the normal **shichi-ji**, especially on the telephone and in business conversations so as not to be confused with **ichi-ji** 'one o'clock.'

▶ **36.1**

Numbers from both series are used in naming and counting the days of the month, the forms for which are identical; e.g. **futsu-ka** can mean either 'the second day' or 'two days.' **Tsui-tachi** 'the first day' is an exception. It is derived from **tsuki** 'month' + **tachi** 'stand, start' by loss of the 'k'. 'One day' is expressed as **ichi-nichi**, with the Chinese series number **ichi** 'one,' followed by **nichi** 'day,' a classifier of Chinese origin. **Ka** 'day' is a classifier of Japanese origin, and it is used with

Japanese series numbers. For the second through the tenth, fourteenth, twentieth, and twenty-fourth day, the numbers and the classifier **-ka** is used, and number + **nichi** is used for the rest.

1: **tsui-tachi** 'first day,' **ichi-nichi** 'one day';

2: **futsu-ka**	3: **mik-ka**	4: **yok-ka**
5: **itsu-ka**	6: **mui-ka**	7: **nano-ka**
8: **yoo-ka**	9: **kokono-ka**	10: **too-ka**
11: **juu-ichi-nichi**	12: **juu-ni-nichi**	13: **juu-san-nichi**
14: **juu-yok-ka**	15: **juu-go-nichi** . . .	
20: **hatsu-ka**	21: **ni-juu-ichi-nichi**	22: **ni-juu-ni-nichi** . . .
23: **ni-juu-san-nichi**	24: **ni-juu-yok-ka**	25: **ni-juu-go-nichi** . . .
29: **ni-juu-ku-nichi**	30: **san-juu-nichi** . . .	

▶ **36.2**

Numbers 11 to 99

For numbers above 10, the Chinese series is used. The word for '11' is **juu ichi**, from **juu** '10' and **ichi** '1,' '12' is **juu ni**, from **juu** '10' and **ni** '2,' and so on. The multiples of 10 are formed as **ni** '2' **juu** '10' for '20,' **san** '3' **juu** '10' for '30,' etc. '98' is pronounced **kyuu** '9' **juu** '10' **hachi** '8.'

11: **juu ichi**	21: **ni juu ichi**	40: **yon/shi juu**
12: **juu ni**	22: **ni juu ni**	50: **go juu**
13: **juu san**	23: **ni juu san**	60: **roku juu**
14: **juu shi/yon**	24: **ni juu shi/yon**	70: **nana juu**
15: **juu go**	25: **ni juu go**	80: **hachi juu**
16: **juu roku**	26: **ni juu roku**	90: **kyuu juu**
17: **juu shichi/nana**	27: **ni juu shichi/nana**	
18: **juu hachi**	28: **ni juu hachi**	
19: **juu ku/kyuu**	29: **ni juu ku/kyuu**	
20: **ni juu**	30: **san juu**	

Numbers 100 and up

The word for 'hundred' is **hyaku**. The initial consonant 'h' changes to 'b' following **san** 'three' and **nan** 'what,' yielding **san byaku** '300' and **nan byaku** 'how many hundreds.' The initial 'h' changes to 'p' with **roku** 'six' and **hachi** 'eight,' and the numbers are respectively pronounced **rop** and **hap**, yielding **rop pyaku** '600' and **hap pyaku** '800.'

100: **hyaku**	200: **ni hyaku**	300: **san byaku**
400: **yon hyaku**	500: **go hyaku**	600: **rop pyaku**
700: **nana hyaku**	800: **hap pyaku**	900: **kyuu hyaku**

Three-digit numbers are expressed as the combination of hundreds, tens, and ones. For example, '368' consists of **san byaku** '300', **roku juu** '60' and **hachi** '8,' and is pronounced as **san byaku roku juu hachi**.

The word for 'thousand' is **sen**. The initial consonant 's' changes to 'z' following **san** 'three' and **nan** 'what,' yielding **san zen** '3000' and **nan zen** 'how many thousands.'

1,000: **(is) sen**	2,000: **ni sen**	3,000: **san zen**
4,000: **yon sen**	5,000: **go sen**	6,000: **roku sen**
7,000: **nana sen**	8,000: **has sen**	9,000: **kyuu sen**

The word for 'ten thousand' is **(ichi) man**, with a new unit name. There is no such word as *__juu sen__, a literal translation of 'ten thousand.'

10,000: **ichi man**	20,000: **ni man**	30,000: **san man**
40,000: **yon man**	50,000: **go man**	60,000: **roku man**
70,000: **nana man**	80,000: **hachi man**	90,000: **kyuu man**

The unit name changes by each digit up to **ichi man** '10,000.' Then it changes when the digit increases by four, or at every four zeros.

1	ichi	10,000,000	(is)sen man
10	juu	100,000,000	ichi oku
100	hyaku	1,000,000,000	juu oku
1,000	sen or is sen	10,000,000,000	hyaku oku
10,000	ichi man	100,000,000,000	sen oku
100,000	juu man	1,000,000,000,000	it choo
1,000,000	hyaku man		

'0' in a numerical sequence is not pronounced.

205:	ni hyaku go
40,301:	yon man san byaku ichi
6,089,030:	rop pyaku hachi man kyuu sen san juu

Numbers with a decimal point

A decimal point is pronounced as **ten** 'point,' and the number after it is read as a sequence of single digit numbers. The numbers to the left of the decimal point are pronounced as explained in **16.1**. Zero (0) is pronounced as **ree** or **zero** when it is the only number to the left of the decimal point.

0.5:	ree ten go	0.14:	ree ten ichi yon
9.72:	kyuu ten nana ni	40.863:	yon jut ten hachi roku san

Unlike in spoken English, in which zero is often omitted and '0.5' is pronounced simply as 'point five', Japanese does not omit 0 in either speech or writing.

Fractions

When reading fractions, the whole is pronounced first, followed by the part.

1/2:	ni bun no ichi	half
2/3:	san bun no ni	two thirds
3/4:	yon bun no san	three quarters

16.2 | Types and meanings of classifiers

In Japanese, a quantity is expressed by a number followed by a classifier (also called counter). Classifiers are not used with adverbs that express quantities (e.g. **subete** 'all,' **hotondo** 'almost all'). In English a classifier is used when describing the quantity of items classified as mass nouns (nouns that are not countable); e.g. 'three grains of rice,' 'two loaves of bread,' 'four sheets of paper.' In Japanese, classifiers are used when talking about both things that can and cannot be counted. The choice of classifier depends on the class of noun.

Class of noun	Classifier	Number + Classifier	
people (men, women, children, teachers)	**ri/nin:**	**hito ri** **futa ri** **san nin**	one two three
small animals and insects (frogs, mice, flies, dogs, cats)	**hiki:**	**ip piki** **ni hiki** **san biki**	one two three
large animals (horses, cows, bears, lions)	**too**	**it too** **ni too** **san too**	one two three
thin flat objects (paper, plates, shirts, sliced ham)	**mai**	**ichi mai** **ni mai** **san mai**	one two three
long and narrow objects (pens, umbrellas, fingers, trees, films)	**hon**	**ip pon** **ni hon** **san bon**	one two three

Class of noun	Classifier	Number + Classifier	
large machines and vehicles (cars, bicycles, copy machines)	**dai**	**ichi dai** **ni dai** **san dai**	one two three
bound objects (books, dictionaries, photo albums)	**satsu**	**is satsu** **ni satsu** **san satsu**	one two three
things measured by spoons, cups, glasses, buckets	**hai**	**ip pai** **ni hai** **san bai**	one two three
chunky or round objects, things in general (candies, apples, boxes, balls)	**ko**	**ik ko** **ni ko** **san ko**	one two three
chunky or round objects, intangible things and concepts (apples, problems, hopes, recipes)	**tsu**	**hito tsu** **futa tsu** **mit tsu**	one two three

When classifiers are attached, the pronunciation of some numbers and/or classifiers changes, e.g. **ichi + hon → ip pon** 'one long object,' **ichi + satsu → is satsu** 'one bound object,' **san + hiki → san biki** 'three small animals.'

The most general classifier of Japanese origin is **tsu**, used with native numbers. It is particularly appropriate when counting small, round or chunky objects (e.g. apples, cups), but it can be used with almost any object in place of a specific classifier when speaking informally. Television, chairs, and dressers, for example, are supposed to be counted with specially designated classifiers, but **tsu** is commonly used instead. Tsu is also used referring to orders at restaurants and coffee shops; e.g. **tenpura mit-tsu** 'three tempuras,' **koohii hito-tsu** 'one coffee.'

When the number is larger than nine, things that are normally counted with **tsu** appear without a classifier; e.g. **Kanji o hyaku oboeta** 'I learned 100 **kanji**.' It is possible to switch to **-ko** in this and many other cases; e.g. **Kanji o hyak-ko oboeta** 'I learned 100 kanji.' Ages 9 and under can be counted with **tsu**; e.g. **kokono-tsu** '9 years old.' Over 9, ages can be given without any classifier or with **sai** 'year(s) old'; e.g. **too** or **jus-sai** '10 years old,' **san-juu-ichi** or **san-juu-is-sai** '31 years old.' (**-Sai** can be used with any age, from one year old.)

Other groups of classifiers

Units of measurement

miri meetoru	millimeter
senchi	centimeter
meetoru	meter
guramu	gram
kiro	kilogram/kilometer
miri rittoru	milliliter
rittoru	liter

Duration

byoo	second
fun	minute
jikan	hour
nichi (kan)	day
shuukan	week
ka getsu	month
nen (kan)	year
seeki	century

Frequency

do	times
kai	times

Currency

en	Japanese yen
doru	dollar
sento	cent
yuuro	euro
pondo	pound (sterling)

There is a classifier **sen** to express amounts less than **ichi en** 'one yen,' used for currency exchange rates and stock prices. 100 **sen** is equivalent to **ichi en** 'one yen.'

Different classifiers may be used with the same noun.

ご飯が一粒残った。
Gohan ga hito tsubu nokotta.
One grain of rice remained.

ご飯を一杯食べた。
Gohan o ippai tabeta.
I ate a bowl of rice.

ご飯を一キロ使った。
Gohan o ichi kiro tsukatta.
I used one kilogram of rice.

16.3   Position of numbers and classifiers

The number always precedes the classifier. Although the position of the number + classifier combination in a sentence depends on various factors, the canonical position is after the noun it modifies. The case particle is attached to the noun and the number + classifier chunk follows it. Case particles are not usually attached to the number + classifier phrase indicating an amount.

本を3冊買った。
Hon o san satsu katta.
I bought three books.

子供が2人遊んでいる。
Kodomo ga futari asonde iru.
Two children are playing.

姉が一人と弟が二人いる。
Ane ga hitori to otooto ga futari iru.
I have one older sister and two younger brothers.

A quantifier marked with **no** (pre-nominal form of the copula) can appear before the associated noun.

三匹の子ぶた
san biki no kobuta
three little pigs

狼と7匹の子やぎ
ookami to nana hiki no koyagi
a wolf and seven kid goats

一杯のかけそば
ip pai no kakesoba
one bowl of soba noodles

The [number + classifier **no** N] sequence is appropriate when the quantified objects, people, etc. have particular significance to the narrative and are treated as a group. It is often used in the titles of stories or written materials. Such a sequence can be connected to another with **to** 'and.'

> 花瓶に５本のバラと３本のガーベラを一緒に飾った。
> **Kabin ni go hon no bara to san bon no gaabera o isshoni kazatta.**
> I arranged five roses and three gerberas together in the vase.

The quantifier can also be placed before the noun it quantifies without adding **no**. Such a move has the effect of emphasizing the number + classifier phrase or making the sentence sound not well planned. The [number + classifier + N] sequence cannot be connected to another sequence of the same type. Thus, one cannot say *Ni hon enpitsu to san satsu hon o katta to mean 'I bought two pencils and three books.'

> スーパー で二個りんごを買った。
> **Suupaa de ni ko ringo o katta.**
> I bought two apples at a supermarket.

When the number + classifier phrase quantifies a noun marked by a postposition such as **to** 'with,' **ni** 'for,' and **kara** 'from,' the phrase is placed between the noun and the postposition.

> 友達二人と出かけた。
> **Tomodachi futari to dekaketa.**
> I went out with two friends.

> 先生三人から推薦状をもらった。
> **Sensee san nin kara suisenjoo o moratta.**
> I received letters of recommendation from three teachers.

17

Compounds

Nominal compounds

The following compounds are examples of those combining two nouns. Some nominal compounds maintain the original meaning of each noun. In other nominal compounds the second noun functions as a suffix.

- N1 + N2

    ◆ [N1 modifies N2] or [N1 and N2]

    本棚 **hon-dana** 'bookshelf' (**hon** 'book' + **tana** 'shelf/shelves')
    食品部門 **shokuhin-bumon** 'food department' (**shokuhin** 'food' + **bumon** 'section/department')
    三人部屋 **sannin-beya** 'a room for three people' (**sannin** 'three people' + **heya** 'room')
    草木 **kusa-ki** 'grass and trees' (**kusa** 'grass' + **ki** 'tree')
    物事 **mono-goto** 'things' (**mono** 'thing' + **koto** 'thing')

    ◆ N2 functions as a suffix

    バス代 **basu-dai** 'bus-fare'
    若者向け **wakamono-muke** 'targeted at young people'
    入場料 **nyuujoo-ryoo** 'entrance fee'

Some nominal compounds are created by the pattern V + N.

- V(stem) + N

    生け花 **ike-bana** 'arranged flowers' (or 'flower arrangement')
    やり残し **yari nokoshi** 'things left undone'
    食べ物 **tabe-mono** 'food'
    飲み物 **nomi-momo** 'drink'
    買い物 **kai-mono** 'shopping'
    食べ方 **tabe-kata** 'the way to eat'
    挿し絵 **sashi-e** 'illustration' (lit. 'inserted picture')

Adjectival compounds

Some compounds are created by the pattern V(stem) + adj.

- V(stem) + adj.

    書きやすい **kaki-yasui** [write+easy] 'easy to write'
    歩きにくい **aruki-nikui** [walk+difficult] 'difficult to walk'
    誇り高い **hokori-takai** [be proud+high] 'proudly'
    待ち遠しい **machi-dooshii** [wait+impatient] 'can hardly wait'
    寝苦しい **ne-gurushii** [sleep+hard] 'difficult to sleep'

■   N + adj.

心細い **kokoro-bosoi** [heart+narrow] 'insecure'
心安らか **kokoro-yasuraka** [heart+peaceful] 'peaceful'
心苦しい **kokoro-gurushii** [heart+painful] 'sorry'
涙もろい **namida-moroi** [tears+weak] 'easy to cry'
生ぬるい **nama-nurui** [raw+tepid] 'lukewarm'
根深い **ne-bukai** [root+deep] 'inveterate/deep-rooted'

17.3 Verbal compounds

Two verbs can be combined to create verbal compounds. In one type, each of the two verbs contributes equally ('do V1 and do V2'). In another, the first verb describes how the second verb (i.e. main verb) is carried out.

■   V1 + V2: do V1 and V2; or V2 is the main verb

持ち出す **mochi-dasu** [hold+take out] 'take out'
飛び出す **tobi-dasu** [jump+go out] 'run out'
書き写す **kaki-utsusu** [write+copy] 'copy; transcribe'
飛び越える **tobi-koeru** [jump+go over/pass] 'jump over'
呼び止める **yobi-tomeru** [call+stop] 'call out for someone to stop'
作り直す **tsukuri-naosu** [make+fix] 'remake'
聞き返す **kiki-kaesu** [question+return] 'question again'
引き起こす **hiki-okosu** [draw+cause] 'trigger'
取り戻す **tori-modosu** [get+return (something)] 'retrieve/take back'

In yet another type, the first verb functions as the main verb, and the second verb as an auxiliary (helping) verb.

■   V1 + V2: V1 is the main verb

食べかける **tabe-kakeru** [eat+hang] 'take a bite/start to eat'
怒鳴りつける **donari-tsukeru** [shout+attach (transitive)] 'yell at'
泣きつく **naki-tsuku** [cry+adhere] 'beg desperately'
飲み過ぎる **nomi-sugiru** [drink+exceed] 'over drink'
押し込む **oshi-komu** [push+get into] 'put something into'
降り出す **furi-dasu** [rain+begin] 'start to rain (all of sudden)'
書きあげる **kaki-ageru** [write+raise] 'complete writing something'
炊きあがる **taki-agaru** [boil+rise] '(rice) is cooked'

18

Formal nouns

Formal nouns are so called because they are nouns only in form. They must always be modified, such as by a demonstrative (e.g. **sonna** 'that kind of') and a clause, and cannot stand alone. There are a variety of formal nouns in Japanese.

18.1 *koto*

Koto (lit. 'thing') refers to intangible and abstract things such as facts, concepts, and information. **Koto** as a formal noun turns a clause into a noun phrase. The predicate in the **koto** clause must appear in plain form. **Koto** is used to describe events, actions, or information in a rather formal, abstract and general way, and hence it often occurs with verbs of learning, deduction and thinking.

▶ 26

山田さんが有名な学者であることを知っていますか。
Yamada-san ga yuumee na gakusha de aru koto o shitte imasu ka.
Do you know that Mr/Ms Yamada is a famous scholar?

冬になると鬱病になる人が増えることがわかった。
Fuyu ni naru to utsubyoo ni naru hito ga fueru koto ga wakatta.
I realized that people get depressed more in winter.

今すぐ日本の景気をよくすることは難しい。
Ima sugu Nihon no keeki o yoku suru koto wa muzukashii.
It is difficult to improve Japan's economy in a short period.

日本人にとって正月を家族と過ごす事はとても大切なことです。
Nihonjin ni totte shoogatsu o kazoku to sugosu koto wa totemo taisetsu na koto desu.
It is important for Japanese people to spend time together with their family on New Year's Day.

趣味はドライブに行っておいしいものを食べることです。
Shumi wa doraibu ni itte oishii mono o taberu koto desu.
My hobby is to go for a drive and to eat delicious food.

Koto is also used in several constructions when talking about one's experience, ability, decision, etc. They include (V(plain nonpast) + **koto**) **ni suru** 'to decide to', (V(plain nonpast) + **koto**) **ni naru** 'it is decided to', (V(plain) + **koto**) **ga dekiru** 'can, it is possible to', (V(plain past) + **koto**) **ga aru** 'to have the experience of doing something,' and (V(plain nonpast) + **koto**) **ga aru** 'there are times when.'

▶ 44; 51.1; 86.2

三月にアメリカへ出張することになりました。
Sangatsu ni Amerika e shutchoo suru koto ni narimashita.
It has been decided that I will go on business to the U.S. in March.

今年で会社を辞めることにしました。
Kotoshi de kaisha o yameru koto ni shimashita.
I have decided to resign from my company this year.

三か国語を話すことができます。
San-ka-kokugo o hanasu koto ga dekimasu.
I can speak three languages.

沖縄に行ったことがあります。
Okinawa ni itta koto ga arimasu.
I have been to Okinawa.

時々暑くて眠れないことがあります。
Tokidoki atsukute nemurenai koto ga arimasu.
There are times when I can't sleep because it is too hot.

18.2 *no*

18.2.1 *no*

No functions as a nominalizer by making a clause into a noun phrase. **No** is used when the main verb expresses perceptions, concrete actions or events, including verbs of seeing and hearing, discovery, helping and stopping.

▶ **26.1**

私は田中さんがバイオリンを弾くのを聴いた。
Watashi wa Tanaka-san ga baiorin o hiku no o kiita.
I heard Mr/Ms Tanaka play the violin.

私は佐藤さんが彼女と会っているのを見た。
Watashi wa Satoo-san ga kanojo to atte iru no o mita.
I saw Mr Sato meeting with his girlfriend.

休みの日はゆっくり散歩するのが好きだ。
Yasumi no hi wa yukkuri sanpo suru no ga suki da.
I love taking a stroll when I have a day off.

山田さんが帰ってくるのを待ちましょう。
Yamada-san ga kaette kuru no o machimashoo.
Let's wait for Mr/Ms Yamada to return.

病気になってから、タバコをすうのをやめました。
Byooki ni natte kara tabako o suu no o yamemashita.
I have given up smoking since I got sick.

A **no**-clause can function as an object, as in the above examples. It can also function as the subject of the sentence.

一流の大学に入るのは難しい。
Ichiryuu no daigaku ni hairu no wa muzukashii.
Getting into a first-rate university is difficult.

たばこをすうのは体によくない。
Tabako o suu no wa karada ni yokunai
Smoking is not good for one's health.

There are cases where both **no** and **koto** can be used. However, there is a difference in meaning and context. See **26.1** for details.

no da/desu

No very frequently occurs followed by a copula **da** or **desu** as in **n da, n desu, no da, no desu** or **no**, at the end of sentences. Its basic function is to mark information as known or to present the information as accessible. The actual effect of this expression, however, varies greatly depending on the situation and sentence types.

Most often the sentence with **no da** gives an explanatory tone.

> A: どうして来なかったんですか。
> **Dooshite konakatta n desu ka.**
> Why is it that you did not come?

> B: へんな物を食べたせいかお腹が痛かったんです。
> **Hen na mono o tabeta see ka onaka ga itakatta n desu.**
> (It is that) I had a stomachache, perhaps because I ate something bad.

B is explaining why he/she did not come.

> 石川: 田中君、剣道にこってるみたいだね。
> **Ishikawa: Tanaka-kun, kendoo ni kotteru mitai da ne.**
> Tanaka-kun, it seems like you are really into kendo.

> 田中: うん、とっても面白いんだ。
> **Tanaka: Un, tottemo omoshiroi n da.**
> Yeah, it is really interesting.

In questions, **no da** is used when one forms an assumption based on what one observes or knows and then asks whether that assumption is correct.

> 風邪をひいたんですか。
> **Kaze o hiita n desu ka.**
> (Is it that) you caught a cold? (Am I correct in assuming you caught a cold?)

This sentence might be uttered when the speaker observes that the addressee is coughing, for example.

> パーティーへ行くんですか。
> **Paatii e iku n desu ka.**
> Are you going to the party? (Am I correct in assuming that you are going to the party?)

One might say this when one observes that the addressee is all dressed up. Such an assumption does not exist with a sentence without **no da**.

No often creates a sense of shared feeling or rapport between the speaker and the addressee, and hence it often gives a soft, less imposing tone. It is very frequently used in giving background information for what comes next or as an introduction to more important information that comes next. This is generally the case for phrases such as **n desu kedo** and **n desu ga**.

> ちょっと話したいことがあるんだけど、
> **Chotto hanashitai koto ga aru n da kedo,**
> I have something I want to talk to you about, . . .

> ちょっと伺いたいことがあるんですが、よろしいでしょうか。
> **Chotto ukagaitai koto ga aru n desu ga, yoroshii deshoo ka.**
> I have something I would like to ask you. Is it OK?

> あしたコンパがあるんだけど、行かない？
> **Ashita konpa ga aru n da kedo, ikanai?**
> There is a social tomorrow. Won't you come?

It should be noted, however, that **no da**, when used with **kara**, gives a strong reproachful tone.

せっかく私が作った<u>ん</u>だから、こわさないでください。
Sekkaku watashi ga tsukutta <u>n</u> da kara, kowasanaide kudasai.
I took so much trouble to make it, so please don't break it.

若い<u>ん</u>だから、もうちょっと頑張ってください。
Wakai <u>n</u> da kara, moo chotto ganbatte kudasai.
(The fact is that) you are young, so try a little harder.

The last sentence might be said to someone who is not trying very hard.

18.3 | *mono*

Mono and its colloquial form **mon** literally refer to 'tangible things' and have many idiomatic expressions as a formal noun modified by the preceding clause. In these expressions, **mono** is often associated with emotions of the speaker and is used to convey nostalgic feeling, strong desire, conviction and the like. The following are some examples.

(a) General truth/conviction
V nonpast plain + **mono da/desu** conveys what the speaker/writer thinks is generally the case.

努力すればだれでも成功するものです。
Doryoku sureba dare demo seekoo suru mono desu.
If you try hard, you should succeed.

年を取ると忘れっぽくなるものです。
Toshi o toru to wasureppoku naru mono desu
It is generally the case that when you grow old, you become forgetful.

This construction can also be used to order the addressee to do something by stressing what s/he is saying as a general truth or a social norm.

ご近所の人に会ったら、ご挨拶するものですよ。
Go-kinjo no hito ni attara go-aisatsu suru mono desu yo.
When you meet your neighbors, you are supposed to greet them.

もらったら、お返しするもんですよ。
Morattara okaeshi suru mon desu yo.
When you receive a gift from someone, you should give a return gift.

(b) Nostalgic reminiscence
When the predicate preceding **mono desu** is in the past tense, it is often used when the speaker recalls something with a kind of nostalgic or sentimental feeling.

子供の頃はこの川で魚釣りをしたものです。
Kodomo no koro wa kono kawa de sakanatsuri o shita mono desu.
I used to fish in this river when I was a kid.

この辺は昔、店がたくさんあってにぎやかだったものです。
Kono hen wa mukashi, mise ga takusan atte nigiyaka datta mono desu.
This area used to be bustling with many shops.

(c) Desire
V + **tai mono desu ne** is used to state one's desire emphatically.

The speaker expresses his/her strong feeling.

一度アフリカに行ってみたいものですね。
Ichido Afurika ni itte mitai mono desu ne.
I would really like to go to Africa once!

(d) Strong negative feeling

Mono/mon (desu) ka with a falling intonation expresses the speaker's strong negation.

そんなこと、あるもの/もんですか。
Sonna koto aru mono/mon desu ka.
How can that be! (= That is impossible).

あんな所、行くもの/もんですか。
Anna tokoro iku mono/mon desu ka.
How can I go there! (= That is impossible).

(e) Justifying a reason

Mon at the end of the sentence can express the speaker's justification of his/her action. The expression tends to be used by younger women or children.

A: どうして食べないの？
Dooshite tabenai no?
Why don't you eat it?

B: だって、おいしくないんだ<u>もん</u>。
Datte, oishikunai n da <u>mon</u>.
Because it's not tasty.

(f) Giving a reason

S **mon(o) desu/da kara** can be used to give a reason. In such a case, the reason is a personal one, not known to the other party.

A: 遅い！遅い！
Osoi! Osoi!
You are late! You are late!

B: ごめん。道が込んでいたもんだから。
Gomen. Michi ga konde ita mon da kara.
Sorry. It's because the traffic was slow.

松田： あら、本田さん、いらっしゃい。
Matsuda: Ara, Honda-san, irasshai.
Oh, hi, Honda-san. Welcome!

本田： あのう、ちょっと近くに来たものですから…
Honda: Anoo, chotto chikaku ni kita mono desu kara...
Um, since I was in the neighborhood...

18.4 *yoo*

Yoo has various idiomatic uses. V(plain nonpast) + **yoo ni suru** indicates the speaker's conscious effort and is equivalent to the English meaning of 'make an effort to.'

甘い物は食べないようにしています。
Amai mono wa tabenai yoo ni shite imasu.
I am trying not to eat sweet things.

V(plain nonpast) + **yoo ni naru** 'reach the point where' expresses a gradual change in abilities, habits, or conditions.

このごろ肉より魚を食べるようになりました。
Kono goro niku yori sakana o taberu yoo ni narimashita.
I have come to eat more fish than meat lately.

健康のために運動するようになりました。
Kenkoo no tame ni undoo suru yoo ni narimashita.
For the sake of my health I started exercising.

Yoo ni naru is similar to **koto ni naru** in the sense that both express some change or result. However, they are different in the sense that **koto ni naru** implies that some decision was made, while **yoo ni naru** simply describes a gradual change.

Yoo ni can also introduce a manner clause as in the following examples.

先日お話ししたように、今週の金曜日から留守にします。
Senjitsu o-hanashi shita yoo ni, konshuu no kin'yoobi kara rusu ni shimasu.
As I mentioned the other day, I will be out of town from this Friday.

北海道は「日本のウィスコンシン」と呼ばれるように、湖が多くてきれいです。
Hokkaidoo wa 'Nihon no Wisukonshin' to yobareru yoo ni, mizuumi ga ookute kiree desu.
As Hokkaido is called 'the Wisconsin of Japan,' it has many lakes and is pretty.

tokoro

Tokoro meaning 'place' can be used as a formal noun in various contexts. It highlights a particular point of time or aspect of an event, action, or process:

Expressions focusing on the aspect of process:

今会社から帰ったところです。
Ima kaisha kara kaetta tokoro desu.
I (have) just returned from work.

今出かけるところです。
Ima dekakeru tokoro desu.
I am about to leave.

兄の日記を読んでいるところを見られてしまった。
Ani no nikki o yonde iru tokoro o mirarete shimatta.
I was caught (at the moment) when I was reading my brother's diary.

Other expressions:

今日はお忙しいところをお集りいただき、ありがとうございます。
Kyoo wa o-isogashii tokoro o o-atsumari itadaki, arigatoo gozaimasu.
Thank you for coming today, (at a time) when you must be busy.

夕ご飯を食べているところに父から電話があった。
Yuugohan o tabete iru tokoro ni chichi kara denwa ga atta.
There was a call from my father, (at the time) when I was eating dinner.

その仕事が終わったところで、一休みしましょう。
Sono shigoto ga owatta tokoro de, hitoyasumi shimashoo.
Let's take a break, (at the point) when you are finished with the job.

▶ 23.3; 27.4.2

wake

Wake 'reason' is often used with the copula as in **wake da/desu**. Preceded by a clause, this phrase expresses the speaker's logical or deductive judgment on what has been said or observed.

(1) V(plain) **wake da**
　　　［飲む/飲んだ］わけだ
　　　　　　　　　　　　　　　　　　　[nomu/nonda] **wake da**

(2) Adj. **(i)**(plain) **wake da**
　　　［高い/高かった］わけだ
　　　　　　　　　　　　　　　　　　　[takai/takakatta] **wake da**

(3) Adj **(na)/datta wake da**
　　　［上手な/上手だった］わけだ
　　　　　　　　　　　　　　　　　　　[joozuna/joozu datta] **wake da**

(4) N **to yuu/datta wake da**
　　　［学生という/学生だった］わけだ
　　　　　　　　　　　　　　　　　　　[gakusee to yuu/gakusee datta] **wake da**

- **wake da**: no wonder, that is why, that explains

    A:　来年アメリカに留学するつもりです。
    　　Rainen Amerika ni ryuugaku suru tsumori desu.
    　　I am planning to study in America next year.

    B:　それで今、一生懸命英語を勉強しているわけですね。
    　　Sorede ima isshookenmee Eego o benkyoo shite iru wake desu ne.
    　　No wonder you are studying English so hard.

In this example, on the basis of what he has heard, Speaker B draws the conclusion that it is no wonder A studies English so hard.

    A:　山田さん、今旅行中ですよ。
    　　Yamada-san, ima ryokoo-chuu desu yo.
    　　Mr/Ms Yamada is on a trip now.

    B:　それで、昨日会議に来なかったわけですね 。
    　　Sorede kinoo kaigi ni konakatta wake desu ne.
    　　No wonder he was not at the meeting yesterday.

Here, based on what speaker A said about Mr/Ms Yamada, speaker B deduces the reason why speaker A did not attend the meeting yesterday.

- **wake da**: that means

    A:　妻は明日から２週間ギリシャに行きます。
    　　Tsuma wa ashita kara nishuukan Girisha ni ikimasu.
    　　My wife is going to Greece tomorrow for two weeks.

    B:　じゃあ、今月の末まで家にいらっしゃらないわけですね。
    　　Jaa, kongetsu no sue made ie ni irassharanai wake desu ne.
    　　Then, (that means) she will not be home till the end of this month.

Here speaker B makes the deduction 'speaker A's wife will not be home till the end of the month,' by referring to what speaker A has said.

    A:　卒業論文の締め切りがあと２週間なんです。
    　　Sotsugyoo ronbun no shimekiri ga ato nishuukan na n desu.
    　　Two more weeks are left till the deadline for my graduation thesis.

    B:　ということは、今月はとても忙しいわけですね。
    　　To yuu koto wa, kongetsu wa totemo isogashii wake desu ne.
    　　That means you must be very busy this month.

In this example speaker B concludes that speaker A must be very busy because he has to finish his thesis in two weeks.

▶ **47.1; 73.1; 78.1.2**

tsumori

Tsumori is a formal noun and cannot be used independently. It must be preceded by a clause or a demonstrative. The most common meaning of **tsumori** is to express the speaker's intention to carry out a future action. Hence verbs used for this type of **tsumori** must concern the speaker's controllable actions.

> 来年心理学を勉強するつもりです。
> **Rainen shinrigaku o benkyoo suru tsumori desu.**
> I am going to study psychology next year.

> 週末は友達とドライブに行くつもりです。
> **Shuumatsu wa tomodachi to doraibu ni iku tsumori desu.**
> I am going out for a drive with my friends on the weekend.

> A: 明日の集会に行きますか。
> **Ashita no shuukai ni ikimasu ka.**
> Are you going to the meeting tomorrow?

> B: はい、そのつもりです。
> **Hai, sono tsumori desu.**
> Yes, I intend to.

Tsumori can be negated in two ways, V-**nai** + **tsumori** 'to intend not to do . . .' and V + **tsumori ga/wa nai** 'to have no intention of doing . . .' The latter expresses much stronger negative determination than does the former.

> もう酒は飲まないつもりです。
> **Moo sake wa nomanai tsumori desu.**
> I do not intend to drink sake any more.

> もう酒を飲むつもりはありません。
> **Moo sake o nomu tsumori wa arimasen.**
> I have no intention of drinking sake any more.

When the predicate of the clause is not associated with future actions, **tsumori** expresses the subject's belief, which often is not shared by others. In these cases, the preceding element of **tsumori** is an action verb (past tense), a stative verb, an adjective, or a noun + **no**.

> 先週お渡ししたつもりですが。
> **Senshuu owatashi shita tsumori desu ga.**
> I think I gave it to you last week, but . . .

> 彼はあれでもハンサムなつもりなんです。
> **Kare wa are demo hansamu na tsumori nan desu.**
> He thinks he is handsome (even though he is not).

> 私は７７歳ですが、まだまだ若いつもりです。
> **Watashi wa nanajuunana sai desu ga, madamada wakai tsumori desu.**
> Although I am 77 years old, I think of myself as still young.

> 全部わかっているつもりになっている。
> **Zenbu wakatte iru tsumori ni natte iru.**
> (He) thinks he knows everything.

> あれで女優のつもりだ。
> **Are de joyuu no tsumori da**.
> And she thinks she is an actress!

▶ 45.1

hazu

Hazu is a formal noun, which must be modified by demonstratives or clauses. Clause + **hazu da** means 'to be expected, to be supposed to.' The expression refers to the speaker's expectation or anticipation, which are presented as natural outcomes of reasoning. Since **hazu** expresses the speaker's natural expectation based on some reliable information, it cannot be used to refer to his/her own volitional actions.

> A: お父さん、いる？
> **Otoosan, iru?**
> Is Dad there?

> B: ６時頃家を出たから、そっちに着いているはずだけど。
> **Rokuji goro ie o deta kara, sotchi ni tsuite iru hazu dakedo.**
> He left home around six, so he should be there.

> A: まだ来てないよ。
> **Mada kite nai yo.**
> He is not here yet.

> B: そんなはずないよ。もう２時間たっているよ。
> **Sonna hazu nai yo. Moo ni-jikan tatte iru yo.**
> That shouldn't be. It has been two hours (since he left the house).

In this example speaker B expects his father to be there. This expectation is based on the facts that his father left home about six o'clock and that it usually does not take two hours to get there. In response to speaker A's reply that his father is not there yet, speaker B says that it shouldn't be so.

> A: 田中さん、昨日の同窓会に出席したか知ってる？
> **Tanaka-san, kinoo no doosookai ni shusseki shita ka shitte ru?**
> Do you know whether Mr/Ms Tanaka attended the reunion yesterday?

> B: クラスメートに会いたいって言って（い）たから、出たはずだよ。
> **Kurasumeeto ni aitai tte itte (i)ta kara, deta hazu da yo.**
> He/she should have because he/she said he/she wanted to see his/her classmates.

In this example speaker B expects that Mr Tanaka did attend the reunion party. She makes an assumption based on the conversation she had with Mr Tanaka.

> そのケーキはよく売れているから、おいしいはずですよ。
> **Sono keeki wa yoku urete iru kara, oishii hazu desu yo.**
> The cake must be tasty, because it sells very well.

Here the speaker expects/assumes that the cake is delicious because it has been popular and sells well.

Other frequently used formal nouns

There are other frequently used formal nouns. They include **bakari**, **dake**, and **tame**.

bakari

Bakari has various meanings.

- V (past plain) **bakari** means 'just did something' and emphasizes the immediacy in time.

  今家に着いたばかりです。
  Ima ie ni tsuita bakari desu.
  I (have) just got home.

父は買ったばかりのスーツを着て出かけた。
Chichi wa katta bakari no suutsu o kite dekaketa.
My father went out in the suit that he had just recently bought.

■ N **bakari**: 'just, nothing but', 'all s/he eats, buys etc., is . . .' (exaggeration)

うちの子は肉ばかり食べています。
Uchi no ko wa niku bakari tabete imasu.
My child eats nothing but meat.

■ V-**te bakari iru** 'one does nothing but . . .', 'all one does seems to be . . .' (exaggeration)

毎日ビデオゲームをしてばかりいます。
Mainichi bideo geemu o shite bakari imasu.
(He) does nothing but play video games every day.

■ Number **bakari**: approximately, about (sounds a little affected)

五分ばかり待ちました。
Gofun bakari machimashita.
(I) waited about five minutes.

▶ 81.2

dake

Dake meaning 'only, just' minimizes the amount, action, state, etc. that precedes it.

五分話しただけではどんな人かわかりません。
Gofun hanashita dake de wa donna hito ka wakarimasen.
You can't tell what kind of person (he) is by just talking with (him) for five minutes.

一つだけ質問してもいいですか。
Hitotsu dake shitsumon shite mo ii desu ka.
May I ask just one question?

あのレストランは雰囲気がいいだけです。料理はあまりおいしくありません。
Ano resutoran wa fun'iki ga ii dake desu. Ryoori wa amari oishiku arimasen.
The only good thing about that restaurant is that it has a nice atmosphere. The food is not too good.

In some contexts, **dake** indicates an amount 'that much.'

どうぞ、好きなだけ取ってください。
Doozo, suki na dake totte kudasai.
Please take as much as you want.

あれだけ親切な人も珍しい。
Are dake shinsetsu na hito mo mezurashii.
Such a generous person is rare.

▶ 10.3

tame

Clause + **tame** can express purpose or reason.

▶ 47

In the purpose construction CLAUSE1 **tame ni** CLAUSE2 ('in order to do V1, (one) does V2'), V1 must be in plain form in nonpast tense while V2 can be in plain or **desu/masu** form and in any tense. Also, the subject of V1 and V2 must be the same.

（私は）日本文化の研究をするために日本へ行きます。

(Watashi wa) Nihon bunka no kenkyuu o suru tame ni Nihon e ikimasu.

I am going to Japan in order to do research on Japanese culture.

In the reason construction CLAUSE1 **tame ni** CLAUSE2 ('due to the fact that CLAUSE 1, CLAUSE 2 results'), the predicate in both clauses can be anything – verb, adjective or copula, and the tense does not matter. **Tame** in this usage is appropriate in formal speech and in writing.

このあたりは化学薬品の工場が多いために空気が汚染されている。

Kono atari wa kagaku yakuhin no koojoo ga ooi tame ni kuuki ga osen sarete iru.

Because this area has many chemical factories, the air is polluted.

When **tame** is modified by a noun, **N no tame** can express purpose, reason or benefit.

これは登山のための靴です。(purpose)

Kore wa tozan no tame no kutsu desu.

These are shoes for mountain climbing.

大雪のためにフライトがキャンセルされた。(reason)

Ooyuki no tame ni furaito ga kyanseru sareta.

The flight was canceled because of heavy snow.

彼は家族のために一生懸命働いた。(benefit)

Kare wa kazoku no tame ni isshoo kenmee hataraita.

He worked very hard for his family.

▶ 47.3

19

Auxiliary verbs

19.1 General remarks on auxiliary verbs

Auxiliary verbs in Japanese are attached to the **te**-form or the stem of the main verb. An auxiliary verb has its own meaning when it is used as the main verb, but as an auxiliary verb, it often loses its original meaning. Auxiliary verbs add aspectual meaning to the action/event denoted by the main verb. They are conjugated to express past/nonpast tense, affirmative/negative distinction, and formal/informal styles. When responding to a question with V-**te**/V-stem + auxiliary structure, the main verb needs to be repeated with the auxiliary verb.

19.2 V-*te* + auxiliary verbs

19.2.1 V-*te iru*

Meanings expressed by V-**te iru** are: 1. action in progress; 2. resultant state; 3. habitual/repeated action; and 4. experience. Its meaning depends on the types of verb used or the context in which it is used. In casual speech, the vowel **i** in the auxiliary **iru** is often omitted, resulting in V-**te ru**.

Action in progress
When the main verb is a durative action verb, V-**te iru** indicates that the action denoted by the main verb is in progress at a given moment. Durative action verbs are verbs that denote an action that takes some time to perform; e.g. **taberu** 'to eat,' **nomu** 'to drink,' **utau** 'to sing,' **kaku** 'to write,' **miru** 'to watch,' **matsu** 'to wait' and **aruku** 'to walk.' Motion verbs, e.g. **iku** 'to go' and **kuru** 'to come' do <u>not</u> belong to this group.

> 子供が公園で遊んでいる。
> **Kodomo ga kooen de asonde iru.**
> Children are playing in the park.

> 今勉強している。
> **Ima benkyoo shite iru.**
> I'm studying right now.

> 夕べの10時には家で本を読んでいました。
> **Yuube no juuji ni wa ie de hon o yonde imashita.**
> I was reading a book at 10 o'clock last night.

Resultant state
When the main verb is a change-of-state or a momentary verb or an intransitive verb, V-**te iru** expresses the state which the subject is in as a result of the past action/event denoted by the verb. Change-of-state verbs express actions or events after which the subject's state changes; e.g. **shinu** 'to die,' **kekkon suru** 'to marry,' **owaru** 'for something to end,' **shiru** 'to find out,

learn,' **tatsu** 'to stand up,' **futoru** 'to gain weight,' **yaseru** 'to lose weight' and **aku** 'open (intransitive).'

同僚は結婚している。
Dooryoo wa kekkon shite iru.
My colleague is married.

この虫はもう死んでいる。
Kono mushi wa moo shinde iru.
This bug is already dead.

窓が開いている。
Mado ga aite iru.
The window is open.

Motion verbs such as **iku** 'to go' and **kuru** 'to come' also express a resultant state in the **-te iru** construction.

父は今会社に行っています。
Chichi wa ima kaisha ni itte imasu.
My father is at work now.

友達が来ています。
Tomodachi ga kite imasu.
My friend has come and is here.

Transitive verbs in the passive form are intransitive as a composite, and express a resultant state in the **-te iru** construction.

鍵が壊されている。
Kagi ga kowasarete iru.
The lock has been broken (and it is broken).

Habitual/repeated action

In some contexts, V-*te* **iru** is interpreted as a habitual or repeated action. This type of sentence often includes adverbs of frequency; e.g. **mainichi** 'every day' **yoku** 'often' **maitoshi** 'every year' and **itsumo** 'always.'

健康のために毎朝歩いている。
Kenkoo no tame ni maiasa aruite iru.
I walk every morning for my health.

妹は電車で高校にかよっています。
Imooto wa densha de kookoo ni kayotte imasu.
My younger sister commutes to high school by train.

Experience

When V-*te* **iru** is used with adverbs like **sudeni** 'already' and **moo** 'already' or adverbial phrases indicating a specific time in the past, it expresses a person's past experience that is somehow relevant to the speaker at present, especially when checking a document.

田中さんは3年前に留学している。
Tanaka-san wa sannen mae ni ryuugaku shite iru.
Mr/Ms Tanaka studied abroad three years ago.

佐藤さんは去年新車を買っています。
Satoo-san wa kyonen shinsha o katte imasu.
Mr/Ms Sato bought a brand new car last year.

In these examples, the auxiliary verb **iru** remains in the nonpast form even though it expresses a past experience. The temporal adverbs are needed to indicate that they are talking about a past event.

V-**te** plus the negative form of the auxiliary verb **iru** is used especially with the adverb **mada** 'yet' to express that one has not done something yet.

> （まだ）昼ご飯を食べていません。
> **(Mada) hirugohan o tabete imasen**.
> I have not eaten lunch (yet).

▶ 12.1; 12.2; 37.5; 37.6; 37.7; 37.11; 44.2

19.2.2 V-*te aru*

V-**te aru** expresses a state that results from somebody's action without stating the agent of the verb. It implies the volition of the person who performed the action, i.e. someone did it for some purpose. It is typically used with transitive verbs. The direct object of the main verb is marked by -**ga** in V-**te aru** sentences.

> ケーキが買ってあります。
> **Keeki ga katte arimasu.**
> A cake has been bought.

> 部屋がかたづけてあった。
> **Heya ga katazukete atta.**
> The room had been tidied up.

The verbs that are not used in V-**te aru** sentences are: stative verbs (e.g. **aru/iru** '(for inanimate/ animate things) to exist,' **dekiru** 'can do'); copula; verbs that express actions that cannot be done volitionally (e.g. **wasureru** 'to forget' and **ushinau** 'to lose'); and verbs that denote actions that do not imply a predetermined end point or result (e.g. **utau** 'to sing,' **unten suru** 'to drive' and **aruku** 'to walk').

Transitive V-**te aru** and intransitive V-**te iru** both describe a state, but while V-**te iru** simply describes the state of the subject noun, as in example (a) below, V-**te aru** implies that the state described is a result of something someone did for some purpose, as in example (b).

> (a) 窓が開いています。
> **Mado ga aite imasu.**
> The window is open.

> (b) 窓が開けてあります。
> **Mado ga akete arimasu.**
> The window is open. (Someone left it open for some purpose.)

▶ 12.1; 12.2

19.2.3 V-*te miru*

V-**te miru** means 'to do something to see what will happen.' To use this expression, the action has to be performed. If it is not possible to complete the action, i.e. if one tried but couldn't do it, the volitional form of the verb + **to suru** construction is used instead.

> 激辛ラーメンを食べてみた。
> **Gekikara raamen o tabete mita.**
> I tried super spicy ramen. (Lit. I ate super spicy ramen to see how it was.)

> 新しいドレスを着てみた。
> **Atarashii doresu o kite mita.**
> I tried on the new dress. (Lit. I put on the new dress to see how it looked.)

> ドアをノックしてみた。
> **Doa o nokkushite mita.**
> I knocked on the door to see what would happen.

朝5時に起きてみた/起きようとしたけど、起きられなかった。

Asa goji ni ~~okite mita~~/**okiyoo to shita kedo, okirarenakatta.**

I tried to get up at five a.m., but I could not wake up.

▶ 72.4

19.2.4 *V-te oku*

V-**te oku** expresses that the subject does something as preparation for future purpose so that there will be no regret. Another meaning is to keep some state as is for some purpose.

ホテルを予約しておいた。

Hoteru o yoyaku shite oita.

I reserved a hotel.

傘を買っておきました。

Kasa o katte okimashita.

I bought an umbrella.

暑かったので、窓を開けておいた。

Atsukatta node, mado o akete oita.

I kept the window open because it was hot.

Unlike the V-**te aru** construction (see **19.2.2**), the agent of the action denoted by the main verb can be expressed as the subject in the V-**te oku** construction.

母は晩ご飯を作っておいた。

Haha wa bangohan o tsukutte oita.

My mother made dinner in advance.

▶ 12.1

19.2.5 *V-te shimau*

V-**te shimau** expresses that the subject does something completely, regrettably, or inadvertently. The interpretation of V-**te shimau** sentences depends on the context and one's understanding of the situation.

友達の宿題をやってしまった。

Tomodachi no shukudai o yatte shimatta.

I did my friend's homework completely/regrettably/inadvertently.

If we assume that the speaker thinks doing another person's homework is wrong, we may interpret this sentence as 'I regrettably did my friend's homework.' If we know that s/he did a friend's homework by mistake, it would mean 'I inadvertently did my friend's homework.' Consider the next example:

暇だったから、宿題をやってしまった。

Hima datta kara, shukudai o yatte shimatta.

Because I had free time, I did my homework completely.

Given the context (having free time), we may interpret **shukudai o yatte shimatta** as 'I did my homework completely' rather than 'regrettably' or 'inadvertently,' though these are still possible interpretations. Another example is:

会社をさぼったのに本屋で同僚に会ってしまった。

Kaisha o sabotta noni hon'ya de dooryoo ni atte shimatta.

I skipped work, but I ran into my colleague at a bookstore regrettably/inadvertently.

Knowing that the agent skipped his/her work, 'running into a colleague' is interpreted as 'regrettable' or 'inadvertent.'

In casual speech, the pronunciation V-**te shimau** may change as follows:

-te shimau → chau	**-de shimau → jau**
食べてしまう → 食べちゃう	飲んでしまう → 飲んじゃう
tabete shimau → tabe chau	**nonde shimau → non jau**
eat	drink

▶ **57.4; 67.2**

19.2.6 **V-te kuru**

Kuru as a main verb means 'to come,' indicating a motion toward the speaker. V-**te kuru** expresses how the action/event denoted by the main verb relates to the speaker in a spatial or temporal sense.

Meanings expressed by V-te kuru:

(1) 'to do something and come back; to go and do something and come back'
Main verb = action verb

> 弟が飲み物を買ってきた。
> **Otooto ga nomimono o katte kita.**
> My brother went to buy drinks (and came back).

> 明日、様子を見てくる。
> **Ashita, yoosu o mite kuru.**
> I will go tomorrow and see how things are.

(2) Continuation of action/event from some point in the past to the present.

> ずっと魚屋で魚を買ってきたので、スーパーの魚は食べられない。
> **Zutto sakanaya de sakana o katte kita node, suupaa no sakana wa taberarenai.**
> I've always bought fish at fish markets, so I can't eat fish from supermarkets.

> その番組は小さい時から見てきた。
> **Sono bangumi wa chiisai toki kara mite kita.**
> I have been watching the program since I was little.

(3) 'to begin to change'
Main verb = verb of process/change

> 雨が降ってきた。
> **Ame ga futte kita.**
> It has begun to rain.

> 物価があがり生活が苦しくなってきた。
> **Bukka ga agari seekatsu ga kurushiku natte kita.**
> Prices have gone up and life has begun to get difficult.

> 最近やせてきた。
> **Saikin yasete kita.**
> I have begun to lose weight.

▶ **50.3**

19.2.7 **V-te iku**

When it is the main verb, **iku** 'to go' denotes a motion away from the speaker. V-**te iku** indicates a spatial, temporal, or psychological movement of the action/event denoted by the main verb in a direction away from the speaker.

Meanings expressed by V-*te iku*:

(1) 'do something and go'

> 服が汚れたから、着替えていく。
> **Fuku ga yogoreta kara, kigaete iku.**
> My clothes (have) got dirty, so I will change and go.

> 友達の家にケーキを買っていった。
> **Tomodachi no ie ni keeki o katte itta.**
> I bought cake and went to my friend's house.

(2) 'continue to do . . . ; continue to change'
Main verb = verb of process/change

> 夫婦がうまくやっていく方法が知りたい。
> **Fuufu ga umaku yatte iku hoohoo ga shiritai.**
> I want to know a method for a married couple to continue to get along.

> これからもがんばっていきたいです。
> **Kore kara mo ganbatte ikitai desu.**
> I want to continue doing my best from now on as well.

(3) 'to occur gradually'

> 時代と共にさまざまな製品が我々の生活から消えていくでしょう。
> **Jidai to tomo ni samazama na seehin ga wareware no seekatsu kara kiete iku deshoo.**
> Over time, various products will gradually disappear from our daily life.

(4) 'to be changing' (process of change)

> 大量生産で製品が劣化していった。
> **Tairyooseesan de seehin ga rekka shite itta.**
> Due to mass production, the product quality went down.

> 夫は薬の副作用で痩せていった。
> **Otto wa kusuri no fukusayoo de yasete itta.**
> My husband went on losing weight due to side effects of the medicine.

▶ 50.3

19.2.8 V-*te* + benefactives

Benefactives are verbs such as **ageru** 'to give,' **kureru** 'X gives me,' and **morau** 'to receive.' See **12.7** for the use of these verbs in the giving and receiving of objects. The same rules apply to the use of V-**te** + benefactives, which expresses the giving and receiving of a favor/benefit.

■ **V-te ageru/sashiageru/yaru: 'to do something as a favor'**

The subject of the V-**te ageru/sashiageru/yaru** sentence is the giver of a favor. The recipient is someone other than the speaker or his/her in-group.

> <u>not</u> *田中さんは私に車を貸してあげた。
> ***Tanaka-san wa watashi ni kuruma o kashite ageta.**
> Mr/Mr Tanaka lent me a car.

However, when the speaker is the giver, the recipient can be someone in the speaker's in-group.

> 私は妹に朝ご飯を作ってあげた。
> **Watashi wa imooto ni asagohan o tsukutte ageta.**
> I made breakfast for my younger sister.

V-**te ageru** is used when the social status of the subject/giver is equal or higher than that of the recipient of the benefit. The recipient is marked by the particle **ni** when the recipient is an indirect object.

研さんは美奈さんに英語を教えてあげました。
Ken-san wa Mina-san ni Eego o oshiete agemashita.
Ken taught English to Mina as a favor.

私は友達にお金を貸してあげた。
Watashi wa tomodachi ni o-kane o kashite ageta.
I lent money to my friend as a favor.

If the recipient is the direct object of the main verb, it is marked by **o**.

私は友達を応援してあげた。
Watashi wa tomodachi o ooen shite ageta.
I cheered my friend on as a favor.

親は子供をほめてあげた。
Oya wa kodomo o homete ageta.
The parent praised his/her child for the child's benefit.

The recipient is marked with **to** 'with' in the following example.

私は弟と映画を見てあげた。
Watashi wa otooto to eega o mite ageta.
I watched the movie with my younger brother as a favor.

In other cases, the recipient is indicated by **no tame ni** 'for the sake of.'

私は友達のためにノートをコピーしてあげた。
Watashi wa tomodachi no tame ni nooto o kopii shite ageta.
I copied my notes for my friend.

父は母のために買い物をしてきてあげた。
Chichi wa haha no tame ni kaimono o shite kite ageta.
My father went and did the shopping for my mother.

V-**te sashiageru** is used if the social status of the recipient is higher than that of the giver's.

おばあさんの荷物を運んでさしあげた。
Obaasan no nimotsu o hakonde sashiageta.
I carried the elderly woman's luggage for her.

私はお客様にお茶を入れてさしあげた。
Watashi wa okyaku-sama ni ocha o irete sashiageta.
I made tea for the customer.

When the utterance is directed towards the recipient of the favor, V-**te ageru/sashiageru** is often avoided because it sounds as if the speaker is demanding the recipient's gratitude by making it explicit that the speaker did the action as a favor. In such a case, the humbling form, **o**-V(stem)-**suru** is used.

お茶をお入れします。
O-cha o o-ire shimasu.
I will make some tea for you.

▶ 29

V-**te yaru** may be used when the giver's social status is higher than the recipient's. However, some people, especially female speakers of Japanese, frequently use V-**te ageru** in those cases, possibly because V-**te yaru** may be perceived by others as too rough.

弟に事情を説明してやった。
Otooto ni jijoo o setsumee shite yatta.
I explained the circumstances to my younger brother.

犬にパンをわけてやった。
Inu ni pan o wakete yatta.
I shared my bread with the dog.

V-te yaru is often used to express the giving of a negative action.

絶対に思い知らせてやる。
Zettai ni omoi-shirasete yaru.
I will definitely take revenge.

彼をひどい目に遭わせてやる。
Kare o hidoi me ni awasete yaru.
I will make him suffer.

■　**V-te kureru/kudasaru: 'X gives me the favor of doing . . .'**

The subject of a V-te kureru/kudasaru sentence is the giver of a favor. In declarative sentences, the recipient of the favor is the speaker or someone in his/her in-group. **V-te kureru** is used when the social status of the subject/giver is equal or lower than that of the recipient of the favor. The recipient is marked by a particle appropriate in relation to the main verb. If the recipient is the indirect object of the main verb, for example, it is marked by **ni**. When it is the speaker him/herself, it is often omitted.

父が（私に）車を買ってくれた。
Chichi ga (watashi ni) kuruma o katte kureta.
My father bought me a car for my benefit.

母が（私に）プレゼントを送ってくれた。
Haha ga watashi ni purezento o okutte kureta.
My mother sent me a present for my benefit.

友達が弟に英語を教えてくれた。
Tomodachi ga otooto ni Eego o oshiete kureta.
My friend taught English to my younger brother for his benefit.

If the recipient is the direct object of the main verb, it is marked by **o**.

みんなが私の家族を歓迎してくれた。
Minna ga watashi no kazoku o kangee shite kureta.
Everyone welcomed my family.

いつも両親が（私を）支えてくれる。
Itsumo ryooshin ga watashi o sasaete kureru.
My parents always support me (which I appreciate).

When the recipient is neither the direct or indirect object of the main verb but needs to be specified in the sentence, **no tame ni** 'for the sake of' can be used.

母が私のために先生に尋ねてくれた。
Haha ga watashi no tame ni sensee ni tazunete kureta.
My mother asked the teacher for my sake.

V-te kudasaru is used when the giver is the recipient's social superior or someone worthy of respect.

先生が私のために推薦状を書いてくださった。
Sensee ga watashi no tame ni suisenjoo o kaite kudasatta.
My teacher wrote a recommendation letter for me.

In interrogative sentences, the recipient can be a second person, 'you'.

友達は何をしてくれた？
Tomodachi wa nani o shite kureta?
What did your friends do for you?

子供の頃、お父さんは一緒に遊んでくださいましたか。
Kodomo no koro, otoosan wa isshoni asonde kudasaimashita ka.
Did your father play with you when you were a child?

■ **V-te morau/itadaku: 'to receive the favor of doing . . .'**

The subject of V-**te morau/itadaku** sentences is the recipient of a favor. The giver of the favor is marked by **ni** (or sometimes **kara**). The giver in V-**te morau/itadaku** sentences cannot be the speaker. V-**te morau/itadaku** can be used when the recipient receives a favor by asking for it. However, it is possible to use it when such is not the case. V-**te morau** is used when the recipient's social status is equal to or higher than that of the giver's.

誠くんは友達に本を貸してもらった。
Makoto-kun wa tomodachi ni hon o kashite moratta.
Makoto asked his friend to lend him a book, which he did. / For Makoto's sake,
his friend lent him a book.
(Lit. Makoto received the favor of his friend's lending him a book.)

私は母に料理を教えてもらった。
Watashi wa haha ni ryoori o oshiete moratta.
I asked my mother to teach me how to cook and she taught me. / I had my mother
teach me how to cook.
(Lit. I received the favor of my mother's teaching me how to cook.)

When the giver's social status is higher than that of the recipient's, V-**te itadaku** is used.

私は友達のお母さんにケーキを作っていただいた。
Watashi wa tomodachi no okaasan ni keeki o tsukutte itadaita.
My friend's mother made a cake for me.

母は上司の方にうちまで送っていただいた。
Haha wa jooshi no kata ni uchi made okutte itadaita.
My mother's boss brought her home as a favor.

▶ 43

19.3 | Frequently used verb stem + auxiliary verbs

19.3.1 | V(stem) + *-hajimeru/-dasu* 'begin doing . . .'

Both V(stem)-**hajimeru** and V(stem)-**dasu** denote the meaning of 'begin to do something.'

雨が降りはじめた。   雨が降りだした。
Ame ga furi-hajimeta.   **Ame ga furi-dashita.**
It began to rain.   It began to rain.

While V(stem)-**dasu** implies the abruptness of the event and reflects the speaker's surprise about the event, V(stem)-**hajimeru** simply describes the event without such implications. When the action denoted by the main verb can be controlled by the agent's volition, **-dasu** cannot be used.

私は晩ご飯を作り~~出した~~/はじめた。
Watashi wa bangohan o tsukuri-~~dashita~~/hajimeta.
I began making dinner.

私は映画を見~~出した~~/はじめた。
Watashi wa eega o mi-~~dashita~~/hajimeta.
I started to watch the movie.

V(stem)-**hajimeru/-dasu** is not usually used with change-of-state verbs unless the subject is interpreted as plural.

姉/大学時代の友達が結婚しはじめた。
~~Ane~~/daigaku jidai no tomodachi ga kekkon shi-hajimeta.
~~My sister~~/My friends from college began to get married.

５時をすぎると田中さん/お客さんが来はじめた。
Goji o sugiru to ~~Tanaka-san~~/okyaku-san ga ki-hajimeta.
~~Mr/Ms Tanaka~~/Customers began to show up after five p.m.

When the main verb denotes an action that can be controlled by the agent's volition, V(stem)-**dasu** expresses the meaning of 'out' or 'up' as in the following examples.

母は新しい商品を作り出した。
Haha wa atarashii shoohin o tsukuri-dashita.
My mother made up a new product.

妹は買う物を書き出した。
Imooto wa kau mono o kaki-dashita.
My sister wrote out things to buy.

▶ 17.3; 50.4.2

V(stem) + -*owaru* 'finish doing . . .'

V(stem)-**owaru** expresses that the action denoted by the main verb is completed.

本を読みおわった。
Hon o yomi-owatta.
I finished reading the book.

宿題をやりおわったら、出かける。
Shukudai o yariowattara, dekakeru.
I will go out after I finish doing my homework.

父は朝食を食べ終わると、会社に向かった。
Chichi wa chooshoku o tabe-owaru to, kaisha ni mukatta.
When my father finished eating breakfast, he left for work.

V(stem) + -*sugiru* 'to overdo . . .'

Sugiru as a main verb means 'to pass, to go beyond.' V(stem)-**sugiru** expresses 'to do something excessively.'

今日は食べすぎた。	最近の子供はテレビを見すぎる。
Kyoo wa tabe sugita.	**Saikin no kodomo wa terebi o mi-sugiru.**
I ate too much today.	Kids nowadays watch too much TV.

The auxiliary -**sugiru** can be used with the negative form of the main verb. Take the plain negative form of the main verb and change the final -**i** to **sa-sugiru**.

Plain neg.	-sugiru form
見な~~い~~	見なさすぎる
mina~~i~~	**minasa sugiru**
not see	see too little

父は自分の意見を言わなさすぎます。
Chichi wa jibun no iken o iwanasa sugimasu.
My father keeps his opinion to himself excessively.

妹は勉強しなさすぎる。
Imooto wa benkyoo shinasa sugiru.
My sister studies too little.

The auxiliary **-sugiru** is also used with adjectives, expressing that the state is excessive. Take the final **-i** from **i**-adjectives and attach **-sugiru**.

> この服は大きすぎる。
> **Kono fuku wa ooki-sugiru.**
> These clothes are too large.

> 暑すぎて眠れない。
> **Atsu sugite nemurenai.**
> It's too hot to sleep.

Attach **-sugiru** to a **na**-adjective without the copula.

> 図書館は静かすぎる。
> **Toshokan wa shizuka-sugiru.**
> The library is too quiet.

> 寮は賑やかすぎます。
> **Ryoo wa nigiyaka sugimasu.**
> The dorm is too noisy.

▶ 17.3

19.3.4 | V(stem) + -uru/-eru 'there is a possibility of doing . . .'

V(stem) **-uru/-eru** expresses that there is a possibility that the action, state, or event described by the main verb may be realized. It is primarily used in writing. It cannot be used to express one's ability.

> 事故はいつでも起こりうる。
> **Jiko wa itsu demo okori uru.**
> Accidents can occur anytime.

> 嘘もつきえたが、真実をのべた。
> **Uso mo tsuki eta ga, shinjitsu o nobeta.**
> I could have lied, but I told the truth.

The auxiliary **-uru** appears only in the plain nonpast affirmative form, but **-eru** can be conjugated like any other verb.

	Non past		Past	
	Plain	*Polite*	*Plain*	*Polite*
Aff.	**-uru/eru**	**-emasu**	**-eta**	**-emashita**
Neg.	**-enai**	**-emasen**	**-enakatta**	**-emasen deshita**

Stative verbs, such as **aru** 'exist' and **wakaru** 'understand,' can be used with the auxiliary **-uru/eru** to express possibility.

> そんなことはありえない。
> **Sonna koto wa ari enai**
> Such things cannot possibly happen.

> その可能性はありうる。
> **Sono kanoosee wa ari uru.**
> That possibility can exist.

▶ 12.6; 53.1.2

20

The causative construction

The causative construction expresses the idea that one person causes someone else to do something by physically forcing, applying psychological pressure, ordering, plotting, giving permission, or by not intervening.

20.1 | Causative forms

The following explains how to produce the plain nonpast affirmative causative form from the dictionary form of the verb.

Irregular verbs

Dict. form		Causative form
suru 'to do'	→	**saseru**
kuru 'to come'	→	**kosaseru**

U-verbs
Delete the final **-u** and add **-aseru**; if a vowel precedes the final **-u**, add **-waseru**.

Dict. form		Causative form
yomu 'to read'	→	**yom<u>aseru</u>**
kaku 'to write'	→	**kak<u>aseru</u>**
utau 'to sing'	→	**uta<u>waseru</u>**

Ru-verbs
Delete the final **-ru** and add **-saseru**.

Dict. form		Causative form
taberu 'to eat'	→	**tabe<u>saseru</u>**
kakeru 'to hang'	→	**kake<u>saseru</u>**

NOTE | Once any verb is in the causative form, it conjugates like a **ru**-verb.

▶ **12.1**

A shortened version of the causative form, in which the final **-eru** is replaced by **-u**, is also used.

Causative form		Shortened causative form	
saseru	→	**sasu**	'to make X do'
kosaseru	→	**kosasu**	'to make X come'
yomaseru	→	**yomasu**	'to make X read'
tabesaseru	→	**tabesasu**	'to make X eat'

The shortened causative conjugates like **u**-verbs (**12.1**).

Most stative verbs, e.g. **aru** 'for inanimate things to exist,' **iru** 'need,' **niau** 'look good, suit' and potential verbs, are not used in the causative form.

20.2 Regular (productive) causative

Structure: causer-**ga/wa**   causee-**o/ni**   intransitive V-**(s)aseru**
Structure: causer-**ga/wa**   causee-**ni**   transitive V-**(s)aseru**

The causer is the person who makes the causee perform the action denoted by the verb. The causee is the one who performs the action denoted by the verb. When the verb is intransitive, the causee may be marked by the particles **o** or **ni**. When the verb is transitive, the causee must be marked by **ni**. The regular causative sentences with an **o**-marked causee are called **o**-causative and those with a **ni**-marked causee are called **ni**-causative.

> 親が子供に/を宿題をさせた。
> **Oya ga kodomo ni/o shukudai o saseta.**
> The parent made the child do homework.

> 私は妹に/を昼ご飯を作らせた。
> **Watashi wa imooto ni/o hirugohan o tsukuraseta.**
> I made my sister make lunch.

> 妻は夫に/を買い物に行かせた。
> **Tsuma wa otto ni/o kaimono ni ikaseta.**
> The wife let/made her husband go shopping.

When both **o** and **ni** are possible markers for the causee, the **o**-causative sentence tends to express more coercive meaning than the **ni**-causative sentence. In the above example, **otto o ikaseta** might mean that the husband did not want to go shopping but the wife made him go. With **ni**, on the other hand, it might mean that the husband was quite willing to go shopping, and the wife let him go.

20.3 Adversative causative

Structure: causer-**wa/ga**   causee-**o**   intransitive V-**(s)aseru**.

In adversative causative sentences, the causee is marked with **o**, just like **o**-causatives. However, they are not interpreted as having a coercive meaning. The subject (i.e. causer) in the adversative causative is not directly involved in causing the event. The adversative causative sentence expresses the idea that the subject of the sentence feels somehow responsible for an action carried out by the causee or for an event which affects the causee. The action/event denoted by the verb is usually something that has an adverse effect on the subject.

> 私は仲間を死なせてしまったことを後悔している。
> **Watashi wa nakama o shinasete shimatta koto o kookai shite iru.**
> I regret that I let my friend die.

In this sentence, '**nakama**' died for some reason, and '**watashi**' thinks that there might have been something she/he could have done to prevent the death. Therefore, even though '**watashi**' did not kill '**nakama**,' '**watashi**' feels like she/he caused the death. The sentence structure of the adversative causative is the same as the **o**-causative. It is therefore possible to interpret the example given here as though it is **o**-causative, i.e. '**watashi**' made his/her friend die, for example, by not giving obviously needed help.

20.4 Causatives + benefactives

When causatives combine with benefactives, they express the meaning of 'to permit/let' and lose the coercive meaning. It is used when the causer lets the causee do what the causee wants to do. By using the benefactives in combination with the causatives, the speaker acknowledges that there is some benefit given or received in the action/event denoted by the main verb.

▶ **12.7; 19.2.8; 43**

20.4.1 Causative *te* + *ageru/sashiageru*: 'to let X do . . .'

Structure: causer-**wa/ga**   causee-**ni**   V-causative **te**-form + **ageru**

The causer knows or assumes the causee's intention or desire to do the action denoted by the main verb and allows the action to take place.

私は友達にコンピューターを使わせてあげた。
Watashi wa tomodachi ni konpyuutaa o tsukawasete ageta.
I let my friend use the computer.

母親は子供を遊びに行かせてあげた。
Hahaoya wa kodomo o asobi ni ikasete ageta.
The mother let her child go to play.

When the causee is the causer's social superior or someone worthy of respect, **sashiageru** may be used instead of **ageru**.

私たちはお客様にお土産を持たせてさしあげた。
O-kyaku-sama ni o-miyage o motasete sashiageta.
We had our guests take a souvenir gift.

In the above example, the speaker is reporting to someone that she/he gave a souvenir gift to his/her guests. Importantly, the speaker is not talking to the guests themselves. Causative-**te sashiageru** is not appropriate when the speaker is talking to his/her superior about actions that benefit the superior. For example, if you are talking to your guest about letting him/her take a souvenir, the exalting form should be used.

▶ **12.7; 19.2.8; 29.2**

お客様、お土産をお持ちになってください。
O-kyaku-sama, o-miyage o o-mochi ni natte kudasai.
Please take the souvenir with you.

not   *お客様、お土産を持たせてさし上げます。
        *O-kyaku-sama, o-miyage o motasete sashiagemasu.
        We will have you take the souvenir with you (as a favor).

20.4.2 Causative *te* + *kureru/kudasaru*: 'someone lets me do . . .'

Structure: causer-**wa/ga**   causee-**ni**   V-(causative) **te**-form + **kureru/kudasaru**

To combine **kureru/kudasaru** with the causative-**te** form, the causer must be someone other than the speaker and the causee must be the speaker or someone close to the speaker (e.g. family members).

A causative + **kureru/kudasaru** sentence expresses the speaker's gratitude towards the causer who allowed the causee to do the action denoted by the main verb. When the causer is the causee's social superior or someone worthy of respect, **kudasaru** is used instead of **kureru**.

▶ **12.7; 19.2.8**

同僚が（私に）手料理を食べさせてくれた。
Dooryoo ga (watashi ni) teryoori o tabesasete kureta.
My colleague let me eat his/her homemade dish.

先生が妹にノートを写させてくださった。
Sensee ga imooto ni nooto o utsusasete kudasatta.
The teacher let my younger sister copy his/her notebook.

20.4.3 **Causative *te* + *morau/itadaku*: 'to be permitted to do . . .'**

Structure: causee-**wa**/**ga** causer-**ni** V(causative) **te**-form + **morau/itadaku**

This structure is different from the other causative structures in that the subject is the causee rather than the causer. It expresses that the causee receives the favor of the causer's letting him/her do the action denoted by the main verb. It implies that the causee asked for and was granted permission.

（私は）両親に留学させてもらった。
(Watashi wa) ryooshin ni ryuugaku sasete moratta.
I had my parents let me study abroad.

The above example expresses that **watashi** 'I' received from the parents the favor of being allowed to study abroad. The causer (**ryooshin** 'parents') is marked by the particle **ni** and the causee (**watashi** 'I') is marked by **wa**.

When the causer is the causee's social superior or someone worthy of respect, **itadaku** is used instead of **morau**.

▶ **12.7; 19.2.8**

（私は）上司に極秘書類を読ませていただいた。
(Watashi wa) jooshi ni gokuhi-shorui o yomasete itadaita.
My boss let me read the top-secret document.

When **itadaku** is used with the causative **te**-form, the causee/subject is usually the speaker or the speaker's in-group member.

20.5 # Other ways to express causative meaning

20.5.1 ## Lexical causative

Transitive verbs that have morphologically related intransitive counterparts are called lexical causatives. They contrast with their intransitive counterparts by expressing causation. Some examples of transitive–intransitive pairs are given below.

▶ **12.2**

Transitive (lexical causative)	Intransitive
kesu 'to turn off (something)'	**kieru** 'to go off/out'
akeru 'to open (something)'	**aku** '(for something) to open'
okosu 'to wake up (someone)'	**okiru** '(for someone) to wake up'

Transitive verbs express that someone causes something to happen; e.g. 'to turn off the light' means that someone causes the light to turn off. Intransitive verbs express that something happens (the existence of a causer is of no concern); e.g. 'The light turned/went off.'

Intransitive verbs that have lexical causative counterparts can have the regular (productive) causative form as well. In such cases, the lexical causative and the regular causative sentences express slightly different meanings.

Intransitive	子供たちがお風呂に入った。 **Kodomo-tachi ga o-furo ni haitta.** The kids took a bath.
Lexical causative	私は子供たちをお風呂にいれた。 **Watashi wa kodomo-tachi o o-furo ni ireta.** I bathed the kids.
Regular causative	私は子供たちをお風呂に入らせた。 **Watashi wa kodomo-tachi o o-furo ni hairaseta.** I made the kids take a bath.

In the lexical causative example, '**watashi**' physically takes part in bathing the children, for example, by taking their clothes off, scrubbing them, and so on. In the regular causative example, '**watashi**' makes the children take a bath by just ordering them to do so.

20.5.2 | ### Adjective-*ku/ni* + *suru*

The adjective **ku/ni** + **suru** construction expresses the meaning of 'make X be something,' in which 'something' is a property expressed by the adjective.

I-adjective

> **akarui** 'bright' → **akaruku suru** 'make it bright'
> **atarashii** 'new' → **atarashiku suru** 'make it new'

Na-adjective

> **kiree** 'clean' → **kiree ni suru** 'make it clean'
> **hade** 'gaudy' → **hade ni suru** 'make it gaudy'

Example sentences:

> 私たちは建物を新しくした。
> **Watashi-tachi wa tatemono o atarashiku shita.**
> We remodeled the building. (Lit. We made the building new.)

> 母は部屋をきれいにした。
> **Haha wa heya o kiree ni shita.**
> My mother cleaned the room. (Lit. My mother made the room clean.)

NOTE | The transitive construction NOUN (X) **o** NOUN (Y) **ni suru** 'make X become Y' also expresses a causative meaning; e.g. **gakkoo o danjo kyoogaku ni suru** 'make the school co-ed,' to be contrasted with the intransitive counterpart, NOUN (X) **ga** NOUN (Y) **ni naru** 'X becomes Y.'

21

The passive construction

In active sentences, the subject is the agent that performs the action denoted by the verb. In passive sentences, the subject is the receiver of the action, and the agent may or may not be expressed in the sentence. There are two types of passive constructions in Japanese, direct (regular) and indirect (adversative).

21.1 Passive forms

The verb ending changes to passive form as follows:

Ru-verbs: final **-ru** changes to **-rareru**.

Dict. Form		Passive	Dict. Form		Passive
miru 'see'	→	**mirareru**	**taberu** 'eat'	→	**taberareru**

U-verbs: final **-u** changes to **-areru**. For **-u** verbs whose dictionary forms end in **u** (う) (e.g. **ka-u** 'to buy'), insert 'w' as in **kaw-areru**.

Dict. Form		Passive	Dict. Form		Passive
toru 'take'	→	**torareru**	**matsu** 'wait'	→	**matareru**
yomu 'read'	→	**yomareru**	**suu** 'inhale'	→	**suwareru**

Irregular verbs change as follows:

Dict. Form		Passive	Dict. Form		Passive
suru 'do'	→	**sareru**	**kuru** 'come'	→	**korareru**

Once verbs are in the passive form, they conjugate like **ru**-verbs (see **12.1**).

Stative verbs; e.g. **aru** '(for inanimate things) to exist,' **iru** 'need,' and **dekiru** 'can do,' are not used in passive constructions except for **iru** '(for animate things) to exist.'

21.2 Regular passive

■   **Sentence structure**:   subject-**wa/ga**   agent-**ni**   transitive V(passive)

In the active sentence, the subject is the agent of the action denoted by the verb and the direct object is the receiver of the action. In regular passive sentences, the object of the active sentence becomes the subject (marked by **wa** or **ga**), and the agent, if it is expressed, is marked by the particle **ni** 'by.' Only transitive verbs can be used in the regular passive.

The following sentences exemplify an active sentence with a direct object and its passivized sentence.

Active 洋子さんは研さんをなぐさめた。
Yooko-san wa Ken-san o nagusameta.
Yoko consoled Ken.
Subject = Agent = Yoko; DO = Ken.

Passive 研さんは洋子さんになぐさめられた。
Ken-san wa Yooko-san ni nagusamerareta.
Ken was consoled by Yoko.
Subject = Receiver of action = Ken; Agent = Yoko.

As shown above, **Ken-san** – the direct object of the first (active) sentence – becomes the subject in the second (passive) sentence. Note also that the agent, **Yooko-san**, is indicated by the particle **ni**.

Some other examples are listed below.

武史さんは同僚に褒められました。
Takeshi-san wa dooryoo ni homeraremashita.
Takeshi was praised by his colleague.

妹は先生にしかられたそうです。
Imooto wa sensee ni shikarareta soo desu.
I hear that my little sister was reprimanded by her teacher.

One of the most frequently used verbs in the passive construction is the verb **iu** 'to say.'

子供の頃、よく親に勉強しなさいと言われました。
Kodomo no koro, yoku oya ni benkyoo shinasai to iwaremashita.
When I was a child, I was often told to study by my parents.

渋谷は若者の街と言われています。
Shibuya wa wakamono no machi to iwarete imasu.
Shibuya is said to be a town for young people.

The passive form is also used as an honorific expression. See **29.3** for explanation and examples of honorific usage of V-**(r)areru** form.

21.3 *ni yotte* passive

■ **Sentence structure:** subject-**wa**/**ga**   agent-**ni yotte**   transitive V(passive)

In some cases the agent of a regular passive sentence (but not of an adversative passive sentence) is marked by **ni yotte** 'by.' The **ni yotte** passive construction can be used in the following cases.

Product/creation: the subject is something that is produced or created

この小説は夏目漱石によって（not に）書かれた。
Kono shoosetsu wa Natsume Sooseki ni yotte (not ni) kakareta.
This novel was written by Soseki Natsume.

Formal or impersonal statements

優秀な学生たちは教師たちによって（に is also possible）賞賛された。
Yuushuu na gakusee-tachi wa kyooshitachi ni yotte (ni is also possible) shoosan sareta.
Outstanding students were commended by the teachers.

A similar passive sentence does not allow **ni yotte** when it is personal and informal.

私は今日先生たちに/~~によって~~褒められた。
Watashi wa kyoo sensee-tachi ni/~~ni yotte~~ homerareta.
I was commended by the teachers today.

In cases where both **ni** and **ni yotte** are possible markers of the agent of a passive sentence, the choice is stylistic: **ni yotte** is more formal and literary.

> 遭難者たちが自衛隊に/によって救出された。
> **Soonansha-tachi ga jieetai ni/ni yotte kyuushutsu sareta.**
> Survivors were rescued by the Self-Defense Force.

21.4 Adversative passive

The adversative passive sentence expresses that the subject of the sentence is affected, usually adversely, by what is expressed in the rest of the sentence. The subject of an adversative passive sentence is not an overt constituent of the corresponding active sentence but is the indirect receiver of the act performed by the agent. That is, someone who does not appear in the corresponding active sentence is added to the sentence as the subject when making the adversative passive sentence. Both transitive and intransitive verbs can be used in adversative passive sentences.

21.4.1 Adversative passive with transitive verb

- **Basic structure**:   subject-**wa/ga**   agent-**ni**   DO-**o**   transitive V(passive)

When the verb of an adversative passive sentence is transitive, the direct object (DO) of the corresponding active sentence remains the DO in the adversative passive construction.

> Active   親が日記を読んだ。
> **Oya ga nikki o yonda.**
> My parent read the diary.
> Subject = Agent = parent; DO = diary
>
> Passive   私は親に日記を読まれた。
> **Watashi wa oya ni nikki o yomareta.**
> I was adversely affected by my parent's reading my diary.
> (Lit. I was read my diary by my parent.)
> Subject = person affected = I; Agent = parent; DO = diary

In the adversative passive sentence above, the person indirectly affected by the action, **watashi**, is added to the sentence as the subject, even though he/she does not appear in the active sentence. The agent of the action in the adversative passive is marked by the particle **ni**, as in the regular passive. The meaning denoted by this type of passive is similar to what is expressed by English passive sentences formed by using *get*.

> 私はルームメイトに車を使われた。
> **Watashi wa ruumumeeto ni kuruma o tsukawareta.**
> My roommate used my car and I was adversely affected. (I got my car used by my roommate.)

> 友達はすりに財布を盗まれた。
> **Tomodachi wa suri ni saifu o nusumareta.**
> My friend got his wallet stolen by a pick-pocket.

21.4.2 Adversative passive with intransitive verb

- **Basic structure**:   subject-**wa/ga**   agent-**ni**   intransitive V-(passive)

When the verb is intransitive, there is no direct object. The person indirectly affected by the action is added to the sentence as the subject, and the agent of the action is marked by the particle **ni**, as in the regular passive. There is no direct translation of this type of passive into English because English intransitive verbs do not have a passive form. The meaning denoted in this type of passive is often expressed by 'on me/him/her' etc. in English.

Active 雨が降った。
Ame ga futta.
It rained.
Subject = Agent = rain

Passive 私は雨に降られた。
Watashi wa ame ni furareta.
It rained on me (Lit. I was rained on.)
Subject = I = person affected; Agent = rain.

Active 子供が泣いた。
Kodomo ga naita.
The child cried.
Subject = Agent = child

Passive 私は子供に泣かれた。
Watashi wa kodomo ni nakareta.
The child cried on me. (Lit. I was cried by the child.)
Subject = I = person affected; Agent = child.

Although it is most common to use the adversative passive when the subject is negatively affected, it is also possible to use it when the subject is positively affected.

母親は教師に子供のことを褒められて喜んだ。
Hahaoya wa kyooshi ni kodomo no koto o homerarete yorokonda.
The mother was delighted because the teacher spoke well of her child.
(Lit. The mother was delighted to be praised about her child by the teacher.)

21.4.3 Passive sentence with inanimate subject

An inanimate entity can be the subject of a regular passive sentence in Japanese, just as in English, but an inanimate subject is not used in Japanese as commonly as it is in English when a human agent is explicitly included in the sentence.

Active 子供が窓ガラスを割った。
Kodomo ga mado garasu o watta.
A child broke the window.
Subject = Agent = a child, DO = the window

Passive 窓ガラスが子供に割られた。
Mado garasu ga kodomo ni warareta.
The window was broken by a child.
Subject = the window, Agent = a child

When a human agent needs to be included in the passive sentence, it is more common to use the adversative passive with a human subject instead of making the inanimate entity the subject of the regular passive.

隣人は子供に窓ガラスを割られた。
Rinjin wa kodomo ni mado garasu o warareta.
My neighbor was negatively affected by some kid's breaking his/her window.

An inanimate entity is commonly used as the subject of a passive sentence when the agent is also inanimate or the agent is not stated in the sentence.

舟が波にさらわれた。
Fune ga nami ni sarawareta.
The boat was swept away by the waves.

最近は幼い子供たちの間でも、携帯電話が使われている。
Saikin wa osanai kodomo-tachi no aida demo, keetai denwa ga tsukawarete iru.
Recently, cell phones are used even among small children.

Causative passive

Causative passive sentences express that the subject of the sentence is made/forced to do something by someone. The verb form changes as follows:

	Dict. Form	Causative passive
Irregular verbs	**suru** 'do'	**sase-rareru**
	kuru 'come'	**kosase-rareru**
Ru-verbs: Change final **-ru** to **sase-rareru**.		
	kiru 'wear'	**ki-sase-rareru**
	taberu 'eat'	**tabe-sase-rareru**

U-verbs: There are two ways of deriving causative passive forms. One way is to change final **-u** to **-ase-rareru**. Another way is to change **-u** to **-asareru**. The latter shorter form is more common in speech.

yomu 'read'	**yom-ase-rareru; yom-asareru**
iku 'go'	**ik-ase-rareru; ik-asareru**

NOTE

(1) With **-u** verbs ending in **u** (う), as in **kau** 'to buy,' change **-u** to **-w-aserareru** or **-w-asareru**.

kau 'buy'	**kaw-aserareru** or **kaw-asareru**
tsukau 'use'	**tsukaw-aserareru** or **tsukaw-asareru**

(2) When the final syllable of **-u** verbs ends with **-su**, only the longer form **-ase-rareru** form exists. The causative passive form for **hanasu** 'talk, speak,' therefore is **hanas-ase-rareru**.

Once in the causative passive form, all verbs conjugate like a **ru**-verb. (see **12.1**)

■　**Sentence structure of causative passive:**

agent (forced performer of the action) **wa/ga** forcer **ni** DO **o** V(causative passive)

> 私は母に部屋を掃除させられた。
> **Watashi wa haha ni heya o sooji saserareta.**
> I was made to clean the room by my mother.

> 子供たちは毎日宿題をさせられます。
> **Kodomo-tachi wa mainichi shukudai o saseraremasu.**
> Children are made to do their homework everyday.

If the agent is forced to do something due to circumstances, expressions similar to 'have to' or 'cannot help doing' are used instead of the causative passive construction.

> 急に大雨が降り出したので、ずぶぬれになるしかなかった。
> **Kyuu ni ooame ga furidashita node, zubunure ni naru shika nakatta.**
> It started to pour suddenly, so we couldn't help getting soaked.

> 車が故障して、タクシーに乗らなければならなかった。
> **Kuruma ga koshoo shite, takushii ni noranakereba naranakatta.**
> My car broke down and I had to take a taxi.

21.6 Other ways to express passive meaning

Some verbs express a passive meaning even though they are not in the passive form.

21.6.1 Intransitive verbs that are passive in meaning

Intransitive verbs such as **kimaru** 'to be decided,' **naoru** 'to be cured,' and **kandoo suru** 'to be moved' are passive in meaning.

結婚式の日取りが決まった。
Kekkonshiki no hidori ga kimatta.
The wedding date was decided.

病気が治った。
Byooki ga naotta.
The illness was cured.

21.6.2 Some verbal nouns + *ni naru*

Some expressions with verbal noun + **ni naru** express a passive meaning, though such examples are limited in number.

上司にご馳走になった。
Jooshi ni go-chisoo ni natta.
I was treated to dinner by my boss.

病気のとき、皆のお世話になった。
Byooki no toki, minna no osewa ni natta.
When I was sick, I was taken care of by everyone.

▶ 7.1.2

21.6.3 Verb (plain nonpast) + *koto ni naru*

The V(plain nonpast) + **koto ni naru** sturucture is used to express that something was decided by external forces or circumstances or in consultation with someone else.

留学することになった。
Ryuugaku suru koto ni natta.
It was decided that I would study abroad.

来月引っ越すことになりました。
Raigetsu hikkosu koto ni narimashita.
It has been decided that we will move next month.

▶ 86.2

21.6.4 Causative *te*-form + *morau*

The **te**-form of a causative verb used with the auxiliary verb **morau** expresses 'to be allowed to do.'

▶ 20.4.3

私はピアノを習わせてもらった。
Watashi wa piano o narawasete moratta.
I was allowed to take piano lessons. (My parents let me take piano lessons.)

私は学生時代に留学させてもらいました。
Watashi wa gakusee jidai ni ryuugaku sasete moraimashita.
I was allowed to study abroad when I was a student.

21.7 | **Understanding causative, adversative passive and causative passive sentences**

Below is a comparison of causative, adversative passive and causative passive constructions.

Causative:	X **wa/ga** Y **ni/o** V-**(s)aseru** 'X makes Y do V' (Y = doer).
Adversative passive:	X **wa/ga** Y **ni** V-**(r)areru** 'X is adversely affected by Y's doing V' (Y = doer).
Causative passive:	X **wa/ga** Y **ni** V-**(s)ase-rareru** 'X is forced to do V by Y' (X = doer).

The following sentences illustrate these patterns. In all of these sentences, Hanako is the one who sang a song.

(1) 太郎は花子に歌を歌わせた。 (causative)
     Taroo wa Hanako ni uta o utawaseta.
     Taro made Hanako sing a song.

(2) 太郎は花子に歌を歌われた。 (adversative passive)
     Taroo wa Hanako ni uta o utawareta.
     Hanako sang a song (and Taro was bothered by it.)

(3) 花子は太郎に歌を歌わせられた。 (causative passive)
     Hanako wa Taroo ni uta o utawaserareta.
     Hanako was made to sing a song by Taro.

In the causative sentence, Taro (the subject) is the causer and Hanako (the indirect object) is the doer. Normally, the sentence means that Hanako did not want to sing, but was forced to sing. In the adversative passive sentence, Taro (the subject) is the person who is negatively affected by Hanako's singing. Perhaps Hanako is bad at singing and Taro did not want to hear her singing. In the causative passive sentence, Hanako (the subject) was made to sing a song. The implication is that Hanako did not want to sing.

22

Conjunctions and connectives

There are many different ways to connect sentences. Conjunctions, or conjunctive particles, connect two or more clauses into one sentence. Connectives, on the other hand, are independent words or phrases that express how one sentence relates to another sentence.

22.1 *te*-form as a conjunction

The **te**-form of any predicate can be used as a conjunction. When the predicate is a **na**-adjective or a noun, the **te**-form of the copula (i.e. **de**) is used. See **13.3** for the **te**-form of adjectives and **12.1** for the **te**-form of verbs. The **te**-form can be used to express a simple coordination ('and'), a causal relation ('and so'), or a sequential relation ('and then') of the conjoined clauses.

▶ 37.4

(a) Simple coordination ('and')

父は教師で母は会計士です。
Chichi wa kyooshi de haha wa kaikeeshi desu.
My father is a teacher and my mother is an accountant.

このレストランは安くておいしいです。
Kono resutoran wa yasukute oishii desu.
This restaurant is inexpensive and delicious.

週末、井田さんは映画を見て、森さんは買い物をした。
Shuumatsu, Ida-san wa eega o mite, Mori-san wa kaimono o shita.
On the weekend, Mr/Ms Ida watched a movie and Mr/Ms Mori went shopping.

(b) Causal relation ('and so')

Depending on the meaning expressed by the clauses connected with the **te**-form, the first clause may be interpreted as the cause or reason for the second clause.

▶ 48.3

頭が痛くて、勉強ができません。
Atama ga itakute, benkyoo ga dekimasen.
I have a headache, so I can't study.

悲しい映画を見て、泣いてしまった。
Kanashii eega o mite, naite shimatta.
I watched a sad movie and I couldn't help crying.

When two adjectives are connected using the **te**-form, the first one tends to be interpreted as the cause or reason for what is expressed by the second adjective. Because of this tendency, the adjective that expresses the more objective concept tends to precede the adjective that expresses the speaker's evaluation, such as, **omoshiroi** 'interesting,' **tsumaranai** 'boring,' **oishii** 'tasty,' and **mazui** 'taste horrible.' The adjective **ii** 'good' always comes at the end when used with other adjectives. The first adjective tends to be interpreted as the reason for the speaker's evaluation.

ここは静かでいいですね。
Koko wa shizuka de ii desu ne.
This place is quiet and nice.

この町は小さくてつまらないです。
Kono machi wa chiisakute tsumaranai desu.
This town is small and boring.

甘い物はきらいなんですが、このケーキは甘くなくておいしいですね。
Amai mono wa kirai na n desu ga, kono keeki wa amakunakute oishii desu ne.
I don't like sweets, but this cake is not sweet and it's tasty.

(c) Sequential relation ('and then')

The **te**-form of verbs can also express multiple actions carried out by the same person in sequence.

夫は毎朝七時に起きて、ニュースを聞きます。
Otto wa maiasa shichiji ni okite, nyuusu o kikimasu.
My husband gets up at 7 o'clock every morning, and listens to the news.

昨日は、買い物をして、映画をみて、レストランで食事をした。
Kinoo wa, kaimono o shite, eega o mite, resutoran de shokuji o shita.
Yesterday, I went shopping, watched a movie, and had a meal at a restaurant.

When a motion verb like **iku** 'to go' or **kuru** 'to come' is used in the **te**-form followed by an action verb, it indicates that the action takes place where one goes or comes to.

図書館に行って本を借りた。
Toshokan ni itte hon o karita.
I went to the library and borrowed a book.

友達がうちに来てテレビを見た。
Tomodachi ga uchi ni kite terebi o mita.
My friend came to my house and watched TV.

NOTE | In writing and in formal speech, the verb stem is used instead of the verb **te**-form for conjunction.

春が去り、夏が来た。
Haru ga sari, natsu ga kita.
Spring left and summer came.

私はいつもどおりに会社に行き、仕事をした。
Watashi wa itsumo doori ni kaisha ni iki, shigoto o shita.
I went to the office as always and worked.

22.2 Coordinate conjunctions and connectives

22.2.1 *shi*

The conjunctive particle **shi** 'and' is used to list activities or states. The predicate preceding **shi** usually takes the plain form.

働く女性は、仕事もするし、家事もする。
Hataraku josee wa, shigoto mo suru shi, kaji mo suru.
Working women not only work but do the housework too.

小野さんは親切だし、頭もいいし、すばらしい人ですね。
Ono-san wa shinsetsu da shi, atama mo ii shi, subarashii hito desu ne.
Mr/Ms Ono is kind as well as smart, so he/she is a wonderful person, isn't he/she?

When clauses are coordinated with **shi**, the semantic particle **mo** tends to be used in place of the case particles **ga** and **o**. For instance, **atama *mo* ii** 'is also smart' is used instead of **atama *ga* ii** 'is smart' in the above example.

The **shi** clause is often used to list reasons or causes for the main clause.

お金もないし、仕事もないし、ぜいたくはできない。
Okane mo nai shi, shigoto mo nai shi, zeetaku wa dekinai.
I can't allow myself any luxuries because I don't have money and I don't have a job.

疲れていたし、宿題もあったし、出かけませんでした。
Tsukarete ita shi, shukudai mo atta shi, dekakemasen deshita.
I was tired, and I had homework, so I didn't go out.

22.2.2 V-*ba*-form

Clauses conjoined with the V-**ba**-form express 'to do X as well as Y' or 'some do X and some do Y.'

ビールも飲めば、日本酒も飲む。
Biiru mo nomeba, nihonshu mo nomu.
I drink beer as well as Japanese sake.

犬が好きな人もいれば、猫が好きな人もいる。
Inu ga suki na hito mo ireba, neko ga sukina hito mo iru.
Some people like dogs and some people like cats.
(Lit. There are people who like dogs as well as people who like cats.)

雪が降る日もあれば、降らない日もある。
Yuki ga furu hi mo areba, furanai hi mo aru.
Some days it snows and some days it doesn't.
(Lit. There are days it snows as well as days it doesn't snow.)

▶ 24.2

22.2.3 ...*toka* ...*toka suru*

The conjunctive particle **toka** is used to list activities non-exhaustively as examples, i.e. 'to do things like X and Y.' The tense of the whole sentence is expressed by the final verb **suru**. The verb preceding **toka** takes the plain nonpast tense form regardless of the tense expressed by **suru**.

分からない時は、人に聞くとかネットで調べるとかする。
Wakaranai toki wa, hito ni kiku toka netto de shiraberu toka suru.
When I don't know, I do things like asking others and searching on the Internet.

学生時代はよく映画を見るとかケーキを焼くとかしました。
Gakusee jidai wa yoku eega o miru toka keeki o yaku toka shimashita.
I often did things like watching movies and baking cakes during my college years.

22.2.4 V-*tari* V-*tari suru*

The conjunction with the V-**tari** (plain past tense form + **ri**) structure is also used to list activities non-exhaustively as examples, i.e. 'to do things like X and Y.' The tense of the whole sentence is expressed by the final verb **suru**. The verb in the **-tari -tari** structure always takes the plain past tense form regardless of the tense expressed by **suru**.

休みの日は本を読んだり映画を見たりします。
Yasumi no hi wa hon o yondari eega o mitari shimasu.
On my day off, I do things like read books and watch movies.

週末は友達と会ったり買い物をしたりした。
Shuumatsu wa tomodachi to attari kaimono o shitari shita.
On the weekend, I did things like meet with my friends and go shopping.

22.2.5 Coordinate connectives

Connective phrases such as **soshite**, **sorekara**, **soreni** and **mata** can be used to list actions and states, with the sense of 'and' and 'also.' They may be used with a conjunctive particle.

明日の授業に写真を持って来てください。それから、宿題も忘れないでください。
Ashita no jugyoo ni shashin o motte kite kudasai. Sorekara, shukudai mo wasurenaide kudasai.
Please bring a photo for tomorrow's class. Also, please don't forget your homework.

歴史漫画はおもしろい。そして歴史の勉強にもなる。
Rekishi manga wa omoshiroi. Soshite rekishi no benkyoo ni mo naru.
History comics are fun. And you can also learn history.

私は漢字が苦手だし、それに、カタカナもよく忘れます。
Watashi wa kanji ga nigate da shi, soreni, katakana mo yoku wasuremasu.
I'm bad at **kanji**, and also, I often forget **katakana**.

夏はキャンプに行ったり、また、海水浴にもよく行く。
Natsu wa kyanpu ni ittari, mata, kaisuiyoku ni mo yoku iku.
During summer, we go camping and we also often go to the sea to swim.

When **soshite** and **sorekara** are used to express actions carried out by the same person, they express that those actions are carried out in sequence. See the next section for sequential connectives.

22.3 Sequential conjunctions and connectives

The V-**te** form is the most commonly used sequential conjunction. See examples in **22.1**. Sequential connectives indicate that events described by two adjacent sentences occur in sequence; e.g. **soshite** 'and,' **sorekara** 'and then,' **sorede** 'and,' and **de** 'and.' While **soshite** and **sorekara** are used both in (formal) writing and in speaking, **sorede** and **de** are used mainly in speaking.

学校に行った。そして試験を受けた。
Gakkoo ni itta. Soshite shiken o uketa.
I went to school. And I took the exam.

昨日はジョギングをした。それから、家で洗濯をした。
Kinoo wa jogingu o shita. Sorekara, uchi de sentaku o shita.
Yesterday, I went jogging. And then, I did the laundry at home.

ケーキを5個買った。で、全部一人で食べた。
Keeki o goko katta. De, zenbu hitori de tabeta.
I bought five pieces of cake. And I ate them all by myself.

22.4 Causal conjunctions and connectives

Commonly used causal conjunction particles are **kara** 'because,' **node** 'because' and **tame** 'due to.' See **47.3** and **47.4** for examples and usages of these conjunctions.

Causal connectives express the cause and result relationship between sentences.

In many cases, the first sentence expresses the cause/reason and the causal connective precedes the second, result sentence; e.g. **dakara** 'so (informal),' **sorede** 'so,' **sono tame** 'due to that (formal),' **shitagatte** 'consequently (writing),' **sore yue** 'therefore (writing),' and **yue ni** 'hence (writing).'

> お金がない。だから車が買えない。
> **Okane ga nai. Dakara kuruma ga kaenai.**
> I don't have money. So I cannot buy a car.

> 約束を忘れていた。それで待ち合わせに行かなかった。
> **Yakusoku o wasurete ita. Sorede machi-awase ni ikanakatta.**
> I had forgotten the appointment. So I didn't go to the meeting place.

> 会社が倒産した。したがって、ボーナスは出ない。
> **Kaisha ga toosan shita. Shitagatte, boonasu wa denai.**
> The company went bankrupt. Therefore, bonuses won't be paid.

22.5 Concessive conjunctions and connectives

When two clauses contrast in meaning or when the second clause expresses what is not expected from the first clause, the two clauses may be connected by concessive connectives or conjunctions. Some of the commonly used concessive conjunctions and connectives are listed below.

22.5.1 *keredo(mo)/kedo* (colloquial) 'but, although'

> お金はあまりないけど、幸せです。
> **Okane wa amari nai kedo, shiawase desu.**
> I don't have much money, but I am happy.

> スミスさんは日本に住んでいたけれど（も）、日本語が話せません。
> **Sumisu-san wa Nihon ni sunde ita keredo(mo), Nihongo ga hanasemasen.**
> Mr/Ms Smith lived in Japan, but he/she can't speak Japanese.

22.5.2 *ga* 'but' (formal/written)

> あのレストランはおいしいですが、ちょっと高いです。
> **Ano resutoran wa oishii desu ga, chotto takai desu.**
> That restaurant is good, but it is a little expensive.

▶ See **39** for more examples and explanations about the use of **keredo(mo)/kedo** and **ga**.

22.5.3 *noni* 'although, despite the fact that'

> スミスさんは日本に住んでいたのに、日本語が話せません。
> **Sumisu-san wa Nihon ni sunde ita noni, Nihongo ga hanasemasen.**
> Despite the fact that Mr/Ms Smith lived in Japan, he/she can't speak Japanese.

Compared with **keredo(mo)** and **ga**, which express contrast objectively, **noni** expresses contrast more subjectively. **Noni** is used to express the speaker's various sentiments such as surprise, frustration, and complaints.

(a) 勉強したけれど、できなかった。
 Benkyoo shita keredo, dekinakatta.
 I studied, but did not do well.

(b) 勉強したのに、できなかった。
 Benkyoo shita noni, dekinakatta.
 Even though I studied, I did not do well.

While (a) with **keredo** is an objective statement about what happened, (b) with **noni** indicates that the speaker is frustrated that he/she did not do well, and that he/she feels he/she should have done better because he/she had studied.

22.5.4 *te mo* 'even if, even though'

The **te**-form of a copula, adjective, or verb + **mo** is used to express the meaning of 'even though' or 'even if' depending on the situation.

> 日本食はたくさん食べても太らないようです。
> **Nihonshoku wa takusan tabete mo futoranai yoo desu.**
> It seems that, with Japanese food, even if you eat a lot, you don't gain weight.

> 先生に聞いても分からなかった。
> **Sensee ni kiite mo wakaranakatta.**
> I did not understand even though I asked the teacher.

When a **-te mo** clause contains question words, it means 'no matter who/what/where/how much, etc.'

> 源氏物語は何度読んでも面白い。
> **Genji monogatari wa nando yonde mo omoshiroi.**
> 'The Tale of Genji' is interesting no matter how many times I read it.

> 「羅生門」という映画は、だれが見ても面白いだろう。
> **Rashoomon to yuu eega wa dare ga mitemo omoshiroi daroo.**
> The movie 'Rashomon' will be interesting to whoever watches it.

22.5.5 V-*ta tte* 'even if, even though'

V-**tatte** (-**ta** is the same as the past tense form) is similar in meaning to -**te mo**. While -**temo** can be used in both speech and (formal) writing, -**tatte** is only used in colloquial speech and sounds more emotive than -**temo**.

> 失敗したって大丈夫！
> **Shippai shi-tatte daijoobu!**
> Even if you fail, no problem!

> 今さら謝ったって遅い。
> **Ima sara ayamat-tatte osoi.**
> It's too late to apologize now.

22.5.6 *kuse ni* 'although'

Kuse ni expresses the speaker's strong feeling of displeasure, disgust, contempt or the like. Such negative feelings are based on the speaker's belief and/or stereotypes.

> お金がないくせに高いものばかり買っている。
> **O-kane ga nai kuse ni takai mono bakari katte iru.**
> (He) buys only expensive things although (in spite of the fact that) he does not have any money.

> 知らないくせに知っているように言うのはよくない。
> **Shiranai kuse ni shitte iru yoo ni iu no wa yokunai.**
> It's not good to say things that you don't know as if you knew them.

22.5.7 *monono* 'although'

Monono is used mainly in (formal) writing. It follows the plain forms of verbs and **i**-adjectives. When **monono** follows a predicative noun, N **de aru monono** is used; when it follows a **na**-adjective, adj.-**na monono** is used.

> 毎日運動しているものの、なかなか体重が減らない。
> **Mainichi undoo shite iru monono, nakanaka taijuu ga heranai.**
> Although I am exercising every day, I am not losing weight quickly.

友達がいいアニメだと言うから見たものの、よくわからなかった。
Tomodachi ga ii anime da to yuu kara mita monono, yoku wakaranakatta.
I watched the anime because my friend said it was good, but I did not understand it well.

22.5.8 *nagara* 'although'

Nagara has two interpretations depending on what precedes it . When **nagara** follows action verbs (e.g. **tabe-nagara mita**), it means that two actions occur simultaneously (e.g. watching while eating). When it follows a predictive noun, an adjective, or a stative verb, it means 'although.'

ここは小さい町ながら活気がある。
Koko wa chiisai machi nagara kakki ga aru.
Although this is a small town, it is lively.

忙しいながら楽しい毎日です。
Isogashii nagara tanoshii mainichi desu.
Although I am busy, I am enjoying my days.

残念ながら、今日はパーティーに行けません。
Zannen nagara, kyoo wa paatii ni ikemasen.
I am sorry but I can't go to the party today.

知っていながら教えてくれない。
Shitte i-nagara oshiete kurenai.
Although (he) knows (it), (he) won't tell me.

22.5.9 Concessive connectives

Like concessive conjunctions, concessive connectives are used to express contrast. A concessive connective begins a sentence that opposes the statement made in the preceding sentences. Commonly used concessive connectives include **demo** 'but (spoken),' **dakedo** 'but (spoken),' **shikashi** 'but (written),' **daga** 'but (written),' **tokoroga** 'however (written),' **sono hanmen** 'on the other hand,' **gyakuni** 'in contrast; on the contrary,' **ippoo** 'on the other hand' and **sore ni taishite** 'in contrast.' See **39.2** for examples and usages.

22.6 Disjunctive conjunctions and connectives

To connect clauses disjunctively, a disjunctive particle **ka** or **nari** can be used.

22.6.1 *. . . ka . . . ka suru*

The structure X **ka** Y **ka suru** is used to express 'do X or do Y.'

小野さんは銀行でお金をおろすか借りるかしたようです。
Ono-san wa ginkoo de o-kane o orosu ka kariru ka shita yoo desu.
It appears that Mr/Ms Ono either withdrew or borrowed money from the bank.

来年は新しい家を買うか建てるかするつもりだ。
Rainen wa atarashii ie o kau ka tateru ka suru tsumori da.
Next year, I intend to buy or build a new house.

The tense of the coordinated clauses is expressed by the final verb **suru**, and the verb before **ka** generally takes the nonpast form regardless of the tense of the final **suru**. However, when the final **suru** is in the past tense, the verb before **ka** may appear in the past tense.

小野さんは銀行でお金をおろしたか借りたかしたようです。
Ono-san wa ginkoo de o-kane o oroshita ka karita ka shita yoo desu.
It appears that Mr/Ms Ono either withdrew or borrowed money from the bank.

... nari ... nari suru

The disjunctive structure X **nari** Y **nari suru** expresses 'to do things like X or Y.' The tense of the disjunctive clauses is expressed by the final verb **suru**. The verb before **nari** is always in the plain nonpast form regardless of the tense of the final **suru**.

> 要らないものは、しまうなり、捨てるなりした。
> **Iranai mono wa, shimau nari, suteru nari shita.**
> As for the things I don't need, I did things like put them away or throw them away.

> 人に聞くなり調べるなりして、答えをだすべきだ。
> **Hito ni kiku nari shiraberu nari shite, kotae o dasu beki da.**
> You should find the answer by doing things like asking others or looking it up.

Disjunctive connectives

Disjunctive connectives such as **matawa**, **aruiwa**, **moshikuwa**, and **soretomo**, all meaning 'or, alternatively,' can can be used along with disjunctive particles or by themselves.

> レポートは明日の授業で提出するか、または、メールで送ってください。
> **Repooto wa ashita no jugyoo de teeshutsu suru ka, matawa, meeru de okutte kudasai.**
> Please turn in your paper in class tomorrow or email it to me.

> コーヒー、飲む？ それとも、お茶のほうがいい？
> **Koohii, nomu? Soretomo, o-cha no hoo ga ii?**
> Want coffee? Or would you prefer tea?

22.7 Other connectives

Summary/rephrase

Connectives such as **tsumari** 'in short,' **sunawachi** 'that is to say (literary),' and **yoosuruni** 'to sum up' are used to begin a sentence that summarizes or rephrases the preceding sentence(s).

> イベントには大勢の客が押し寄せた。つまり大成功だった。
> **Ibento ni wa oozee no kyaku ga oshiyoseta. Tsumari daiseekoo datta.**
> 'The event drew a large audience. In short, it was a great success.'

> 田中さんは事故のことを何も覚えていない、要するに、記憶喪失です。
> **Tanaka-san wa jiko no koto o nanimo oboete inai, yoosuruni, kiokusooshitsu desu.**
> Mr/Ms Tanaka does not remember anything about the accident; in other words, he/she suffers from amnesia.

Addition

Connectives such as **sono ue** 'what's more,' **sara ni** 'what's more' and **shikamo** 'furthermore' are used to introduce a sentence that expresses additional information.

> 風邪をひいた。その上、財布を落としてしまった。
> **Kaze o hiita. Sono ue, saifu o otoshite shimatta.**
> I caught a cold. What's more, I lost my wallet.

> 明日は期末試験がある。しかも、私の苦手な科目だ。
> **Ashita wa kimatsu shiken ga aru. Shikamo, watashi no nigate na kamoku da.**
> I have a final exam tomorrow. Furthermore, it's my weakest subject.

Change of topic

Connectives such as **sate** 'now,' **tokorode** 'by the way,' **sore dewa** 'now, well then (formal)' and **soreja** 'now, well then (informal)' **jaa** 'well then (informal)' are used to bring up a new topic of discussion.

> ところで、週末は何か予定がありますか。
> **Tokorode, shuumatsu wa nanika yotee ga arimasu ka.**
> By the way, do you have any plans for the weekend?

> さて、みなさんの意見はまとまりましたか。
> **Sate, minasan no iken wa matomarimashitaka.**
> Now, have you all reached a consensus?

> それでは、自己紹介をしてもらいましょう。
> **Soredewa, jiko shookai o shite moraimashoo.**
> Well then, please introduce yourselves.

tatoeba 'for example'

> 野菜を作っています。例えば、胡瓜とか、人参です。
> **Yasai o tsukutte imasu. Tatoeba, kyuuri toka, ninjin desu.**
> I'm growing vegetables. Like, for example, cucumbers and carrots.

> バザーで売れそうなもの、例えば、状態のいい古着や食器類などを寄付してください。
> **Bazaa de uresoo na mono, tatoeba, jootai no ii furugi ya shokkirui nado o kifu shite kudsai.**
> Please donate things to be sold at our thrift sale, for example, used clothes in good condition and dishes.

23

Temporal clauses

23.1 *toki (ni)* 'when'

Toki 'time' is a noun used in time expressions such as 'at/during the time of X' and 'when X.' The predicate of the clause appears in the noun-modifying form.

▶ 7.2; 25

When the predicate of a **toki** clause is stative (a noun, adjective, or stative verb) it is usually nonpast even when the whole sentence is past tense.

- **Noun *no toki (ni)***

  妹が高校生の時（に）たまに一緒にでかけた。
  Imooto ga kookoosee no toki (ni) tamani isshoni dekaketa.
  When my younger sister was a high school student, we went out together occasionally.

- **Adjective *toki (ni)***

  若い時（に）いろいろな経験をした。
  Wakai toki (ni) iroiro na keeken o shita.
  I had various experiences when I was young.

  みんながひまな時（に）集まりましょう。
  Minna ga hima na toki (ni) atsumarimashoo.
  Let's get together when everyone is free.

- **Stative verb *toki (ni)***

▶ 12.3

  試験がある時（に）徹夜で勉強した。
  Shiken ga aru toki (ni) tetsuya de benkyoo shita.
  I studied all night when I had exams.

  両親がいる時（に）相談した。
  Ryooshin ga iru toki (ni) soodan shita.
  I consulted my parents when they were home.

- **Non-stative verb *toki (ni)***

When the predicate of the temporal clause is a non-stative verb, the form of the predicate is determined as follows: if the event in the temporal clause is completed before the event expressed in the main clause, the past tense (in pre-nominal form) is used; if not completed, the nonpast form is used in the temporal clause regardless of the tense of the main clause. See **27.4.2.2** for more examples and explanations about the tense in the **toki** clause.

  ちょうど家に着いた時（に）電話が鳴った。
  Choodo uchi ni tsuita toki (ni) denwa ga natta.
  The phone rang right when I got home.

本を読む時（に）眼鏡をかけます。
Hon o yomu toki (ni) megane o kakemasu.
I put on my glasses when I read.

23.2 'Before,' 'after,' and 'while'

There are various expressions that indicate the temporal meaning 'before,' 'after,' and 'while.'
See **46** for detailed explanations and example sentences.

前に	**mae ni**	'before'
あとで	**ato de**	'after'
あいだ（に）	**aida (ni)**	'while, during'
うちに	**uchi ni**	'while, before'

23.3 *tokoro (o/e/ni)* 'when (and where)'

The noun **tokoro** literally means 'place.' When it is used to form a clause, the interpretation
is similar to **toki (ni)** 'when X,' but the focus of the **tokoro** clause is more on the situation or
the state than when it occurs. What particle follows **tokoro** depends on the main clause.

■ **Clause + *tokoro o***

The particle **o** follows **tokoro** when the event expressed in the main clause directly interrupts
or intervenes in the event expressed in the temporal clause.

私たちが道に迷っているところを、親切な人が助けてくれた。
**Watashi-tachi ga michi ni mayotte iru tokoro o, shinsetsu na hito ga tasukete
kureta.**
A kind person helped us when we were lost.

たばこをすっているところを母にみつかってしまった。
Tabako o sutte iru tokoro o haha ni mitsukatte shimatta.
My mother found me smoking (unfortunately.)

帰ろうとしたところを呼び止められた。
Kaeroo to shita tokoro o yobi-tomerareta.
I was stopped right when I was about to go home.

■ **Clause + *tokoro ni/e***

The particles **ni** or **e** follow **tokoro** when the main clause expresses that something or someone
comes into existence where the event in the temporal clause is taking place. Verbs that are
often used in the main clause in this structure are **kuru** 'to come,' V-**te kuru** 'to come to be,'
arawareru 'to appear,' and so on.

皆で相談しているところに田中さんが現れた。
Minna de soodan shite iru tokoro ni Tanaka-san ga arawareta.
Mr/Ms Tanaka showed up when we were having our discussion.

寝ようとしているところに電話がかかって来た。
Neyoo to shite iru tokoro ni denwa ga kakatte kita.
The telephone rang when I was about to go to sleep.

► 18.5

24

Conditional clauses

There are four major conditional clauses, marked by **to**, **ba**, **tara** and **nara**. They express the meaning of 'if' and/or 'when'. **To** and **tara** can refer to events in the past and express the meaning of 'when'.

► 55 for more discussion of similarities and differences among these forms.

24.1 | *to* 'if, when, whenever'

In S1 **to** S2, S2 represents a natural, logical, or inevitable consequence of S1. **To** clauses are formed by adding **to** to the plain nonpast forms of verbs, adjectives, and the copula.

	Plain nonpast form	*To conditional*
ru-verbs	寝る **neru** 'to sleep'	寝ると **neru to**
u-verbs	読む **yomu** 'to read'	読むと **yomu to**
Irregular verbs	来る **kuru** 'to come'	来ると **kuru to**
	する **suru** 'to do'	すると **suru to**
-(i) adjectives	高い **takai** 'to be expensive'	高いと **takai to**
(**na** adj. +) **desu**	（静か）だ **(shizuka) da** 'to be (quiet)'	～だと **da to**
(noun +) **desu**	（学生）だ **(gakusee) da** 'to be (student)'	～だと **da to**

Natural consequence

この辺は冬になると、雪がたくさん降る。
Kono hen wa fuyu ni naru to, yuki ga takusan furu.
When the winter comes, it snows a lot in this area.

毎年4月になると、桜の花がきれいだ。
Maitoshi shigatsu ni naru to, sakura no hana ga kiree da.
Every year, when it's April, the cherry blossoms are beautiful.

あの角を右に曲がると、大きなスーパーが見えます。
Ano kado o migi ni magaru to, ookina suupaa ga miemasu.
When you turn right at the corner, you will see a big supermarket.

Inevitable consequence

甘いものばかり食べていると、太りますよ。
Amai mono bakari tabete iru to futorimasu yo.
If you eat nothing but sweets, you will get fat.

この薬を飲むと、眠くなります。
Kono kusuri o nomu to, nemuku narimasu.
When you take this medicine, you will get sleepy.

24.2 *ba* and *nara* 'if, provided that'

Ba indicates a condition–consequence relation and expresses the meaning of 'provided that.'
Ba forms are obtained as follows. With ALL types of verbs: the final **-u → -eba**. With **i** adjectives:
-i → kereba. With the copula: (noun/**na** adjective) **da** → (noun/**na** adjective) **nara(ba)**.

	Plain nonpast form	*Ba conditional*
ru-verbs	寝る **neru** 'to sleep'	寝れば **nereba**
u-verbs	読む **yomu** 'to read'	読めば **yomeba**
Irregular verbs	来る **kuru** 'to come'	来れば **kureba**
	する **suru** 'to do'	すれば **sureba**
-i adjectives	高い **takai** 'expensive'	高ければ **takakereba**
(negative form)	高くない **takakunai** 'not expensive'	高くなければ **takakunakereba**
(**na** adj. +) **desu**	（静か）だ **(shizuka) da** 'to be (quiet)'	～なら（ば）**nara(ba)**
(noun +) **desu**	（学生）だ **(gakusee) da** 'to be (student)'	～なら（ば）**nara(ba)**

Ba expresses a necessary condition in which the event described in the main clause is to occur
or to be true.

これを見れば、わかります。
Kore o mireba, wakarimasu.
If you look at this, you will understand.

日本で勉強すれば、日本語が上手になります。
Nihon de benkyoo sureba, Nihongo ga joozu ni narimasu.
If you study in Japan, your Japanese will improve.

安ければ、買います。
Yasukereba, kaimasu.
If it is inexpensive, I will buy it.

健康なら（ば）、それで十分です。
Kenkoo nara, sore de juubun desu.
As long as I am in good health, that will be enough.

１８歳以上の人なら、誰でも応募できます。
Juuhachi sai ijoo no hito nara, dare demo oobo dekimasu.
If you are over 18 years old, you (lit. anyone) can apply.

24.3 *tara* 'if/when'

Tara has both a temporal meaning 'when' and a conditional meaning 'if'. The clause + **tara**
structure is formed by adding **ra** to the past plain forms of predicates.

	Plain past	*Conditional forms*
ru verbs	食べた **tabeta** 'ate'	食べたら **tabetara**
u verbs	書いた **kaita** 'wrote'	書いたら **kaitara**
irregular verbs	した **shita** 'did'	したら **shitara**
	来た **kita** 'came'	来たら **kitara**
i adjectives	寒かった **samukatta** 'was/were cold'	寒かったら **samukattara**
negative	食べなかった **tabenakatta** 'did not eat'	食べなかったら **tabenakattara**
(**na** adj. +) **desu**	（有名）だった **(yuumee) datta** 'was/were famous'	～だったら **dattara**
(noun +) **desu**	（休み）だった **(yasumi) datta** 'was a holiday'	～だったら **dattara**

When the event described in the **tara** clause is certain to occur, it expresses the meaning of 'when.' If the situation is uncertain, the **tara** clause expresses the meaning of 'if.'

- 'when'

  春になったら必ず帰るからね。
  Haru ni nattara kanarazu kaeru kara ne.
  When spring comes, I will be back for sure.

  学期が始まったら忙しくなるから、今のうちにゆっくりしておこう。
  Gakki ga hajimattara isogashiku naru kara, ima no uchi ni yukkuri shite okoo.
  When the semester starts, I will be busy, so I will spend some relaxing time now.

- 'if'

  今度失敗したら、もうチャンスはない。
  Kondo shippai shitara, moo chansu wa nai.
  If I fail this time, there won't be any more chances.

  インターンシップがもらえたら、日本に行きます。
  Intaanshippu ga moraetara, Nihon ni ikimasu.
  If I can get an internship, I will go to Japan.

The **-tara** clause can also express an event or a situation which is contrary to facts.

もしあの時あの電車に乗っていたら、死んでいたかもしれません。
Moshi ano toki ano densha ni notte itara, shinde ita kamo shiremasen.
If I had taken the train that day, I might have been killed.

もし私があなただったら、行かないと思う。
Moshi watashi ga anata dattara, ikanai to omou.
If I were in your place, I don't think I would go.

In S1 **tara** S2, when S2 is in the past tense, S2 indicates something beyond the speaker's control and/or an unexpected event.

お風呂に入ったら、電話がなった。
Ofuro ni haittara, denwa ga natta.
When I had just got into the bath, the phone rang.

窓を開けたら、虫が入ってきた。
Mado o aketara, mushi ga haitte kita.
When I opened the window, bugs came in.

The examples below are ungrammatical because the consequence expressed in the main clause is controllable by the speaker and is not something unexpected.

*お風呂に入ったら、歌を歌った。
*Ofuro ni haittara, uta o utatta.
When I took a bath, I sang a song.

*窓を開けたら、新鮮な空気をすった。
*Mado o aketara, shinsen na kuuki o sutta.
When I opened the window, I took a deep breath of fresh air.

(no) nara 'if it is the case' (assertion)

Clause **nara** is used when the speaker makes an assumption based on what has been said and/or what can be surmised from the context.

> A: もうそろそろ、車を買い替えようと思っているんですが . . .。
> **Moo sorosoro kuruma o kaikaeyoo to omotte iru n desu ga . . .**
> I am thinking of replacing my car with a new one . . .

> B: 車を買うなら、いいディーラーを知っていますよ。
> **Kuruma o kau nara, ii diiraa o shitte imasu yo.**
> If you are buying a car, I know a good car dealer.

In the above example, the conditional clause 'if you are buying a car' in speaker B's remark is based on what speaker A has just said.

> A: アメリカに留学しようと思っているんですが . . .。
> **Amerika ni ryuugaku shiyoo to omotte iru n desu ga . . .**
> I am thinking of studying in America, but . . .

> B: アメリカに留学するなら、TOEFLを受けなければなりません。
> **Amerika ni ryuugaku suru nara, TOEFL o ukenakereba narimasen.**
> If you are going to study in America, you need to take the TOEFL exam.

▶ **55** for differences among the conditionals

25

Relative (noun modifying) clauses

A sentence can modify a noun, and in such a case, the noun is called the 'head' and the sentence the 'relative clause.'

Features of Japanese relative clauses

Relative clauses in Japanese have the following characteristics.

1. The predicate of a relative clause is in the plain form.
2. A relative clause precedes its head noun.
3. There are no relative pronouns such as 'who,' 'which,' and 'that'.

In the following examples, relative clauses are indicated by [ ] and the head noun is underlined.

(a) ［あそこにいる］人は田中さんです。
     [Asoko ni iru] <u>hito</u> wa Tanaka-san desu.
     The person who is there is Mr/Ms Tanaka.

(b) ［母が作る］カレーはおいしいです。
     [Haha ga tsukuru] <u>karee</u> wa oishii desu.
     The curry that my mother makes is tasty.

(c) ［日本人がバレンタインデーに贈り物をあげる］人は恋人に限られていません。
     [Nihonjin ga Barentaindee ni okurimono o ageru] <u>hito</u> wa koibito ni kagirarete imasen.
     The people to whom the Japanese give presents on Valentine's Day are not limited to their sweethearts.

In most cases the head noun has a grammatical relation with the predicate of its relative clause. For example, in (a), the head noun **hito** 'person' is the subject of the verb **iru** 'to exist' as in **hito ga asoko ni iru** 'There is a person over there.' In (b), **karee** 'curry' is the direct object of the verb **tsukuru** 'to make' as in **haha ga karee o tsukuru** 'My mother makes curry.' In (c), **hito** 'person' is the indirect object of **ageru** 'to give' as in **Nihonjin ga Barentaindee ni hito ni okurimono o ageru** 'The Japanese give gifts to people on Valentine's Day.'

Another characteristic of a Japanese relative clause is that the particle **ga** can be optionally changed to **no**.

母の作るカレーはおいしいです。
Haha no tsukuru karee wa oishii desu.
The curry that my mother makes is tasty.

最近日本語のできる外国人が増えた。
Saikin Nihongo no dekiru gaikokujin ga fueta.
In recent years, the number of foreigners who speak Japanese has increased.

NOTE | If the particle **wa** appears in a relative clause, its function is contrastive, not indicating a topic.

［人の前では言えない］ことも家族には言える。
[Hito no mae de wa ienai] koto mo kazoku ni wa ieru.
Even things I can't say in public, I can tell my family.

▶ 27.4.1

25.2 Gapless relative clauses

Japanese has another type of relative clause where there is no specific grammatical relation between the head noun and the predicate in the relative clause.

(d) 魚を焼くにおい
sakana o yaku nioi
the smell of fish being grilled. / Lit. the smell that someone grills fish.

(e) ピアノをひいている音
piano o hiite iru oto
the sound of (someone) playing the piano. / Lit. the sound that (someone) is playing the piano.

(f) 触った感じ
sawatta kanji
the feeling one gets by touching. / Lit. the feeling that (someone) has touched.

In (d), for example, the head noun **nioi** 'smell' does not bear any grammatical relation (such as subject, object, direction, etc.) to the verb **yaku** 'to grill, bake.' Rather, **nioi** is something which is produced as a result of what is described in the relative clause. Similarly, in (f), the head noun **kanji** 'feeling' is what is brought about as a result of touching (something). In this type of relative clause, there is a semantic/pragmatic connection between the head and the relative clause.

26

Complement clauses

A complement clause is a clause that is required, i.e., not optional, as a constituent of a larger sentence. It functions like a noun phrase required by the predicate of the main clause.

no and *koto* '. . . ing, that . . .'

Both **no** '. . . one(s), thing(s)' and **koto** 'fact(s), intangible thing(s)' nominalize a clause, i.e. turn a clause into a noun phrase. In English, this is done by using the gerund '-ing,' as in 'Eating breakfast is important'; by using 'to,' as in 'To eat breakfast is important'; or by using 'that,' as in 'That I ate breakfast is true.' When a clause is nominalized, it can be used in the position in a sentence that a noun phrase commonly occupies, such as the subject and object positions. The topic particle **wa** cannot be used within the nominalized clause, and therefore the subject must be marked by **ga**.

朝ご飯を食べるの/ことは健康にいい。
Asagohan o taberu no/koto wa kenkoo ni ii.
Eating breakfast is good for one's health.

誰も私が/は朝ご飯を食べたの/ことを知らない。
Dare mo watashi ga/wa asagohan o tabeta no/koto o shiranai.
Nobody knows that I ate breakfast.

詩を書くの/ことが好きだ。
Shi o kaku no/koto ga suki da.
I like writing poems.

The predicate preceding **no** or **koto** needs to be in its pre-nominal form. However, when the predicate preceding **no** or **koto** is a nominal predicate, the pre-nominal copula **no** cannot be used. Instead, the copula **de aru** is used.

▶ 5.2.1

母が弁護士であるの/ことを誇りに思う。
Haha ga bengoshi de aru no/koto o hokori ni omou.
I am proud that my mother is a lawyer.

テストが簡単なの/ことを喜んだ。
Tesuto ga kantan na no/koto o yorokonda.
We were glad that the test was easy.

no and **koto** can be used interchangeably in many cases, but they induce slightly different interpretations. When **no** is used, the sentence indicates that the speaker empathizes with what is expressed by the **no** clause. On the other hand, the use of **koto** indicates the speaker's lack of empathy or his/her distant feeling towards what is denoted by the **koto** clause. In short, the sentence with the nominalizer **no** sounds more subjective or personal and the sentence with the nominalizer **koto** sounds more objective or general. Another difference is that **no** is used when the nominalized sentence expresses something concrete or perceptible, while **koto** is commonly used when the nominalized clause expresses something more abstract.

▶ See 18.1 for idiomatic expressions that only appear with **koto**.

Only **no** is used when the clause is a complement of verbs of sense perception (e.g. **miru** 'to see,' **kiku** 'to listen/hear,' **kikoeru** 'to be audible'), discovery (e.g. **mitsukeru** 'find' and **mitsukaru** 'to be found'), and direct interaction (e.g. **tasukeru** 'to rescue,' **tetsudau** 'to help' and **tomeru** 'to stop').

The complement of these verbs expresses a concrete or perceptible event.

隣人が家を出るの/~~こと~~を見た。
Rinjin ga ie o deru no/~~koto~~ o mita.
I saw my neighbor leaving the house.

子供がテレビを見るの/~~こと~~をとめた。
Kodomo ga terebi o miru no/~~koto~~ o tometa.
I stopped the child from watching TV.

Koto tends to be used to nominalize the complement of verbs denoting an abstract thinking process or deduction, such as **narau** 'to learn,' **kangaeru** 'to think,' **meejiru** 'to command' and **suitee suru** 'to deduce.'

娘に早く就職させることを考えた。
Musume ni hayaku shuushoku saseru koto o kangaeta.
I thought about making my daughter get a job soon.

日本語では一つの漢字に複数の読み方があることを習った。
Nihongo de wa hitotsu no kanji ni fukusuu no yomikata ga aru koto o naratta.
I learned that one Chinese character has multiple readings in Japanese.

In nominal (copulative) sentences (i.e. X **wa** Y **da/desu** 'X is Y,') only **koto** can be used to nominalize a clause that occupies the Y position.

▶ 5.2; 18.1

問題は金だ。
Mondai wa kane da.
The problem is money.

問題は金がないこと/~~の~~だ。
Mondai wa kane ga nai koto/~~no~~ da.
The problem is that there is no money.

26.2 *to/tte*

to is a particle that introduces a quotation or a sound related to someone/something doing something. It is often used with verbs like **yuu** (originally **iu**) 'to say,' **omou** 'to think,' **kiku** 'to hear,' **kaku** 'to write,' **sakebu** 'to shout,' **naku** 'to cry,' and **naru** 'to ring.' The clause preceding **to** appears in the plain form. The tense in the complement clause does not have to agree with the tense of the main verb. Nonpast form in the complement clause indicates non-completion of the action/event denoted in the complement clause at the time of the action/event denoted by the main verb.

同僚は明日は会議があると言った。
Dooryoo wa ashita wa kaigi ga aru to itta.
My colleague said that there would be a meeting tomorrow.

今日は雨が降ると思います。
Kyoo wa ame ga furu to omoimasu.
I think that it'll rain today.

明日は晴れると聞きました。
Ashita wa hareru to kikimashita.
I heard that tomorrow would be sunny.

誰かが「火事だ」と叫んだ。
Dare ka ga 'kaji da' to sakenda.
Someone yelled 'Fire!'

When speaking casually, **to** is often pronounced as **tte** or **te** (when preceded by the syllabic **n**).

友達が遊びに来るって言った。
Tomodachi ga asobi ni kuru tte itta.
My friend said she would come to visit.

君はお母さんから何て聞いた？
Kimi wa okaasan kara nan te kiita?
What did you hear from your mom?

目覚まし時計がビービーって鳴った。
Mezamashi dokee ga biibii tte natta.
The alarm clock went off 'beep beep.'

The perception verb **kiku** 'hear' can take a clausal complement nominalized by **no**, but what is expressed differs from what the **-to** clause (quotation) denotes.

(a)　父がうちを出て行くのを聞いた。
　　Chichi ga uchi o dete iku no o kiita.
　　I heard my father leaving home.

(b)　父がうちを出て行くと聞いた。
　　Chichi ga uchi o dete iku to kiita.
　　I heard that my father was leaving home.

In (a), the speaker believes that his/her father left home and he/she heard the sound of it. In (b), it merely expresses that the speaker heard that his/her father was leaving. What is denoted by the **-to** clause is not assumed to be a fact by the speaker; it simply reports or quotes (directly or indirectly) what is said, heard, or thought.

26.3 Embedded questions

A question sentence can be a complement of predicates such as verbs of knowing (**shitte iru** 'to know'), understanding (**wakaru** 'to understand,' **rikai suru** 'to understand'), asking (**kiku** 'to ask,' **tazuneru** 'to inquire,' **shitsumon suru** 'to ask a question'), examining (**kangaeru** 'to think,' **kakunin suru** 'to confirm,' **kooryo suru** 'to consider'), remembering (**omoidasu** 'to recall'), forgetting (**wasureru** 'to forget'), explaining (**setsumee suru** 'to explain') and deciding (**kimeru** 'to decide,' **kettee suru** 'to decide'). When a yes or no question is the complement, the question clause appears in the plain form followed by **ka doo ka** ('whether or not'). It is then placed before the main verb. **Doo ka** is optional in an informal style speech.

休みがとれますか。 (yes or no question)
Yasumi ga toremasu ka.
Can I take a day off?

休みがとれるかどうかききたい。 (embedded question)
Yasumi ga toreru ka doo ka kikitai.
I want to ask whether or not I can take a day off.

The plain affirmative form of the copula **da** is deleted before **ka** in an embedded question.

道子さんは学生ですか。(yes or no question)
Michiko-san wa gakusee desu ka.
Is Michiko a student?

道子さんが学生かどうか知らない。
Michiko-san ga gakusee ka doo ka shiranai.
I don't know if Michiko is a student.

勉強しなくてもいいのですか。(yes or no question)
Benkyoo shinakute mo ii no desu ka.
Is it the case that I don't have to study?

勉強しなくてもいいのかどうか聞きました。(embedded question)
Benkyoo shinakute mo ii no ka doo ka kikimashita.
I asked if it's the case that I don't have to study.

If the embedded question is a WH-question (see **32.2**), the complement clause appears in the plain form followed by **ka**. **Doo ka** cannot be used in an embedded WH-question. The plain affirmative form of the copula **da** is deleted before **ka**.

空港までどうやって行きますか。(WH-question)
Kuukoo made doo yatte ikimasu ka.
How do I get to the airport?

空港までどうやって行くか分からない。(embedded question)
Kuukoo made doo yatte iku ka wakaranai.
I don't know how to get to the airport.

どうして分からないのですか。(WH-question)
Dooshite wakaranai no desu ka.
Why don't you understand?

どうしてわからないのか尋ねた。(embedded question)
Dooshite wakaranai no ka tazuneta.
I asked why he/she doesn't understand.

When the main verb is a verb of asking, the quotation particle **to** may be used following the embedded question.

友達に明日のパーティーに行くかと聞いた。
Tomodachi ni ashita no paatii ni iku ka to kiita.
I asked if my friend was going to the party tomorrow.

明日のテストは難しいかと尋ねた。
Ashita no tesuto wa muzukashii ka to tazuneta.
I asked if tomorrow's test is difficult.

27

Tense and aspect

Tense and aspect in Japanese

Two tense forms are distinguished in Japanese: past and nonpast. The past tense is formed by attaching a derivational suffix **-ta**. The nonpast (plain) forms are **da** for the copula and **-na** adjectives, **-i** for i-adjectives, and **-ru/-u** for verbs.

▶ **12.1; 13**

While tense indicates the time when an action or event takes place, aspect indicates how the action or event is viewed, such as ongoing, completed, not completed, or repeated. Aspect is generally indicated in Japanese by auxiliary verbs such as **-te iru**, **-te aru**, and **-te shimau**.

▶ **19.2**

Sometimes, tense forms also indicate aspect, such as completion vs. non-completion. In sentence (a) below, **-ta** marks past tense, while in sentence (b) **-ta** indicates completion (i.e. perfective aspect.)

  (a) きのう料理をしました。
       Kinoo ryoori o shimashita.
       I cooked yesterday.

  (b) もう料理をしました。
       Moo ryoori o shimashita.
       I have already done the cooking.

Tense in the main clause

For verbs, **-ta** indicates past actions, events, and states, and **-ru/u**, present habitual actions and events or future actions and events. Examples are provided below in informal and formal styles.

  去年日本に行った/行きました。
  Kyonen Nihon ni itta/ikimashita.
  I went to Japan last year.

  毎年日本に行く/行きます。
  Mainen Nihon ni iku/ikimasu.
  I go to Japan every year.

  来年日本に行く/行きます。
  Rainen Nihon ni iku/ikimasu.
  I will go to Japan next year.

  私が子供の時、家は東京にあった/ありました。
  Watashi ga kodomo no toki, ie wa Tookyoo ni atta/arimashita.
  When I was a child, our house was in Tokyo.

家は東京にある/あります。
Ie wa Tookyoo ni aru/arimasu.
My house is in Tokyo.

日本語が話せる/話せます。
Nihongo ga hanaseru/hanasemasu.
I can speak Japanese.

Note that with an action verb such as **iku** 'to go,' the nonpast tense form describes either a habitual action or a future action. On the other hand, with stative verbs such as **aru** 'to exist' and **hanaseru** 'can speak,' the nonpast tense form only describes a current state.

27.3 Tense in a coordinate clause

When two clauses are conjoined by the **-te** form, the tense of the main predicate indicates the tense of both clauses. The **-te** form does not indicate tense by itself. In the following examples, in the first example, the speaker actually went to Japan, since the main verb **benkyoo shita** is in the past tense. In the second example, on the other hand, the main verb is in the nonpast tense, and so 'going to Japan,' as well as 'studying Japanese,' will happen in the future.

▶ 22.1

日本に行って、日本語を勉強した。
Nihon ni itte, Nihongo o benkyoo shita.
(I) went to Japan and studied Japanese.

日本に行って、日本語を勉強する。
Nihon ni itte, Nihongo o benkyoo suru.
(I) will go to Japan and study Japanese.

When two clauses are conjoined by other conjunctions such as **shi** 'and also' and **ga**, but each clause indicates the tense independently.

▶ 22.2.1; 22.5.2

きのう試験があったし、今日はアルバイトがあるし、休む暇もない。
Kinoo shiken ga atta shi, kyoo wa arubaito ga aru shi, yasumu hima mo nai.
I had an exam yesterday and have a part time job to do today, and I have no time to rest.

27.4 Tense in relative and temporal clauses

The tense markers **-ta** and **-ru/-u** in relative and temporal clauses do not necessarily indicate the actual time when an event occurs or when a certain condition is true. Rather, **-ta** indicates that an event has been <u>completed</u> before the main event, and **-ru/-u** indicates that an event has <u>not been completed</u> before the main event or that a state holds <u>simultaneously</u> with the main action.

27.4.1 Tense in relative clauses

(a) 日本に行った人に会った。
Nihon ni itta hito ni atta.
I met a person who had been to Japan.

(b) 日本に行く人に会った。
Nihon ni iku hito ni atta.
I met a person who will be going to Japan / I met a person who was going to go to Japan.

In relative clauses, **-ta** most often indicates that an action was completed before the main action. Thus, in (a), the person had gone to Japan before the speaker met him/her. On the other hand, in (b), the use of nonpast tense form **-u** indicates that the person had not been to Japan when the speaker met him/her. **-u** simply indicates that the person's going to Japan had not taken place at the time of meeting, but may have since. Hence, in (b) it is ambiguous whether the person has gone to Japan at the time of the speaker uttering this sentence.

(c) 私は毎日母が作ったお弁当を食べる。
Watashi wa mainichi haha ga tsukutta obentoo o taberu.
Every day I eat a boxed lunch that my mother prepares.

Here, **-ta** in the relative clause indicates that the mother's preparing lunch precedes the speaker's eating.

(d) あした来た人にはアイスクリームをごちそうします。
Ashita kita hito ni wa aisukuriimu o gochisoo shimasu.
I will treat whoever comes tomorrow to ice cream.

Again, in (d), the person has not come yet. The person will come tomorrow, but 'coming' will take place before being treated to ice cream. Hence, **-ta** is used.

(e) 着物を着ている人も見かけました。
Kimono o kite iru hito mo mikakemashita.
I also saw people wearing kimonos.

In (e), **-ru** is used because 'wearing kimonos' and 'seeing' were concurrent.

(f) クラスにハワイに別荘のある生徒がいた。
Kurasu ni Hawai ni bessoo no aru seeto ga ita.
In my class there was a student who had a vacation house in Hawaii.

In (f), the student had a vacation house in Hawaii when he was in the speaker's class. The sentence does not say anything about whether he still has the house in Hawaii now.

▶ 7.2; 25

27.4.2 Tense in temporal clauses

The same basic rules hold both in relative clauses and temporal clauses. Hence, in temporal clauses **-ta** indicates <u>completion</u> and **-ru/-u** indicates <u>non-completion</u> or <u>simultaneity</u>.

27.4.2.1 Tense in 'before' and 'after' clauses

The verb which comes before **mae ni** 'before' is always in the nonpast tense form. This is because in V₁ **mae ni** V₂, V₁ occurs after V₂ (i.e. V₁ is <u>not completed</u> when V₂ occurs.)

▶ 46.1

日本に行<u>く</u>前に日本語を勉強した方がいい。
Nihon ni <u>iku</u> mae ni Nihongo o benkyoo shita hoo ga ii.
It's better to study Japanese before going to Japan.

ご飯を食べ<u>る</u>前に手を洗います。
Gohan o tabe<u>ru</u> mae ni te o araimasu.
I wash my hands before eating.

In V₁ **ato (de)** V₂, on the other hand, V₁ is always in the past tense form. This is because V₁ is always <u>completed</u> before V₂ in this construction.

ご飯を食べ<u>た</u>あと雑談をします。
Gohan o tabe<u>ta</u> ato zatsudan o shimasu.
(We) chat after eating dinner.

お風呂に入っ<u>た</u>あと少し本を読んでから寝ます。
Ofuro ni hait<u>ta</u> ato sukoshi hon o yonde kara nemasu.
After I take a bath, I read a little and then go to sleep.

27.4.2.2 Tense in 'when' clauses

Again, **-ta** in 'when' clauses indicates <u>completion</u>, and **-ru/-u** indicates <u>non-completion</u>.

▶ 23.1

(a) 日本に行った時に買いました。
Nihon ni itta toki ni kaimashita.
I bought it when (after) I went to Japan.

(b) 日本に行く時に買いました。
Nihon ni iku toki ni kaimashita.
I bought it when I went to Japan.

In the above examples, when **-ta** is used, going to Japan happened before buying – i.e. the speaker bought (it) in Japan. On the other hand, when **-ru/-u** is used, the speaker bought (it) either prior to going to Japan or on the way to Japan (such as at the airport).

(c) ご飯を食べる時「いただきます」と言います。
Gohan o taberu toki 'itadakimasu' to iimasu.
When I eat, I say 'itadakimasu.'

(d) 日本人は、ご飯を食べる時おはしを使います。
Nihonjin wa, gohan o taberu toki ohashi o tsukaimasu.
Japanese people use chopsticks when they eat.

(e) ご飯を食べた時「ごちそうさま」と言います。
Gohan o tabeta toki 'gochisoosama' to iimasu.
When I have eaten, I say 'gochisoosama.'

In (c), **-ru** indicates 'prior to eating,' and in (d), **-ru** indicates concurrent actions – i.e. eating and using chopsticks are simultaneous. In (e), one says 'Gochisoosama' when one finishes eating. This is indicated by **-ta**.

In some cases (mostly with stative predicates and adjectives), however, **-ta** in **toki** clauses can simply indicate past time, just as in English.

(f) 日本に住んでいる時は、毎日日本語を使いました。
Nihon ni sunde iru toki wa, mainichi Nihongo o tsukaimashita.
When I lived in Japan, I used Japanese every day.

(g) 日本に住んでいた時は、毎日日本語を使いました。
Nihon ni sunde ita toki wa, mainichi Nihongo o tsukaimashita.
When I lived in Japan, I used Japanese every day.

(h) 値段が安い時に買いました。
Nedan ga yasui toki ni kaimashita.
I bought it when the price was low.

(i) 値段が安かった時に買いました。
Nedan ga yasukatta toki ni kaimashita.
I bought it when the price was low.

In (f) and (g), **-ru** and **-ta** are used respectively. However, the meanings are basically the same. In (g), because the verb expresses a state of being in Japan, the notion of completion is not appropriate here. Hence, **-ta** in (g) indicates a simple past tense. Similarly, sentences (h) and (i) mean the same thing, although (h) is somewhat preferred.

27.4.2.3 **Tense in a *tokoro* clause**

tokoro is a noun meaning 'place,' but it can also be used to indicate a temporal space. Meanings vary depending on the tense of the verb which precedes **tokoro**. When it is in the past tense form, it means 'have just done something.' When it is in the nonpast tense form, it means 'about to do something,' and with the progressive form -**te iru**, it means 'in the midst of doing something.'

> 今電話をかけるところです。
> **Ima denwa o kakeru tokoro desu.**
> I am just about to make a phone call.

> 今電話をかけているところですから、あとで来てください。
> **Ima denwa o kakete iru tokoro desu kara, ato de kite kudasai.**
> I am in the midst of a telephone call, so please come back later.

> 今電話をかけたところです。
> **Ima denwa o kaketa tokoro desu.**
> I have just made a phone call.

▶ 18.5; 23.3

28

Evidential markers

Evidential markers indicate the source of information. For example, stem+**soo** 'look like, seem,' nonpast/past+**soo** 'I hear,' **yoo** 'seem,' **rashii** 'seem, I hear' and **mitai** 'seem,' indicate that what the speaker is saying is an impression, hearsay, inference, or conjecture.

28.1 Adj.(stem) or V(stem) + *soo* 'look like, seem'

The evidential marker **soo** with stem forms of adjectives and verbs expresses the impression one gets based on what one sees, hears, smells, etc.

Looking at a book with an interesting title, one can say the following sentence. The speaker is simply giving his/her impression.

> この本はおもしろそうですね。
> **Kono hon wa omoshiro soo desu ne.**
> This book looks interesting, doesn't it?

The first sentence below may be uttered when one looks at a dark sky, and the second sentence, when seeing a lonely-looking person.

> 今日は雨が降りそうです。
> **Kyoo wa ame ga furi soo desu.**
> It looks like it will rain today.

> 山下さんはいつも寂しそうです。
> **Yamashita-san wa itsumo sabishi soo desu.**
> Mr/Ms Yamashita always looks lonely.

Soo being a **na** adjective, **soo desu** is used at the end of a sentence, and **soo na** to modify a noun.

> おいしそうなケーキをもらいました。
> **Oishi soo na keeki o moraimashita.**
> I received a delicious-looking cake.

> 大変そうですね。
> **Taihen soo desu ne.**
> That sounds tough.

> 楽しそうですね。
> **Tanoshi soo desu ne.**
> That sounds like fun.

Soo cannot be used to express the speaker's conjectures concerning a past event or state. See **yoo** and **rashii** for expressing such conjectures.

145

CLAUSE (plain) + *yoo* 'seem, I gather'

The evidential marker **yoo** expresses conjectures based on evidence gathered through the speaker's observation or first-hand knowledge.

▶ 18.4

経済のクラスは難しいようです。
Keezai no kurasu wa muzukashii yoo desu.
It seems that the economics class is/might be difficult.

この本は学生には高すぎるようです。
Kono hon wa gakusee ni wa taka sugiru yoo desu.
It appears that this book might be too expensive for students.

佐藤さんは会社員のようです。
Satoo-san wa kaishain no yoo desu.
It seems that Mr/Ms Sato might be an office worker.

Yoo can be used to express conjectures concerning a past event or state as well as a present or future event or state.

田中さんはもう帰ったようです。
Tanaka-san wa moo kaetta yoo desu.
It appears to me that Mr/Ms Tanaka may have gone home.

この課題は簡単だったようです。
Kono kadai wa kantan datta yoo desu.
It appears that this assignment might have been easy.

Although both (stem+) **soo** and **yoo** can be used to express a conjecture, when talking about a visual <u>impression</u>, **soo** is used.

このケーキはおいしそうです。
Kono keeki wa oishi soo desu.
This cake looks delicious.

If **yoo** is used, what is expressed is the conjecture reached after considering various pieces of evidence, short of actually eating the cake. The evidence could be that many people were buying it or that the speaker saw many people enjoy eating it.

あそこの店のケーキはおいしいようです。
Asoko no mise no keeki wa oishii yoo desu.
It seems that cake from that shop/restaurant is good.

In informal conversation, **mitai** is often used in place of **yoo**.

この靴はきつすぎるみたいです。
Kono kutsu wa kitsu sugiru mitai desu.
It seems that these shoes are too tight.

Mitai follows the plain form of the predicate, but when the predicate is a noun or a **na**-adjective in the nonpast affirmative form, **mitai** directly attaches to the stem of the **na**-adjective.

退院したばかりなのに、田中さんはもう元気みたいだよ。
Taiin shita bakari na noni, Tanaka-san wa moo genki mitai da yo.
Even though he was just discharged from the hospital, Mr/Ms Tanaka appears well already.

CLAUSE (plain) + *rashii* 'seem, I hear'

The evidential marker **rashii** is similar to **yoo** in that it also expresses a conjecture or an inference. With **rashii**, however, the conjecture is most likely based on what one has read or heard rather than what one has observed. **Rashii** can be used to express conjectures concerning a past event or state as well as a present or future event or state.

When the predicate is a verb or an i-adjective, it takes the plain form before **rashii**.

田中さんは高校の時、留学したらしい。
Tanaka-san wa kookoo no toki, ryuugaku shita rashii.
It seems that Mr/Ms Tanaka studied abroad when he/she was in high school.

噂によると、あの二人はつきあっているらしいです。
Uwasa ni yoru to, ano futari wa tsukiatte iru rashii desu.
According to rumor, it seems that those two are dating.

この大学に入るのはかなり難しいらしいよ。
Kono daigaku ni hairu no wa kanari muzukashii rashii yo.
It seems that getting admitted into this university is very difficult.

The nonpast affirmative form of the copula (i.e. **da**) is deleted preceding **rashii**. (The copula is normally required when nouns and **na** adjectives are used as predicates.)

この病院は有名らしいです。
Kono byooin wa yuumee rashii desu.
It seems that this hospital is well known.

鈴木さんの実家は沖縄らしいです。
Suzuki-san no jikka wa Okinawa rashii desu.
It seems that Mr/Ms Suzuki's parents' home is in Okinawa.

Other forms of the copula **da** (i.e. negative nonpast, affirmative past, and negative past) do appear preceding **rashii**.

田中さんのお母さんは小学校の先生だったらしいです。
Tanaka-san no okaasan wa shoogakkoo no sensee datta rashii desu.
It seems that Mr/Ms Tanaka's mother used to be an elementary school teacher.

健さんはカラオケが好きじゃないらしい。
Ken-san wa karaoke ga suki ja nai rashii.
It seems that Ken does not like karaoke.

CLAUSE (plain) + *soo* 'I hear' (hearsay)

When **soo** follows the plain forms of the predicate, it indicates 'hearsay.'

田中さんは高校の時留学したそうです。
Tanaka-san wa kookoo no toki ryuugaku shita soo desu.
I hear that Mr/Ms Tanaka studied abroad when he/she was in high school.

あのレストランのケーキはおいしいそうです。
Ano resutoran no keeki wa oishii soo desu.
I hear that the cake from that shop/restaurant is delicious.

Summary

In Japanese it is important to distinguish information that one has direct access to from information obtained by hearsay or that one cannot directly experience. When someone asks you how your friend (Nobuko) is doing, for example, you would probably answer using one of the evidential expressions, **rashii**, **yoo**, or hearsay **soo**, unless you have actually seen her. Similarly, what you have heard on the news is usually conveyed as hearsay.

As mentioned in **13.5**, expressing one's own internal state and that of others are also clearly distinguished in Japanese. One can only truly know one's own internal state and not that of others. Therefore, a direct declarative statement can be made only about one's own internal state. One can only *infer* another person's internal state. Therefore, when one talks about another person's internal state (e.g. desire, fear, joy, or sorrow), evidential markers are usually used. The choice will depend on what kind of evidence the speaker is using. As explained in the previous sections, (stem) **soo** expresses the speaker's impression based on visual or other senses. **Yoo** indicates a conjecture that is based on the speaker's various observations, and **rashii** is used when the conjecture is based on circumstantial evidence or information gathered from external sources by reading or hearing.

(a) 田中さんは結婚して幸せそうだ。
Tanaka-san wa kekkon shite shiawase soo da.
Mr/Ms Tanaka looks happy to be married.

(b) 田中さんは結婚して幸せなようだ。
Tanaka-san wa kekkon shite shiawasena yoo da.
I gather that Mr/Ms Tanaka is happy to be married.

(c) 田中さんは結婚して幸せらしい。
Tanaka-san wa kekkon shite shiawase rashii.
I infer (or I hear) that Mr/Ms Tanaka is happy to be married.

Example (a) may be uttered when the speaker actually sees Mr/Ms Tanaka looking happy in his/her marriage. Example (b) may be used when the speaker sees or hears Mr/Ms Tanaka do things that indicate his/her happiness in marriage. Example (c) may be used when the speaker reads or hears about Mr/Ms Tanaka's happy marriage from external sources such as mutual friends and letters.

▶ 58

29

Honorifics (*keego*)

General remarks on Japanese honorifics

Consciously or not, the speaker decides not only what to say, but how to say it in any language. In Japanese, there is a linguistic system called **keego** (honorifics) to be used when speaking politely and deferentially. Consisting of special vocabulary and constructions, honorifics are classified into three major types: *exalting words* (**sonkeego**), *humbling words* (**kenjoogo**), and *polite words* (**teeneego**).

Exalting words are used to refer to the actions, states, and belongings of someone to whom the speaker is expected to show respect, such as his/her superior at work, teachers, and older people. *Humbling words* refer to the actions, states. and belongings of the speaker (and family members). To show one's respect toward the referent (who may be, and often is, the addressee), one can either raise the referent's status by using *exalting verbs* to describe his/her actions (e.g. 'you/esteemed person honorably do(es) . . .') or lower one's own status by using *humbling verbs* for one's own actions (e.g. 'I humbly do . . .'). Basically, *exalting words* are used for one's out-group members who are regarded worthy of respect, and *humbling words* for one's in-group members. The term 'social superior' is used hereafter to refer to a person higher in rank than the speaker in terms of age and/or status.

Neutral verb:	友達は来ます。 **Tomodachi wa kimasu.** My friend will come.
Exalting verb:	課長は<u>いらっしゃい</u>ます。 **Kachoo wa <u>irasshai</u>masu.** The section chief will (honorably) <u>come</u>.
Humbling verb:	私は<u>参り</u>ます。 **Watashi wa <u>mairi</u>masu.** I will (humbly) <u>come</u>.

Polite words

Polite words mostly consist of two types. One type refers to the sentence endings **desu** (with nouns and adjectives) and **masu** (with verbs). They show the psychological and social distance the speaker feels toward the person to whom he/she is speaking. No matter how close the relationship, however, he/she is expected to speak in the **desu/masu** style to his/her social superior. One would use **desu/masu** to one's equal until one feels close to him/her.

Plain endings	Polite endings	
今日は金曜日だ。 **Kyoo wa kin'yoobi da.**	今日は金曜日<u>です</u>。 **Kyoo wa kin'yoobi <u>desu</u>.**	It is Friday today.
とても寒い。 **Totemo samui.**	とても寒い<u>です</u>。 **Totemo samui <u>desu</u>.**	It is very cold.
雪が降っている。 **Yuki ga futte iru.**	雪が降ってい<u>ます</u>。 **Yuki ga futte <u>imasu</u>.**	It is snowing.

The other type of *polite words* is the prefixes **o-** and **go-** (like saying 'honorable such-and-such'), attached to nouns describing a social superior's actions and belongings. **o-** can also be attached to certain adjectives describing a social superior's state.

お車	**o-kuruma**	'car'	お話	**o-hanashi**	'talk'
お若い	**o-wakai**	'young'	お暇	**o-hima**	'free time'
ご住所	**go-juusho**	'address'	ご研究	**go-kenkyuu**	'research'

Generally, **o-** is attached to Japanese native words, and **go-** to words of Chinese origin. Many Chinese-origin words, however, routinely take **o-**, especially everyday words that have been in Japanese for a long time. In principle, neither **o-** nor **go-** is to be attached to loan words from the West. Some loan words that are part of everyday vocabulary do appear with **o-**, though the practice is often frowned upon.

お天気	**o-tenki**	'weather'	お電話	**o-denwa**	'telephone'
おビール	**o-biiru**	'beer'	おタバコ	**o-tabako**	'cigarette, smoking'

29.3 ## Exalting words

Some nouns are categorized as exalting words, including those that appear with the prefix **o-** referring to an object belonging to the addressee and/or esteemed referent.

Neutral			Exalting		
著書	**chosho**	'book'	貴著	**kicho**	'your (honorable) book'
会社	**kaisha**	'company'	貴社	**kisha**	'your (honorable) company'
人	**hito**	'person'	方	**kata**	'esteemed person'
手紙	**tegami**	'letter'	お手紙	**o-tegami**	'your (honorable) letter'

There are a number of special ('suppletive') verbs that express exaltative meaning (see **29.8**). They are all frequently used words such as 'to be,' 'to come,' 'to go,' 'to do,' 'to eat,' and 'to see.' Other verbs can be turned into exalting verbs in one of the two productive constructions, **V-(r)areru** and **o-/go-V ni naru**; e.g. **kak-areru**, **o-kaki ni naru** 'write (exalting).' The subject of an exalting verb is someone other than the speaker, usually his/her social superior, who often coincides with the addressee.

	Neutral	Special	verb-*(r)areru*	*o-/go-V (stem)* **ni naru**
do	**su-ru**	**nasaru**	**s-areru**	—
come	**ku-ru**	**irassharu**	**ko-rareru**	—
see	**mi-ru**	**go-ran ni naru**	**mi-rareru**	—
teach	**oshie-ru**	—	**oshie-rareru**	**o-oshie ni naru**
call	**yob-u**	—	**yob-areru**	**o-yobi ni naru**
use	**riyoo su-ru**	—	**riyoo s-areru**	**go-riyoo ni naru**
be	**de a-ru**	**de irassharu**	**de or-areru**	—

こちらは森さんのお母様で<u>いらっしゃいます</u>。
Kochira wa Mori-san no okaasama <u>de irasshaimasu</u>.
This is Mr/Ms Mori's mother.

先生、明日のパーティに<u>いらっしゃいます</u>（or <u>来られます</u>）か。
Sensee, ashita no paatii ni <u>irasshaimasu</u> (or <u>koraremasu</u>) ka.
Are you coming to the party tomorrow, Professor?

課長はタクシーを<u>お呼びになりました</u>（or <u>呼ばれました</u>）。
Kachoo wa takushii o <u>o-yobi ni narimashita</u> (or <u>yobaremashita</u>).
The section chief called a taxi.

The **-(r)areru** variety sounds more impersonal and less polite than do the special verbs and **o-**verb **ni naru**. It is identical to the passive form (e.g. **kak-areru** 'be written'), and has been gaining in popularity recently over **o-V ni naru** forms, especially among young people, although it can be inappropriate sometimes. For example, **Shachoo wa tabe-rare-mashita ka** meaning 'Did the company president eat?' can potentially sound as though it were in the passive, 'Was the company president eaten?'. In such cases, it is safe to use the special verb **meshiagari-mashita ka** 'Did he/she eat?'

Common abbreviations of **o-/go-**verb **ni naru** include the request form **o-/go-**verb **kudasai**, instead of **o-/go-**verb **ni natte kudasai** 'please do . . . ,' and **o-/go-**verb **desu**, to refer to someone's current state or action in progress.

どうぞ<u>おかけ</u>下さい。（← どうぞ<u>おかけになって</u>下さい。）
Doozo <u>o-kake</u> kudasai. (← Doozo <u>o-kake ni natte</u> kudasai)
Please sit.

社長は只今<u>お出かけ</u>です。　　　（← <u>お出かけになっています</u>。）
Shachoo wa tadaima <u>o-dekake desu</u>. (← Shachoo wa tadaima <u>o-dekake ni natte imasu</u>.)
The company president is out (of the office) now.

クーポンを<u>ご利用</u>ですか。（← <u>ご利用になっています</u>か。）
Kuupon o <u>go-riyoo desu</u> ka. (← Kuupon o <u>go-riyoo ni natte imasu</u> ka.)
Are you using coupons?

29.4 Humbling words

Some nouns are categorized as humbling words.

Neutral			*Humbling*		
著作	**chosaku**	'book'	拙著	**setcho**	'my (bad) book'
会社	**kaisha**	'company'	弊社	**heesha**	'my (modest) company'
人	**hito**	'person'	者	**mono**	'person (in my in-group)'

Like exalting verbs, there are special ('suppletive') humbling forms for certain verbs (see **29.8**). Other verbs can express humility when used in the construction **o-/go-V suru**; e.g. **o-kaki suru** 'write,' **go-setsumee suru** 'explain.' The construction implies that the action is done to or for the benefit of the social superior. Most of the special humbling words imply this. The subject of a humbling verb is always the speaker himself/herself ('I') or his/her family member.

	Neutral	*Special*	*o-/go-V suru*
do	**su-ru**	**itasu**	—
come	**ku-ru**	**mairu**	—
see	**mi-ru**	**haiken suru**	—
teach	**oshie-ru**	—	**o-oshie suru**
guide	**annai su-ru**	—	**go-annai suru**

修理は私が<u>致します</u>。
Shuuri wa watakushi ga <u>itashimasu</u>.
I will fix it.

タクシーを<u>お呼びしましょうか</u>。
Takushii o <u>o-yobi shimashoo ka</u>.
Shall I call a taxi <u>for you</u>?

ここで<u>お待ちします</u>。
Koko de <u>omachi shimasu</u>.
I will wait <u>for you</u> here.

ちょっと<u>ご相談したい</u>ことがありまして . . . 。
Chotto <u>go-soodan shitai</u> koto ga arimashite . . .
'There is something I'd like to ask you about.'

o-/go-V suru is inappropriate when one's action has no bearing on the social superior. In such a case, neutral forms suffice; e.g. **Kinoo wa hon o yomimashita** 'I read a book yesterday.' To express humility while avoiding an implication of benefit for the social superior, one can use verb-**(s)asete itadaku**; e.g. **Hon o yomasete itadakimashita** 'I read the book (since you/social superior graciously let me).' Verb-**(s)aseru** is a causative form 'make/let someone do…,' and **itadaku** is a special humbling verb meaning 'to receive a favor or object for which the speaker is thankful.' As such, the construction implies that someone granted permission.

ここで待た<u>せていただき</u>ます。
Koko de mata<u>sete itadaki</u>masu.
'(With your permission) I will wait here.'

子供は部屋に入ら<u>せていただき</u>ました。
Kodomo wa heya ni haira<u>sete itadaki</u>mashita.
'My child was allowed to enter the room.'

29.5 Hyperpolite words

Humbling verbs have two usages. One implies that the speaker's action involves the social superior; e.g. 'Shall I (humbly) call a taxi <u>for you</u>?' Words in such usage are called *humbling words I* (**kenjoogo I**). There is no such implication in the other usage, called *humbling words II* (**kenjoogo II**) or *hyperpolite words* (**teechoogo**). The speaker uses humbling verbs simply to sound polite.

山田弘の母<u>でございます</u>。
Yamada Hiroshi no haha <u>de gozaimasu</u>.
I am Hiroshi Yamada's mother.

昨日は買い物に<u>参りました</u>。
Kinoo wa kaimono ni <u>mairimashita</u>.
I went shopping yesterday.

Some special verbs have distinct forms for humbling and hyperpolite meanings; e.g. **moosu** 'say' vs. **mooshi-ageru** 'say (to social superior),' **zonjiru** 'know' vs. **zonji-ageru** 'know (social superior).' Verb-**(s)asete itadaku** is often used as a hyperpolite expression when no permission is relevant.

それについては何も<u>存じません</u>。
Sore ni tsuite wa nani mo <u>zonjimasen</u>.
I don't know anything about that.

近くに住まわ<u>せていただい</u>ています。
Chikaku ni sumaw-asete <u>itadaite</u> imasu.
I live near here.

Beautifying words

Beautifying words (**bikago**) are basically nouns with the prefixes **o-** and **go-**; e.g. **o-sake** 'sake,' **o-sooji** 'cleaning,' **go-shuugi** 'congratulatory gift.' Unlike the other categories of honorifics, beautifying words are not necessarily used to be polite or to express respect toward the addressee (or social superior referent). Neither do they lower the status of the speaker or raise that of the addressee (or social superior referent). Another feature of the beautification words is that **o-** and **go-** are attached even to items that belong to the speaker. The user believes that the utterance sounds 'nice, elegant and refined' with such prefixes. The **o-** and **go-** attached to Western loan words, cited in **29.2**, are one type of such examples.

お金	**o-kane**	'money'	お顔	**o-kao**	'face'
お帽子	**o-booshi**	'(my) hat'	お友達	**o-tomodachi**	'(my) friend'
おビール	**o-biiru**	'beer'	おタバコ	**o-tabako**	'cigarette, smoking'

Another type of beautifying words are those that cannot occur without **o-** or **go-**.

おなか	**o-naka**	'stomach (Lit. middle)'	お日様	**o-hi-sama**	'sun'
ご飯	**go-han**	'cooked rice, meal'	ご馳走	**go-chisoo**	'feast'

Honorific usage

As in any language, honorific usage varies greatly from speaker to speaker. With many more forms and rules than those that have been presented above, Japanese honorifics are complicated and difficult even for native speakers. Honorifics are not only used by someone lower in status to someone higher in status, but also in the reverse situation and between equals. The amount and types of honorifics shift all the time within the same conversation and with the same participants, depending on their estimation of how politely to talk at the time, the topic, bystanders, and so on. Traditionally, the ability to use honorifics is regarded as a mark of education, maturity, and status in Japanese society. Those wishing to project such an identity would use honorifics, though to a varying degree, talking to their bosses, colleagues, subordinates, customers, teachers, etc. in formal situations.

(1) 部長A：　　　　これ、拝見してもよろしいですか。
Buchoo A: 　**Kore, haiken shite mo yoroshii desu ka.**
Department chief A: 　May I take a look at this? (with humbling verb)

部長B：　　　　ええ、どうぞご覧（になって）ください。
Buchoo B: 　**Ee, doozo goran (ni natte) kudasai.**
Department chief B: 　Yes, please do take a look. (with exalting verb)

(2) 教師A：　　　　あの方、ご存知ですか。
Kyooshi A: 　**Ano kata go-zonji desu ka.**
Teacher A: 　Do you know that person? (with exalting verb)

教師B：　　　　ええ、存じ上げております。
Kyooshi B: 　**Ee, zonji-agete orimasu.**
Teacher B: 　Yes, I know him/her. (with humbling verb)

The in-group/out-group membership of the speakers is particularly important, but the status is relative and changeable. The basic rule is that one uses exalting words to describe outsiders, and humbling words about insiders. When talking about Boss A with colleagues (and/or with Boss B), A is regarded as an outsider at that moment, and one would use an exalting word about his/her actions. When one talks with customers, however, A is regarded as an in-group member, and a humbling word would be appropriate. If one used an exalting expression instead, it would raise the status of A (insider), and lower the status of the addressee (outsider), which would be rude. If A's spouse walks in, the boss is now considered an outsider (aligned with the spouse), and an exalting word would be appropriate.

(3) To someone who works for the same company:

社長は今出かけて<u>いらっしゃいます</u> or <u>おでかけです</u>。
Shachoo wa ima dekakete irasshaimasu or <u>**o-dekake desu**</u>.
He/she (company president) is out now. (with exalting verb)

(4) To someone from another company:

社長は今出かけて<u>おります</u>。
Shachoo wa ima dekakete orimasu.
He/she (company president) is out now. (with humbling verb)

(5) To the referent's spouse:

社長は今出かけて<u>いらっしゃいます</u> or <u>おでかけです</u>。
Shachoo wa ima dekakete irasshaimasu or <u>**o-dekake desu**</u>.
He/she (company president) is out now. (with exalting verb)

A double use of honorific forms to describe one event is common. Stacking three honorific forms is possible, but not common. In fact, an excessive use of honorifics is considered rude and insulting, characterized as **ingin buree** (unctuous).

お待ちしております。
O-machi shite orimasu.
I'll be waiting for you (humbling construction and humbling verb **oru**)

どんなことを<u>お考えになっていらっしゃる</u>んですか。
Donna koto o <u>o-kangae ni natte irassharu</u> n desu ka.
What are you thinking about? (exalting construction and exalting verb **irassharu**)

When honorific verbs are used, other elements of the sentence are affected, and formal nouns, adverbs, etc. tend to be used.

	Neutral words		*Formal words*	
today	今日	**kyoo**	本日	**honjitsu**
from now on	これから	**korekara**	今後	**kongo**
meal	ご飯	**gohan**	食事	**shokuji**
a minute ago	さっき	**sakki**	先ほど	**sakihodo**

Politeness is conveyed not just by the vocabulary and constructions used, but also by various nonlinguistic elements such as the speaker's gentle demeanor, pleasant tone, and appropriate gestures. To become proficient in honorifics, it will be useful to watch how Japanese people interact with each other and in what type of situations they use honorifics, in real life or in TV dramas, from such a point of view.

Summary of special forms

Regular verbs		Exalting (respectful) verbs	Humbling verbs
行く **iku** 'go'	来る **kuru** 'come'	いらっしゃる **irassharu**	参る **mairu**
いる **iru** 'exist'		いらっしゃる **irassharu**	おる **oru**
言う **iu** 'say'		おっしゃる **ossharu**	申す、申し上げる **moosu, mooshiageru**
する **suru** 'do'		なさる **nasaru**	いたす **itasu**
食べる **taberu** 'eat'	飲む **nomu** 'drink'	召し上がる **meshiagaru**	いただく **itadaku**
見る **miru** 'see'		ご覧になる **goran ni naru**	拝見する **haiken suru**
訪ねる **tazuneru** 'visit'	聞く **kiku** 'ask'		伺う **ukagau**
寝る **neru** 'sleep'		お休みになる **oyasumi ni naru**	
もらう **morau** 'receive'			いただく **itadaku**
あげる **ageru** 'give'			さしあげる **sashiageru**
くれる **kureru** 'give (me)'		くださる **kudasaru**	
知っている **shitte iru** 'know'		ご存知だ **go-zonji da**	存じておる、 **zonjite oru** 存知あげる **zonji ageru**
会う **au** 'meet'			お目にかかる **ome ni kakaru**
N だ N **da** 'be Noun'		N でいらっしゃる N **de irassharu**	N でございます N **de gozaimasu**

Part B

Functions

I

Social interaction and communication strategies

30

Social interaction

In any language, choosing appropriate linguistic forms and strategies according to the context is important for successful communication. The 'context' includes who is talking to whom, when, where, about what, in what way, and why (with what intention). In addition, how the speaker identifies or wishes to project himself/herself at the time affects how he/she speaks. Use of inappropriate speech styles may have serious consequences in Japanese, in which such distinctions as formal–informal and polite–rough are overtly made. The failure to use appropriate communication strategies may also result in being considered rude.

In Japan it is customary for people to bow when they greet someone, introduce themselves, apologize, and so on. Bowing about 30 degrees is considered ordinary, and a person lower in rank is expected to wait to raise his/her head until the social superior does so first.

30.1 Determining the style

There are two main styles in Japanese, formal and informal. *Formal style* is defined as sentences ending in **desu** (with nouns and adjectives), **masu** (with verbs), and their variations (e.g. negative, past tense), and *informal style* as those ending in **da**, **(r)u**, and their variations. They are typically used as follows.

> Informal style: To family members, close friends and colleagues, and children
> Formal style: To social superiors and acquaintances.

Speaking to social superiors, such as people who are higher in rank and/or older, honorific words and constructions (**keego**) are also expected to be used to a varying degree.

During a social interaction, one's communication style often shifts for a variety of reasons. The factors can be divided into three major categories: (a) medium of communication; (b) setting; and (c) participants and referents. These and additional factors, such as the topic of conversation and the presence of bystanders, interact and shape the speaking (or writing) style.

(a) Medium of communication
Spoken and written languages are different in any language, but the difference seems particularly prominent in Japanese. Spoken Japanese displays the following features to a different degree.

- Fragmented with many incomplete sentences and omissions.
- Interactive, accompanied by interactive particles (e.g. **ne**, **yo**), fillers (e.g. **anoo** 'um'), and listener responses (called **aizuchi**; e.g. **hai** 'yes').
- Full of contractions (e.g. **ik-anaku-cha** ← **ik-anaku-te wa** 'I must go').
- The word order may be switched around, and subject, object, time and place words, etc. may appear after the verb, as opposed to the canonical subject–object–verb order.

Both spoken and written languages can be more or less conversational or presentational. For example, chatting with friends is very different from how news reports and formal speeches are presented. The writing style in scholarly articles and newspaper editorials is presentational, containing many Sino-Japanese (**kanji**) words, while texting, e-chat, and e-mail to friends are highly conversational.

▶ 6

(b) Setting

The setting of communication may be formal, informal (casual), business, professional, private, or ritual, among others. A job interview is an example of a formal setting.

(c) Participants and referents

The group membership (i.e. in-group or out-group) of the speaker and other participants, their age, gender, social status, and the relative ranks among them all figure importantly. So does the psychological distance the speaker feels toward the listener and the referent, and this may shift during the same conversation. The speaker's preference to appear in a certain way (e.g. educated, friendly, polite), also affects the choice of linguistic forms, such as honorific (**keego**) and dialect forms.

It will be safe for an adult to speak in formal (**desu/masu**) style when meeting another adult for the first time. If two people close in age and rank become friends, they usually start using informal style at some point. In Japanese culture, no matter how close one may become with someone older and/or higher in status, one does not switch to informal style, unless specifically requested. See **29.7** on how the in-group/out-group membership of the speakers affects speech style.

▶ 6.2; 29

30.2 Greetings

Ohayoo and **ohayoo gozaimasu** are used in the morning (usually before 11 a.m.). The former is used to one's family members and social equals (e.g. close friends, colleagues), while the latter is polite and appropriate to one's boss, teacher, and someone you do not know well. Neither of the greetings used in the afternoon and evening have such a distinction.

おはよう。/ おはようございます。	**Ohayoo. / Ohayoo gozaimasu.**	Good morning.
こんにちは。	**Konnichi wa.**	Good afternoon.
こんばんは。	**Konban wa.**	Good evening.
おやすみなさい。	**Oyasumi nasai.**	Good night.

It is not common in Japan for strangers to exchange 'hello' or 'hi' when they pass each other on the street. Family members do not say **konnichi wa** 'hello' or **konban wa** 'good evening' to each other, though **ohayoo** 'good morning' has no such restriction.

There are many expressions corresponding to 'hello' in English. To announce one's return home or to the office and to welcome someone back, the following phrases are used.

A:	ただいま。	**Tadaima.**	Hello. (I'm now back.)
B:	おかえりなさい。	**Okaeri nasai.**	Hello. (Welcome back.)

The following three dialogues are examples of exchanges between people who have not seen each other in a while. **O-genki desu ka** ('Are you well?') may be added in such a case, like 'How have you been?' in English. The Japanese phrase is also used when there is a legitimate concern about the other party's health, for example, someone who was ill recently.

(1)	先生：	ああ、本田さん、久しぶり。(I)	
	Sensee:	**Aa, Honda-san, hisashiburi.**	
	Teacher:	Oh, Mr/Ms Honda. I haven't seen you in a while.	
	本田：	ご無沙汰しておりまして申し訳ありません。(F)	
	Honda:	**Go-busata shite orimashite mooshiwake arimasen.**	
	Honda:	I'm sorry not to have kept in better touch. (Formal/polite)	

(2) 松井 ： 久しぶりですね。お元気ですか。
Matsui: **Hisashiburi desu ne. O-genki desu ka.**
Matsui: Long time no see. How have you been?

知人 ： ええ、お陰さまで。
Chijin: **Ee, okagesama de.**
Acquaintance: Fine, thank you.

(3) A: お変わりありませんか。
O-kawari arimasen ka.
How have you been? (Lit. Is there not any change?)

B: はい、お陰さまで。
Hai, okagesama de.
Yes, thank you for asking.

Rather than saying **o-genki desu ka** (Lit. 'Are you well?'), Japanese people briefly comment on the weather to someone whom they see often. Common weather-related phrases include **ii tenki desu nee** 'nice weather, isn't it' (when the sun is out even if it is cold), **yoku furimasu nee** 'it's been raining/snowing a lot, hasn't it,' and **samuku/atatakaku narimashita nee** 'it's gotten cold/warm, hasn't it.' The addressee usually responds with **soo desu nee** 'yes' to all of these.

A: おはようございます。
Ohayoo gozaimasu.
Good morning.

B: おはようございます。今日はいい天気ですねぇ。
Ohayoo gozaimasu. Kyoo wa ii tenki desu nee.
Good morning. The weather is nice today, isn't it.

A: そうですねぇ。
Soo desu nee.
Yes, indeed.

30.3 Introducing oneself

The most common phrases to introduce oneself are **hajimemashite** 'how do you do?' (Lit. 'for the first time') and **doozo yoroshiku** 'nice to meet you' (Lit. 'please be nice'). Adults give either their full name or family name, while children may give just their given name.

森 ： 初めまして。森一郎です。どうぞよろしく。
Mori: **Hajimemashite. Mori Ichiroo desu. Doozo yoroshiku.**
Mori: How do you do? I'm Ichiro Mori. Nice to meet you.

In a formal situation, **doozo yoroshiku onegai shimasu** (Lit. 'I humbly request that you be nice') and NAME **to mooshimasu** (Lit. 'I humbly call myself . . .') are used. These are more polite than **doozo yoroshiku** and NAME **desu,** respectively.

町田 ： 初めまして。町田（あゆみ）と申します。
どうぞよろしくお願いします。
Machida: **Hajimemashite. Machida (Ayumi) to mooshimasu.**
Doozo yoroshiku onegai shimasu.
Machida: How do you do? I'm (Ayumi) Machida. It's nice to meet you.

30.4 Introducing others

When introducing someone to another person, the Japanese custom is to introduce the person lower in rank first, then the person higher in rank. In the following example, a college student, Ms Iwai, is introducing her friend Mr Suzuki to Prof. Yamamoto.

岩井：　山本先生、友達の鈴木さんです。
　　　　(to Mr Suzuki) こちらは東京大学の山本先生です。
Iwai:　**Yamamoto-sensee, tomodachi no Suzuki-san desu.**
　　　　(to Mr Suzuki) **Kochira wa Tookyoo Daigaku no Yamamoto-sensee desu.**
Iwai:　Prof. Yamamoto, this is my friend Mr Suzuki.
　　　　(to Mr Suzuki) This is Prof. Yamamoto of Tokyo University.

30.5 Addressing and referring to someone

To address or refer to someone, **-san** is usually attached to family (or sometimes full) names. It can be used regardless of the gender or marital status of the addressee ('Mr, Mrs, Miss, Ms'), but it cannot be used with one's own name because it is a polite suffix. Neither is it used to refer to criminals or those considered not worthy of respect.

田中さん、今日いっしょに映画（を）見ませんか。
Tanaka-san, kyoo issho ni eega (o) mimasen ka.
Mr/Ms Tanaka, would you like to see a movie with me today?

-san can also be attached to given names and certain occupation names.

| 恵子さん | **Keeko-san** | Ms Keiko (woman's given name) |
| 花屋さん | **Hanaya-san** | Mr/Ms florist |

-san is appropriate when addressing or referring to someone who is equal or lower in status, but not to one's social superiors. To the latter, one would use their titles (e.g. **shachoo** 'company president,' **kantoku** 'team manager,' **sensee** 'teacher') or kinship terms (e.g. **okaasan** 'mother,' **oniichan** 'elder brother'). The title **sensee** is used not only to address teachers, but also doctors, lawyers, writers, and the like.

Other suffixes attached to names include **-sama** (more formal than **-san**), **-chan** (diminutive, familiar), and **-kun** (usually to younger males).

-sama is common in business situations addressing or referring to a customer, client or guest, and also in the address line of a letter or an e-mail. The following sentence may be heard in hotels and restaurants, etc.

加藤様、いらっしゃいますか。お電話でございます。 (VF)
Katoo-sama, irasshaimasu ka. O-denwa de gozaimasu.
Is Mr/Ms Kato here? There is a telephone call for you.

-chan is used when addressing or referring to children or one's younger siblings.

太郎ちゃん、いくつ？
Taroo-chan, ikutsu? (I)　　Taro-chan, how old are you?

Grown-ups, especially women, often use first name-**chan** or nickname-**chan** for close friends and family members.

ふみちゃん、今日、映画見に行かない？
Fumi-chan, kyoo, eega mi ni ikanai?
Fumi-chan, do you want to go see a movie today?

The typical use of **-kun** is by male speakers to another male who is socially equal or lower in status. It may also be used by a male boss to female subordinates in a company and by male and female students to male friends.

田中君、きのうのプレゼン、どうだった？
Tanaka-kun, kinoo no purezen, doo datta?
Tanaka-kun, how did your presentation go yesterday?

It is rude to call out-group people by their name alone, without any of the above suffixes attached to it. A bare form is appropriate when one addresses or refers to in-group people; e.g. a family member or someone from one's own company when speaking to outsiders. In addition, male speakers often address their close friends by just family names without any suffixes, which sounds more masculine than rude.

Japanese kinship terms come in pairs depending on to whom one is talking about the family member. Talking inside the family, one would say **otoosan** ('Father') / **papa** ('Dad'), **okaasan** ('Mother') / **mama** ('Mom'), etc., which are also used to address them. Talking to outsiders, adults are supposed to use the formal equivalents **chichi** ('father'), **haha** ('mother'), etc., but it is becoming more and more common for young people to use **otoosan**, **okaasan**, etc., especially in informal situations.

▶ **34.7**

30.6 Visiting someone's home

There are a variety of formulaic expressions used when visiting someone's home. Below are examples of exchanges between a visitor and a host, who are acquaintances.

At the entrance

Guest: ごめんください。 **Gomen kudasai.** Hello.
Host: いらっしゃい（ませ）。 **Irasshai(mase).** Welcome!

Entering the room

Host: どうぞお入りください。 **Doozo o-hairi kudasai.**
Please come in.

Guest: おじゃまします。 **O-jama shimasu.**
Thank you very much. (Lit. I will disturb you.)
or:
失礼します。 **Shitsuree shimasu.**
Excuse me.

Offering food or drink

Host: お茶、いかがですか。 **O-cha, ikaga desu ka.**
Would you care for tea?

Guest: あ、どうぞおかまいなく。 **A, doozo o-kamai naku.**
Oh, please don't bother.
or:
あ、すみません。じゃあ、お願いします。
A, sumimasen. Jaa, o-negai shimasu.
Oh, I feel bad to trouble you, but thank you.

Host: どうぞ召し上がってください。
Doozo meshiagatte kudasai.
Please help yourself.

Guest: すみません。じゃあ、遠慮なくいただきます。
Sumimasen. Jaa, enryo naku itadakimasu.
Thank you very much (Lit. I will receive it without reservation).

Offering another serving

Host:	おかわり／もう少し／もう一杯いかがですか。 **O-kawari / Moo sukoshi / Moo ippai, ikaga desu ka.** Would you like another serving / a little more / another cup (of tea, etc.)?
Guest:	すみません。じゃあ、もう少しいただきます。 **Sumimasen. Jaa, moo sukoshi itadakimasu.** Thank you. I would love to have some more. or: ありがとうございます。でも、もうおなかいっぱいですから ...。 **Arigatoo gozaimasu. Demo, moo onaka ippai desu kara ...** Thank you, but I am full, so ...
Host:	どうぞご遠慮なく。 **Doozo go-enryo naku.** Please feel free. (Lit. Don't hesitate.)

To decline an offer, the guest tends to avoid being direct and end the sentence with **kara** or **node** ('so'), as shown above.

30.7 Leave taking

Sayo(o)nara ('good-bye') may be the best known Japanese phrase for leave taking, but its use is quite restricted. One situation in which it is appropriate is when one leaves and does not expect to see the addressee for a long time. Other common usages are by teachers and students at school (even though they may see each other the next day) and by TV announcers to the audience.

Informal phrases such as the following are used between close friends. Children, especially girls, often say **bai-bai** ('bye') instead.

（それ）じゃあ、また。	**(Sore) jaa, mata.**	See you!
またあした。	**Mata ashita.**	See you tomorrow!

Special phrases are used when temporarily leaving one's home, office, and country.

The person leaving:	いってきます。	**Itte kimasu.** Good-bye! (Lit., I'll go and come back.)
The person staying:	いってらっしゃい。	**Itte rasshai.** Good-bye! (Lit., Go and come back!)

Shitsuree shimasu ('excuse me') is a polite phrase used to one's boss, teacher, **senpai** (one's senior), and the like. There are special expressions for leaving the workplace for the day. Below, the shorter phrase is appropriate for one's colleagues and subordinates, and the longer phrase for one's boss.

The person leaving:	お先に。／お先に失礼します。	**O-saki ni. / O-saki ni shitsuree shimasu.** Good-bye. (Lit. Excuse me for leaving before you.)
The person staying:	お疲れさま。／お疲れさまでした。	**O-tsukare-sama. / O-tsukare-sama deshita.** Good-bye. (Thank you for your hard work.)

O-tsukare-sama deshita (Lit. 'you must be tired') is customarily said to one's colleagues and subordinates, but it is becoming more and more common to say it to one's social superiors. **Go-kuroo-sama (deshita)** (similar to 'Good work!'), however, is still used only to one's subordinates.

Typical exchanges between a visitor and a host, who are acquaintances, are provided below.

Announcing that one must leave

Guest: もう１０時ですね。そろそろ失礼しなくちゃ . . . 。
Moo juuji desu ne. Sorosoro shitsuree shinakucha.
It's already ten o'clock. I should be leaving.

Host: いえ、いえ、どうぞごゆっくりしていらして下さい。
Ie, ie, doozo go-yukkuri shite irashite kudasai.
Oh, no, please stay longer.

Guest: いえ、本当に。今日はありがとうございました。
Ie, hontoo ni. Kyoo wa arigatoo gozaimashita.
Really. Thank you very much for everything today.

Host: いえ、何のおかまいもできませんで . . . 。
Ie, nan no o-kamai mo dekimasen de . . .
Oh, for nothing. (Lit. I couldn't do anything for you.)

At the door

Guest: どうもおじゃましました。では、失礼します。
Doomo o-jama shimashita. Dewa, shitsuree shimasu.
Sorry to have taken so much of your time. (Lit. I disturbed you.)
Good-bye.

30.8 What to say when giving and receiving gifts

When giving and receiving gifts, people use various formulaic expressions depending on the occasion (formal, informal), the relationship between the giver and the receiver (higher, equal, or lower in rank, close or distant), and the content of the gift, among others. To an acquaintance and his/her social superior, it is customary for the giver to minimize the value of the gift out of modesty. In polite situations, both the giver and receiver often speak in incomplete sentences to soften the tone.

これ、つまらないものですが、どうぞ。
Kore, tsumaranai mono desu ga, doozo.
This is just a small gift (Lit. boring thing), but please (accept it).

The receiver would first show hesitation, and then eventually accept it. Below is a sample exchange.

Giver: これ、大したものじゃないんですが、よろしかったら . . . 。
Kore, taishita mono ja nai n desu ga, yoroshikattara. . . .
This is nothing much, but if it is all right with you (please accept it).

Receiver: そんな気を遣っていただかなくても良かったのに . . . 。
Sonna ki o tsukatte itadakanakute mo yokatta noni . . .
Oh, you shouldn't have . . .

Giver: いえ、ほんの気持ちばかりですので . . . 。
Ie, honno kimochi bakari desu node . . .
It's really just a small token, so . . .

Receiver: そうですか。どうもすみません。
Soo desu ka. Doomo sumimasen.
Really? Thank you very much (Lit. I'm sorry).

or: じゃあ、せっかくですから . . . 。ありがとうございます。
Jaa, sekkaku desu kara . . . Arigatoo gozaimasu.
Well, since you kindly brought it . . . Thank you very much.

Speaking to close friends and colleagues and/or in an informal situation, the giver would use less formulaic expressions. The first one below is useful in various situations.

> これ、よかったら....。
> **Kore, yokattara....**
> Here's something for you. (Lit. This, if it's OK.)

Between friends

Giver:	これ、誕生日のプレゼント。気に入ってくれるといいんだけど....。 **Kore, tanjoobi no purezento. Ki ni itte kureru to ii n da kedo...** This is a birthday present for you. I hope you'll like it, but...
Receiver:	え、いいの？ありがとう。 **E? Ii no? Arigatoo.** Oh, really? Thank you.

Between neighbors

Giver:	あのう、甘いものがお好きだって聞いたんで... **Anoo, amai mono ga o-suki da tte kiita n de...** Um, I heard you like sweets, so...
Receiver:	あ、すみません。いつもありがとうございます。 **A, sumimasen. Itsumo arigatoo gozaimasu.** Oh, I feel bad, but thank you very much, as always.

30.9 Congratulating someone

The basic phrase to congratulate someone is **omedetoo**, which by itself can be said to one's family members, friends, and others' children. The polite ending **gozaimasu** is added when speaking to one's acquaintance, boss, teacher, and the like.

> 誕生日、おめでとう。/（お）誕生日、おめでとうございます。
> **Tanjoobi, omedetoo. / (O-)tanjoobi, omedetoo gozaimasu.**
> Happy birthday!

> 卒業、おめでとう。/ ご卒業、おめでとうございます。
> **Sotsugyoo, omedetoo. / Go-sotsugyoo, omedetoo gozaimasu.**
> Congratulations on your graduation!

> ご結婚、おめでとう。/ ご結婚、おめでとうございます。
> **Go-kekkon, omedetoo. / Go-kekkon, omedetoo gozaimasu.**
> Congratulations on your marriage!

▶ 29

30.10 Other formulaic expressions

Expressing empathy and sympathy, as well as appreciation, is highly valued in Japan. To show appreciation for working hard, for example, the sympathetic phrases **o-tsukare-sama (deshita)** 'it must have been tiring' and **go-kuroo-sama (deshita)** ('it must have been difficult') are frequently heard. **O-tsukare-sama (deshita)** can be said to people in the speaker's age group and younger (and sometimes even to one's senior), but **go-kuroo-sama (deshita)** is appropriate only to someone younger and/or lower in rank. (See also 30.7.)

To someone who is having a difficult time, **taihen desu ne** ('It must be tough') is often used. **Kawaisoo** ('poor thing; that's unfortunate') can be used only to people in one's age group and younger. To and about one's elders, **(o-) kinodoku** ('poor thing; that's unfortunate') is more appropriate.

(1)　友人 :　　　　今仕事を探しているんだけど、なかなかなくて . . . 。
　　　Yuujin:　　**Ima shigoto o sagashite iru n da kedo, nakanaka nakute**
　　　Friend:　　　I am looking for a job now, but it's not easy . . .

　　　私 :　　　　　あ、本当。大変だねぇ。
　　　Watashi:　**A hontoo. Taihen da nee.**
　　　I:　　　　　　Really. That's too bad.

　　　友人 :　　　　うん、いろいろ受けたんだけど、だめだった。
　　　Yuujin:　　**Un, iroiro uketa n da kedo, dame datta.**
　　　Friend:　　　Yeah, I applied to many places, but none of them worked out.

　　　私 :　　　　　そう。あんまりがっかりしないようにね。
　　　Watashi:　**Soo. Anmari gakkari shinai yoo ni ne.**
　　　I:　　　　　　Really. Don't be disappointed.

(2)　近所の人 :　　　田中さんのお父さん、ご病気だそうですよ。
　　　Kinjo no hito:　**Tanaka-san no otoosan, go-byooki da soo desu yo.**
　　　Neighbor:　　I heard that Mr/Ms Tanaka's father is ill.

　　　私 :　　　　　そうですか。それはお気の毒ですねぇ。
　　　Watashi:　**Soo desu ka. Sore wa o-ki no doku desu nee.**
　　　I:　　　　　　Really. I am sorry to hear that.

To express condolences, there are set phrases to say and phrases not to say. For example, reduplicated words (e.g. **kasane-gasane** 'again') are avoided, for fear that a death may be repeated. **Zannen desu ne** ('it's too bad; I'm sorry') is also inappropriate on such occasions.

この度は御愁傷様でございます。心からお悔やみを申しあげます。
Kono tabi wa go-shuushoo-sama de gozaimasu. Kokoro kara o-kuyami o mooshiagemasu.
I'm very sorry for your loss. Please accept my sincere condolences.

（お父様の）ご冥福をお祈りしております。
(O-too-sama no) go-meefuku o o-inori shite orimasu.
May he (your father) rest in peace.

To tell people to take care of themselves, different phrases are used depending on the addressee and whether they are currently ill or not. Below, the longer version is more polite than the shorter version.

To someone in poor health

　　　（どうぞ）お大事に。/（どうぞ）お大事になさって下さい。
　　　(Doozo) o-daiji ni. / (Doozo) o-daiji ni nasatte kudasai.
　　　Please take care.

To someone in good health

　　　女 :　　　気をつけてね。/ 元気でね。or 元気でいてね。(informal)
　　　Female:　**Ki o tsukete ne. / Genki de ne. / Genki de ite ne.**

　　　男 :　　　気をつけろよ。/ 元気でな。or 元気でいろよ。
　　　Male:　　**Ki o tsukero yo. / Genki de na. / Genki de iro yo.**
　　　　　　　　Please take care. / Stay healthy. (to family and friends)

　　　男 / 女　　どうぞお元気で。/ お元気でいらして下さい。(formal)
　　　M/F:　　**Doozo o-genki de. / O-genki de irashite kudasai.**
　　　　　　　　Please take care. (to acquaintances and boss, etc.)

Below are common expressions used when someone or something does not seem right. The longer version is appropriate when speaking to one's social superior or someone one does not know well, and the shorter version for one's family and friends.

A: 大丈夫？/ 大丈夫ですか。
Daijoobu? / Daijoobu desu ka.
Are you all right?

or: どうかした？/ どうかしましたか。
Doo ka shita? / Doo ka shimashita ka.
Is there something wrong?

B: 大丈夫。/ 大丈夫です。
Daijoobu. / Daijoobu desu.
I'm OK.

30.11 Using the phone

There are formulaic phrases and protocols for talking on the telephone. In a business setting, for example, the person who answers the phone gives the company and department names often followed by his/her family name, then the caller identifies himself/herself giving his/her affiliation. **Moshi moshi** ('hello; are you there?') is often used during telephone conversations, both business and private types.

プルルルル . . .　　Purururu . . .　　(ringtone)

田中:　紀の丸書店、洋書部（の田中）でございます。
Tanaka: **Kinomaru Shoten, Yoosho-bu (no Tanaka) de gozaimasu.**
This is (Tanaka of) Kinomaru Bookstore Foreign Languages Department.

豊田:　あのう、日本大学の豊田と申しますが、松田さんはいらっしゃいますか。
Toyota: **Anoo, Nihon Daigaku no Toyota to mooshimasu ga, Matsuda-san wa irasshaimasu ka.**
Um, this is Toyota of Nihon University calling. Can I speak to Mr/Ms Matsuda?

田中:　はい、少々お待ち下さい（ませ）。
Tanaka: **Hai, shooshoo o-machi kudasai(mase).**
Yes, (may I ask you to) please wait a minute.

松田:　もしもし、お電話変わりました。松田ですが。
Matsuda: **Moshi moshi, o-denwa kawarimashita. Matsuda desu ga.**
Hello. This is Matsuda speaking now.

or

田中:　申し訳ございません。松田は只今席をはずしておりますが . . .。
Tanaka: **Mooshiwake gozaimasen. Matsuda wa tadaima seki o hazushite orimasu ga . . .**
I'm very sorry. Matsuda just stepped out of the office.

豊田:　そうですか。じゃ、すみませんが、お帰りになったらこちらにお電話下さるようお伝えいただけますか。
Toyota: **Soo desu ka. Ja, sumimasen ga, o-kaeri ni nattara kochira ni o-denwa kudasaru yoo o-tsutae itadakemasu ka.**
I see. I am sorry to bother you, but would you please ask him to call me when he gets back?

Ending a telephone conversation properly is as important as starting it properly. People usually send a signal when they wish to end.

At the end of a business conversation:

A: はい、分かりました。それでは、今日のところはそういうことでよろしかったでしょうか。
Hai, wakarimashita. Sore dewa, kyoo no tokoro wa soo yuu koto de yoroshikatta deshoo ka.
Ok. Would that be all for today, then?

B: はい、では、よろしくお願いします。
Hai, dewa, yoroshiku o-negai shimasu.
Yes, thank you very much in advance.

失礼します。and/or ごめん下さい。
Shitsuree shimasu and/or **Gomen kudasai.**
Good-bye.

At the end of a casual conversation:

A: うん、分かった。じゃ、そろそろ...。
Un, wakatta. Ja, sorosoro ...
OK. Well, then ...

B: うん、じゃ、また。
Un. Ja, mata.
OK. Talk to you again.

31

Basic communication strategies

Speakers use various set phrases and strategies to begin and keep communication going smoothly. This section introduces some of the most commonly used expressions and strategies in Japanese.

31.1 Attracting someone's attention and responding to a call for attention

The easiest way to get someone's attention is to call his/her name or title, such as **X-san** or **sensee** 'teacher.' When you don't know the name or the title of a person, you can use one of the following expressions.

> あのう。
> **Anoo . . .**
> Umm . . .

> あのう、すみませんが . . .
> **Anoo, sumimasen ga . . .**
> Uh, excuse me (but) . . .

> あのう、失礼ですが . . .
> **Anoo, shitsuree desu ga . . .**
> Uh, excuse me/(I am) sorry to be rude (but) . . .

> ちょっと。(I)
> **Chotto.**
> Say!

> ねえ。(I)
> **Nee.**
> Tell you what / Listen,

Anoo (chotto) sumimasen (ga) is probably the most common expression to attract someone's attention. In a more formal situation **Shitsuree desu ga**, which literally means 'to be rude' can be used. To a close friend, **Nee**, which is an interactional particle, can be used. At a restaurant or a store, one can say **Onegai shimasu** 'I request' to catch the attention of a waiter/waitress/sales clerk. **Gomen kudasai** is an appropriate expression when one is at the door of someone's house and wants to get the attention of the resident of the house.

In responding to a call for attention, one can simply say **Hai** 'yes' in a formal situation or **Un?** 'yeah?' in an informal situation. The following expressions can also be used.

> はい、何でしょうか。(F)
> **Hai, nan deshoo ka.**
> Yes, what is it?

> え、何? (I)
> **E, nani?**
> What is it?

31.2 Initiating a conversation

There are many ways of initiating a conversation depending on the situation. You can, for example, initiate a conversation by talking about the weather or things around you. Asking a question is also a common way of initiating a conversation. There are, however, some set phrases that can be used.

> ちょっとお話したいことがあるんですが、(F)
> **Chotto o-hanashi shitai koto ga aru n desu ga,**
> I have something I would like to talk to you about.

> ちょっと話があるんだけど、(I)
> **Chotto hanashi ga aru n da kedo,**
> I have something I want to tell you.

> 今二、三分よろしいでしょうか。(F)
> **Ima ni-san-pun yoroshii deshoo ka.**
> Do you have two or three minutes now?

> 今ちょっといい？(I)
> **Ima chotto ii?**
> Are you free right now?

> 今お忙しいでしょうか。(F)
> **Ima o-isogashii deshoo ka.**
> Are you busy now?

> 今忙しい？(I)
> **Ima isogashii?**
> Are you busy now?

> ちょっとお聞きしたいことがあるんですが、(VF)
> **Chotto o-kiki shitai koto ga aru n desu ga,**
> I have something I would like to ask you.

> ちょっと聞きたいんだけど、(I)
> **Chotto kikitai n da kedo,**
> I want to ask you something.

> お仕事中すみませんが、(F)
> **O-shigoto-chuu sumimasen ga,**
> I am sorry to bother you in the middle of your work,

> 仕事中悪いんだけど、(I)
> **Shigoto-chuu warui n da kedo,**
> I am sorry to bother you in the middle of your work,

► 29

31.3 Ending a conversation

To end a conversation, the following expressions can be used.

> では/じゃ、そろそろこのへんで。
> **Dewa/ja, sorosoro kono hen de.**
> Well . . . , I should be going soon . . .

> では/じゃ、そろそろ。
> **Dewa/ja, sorosoro.**
> Well . . . , (I should be going soon.)

では/じゃ、今日はこんなところで。
Dewa/ja, kyoo wa konna tokoro de.
OK, then, this is it for today.

じゃあね。(I)
Jaa ne.
Ok, then.

31.4 Introducing and developing a topic

31.4.1 Introducing a topic

Topics can be introduced by a phrase such as **jitsu wa** 'actually, to get to the point,' or phrases such as **... no koto na n desu ga/kedo** 'it's about ...'

実は今度の試験のことなんですけど
Jitsu wa kondo no shiken no koto na n desu kedo
Well (lit. actually), it's about the upcoming exam

31.4.2 Changing the topic

Common expressions for changing the topic are:

ところで
tokorode
by the way,

話は変わりますが
hanashi wa kawarimasu ga
not to change the subject,

それはそうと
sore wa soo to
be that as it may,

話は違うけど (I)
hanashi wa chigau kedo
not to change the topic,

31.5 Formal development of a topic

31.5.1 Opening remarks

To present a new topic formally in a lecture or a talk, phrases such as the following can be used.

今日は〜についてお話したいと思います。
Kyoo wa ... ni tsuite o-hanashi shitai to omoimasu.
Today I would like to talk about ...

〜について述べたいと思います。
... ni tsuite nobetai to omoimasu.
I would like to talk about ...

〜に関して考察をしたいと思います。
... ni kanshite koosatsu o shitai to omoimasu.
I would like to look at ...

本日は . . . につきましてお話をさせて戴きます。(VF)
Honjitsu wa . . . ni tsukimashite o-hanashi o sasete itadakimasu.
I should like to talk about . . . today.

▶ **29; 64.1.2**

Establishing a sequence

The most common phrases that express a sequence of points are as follows.

まず始めに
mazu hajime ni
first (of all)

まず最初に
mazu saisho ni
first (of all)

次に
tsugi ni
next

第一に
dai ichi ni
firstly

第二点として
dai ni ten toshite
as my second point / secondly

最後に
saigo ni
lastly

Giving examples

To give examples, use the following phrases.

例えば
tatoeba
for example

いくつか例をあげたいと思います。
Ikutsuka ree o agetai to omoimasu.
I would like to give a few examples.

Summarizing and concluding

To summarize and conclude, use expressions such as the following. Note that the Japanese often end the utterance with **to omoimasu** 'I think,' which softens the assertion.

結論を述べますと、
ketsuron o nobemasu to,
to conclude,

結論として次のことが言えると思います。
Ketsuron toshite tsugi no koto ga ieru to omoimasu.
As a conclusion, I can say the following.

以上のことから〜ということが明らかになると思います。
Ijoo no koto kara . . . to yuu koto ga akiraka ni naru to omoimasu.
From what I've said so far, I believe it is clear that. . . .

以上のことをまとめますと
ijoo no koto o matomemasu to
to summarize (what I have said so far)

つまり〜ということだと思います。
Tsumari . . . to yuu koto da to omoimasu.
In other words, it means . . .

▶ 24.1; 26.2

To end the presentation, you might want to say:

以上です。ご清聴ありがとうございました。
Ijoo desu. Go-seechoo arigatoo gozaimashita.
This concludes my (presentation, speech). Thank you for listening.

これで終わらせていただきたいと思います。
Kore de owarasete itadakitai to omoimasu.
I would like to end (my presentation, speech).

▶ 19.2.8; 20.3.3

31.6 Being vague or indirect

Japanese has many ways of rendering utterances softer and more indirect.

31.6.1 *nanka* 'something'

Nanka (lit. 'something') attached to a noun indicates that the speaker is giving an example.

ラッシュアワーの時なんかもういっぱいで
Rasshuawaa no toki nanka moo ippai de
It's so crowded during the rush hour, for example, and

スーパーでおすしなんかも売っています。
Suupaa de osushi nanka mo utte imasu.
At the supermarket they sell things like sushi.

By using **nanka** the speaker avoids a specific reference and thereby makes the statement more indirect.

Nanka is also used at the beginning and in the middle of a sentence. It softens the tone by adding uncertainty or modesty, though its overuse is frowned upon as is 'like' in English.

Y: なんか月曜日だから全然人がいなくてえ、飲み屋に—
   Nanka getsuyoobi da kara zenzen hito ga inakutee nomiya nii
   Like, because it was Monday, there was no one at the bar,

H: うん。
   Un.

Y: だからなんか、最後まで（・）いてもいいですよとか、延長してもいいですよって。
   Dakara nanka, saigo made (·) ite mo ii desu yo toka, enchoo shite mo ii desu yo tte.
   So, 'you can stay until the closing time,' 'we can extend the closing time.'

H: はーん。
Haan.

Y: お店の人が言ってくれたの。
O-mise no hito ga itte kureta no.
The bar staff told me.

▶ 4.4

31.6.2 *toka, demo*

The use of particles such as **toka** and **demo**, meaning 'or something,' contributes to making an utterance less specific and more vague.

お茶でもいかがですか。
O-cha <u>demo</u> ikaga desu ka.
How about tea or something?

今日は天気がいいから、散歩でもしようかなと思っています。
Kyoo wa tenki ga ii kara, sanpo <u>demo</u> shiyoo ka na to omotte imasu.
It's good weather today, so I am thinking of taking a walk or something.

勉強とかしてるのかな？ (I)
Benkyoo <u>toka</u> shite ru no ka na?
I wonder if (he) is studying or something.

好きな人とかいないの？ (I)
Suki na hito <u>toka</u> inai no?
Don't you have someone you like or something?

▶ 1.3; 22.2.3

This way of using **toka** is more typical of the speech of the younger generation. For the use of **toka** with quotations, see **32.2**.

31.6.3 Stating one's opinion indirectly

In Japanese, it is preferable not to state one's opinion too directly, so expressions such as **. . . n ja nai deshoo ka**, 'I wonder if it's not the case that . . . ,' **. . . ka na to omoimasu**, 'I think that maybe . . .' and similar expressions are used in proffering one's opinion indirectly.

▶ 85

日本に行くなら小さい町の方がいいんじゃないでしょうか。
Nihon ni iku nara chiisai machi no hoo ga ii n ja nai deshoo ka.
If you are going to Japan, I think a smaller town might be better.

大学は大きい大学の方がいいかなと思います。
Daigaku wa ookii daigaku no hoo ga ii ka na to omoimasu.
I think a bigger university might be better.

31.7 Expressing reservation (reluctance)

When someone says **Uun** 'well' or does not respond right away, it generally suggests some reservation or difficulty in responding on the respondent's part. Some of the ways a person indicates reservation or reluctance include:

う～ん。
Uun.
Well.

ちょっと . . . (in response to an invitation)
Chotto . . .
Well . . .

そうですねえ。
Soo desu nee.
Well, let me think.

そうですかねえ。(in response to someone's opinion)
Soo desu ka nee.
I wonder . . .

そうかなあ。(in response to someone's opinion)
Soo ka naa.
Really?

ちょっと考えさせていただけますか。(in response to an invitation or a suggestion)
Chotto kangaesasete itadakemasuka?
Would you let me think a little?

▶ 20.3.3

Requesting repetition

To ask someone to repeat something because you have not heard it right or did not understand it, use one of the following expressions.

すみません、今ちょっとよく聞こえなかったんですが . . . (F)
Sumimasen, ima chotto yoku kikoenakatta n desu ga . . .
I'm sorry, I couldn't hear well, but . . .

すみません。もう一度言っていただけませんか。(VF)
Sumimasen. Moo ichido itte itadakemasen ka.
I am sorry, but could I ask you to say that one more time?

えっ? (I)
E?
Huh.

今何て言った？ (I)
Ima nan te itta?
What did you say just now?

何? (I)
Nani?
What?

Making sure you are understood

To ask if you are being understood, you can use expressions such as the following.

お分かりになったでしょうか。(F)
O-wakari ni natta deshoo ka.
Is it clear (i.e. do you understand)?

言おうとしていること、お分かりいただけたでしょうか。(VF)
Ioo to shite iru koto, o-wakari itadaketa deshoo ka.
Do you understand what I am trying to say?

わかりますか。
Wakarimasu ka.
Do you understand?

わかった？ (I)
Wakatta?
Do you understand?

31.10 Asking how to pronounce or write a word

To ask how to pronounce a word, one may point to the word and say:

これはなんと読みますか。 (F)　　これ、なんて読むの？ (I)
Kore wa nan to yomimasu ka.　**Kore, nan te yomu no?**
How do you read this?　　　　　How do you read this?

▶ 9.1; 26.2

There are many other ways to ask how to pronounce certain words or **kanji**, as demonstrated below. Sentences containing honorific expressions; e.g. **itadaku**, are more formal and polite. Also sentences ending in **ga** or **kedo** 'but' sound less assertive and more polite.

▶ 19.2.8; 26.2; 26.3; 29.3; 31.6

この漢字の読み方を教えていただきたいのですが。 (F)
Kono kanji no yomi kata o oshiete itadakitai no desu ga.
I'd like to ask you to tell me how to read this **kanji**, but . . .

この漢字はなんと読むか、教えていただけませんか/もらえませんか。 (F)
Kono kanji wa nan to yomu ka, oshiete itadakemasen ka/moraemasen ka.
Would you please tell me how to read this **kanji**?

この漢字の読み方を教えてもらいたいんだけど。 (I)
Kono kanji no yomi kata o oshiete moraitai n da kedo.
I want to ask you to tell me how to read this **kanji**, but . . .

これ、なんて読むか、教えてくれる？ (I)
Kore, nan te yomu ka, oshiete kureru?
Can you tell me how to read this?

これ、なんて読むの？ (I)
Kore, nan te yomu no?
How do you read this?

If you want to know the name of an item in Japanese, point to it and say:

▶ 26.2

これは日本語でなんと言いますか。 (F)
Kore wa Nihongo de nan to iimasu ka.
What do you call this in Japanese?

これ、日本語でなんて言うの？ (I)
Kore, Nihongo de nan te yuu no?
What do you call this in Japanese?

▶ 26.2

To ask how to write a word in **hiragana**, **katakana**, or **kanji**, replace the word in the square brackets in the following sentences with the word you intend to write.

▶ 26.2

'**Keetai**' は　平仮名/カタカナ/漢字　でどう書くか、教えていただきたいのですが... (VF)
'Keetai' wa hiragana/katakana/kanji de doo kaku ka, oshiete itadakitai no desu ga ...
I was wondering if you could show me how to write '**keetai**' in **kanji**, but ...

'**Keetai**' は漢字でどう書きますか。(F)
'Keetai' wa kanji de doo kakimasu ka.
How do you write '**keetai**' in **kanji**?

漢字で '**keetai**' と書いていただけませんか。(VF)
Kanji de 'keetai' to kaite itadakemasen ka.
Would you please write '**keetai**' in **kanji**?

'**Keetai**' って漢字でどう書くの？(I)
'Keetai' tte kanji de doo kaku no?
How do you write '**keetai**' in **kanji**?

ここに漢字で '**keetai**' って書いてくれる？(I)
Koko ni kanji de 'keetai' tte kaite kureru?
Could you write '**keetai**' in **kanji** here?

The following sentences exemplify how you may ask for a **kanji** that constitutes one part of a word.

「けいたい」の「けい」はどういう漢字ですか。(F)
Kaisha no 'kee' wa doo yuu kanji desu ka.
What is the **kanji** for '**kee**' in **keetai**?

「けいたい」の「けい」はどう書くの？(I)
Kaisha no 'kee' wa doo kaku no?
How do you write '**kee**' in '**keetai**'?

aizuchi (listener responses)

When conversing in Japanese, **aizuchi** 'listener responses' are used frequently by the listener to let the speaker know that he/she is listening, paying attention, interested in the conversation and/or that s/he would like the speaker to continue. **Aizuchi** take the form of various short expressions often accompanied by slight head nodding. The speaker may feel uncomfortable or ignored if the listener does not give enough **aizuchi**, even if the listener is listening attentively. It is therefore advisable to nod your head from time to time while the other person talks. Use some of the **aizuchi** phrases listed below that are appropriate in the specific context whenever there is a short pause in the other person's utterance. **Aizuchi** occur in both formal and informal conversations.

Types of aizuchi

Showing one is paying attention

Formal

はい。	**Hai.**	Yes.
ええ。	**Ee.**	Yes. (Less formal than **hai**.)
そうですか。	**Soo desu ka.**	I see.

Informal

うん。	**Un.**	Uh-huh.
そう。	**Soo.**	Right.
そうか。	**Soo ka.**	I see.
ふーん。	**Fuun.**	Yeah.

Showing enthusiasm
Aizuchi phrases may be repeated to show enthusiasm.

▶ **31.13**

Formal

はいはい。	**Hai hai.**	Yes, yes.
ええええ。	**Ee ee.**	Yes, yes. (Less formal than **hai**.)

Informal

うんうん。	**Un un.**	Yeah, yeah.
そうそう。	**Soo soo.**	Right, right.

Confirming the speaker's opinion

▶ **10.5**

Formal

そのとおりですね。	**Sono toori desu ne.**	Exactly right.
そうですね。	**Soo desu ne.**	That's right.

Informal

たしかに。	**Tashika ni.**	Certainly.
なるほど。	**Naruhodo.**	I understand.
そうだね。	**Soo da ne.**	That's right.
そうね。	**Soo ne.**	That's right. (Feminine)
やっぱりね。	**Yappari ne.**	As I thought.

Showing surprise

▶ **68**

Formal

そうなんですか。	**Soo na n desu ka.**	Is that the case?
ほんとですか。	**Honto desu ka.**	Is it true?
すごいですねえ。	**Sugoi desu nee.**	That's something! / That's amazing!

Informal

ええ？	**Ee?**	What?
おお！	**Oo!**	Wow!
うわあ！	**Uwaa!**	Wow!
へえ！	**Hee!**	Wow!
すごい！	**Sugoi!**	Great!
ほんと？	**Honto?**	Really?
うそ！	**Uso!**	You're kidding!

Showing reservation (see **31.7**)

Formal and Informal

うーん。	**Uun.**	Hmm . . .

Formal

| どうですかねえ。 | **Doo desu ka nee.** | I wonder (how it is). |
| そうですかねえ。 | **Soo desu ka nee.** | I wonder if that's true. |

Informal

どうかなあ。	**Doo ka naa.**	I wonder (how it is).
そうかなあ。	**Soo ka naa.**	I wonder if that's true.
そう？	**Soo?**	You think?

Showing sympathy

► 10.5

Formal

たいへんですねえ。	**Taihen desu nee.**	That must be tough.
こまりましたねえ。	**Komarimashita nee.**	That's too bad/upsetting.
がっかりですねえ。	**Gakkari desu nee.**	That's disappointing.
お気の毒ですねえ。	**O-kinodoku desu nee.**	I'm sorry to hear that.

Informal

たいへんだねえ。	**Taihen da nee.**	That must be tough.
こまったねえ。	**Komatta nee.**	That's too bad/upsetting.
がっかりだねえ。	**Gakkari da nee.**	That's disappointing.
かわいそうだねえ。	**Kawaisoo da nee.**	Poor thing! / That's a pity.
気の毒だねえ。	**Kinodoku da nee.**	I'm sorry to hear that.

31.12 Fillers (hesitation noises)

Fillers are noises, small words or phrases, such as 'um,' 'er,' 'well,' and 'like,' which are used to fill silences between utterances or to fill pauses when speaking. Commonly used fillers in Japanese are:

えー	**ee**	uh
えーっと	**eetto**	well
あのー	**anoo**	um
そのー	**sonoo**	um
んー	**nn**	er
なんていうか	**nan te yuu ka**	what should I say

31.13 Repetition

Repeating a word or phrase in conversation has various functions, such as acknowledging the other speaker's utterances, agreeing with the speaker, emphasizing, confirming, and clarifying one's own utterances. Repetitions occur frequently in Japanese conversation to show the interlocutors' involvement in the conversation. For example, **aizuchi** phrases are often repeated to express enthusiasm or excitement.

► 31.11

はいはい	**hai hai**	Yes yes.
ええええ	**ee ee**	Yes yes.
そうそう	**soo soo**	Right right.
わかるわかる	**wakaru wakaru**	I totally understand.
まだまだ	**mada mada**	Not yet not yet.
わかったわかった	**wakatta wakatta**	Sure sure.
いくいく	**iku iku**	I'll definitely go.
きたきた	**kita kita**	It came! / It's coming!
はやくはやく	**hayaku hayaku**	Hurry hurry!

Question words in Japanese, such as **dare** 'who,' **doko** 'where,' **nani** 'what,' and **itsu** 'when,' are also repeated in succession by speakers to express excitement.

A:	今日、すごくいいことがあったんだ。
A:	**Kyoo, sugoku ii koto ga atta n da.**
A:	Today, something really good happened.

B:	え、なになに？
B:	**E, nani nani?**
B:	Huh, what is it, what is it? (Lit. what what?)

A speaker may repeat the same word or phrase uttered by a previous speaker to show agreement, excitement, or involvement in the conversation.

子 :	今日の夕飯何？
Ko:	**Kyoo no yuuhan nani?**
Child:	What's today's dinner?

母 :	カレーよ。
Haha:	**Karee yo.**
Mother:	It's curry.

子 :	やったあ、カレー！
Ko:	**Yattaa, karee!**
Child:	Great, it's curry!

Repetition is also used to clarify or to confirm.

A:	次の予約は土曜日です。
	Tsugi no yoyaku wa <u>doyoobi</u> desu.
	Your next appointment is Saturday.

B:	はい、土曜日ですね。
	Hai, <u>doyoobi</u> desu ne.
	Yes, Saturday, right.

川田 :	初めまして、川田です。
Kawada:	**Hajimemashite, <u>Kawada desu</u>.**
Kawada:	How do you do, I'm Kawada.

森 :	ああ、どうも。川田さんですか。森です。
Mori:	**Aa, doomo. <u>Kawada-san desu</u> ka. Mori desu.**
Mori:	Oh, hello. You are Mr/Ms Kawada? I'm Mori.

31.14 Ellipsis

Many parts of a sentence may be omitted when their meaning can be understood from the context. The most frequently omitted part is the topic word of the sentence. Although ellipsis is not obligatory, never omitting the topic phrase makes one sound repetitious.

父は５０才です。（父は）東京に住んでいます。
Chichi wa gojussai desu. (Chichi wa) Tookyoo ni sunde imasu.
My father is 50 years old. (My father) lives in Tokyo.

（私は）田中と申します。（私は）昨日、ここに越してきました。
(Watashi wa) Tanaka to mooshimasu. (Watashi wa) kinoo, koko ni koshite kimashita.
(I) am Tanaka. (I) moved here yesterday.

Nouns that may be expressed with a pronoun in English are usually omitted in Japanese. ( ) indicates omitted phrases in the following examples.

（それは）いいセーターですね。
(Sore wa) ii seetaa desu ne.
(That) is a nice sweater, isn't it.

本を買って、（それを）友達にあげました。
Hon o katte, (sore o) tomodachi ni agemashita.
I bought a book and gave (it) to my friend.

甘い物が好きだけど、（それは）ふとるから、（それを）あまりたべない。
Amai mono ga suki da kedo, (sore wa) futoru kara, (sore o) amari tabenai.
I like sweet things, but (they are) fattening, so I don't eat (them) very much.

▶ See **1.6** on the ellipsis of particles.

31.15 Afterthoughts

Japanese sentences usually end with a predicate followed by inflectional elements. In conversations, however, other parts of speech may be added after the predicate as an afterthought. The particle associated with the noun phrase is optional when added as an afterthought.

本当に疲れたよ、今回の出張（は）。
Hontoo ni tsukareta yo, konkai no shutchoo (wa).
It was really tiring, my business trip this time.

来ましたよ、バス（が）。
Kimashita yo, basu (ga).
It's here, the bus.

あ、忘れちゃった、傘（を）。
A, wasurechatta, kasa (o).
Oh, I forgot, the umbrella.

辞書も使いますよ、時々。
Jisho mo tsukaimasu yo, tokidoki.
I use the dictionary too, sometimes.

▶ **1.3; 10.4**

31.16 Making corrections

Speakers sometimes make mistakes by using an inappropriate word or mispronouncing a word. Some of these errors, if left unattended, can lead to a breakdown in communication. There are various ways for the speaker or the listener to correct what was said.

31.16.1 Self-correction

Replacing a word
When the speaker needs to correct a word he/she used, **ja nakute** (informal) or **de wa naku (te)** (formal) can be used right after the word that needs to be corrected, followed by a replacement word.

たいそう、じゃなくて、体育の時間にサッカーをした。
Taisoo, ja nakute, taiiku no jikan ni sakkaa o shita.
We played soccer during exercise, no, I mean, P. E.

アメリカ、ではなく（て）、欧米諸国の傾向を考えてみましょう。
Amerika, de wa naku, (te) oobeeshokoku no keekoo o kangaete mimashoo.
Let's consider trends in America, no, in America and Europe.

However, in many cases, native speakers' utterances use no particular phrase between the initial word and the replacement other than possibly a short pause or an ('oh').

> <u>たいそう</u>、あ、<u>体育</u>の時間にサッカーをした。
> <u>**Taisoo**</u>, **a,** <u>**taiiku**</u> **no jikan ni sakkaa o shita.**
> We played soccer during the exercise time, oh (I mean), P.E.

Adding more words

In amending a word or phrase, the speaker may add more words to the original word or phrase.

> ケーキ、日本のケーキはおいしいね。
> **Keeki, Nihon no keeki wa oishii ne.**
> Cake, Japanese cake is delicious, isn't it.

> テレビ見る、おかし食べながらテレビ見るのが好きです。
> **Terebi miru, okashi tabenagara terebi miru no ga suki desu.**
> I like watching TV, watching TV and eating snacks at the same time.

31.16.2 Correcting others

When the person you are talking to misunderstands what you have said, the communication may be adjusted by explaining what you meant to say. One of the following phrases may be used to initiate the correction.

> うーん、そうじゃなくて... (I)
> **Uun, soo ja nakute ...**
> Well, it's not that ...

> ごめん、そう言う意味じゃなくて... (I)
> **Gomen, soo yuu imi ja nakute ...**
> Sorry, what I meant isn't that but ...

> すみません、私の説明が足りなかったようですが... (F)
> **Sumimasen, watashi no setsumee ga tarinakatta yoo desu ga ...**
> Excuse me, my explanation appears to have been insufficient, but ...

When someone who is your superior or someone you are not familiar with uses a word or phrase that is wrong, special care needs to be taken when making a correction. One of the following phrases can be used to preface your correction.

> 大変失礼ですが... (F)
> **Taihen shitsuree desu ga ...**
> I'm terribly sorry but ...

> 私が間違っていたら申し訳ないのですが... (F)
> **Watashi ga machigatte itara mooshiwake nai no desu ga ...**
> I'm sorry if I'm wrong but ...

> 私の覚え違いかもしれませんが... (F)
> **Watashi no oboechigai kamo shiremasen ga ...**
> It may be that I don't remember it correctly, but ...

> ちょっと言いにくいのですが... (F)
> **Chotto iinikui no desu ga ...**
> I'm a little hesitant to say this, but ...

The following is an example of correcting others.

> 上司： 来週の会議の準備は進んでいるかね？
> **Jooshi: Raishuu no kaigi no junbi wa susunde iru ka ne?**
> Boss: Are you getting everything ready for the meeting next week?

部下：	はい、あの、私の覚え違いかもしれませんが、会議は再来週では . . . 。	
Buka:	**Hai, ano, watashi no oboechigai kamo shiremasen ga, kaigi wa saraishuu de wa . . .**	
Subordinate:	Yes, sir, well, I may have misremembered, but isn't the meeting the week after next?	
上司：	ああ、そうだったね。	
Jooshi:	**Aa, soo datta ne.**	
Boss:	Oh, that's right.	

To someone you are familiar with or close to, you may use one of the following phrases.

それをいうなら (I)
Sore o yuu nara
You mean to say

ていうか (I)
Te yuu ka
Actually

〜じゃなくて〜でしょ (I)
. . . ja nakute . . . desho
It's not . . . but . . .

Some examples are given below.

亜紀：	うわ、このうどん、細いね。	
Aki:	**Uwa, kono udon, hosoi ne.**	
Aki:	Wow, these udon noodles are thin.	
健：	ていうか、それはうどんじゃなくて、素麺でしょ。	
Ken:	**Te yuu ka, sore wa udon ja nakute, soomen desho.**	
Ken:	Actually, those aren't udon noodles, they're somen noodles.	
祖父：	お前は、お菓子を作るのが上手だから、ソムリエになるといいな。	
Sofu:	**Omae wa, o-kashi o tsukuru no ga joozu da kara, somurie ni naru to ii na.**	
Grandpa:	You are good at making sweets, so you should become a sommelier.	
孫：	おじいちゃん、それを言うなら、パティシエでしょ？	
Mago:	**Ojiichan, sore o yuu nara, patishie desho?**	
Grandchild:	Grandpa, you mean, pâtissier, right?	

31.17 Using and interpreting pauses and silence

Silence plays an important role in Japanese communication. While silence is perceived somewhat negatively in the Western tradition, it is traditionally considered a positive trait in Japanese culture. People of few words are seen as more trustworthy and thoughtful than those of many words.

Common use of silence in Japanese communication

In public situations such as meetings and social gatherings, opinions that disagree with the consensus are generally not openly expressed. A subordinate who disagrees with the opinion expressed by a superior will usually keep silent in order to maintain a harmonious relationship.

Interpreting pauses and silence

Interpreting the meaning of silence is a very difficult task. It could have various meanings, such as thoughtfulness, hesitation, obedience, respect, confusion, defiance, and indifference, to list but a few. The meaning of silence depends on the context of speech, such as who is participating in the communication, what the topic is, and how the communication affects other issues. For instance, if one is giving a lecture/pep-talk to his/her subordinates, the silence from the subordinates may be interpreted as respect, obedience or thoughtfulness. On the other hand, if one asks someone to do a favor but does not get a response, such silence may be interpreted as hesitation, unwillingness, or even defiance. Japanese people often pause during a conversation for various purposes, such as to organize their thoughts, to look for the right word to use, or to analyze what has been said.

31.18 Gaze

Holding the gaze of another person for an extended time is not common in Japanese communication. Prolonged gaze at one's social superior may even be interpreted negatively; e.g. as a sign of contention, discontent, or rebelliousness. While Japanese people do make eye contact, they avert their gaze to look downwards in between eye contact. Studies have shown that North Americans of European descent, for example, perceive a person who looks down to be uninformed, not confident or even dishonest. However, Japanese people often perceive a person who looks down to be respectful. They also tend to look down when they are thinking or deciding what to say.

To indicate your undivided attention to the person to whom you are talking without maintaining prolonged eye contact, you may look towards the other person's neck and use appropriate **aizuchi**.

▶ 31.11

II

Giving and seeking information

32

Questions

32.1 ## Asking and responding to a yes or no question

In Japanese, yes or no questions can be formed by attaching the particle **ka** at the end of the sentence and/or by using a question intonation. There is no change of word order between a declarative sentence and an interrogative sentence.

32.1.1 ### Regular yes or no questions

An interrogative sentence in formal style is formed by attaching **ka** at the end of the sentence (with predicates in polite forms) with a rising intonation. In informal style yes or no questions are usually signaled by utterance-final rising intonation only, without the particle **ka**. By uttering a regular yes or no question, the speaker simply wants to know if what he/she is asking is true or not.

> ビールを飲みますか。 (F)
> **Biiru o nomimasu ka.**

> ビール飲む？ (I)
> **Biiru nomu?**
> Do you drink beer?

Generally **ka** does not directly follow the copula **da** in an independent question, though it can in an embedded question (see **26.3**). Although **ka** can be attached directly to a noun or **na**-adjective, the question would sound very rough.

> あの人（は）日本人か。
> **Ano hito (wa) Nihonjin ka.**
> Is he/she Japanese? (very rough)

32.1.2 ### Yes or no questions with *n(o) desu ka*

When the speaker has some reason/evidence to believe that what he/she is asking might be true, **no desu ka** (or its colloquial form **n desu ka** or **no?**) is attached to the sentence.

> パーティーに行くんですか。 (F)
> **Paatii ni iku n desu ka.**

> パーティーに行くの？ (I)
> **Paatii ni iku no?**
> (Is it the fact that) you are going to the party? / Am I correct in assuming that you are going to the party?

This sentence might be an appropriate question when you observe that the person is all dressed up, and you infer from that that he/she might be going to the party. No such assumption exists in a qestion without **n(o) desu**.

熱があるんですか。
Netsu ga aru n desu ka.
Is it that you have a fever?

While the speaker asks a regular yes or no question **Netsu ga arimasu ka** when he/she does not know whether the hearer has a fever or not, the speaker will say **Netsu ga aru n desu ka** when he/she suspects that the hearer might have a fever (by looking at the hearer's flushed face, etc.).

▶ **18.2.2**

32.1.3 Responding to yes or no questions

32.1.3.1 Affirmative responses

In responding to a yes or no question affirmatively, one can simply say **hai**, **ee**, or **un**, all meaning 'Yes.' One can also repeat a verb or an adjective, but generally other noun phrases are not repeated.

きのうパーティーに行きましたか。(F)	きのうパーティーに行った？(I)
Kinoo paatii ni ikimashita ka.	**Kinoo paatii ni itta?**
Did you go to the party yesterday?	Did you go to the party yesterday?
はい。	うん。
Hai.	**Un.**
はい、行きました。	うん、行った（よ）。
Hai, ikimashita.	**Un, itta (yo).**
Yes, I did.	Yeah, I did.

32.1.3.2 Negative responses

One can respond to a yes or no question negatively by saying **iie**, **ie**, **iya**, **uun**, all meaning 'No.' A possible answer to **Paatii ni ikimashita ka** is:

きのうパーティーに行きましたか。(F)	きのうパーティーに行った？(I)
いいえ。	ううん。
Iie.	**Uun.**
いいえ、行きませんでした。	いや、行かなかった。
Iie, ikimasen deshita.	**Iya, ikanakatta.**
No, I did not go.	No, I didn't.

Sometimes, using an adverb without the verb or adjective is sufficient.

Q: おもしろいですか。
   Omoshiroi desu ka.
   Is it interesting?

A: いいえ、別に。／いいえ、ぜんぜん。
   Iie, betsuni. / Iie, zenzen.
   No, not particularly. / No, not at all.

Adverbs such as **betsuni** or **zenzen** indicate that the negative form follows, so it is not necessary to repeat the predicate.

▶ **14.3; 15.4**

When the question is in the form of N + copula, **Soo desu** 'it is so' is more natural than repeating N + copula.

Q: 日本人ですか。(F)   日本人？(I)
   Nihonjin desu ka.   **Nihonjin?**
   Are you Japanese?   Are you Japanese?

A: はい、そうです。 　　　 うん、そう。
Hai, soo desu. 　　　 **Un, soo.**
Yes, that is right. 　　　 Yeah, that's right.

In answering a **no desu ka** question, it is generally better not to repeat the same words in the question. Simply saying yes or no, using a sentential pronominal word **soo**, or adding further explanation or clarification is appropriate.

Q: 熱があるんですか。
Netsu ga aru n desu ka.
Is it that you have a fever?

A(1): ええ、そうなんです。
Ee, soo na n desu.
Yes, that's right.

A(2): ええ、今朝からちょっと寒気がして...
Ee, kesa kara chotto samuke ga shite ...
Yes, I have been feeling a bit of a chill since this morning ...

32.2 Questions asking for specific content information

Questions seeking 'who,' 'what,' 'where,' 'why,' etc. (WH-questions) are formed by placing interrogative words in appropriate positions in a sentence and adding **ka** at the end of the sentence. In informal style, a rising intonation without **ka** indicates that it is a question. WH-questions, moreover, typically appear in the **n(o) desu** construction.

► 4.3; 18.2.2

だれが来たんですか。(F) 　　　 だれが来たの？(I)
Dare ga kita n desu ka. 　　　 **Dare ga kita no?**
Who came? 　　　 Who came?

何を読んでいるんですか。(F) 　　　 何読んでるの？(I)
Nani o yonde iru n desu ka. 　　　 **Nani yonde ru no?**
What are you reading?

お昼は何にしますか。(F) 　　　 お昼は何にする？(I)
O-hiru wa nan(i) ni shimasu ka. 　　　 **O-hiru wa nan ni suru?**
What will you (or shall we) have for lunch? 　　　 What will you (or shall we) have for lunch?

32.3 Negative questions

32.3.1 Regular negative questions

Negative questions are questions where the main predicate is in the negative form.

田中さんを見ませんでしたか。(F)
Tanaka-san o mimasen deshita ka.

田中さん、見なかった？(I)
Tanaka-san, minakatta?
Didn't you see Mr/Ms Tanaka?

Typically the use of negative questions implies that the speaker thinks or expects the affirmative is the case. In the above sentences, the speaker thinks or expects that the hearer might have seen Tanaka-san. However, when there is strong evidence that the negative action/state holds, negative questions can also imply the speaker's negative assumption as in the following.

この本はおもしろくないですか。
Kono hon wa omoshirokunai desu ka.
Is this book not interesting?

n ja nai desu ka or *n ja arimasen ka*

The phrase **n ja nai desu ka** or **n ja arimasen ka** is a negative counterpart of **n desu ka**.

▶ 15.1

勉強したんじゃないですか。(F)
Benkyoo shita n ja nai desu ka.

勉強したんじゃありませんか。(F)
Benkyoo shita n ja arimasen ka.

勉強したんじゃない？(I)
Benkyoo shita n ja nai.
Isn't it the case that you studied?

勉強しなかったんじゃないですか。(F)
Benkyoo shinakatta n ja nai desu ka.

勉強しなかったんじゃありませんか。(F)
Benkyoo shinakatta n ja arimasen ka.

勉強しなかったんじゃない？(I)
Benkyoo shinakatta n ja nai?
Isn't it the case that you did not study?

These forms (**n ja nai desu ka** or **n ja arimasen ka**) are negative in form but do not add any negative meaning to the sentence. By using these forms, the speaker conveys a strong assumption that what is stated preceding **n ja nai desu ka** or **n ja arimasen ka** is true.

Responding to a negative question

In responding to a negative question in English, the speaker says 'Yes' if the answer one is giving is affirmative, and 'No' if the answer is negative. In Japanese, what is important is the questioner's expectation of what the answer might be. If the questioner is expecting an affirmative answer and the answer is affirmative, **hai** or its variants is used to indicate that the respondent agrees with what the questioner implies or expects. If the questioner expects a negative answer and the answer is negative, again **hai** is used. If the questioner expects an affirmative answer and the answer is negative or vice versa, **iie** 'no' is used indicating that the respondent disagrees with what the questioner expects or assumes.

The speaker expects an affirmative answer.

Q: 田中さんを見ませんでしたか。   田中さん、見なかった？
Tanaka-san o mimasen deshita ka.   **Tanaka-san minakatta?**
Didn't you see Mr/Ms Tanaka?

A: はい、見ました。   うん、見た（よ）。
Hai, mimashita.   **Un, mita (yo).**
Yes, I did.

いいえ、見ませんでした。   ううん、見なかった（よ）。
Iie, mimasen deshita.   **Uun, minakatta (yo).**
No, I didn't.

The speaker expects a negative answer.

Q:	勉強しなかったんじゃないですか。	勉強しなかったんじゃない？
	Benkyoo shinakatta n ja nai desu ka.	**Benkyoo shinakatta n ja nai?**
	Isn't it the case you did not study? (You did not study, right?)	
A:	いいえ、勉強しました（よ）。	ううん、勉強した（よ）。
	Iie, benkyoo shimashita (yo).	**Uun, benkyoo shita (yo).**
	Yes, I did.	
	はい、勉強しませんでした。	うん、勉強しなかった。
	Hai, benkyoo shimasen deshita.	**Un, benkyoo shinakatta.**
	No, I did not.	

32.4 Ways of asking questions less abruptly/more politely

Questions can be prefaced by phrases such as **sumimasen** 'excuse me' or **chotto ukagaitai n desu ga** 'I would like to ask you a question, but. . . .' This makes asking questions less abrupt and consequently more polite.

> すみません、銀行はどこですか。
> **Sumimasen, ginkoo wa doko desu ka.**
> Excuse me, where is the bank?

> ちょっと伺いたいんですが、銀座へはどう行ったらいいんでしょうか。
> **Chotto ukagaitai n desu ga, Ginza e wa doo ittara ii n deshoo ka.**
> I would like to ask you a question, but how can I get to Ginza?

Use of **deshoo** instead of **desu** can also make a question more polite.

> いくらでしょうか。
> **Ikura deshoo ka.**
> How much is it?

▶ 53.2.1

32.5 Other types of questions

32.5.1 'I wonder . . .'

Monologue-type questions such as . . . **ka na** and . . . **kashira** can serve as questions.

> 先生休みかな。
> **Sensee yasumi ka na.**
> I wonder if my teacher is absent.

> 日本語がわかるかしら。
> **Nihongo ga wakaru kashira.**
> I wonder if (he/she) understands Japanese.

Ka na is a more masculine form, while **kashira** is a feminine form. However, these days both men and women use **ka na** in informal speech.

▶ 6.3

32.5.2 *-kke*

This expression is used when the speaker does not remember certain information and tries to recall it by enlisting the addressee's help in recalling the information. It has the sense of 'I seem to remember that . . . , but I am not sure. Can you tell me if it's right?' or 'I don't remember who/what/when, etc. Can you tell me?'. When the predicate is a verb or an **i**-adjective, this form is normally used with the past-tense form.

駅の前に本屋あったっけ。
Eki no mae ni hon'ya atta-kke.
Is there a bookstore in front of the station? I don't remember.

今年のクリスマスは日曜日だっけ。
Kotoshi no kurisumasu wa nichiyoobi da-kke.
Is this year's Christmas on Sunday? I don't remember.

会議は何時からでしたっけ。
Kaigi wa nanji kara deshita-kke.
I don't remember what time the meeting starts. Can you tell me?

去年の冬もこんなに寒かったっけ？
Kyonen no fuyu mo konna ni samukatta-kke?
I don't remember if it was this cold last winter. Was it this cold last winter?

32.5.3 Rhetorical questions

Some question forms are used either as a request or to state one's opinion indirectly.

▶ 72.3; 74.3; 84.1.3

33

Reporting

Direct and indirect quotations

In written Japanese, the direct quotation is generally marked by Japanese quotation marks
(「 」) followed by the particle **to** as in the following sentence.

▶ 26.2

スミスさんは「初めまして」と日本語で言いました。
Sumisu-san wa 'Hajimemashite' to Nihongo de iimashita.
Mr/Ms Smith said, 'How do you do,' in Japanese.

In spoken Japanese, direct and indirect quotations are sometimes difficult to distinguish. However, it is generally the case that if what is quoted has characteristics of an independent utterance, such as polite endings, sentence-final particles, interjections, etc., then it is a direct quote. Indirect quotations generally end in plain forms and do not contain sentence-final particles such as *yo*, *ne*, etc.

田中さんは「月曜日に持ってきます」と言いました。(direct quotation)
Tanaka-san wa 'Getsuyoobi ni motte kimasu' to iimashita.
Mr/Ms Tanaka said, 'I will bring it on Monday.'

田中さんは月曜日に持ってくると言いました。(indirect quotation)
Tanaka-san wa getsuyoobi ni motte kuru to iimashita.
Mr/Ms Tanaka said that he/she will/would bring it on Monday.

田中さんが「フランスのお菓子はおいしいよ」と言いました。(direct quotation)
Tanaka-san ga 'Furansu no okashi wa oishii yo' to iimashita.
Mr/Ms Tanaka said, 'French confectionery is good, I tell you.'

田中さんがフランスのお菓子はおいしいと言いました。(indirect quotation)
Tanaka-san ga Furansu no okashi wa oishii to iimashita.
Mr/Ms Tanaka said that French confectionery is good.

In changing a direct quotation to an indirect quotation, some other adjustments in pronoun and time phrases might have to be made.

田中さんは「私がやります」と言いました。
Tanaka-san wa 'Watashi ga yarimasu' to iimashita.
Mr/Ms Tanaka said, 'I will do it.'

田中さんは自分がやると言いました。
Tanaka-san wa jibun ga yaru to iimashita.
Mr/Ms Tanaka said that he/she will/would do it.

Here the first-person pronoun **watashi** is changed to **jibun** 'self.'

田中さんは「あした宿題を出します」と言いました。
Tanaka-san wa 'Ashita shukudai o dashimasu' to iimashita.
Mr/Ms Tanaka said, 'I will hand in homework tomorrow.'

田中さんは次の日に宿題を出すと言いました。
Tanaka-san wa tsugi no hi ni shukudai o dasu to iimashita.
Mr/Ms Tanaka said that he/she will hand in homework the next day.

Here, a time word has to be changed from 'tomorrow' to 'the next day.'

33.2 Reporting statements

In reporting what others said, the quotation particles such as **to** or its informal variant **tte** are used, followed by verbs of reporting such as **iu** 'to say', **noberu** 'to state', **kaku** 'to write' and the like.

友達が手伝ってくれると言いました。
Tomodachi ga tetsudatte kureru to iimashita.
My friend said that (she) will help me.

友達が手伝ってくれるって言いました。
Tomodachi ga tetsudatte kureru tte iimashita.
My friend said that (she) will help me.

台風で停電になったと新聞に書いてありました。
Taifuu de teeden ni natta to shinbun ni kaite arimashita.
It was written in the newspaper that there was a blackout because of a typhoon.

When the speaker is not quite certain of the exact content of the speech, particles such as **toka** 'something like' or **nante** 'things like' can be used. These particles are sometimes used simply to make one's speech more indirect.

田中さんはアメリカに行くとか言っていました。
Tanaka-san wa Amerika ni iku toka itte imashita.
Mr/Ms Tanaka said something like he/she will go to America.

助詞の間違いが多いなんて言われました。
Joshi no machigai ga ooi nante iwaremashita.
I was told things like I make a lot of mistakes in using particles.

In reporting what someone said, the verbs of saying are often in the **-te iru** form. When these verbs are in simple past tense, the act of saying is focused on rather than the reported fact.

(a) スミスさんは日本に留学すると言っていました。
    Sumisu-san wa Nihon ni ryuugaku suru to itte imashita.
    Mr/Ms Smith said that he/she will go to Japan to study.

(b) スミスさんは日本に留学すると言いました。
    Sumisu-san wa Nihon ni ryuugaku suru to iimashita.
    Mr/Ms Smith said that he/she will go to Japan to study.

Sentence (a) is more appropriate as a hearsay report of what Smith said. Sentence (b) emphasizes Smith's act of actually saying it at a specific time.

In reporting what one has heard or read, other expressions such as [(plain form) **soo da**], **to no koto da/desu** 'I hear that' can be used. Expressions which indicate the source of information include **ni yoru to** 'according to,' **... no hanashi de wa** 'according to what ... says,' **... kara kiita n da kedo** 'I heard it from ...,' or the like.

天気予報によるとあしたは雨だそうです。
Tenkiyohoo ni yoru to ashita wa ame da soo desu.
According to the weather forecast, it is going to rain tomorrow.

新聞の記事によると働く女性が増えているそうだ。
Shinbun no kiji ni yoru to hataraku josee ga fuete iru soo da.
According to the newspaper article, the number of working women is increasing.

ある調査によると国際結婚が増えているとのこと。
Aru choosa ni yoru to kokusai kekkon ga fuete iru to no koto.
According to one survey, international marriage is on the rise.

As the English translations show, in English hearsay, information is not marked with any hearsay marker (except a phrase such as 'according to'). In Japanese, information that one obtains from external sources (i.e. what one has heard, what one has read, etc.) has to be clearly distinguished from the information one knows first-hand, and such information has to be marked by hearsay markers such as (plain form), **soo da** 'I hear.'

33.3 Reporting questions and answers

In reporting questions, embedded questions can be followed by a verb such as **kiku** 'to ask,' **tazuneru** 'to inquire,' **ukagau** (humbling form of **kiku**), or the like. The quotation particle **to** is optional in these cases.

▶ 26.3

友達に宿題があるかどうか（と）聞いたが、友達も知らなかった。
Tomodachi ni shukudai ga aru ka doo ka (to) kiita ga, tomodachi mo shiranakatta.
I asked my friend if we had homework or not, but my friend did not know (the answer) either.

どんな日本食が好きか（と）聞かれて、答えに困った。
Donna Nihonshoku ga suki ka (to) kikarete, kotae ni komatta.
I was asked what kind of Japanese food I like, and I did not know how to answer.

おすしを食べたことがあるかどうか（と）聞かれた。
O-sushi o tabeta koto ga aru ka doo ka (to) kikareta.
I was asked if I had ever eaten sushi.

試験はいつか先生に伺いましょう。
Shiken wa itsu ka sensee ni ukagaimashoo.
Let's ask (our) teacher when the exam is.

Questions and answers can also be reported with appositive clauses **X to yuu** Y, where Y is **shitsumon** 'question,' **kotae** 'answer' or **henji** 'reply.'

日本人にも敬語が難しいかという質問をよくされる。
Nihonjin ni mo keego ga muzukashii ka to yuu shitsumon o yoku sareru.
I often get the question whether Japanese also find honorifics difficult.

暇な時どこに行くかと友達に聞いたら、「猫カフェ」という返事がかえってきた。
Hima na toki doko ni iku ka to tomodachi ni kiitara, 'neko kafe' to yuu henji ga kaette kita.
I asked my friend where she goes when she has free time, and her reply was 'a cat café.'

招待状を出した友達から、出席できないという返事をもらった。
Shootaijoo o dashita tomodachi kara, shusseki dekinai to yuu henji o moratta.
From a friend I sent an invitation to, I received a reply that she cannot attend.

33.4 Reporting commands and requests

33.4.1 As a direct quotation

Commands and requests can be reported by embedding them as a direct quotation of verbs of saying (**iu**), requesting (**tanomu**, **onegai suru**), warning/advising (**chuui suru**), etc.

▶ 26.2; 73; 75

「たばこをやめろ」と言われた。
'Tabako o yamero' to iwareta.
I was told, 'Quit smoking.'

「たばこをやめなさい」と言われた。
'Tabako o yamenasai' to iwareta.
I was told, 'Quit smoking.'

「もう少し静かにしてください」と隣の部屋の人に頼んだ。
'Moo sukoshi shizuka ni shite kudasai' to tonari no heya no hito ni tanonda.
I asked my next door neighbor, 'please be a little quieter.'

「もう少し静かにしてくれませんか」と隣の部屋の人に頼んだ。
'Moo sukoshi shizuka ni shite kuremasen ka' to tonari no heya no hito ni tanonda.
I asked my next door neighbor, 'Won't you please be a little quieter?'

Kudasai is often omitted in a casual request, and so in reporting a request, V-**te** or V-**naide** can be used.

「お金かして」と頼まれた。
'O-kane kashite' to tanomareta.
Someone asked me, 'lend me some money.'

「見ないで」と言った。
'Minaide' to itta.
(I) said, 'Don't look.'

33.4.2 As an indirect quotation

In reporting commands and requests indirectly, plain forms are used (e.g. **ike**, **tabero**, -**te kure**).

もっと野菜を食べろと言われた。
Motto yasai o tabero to iwareta.
I was told to eat more vegetables.

ルームメイトに掃除をしてくれと頼んだ。
Ruumumeeto ni sooji o shite kure to tanonda.
I asked my roommate to clean (the room).

英語で話さないでくれと頼んだ。
Eego de hanasanaide kure to tanonda.
I asked (him/her) not to speak in English.

Another way of reporting commands and requests indirectly is to use **yoo ni**.

子供に早く帰ってくるように言った。
Kodomo ni hayaku kaette kuru yoo ni itta.
I told my child to come back home early.

先生に作文を直してくださるようにお願いした。
Sensee ni sakubun o naoshite kudasaru yoo ni onegai shita.
I asked my teacher to correct my composition.

先生に「あなた」と言わないように注意された。
Sensee ni 'anata' to iwanai yoo ni chuui sareta.
I was advised by my teacher not to say '**anata** you.'

34

Asking and giving personal information

In this chapter, we will talk about different ways of asking and giving personal information. It should be noted that, in asking about others' personal information, the honorific prefix **o** or **go** is used.

▶ 29

34.1 | Name

In Japan, people generally use their last (family) names. First (given) names are usually reserved for very close friends and family members. In giving your name, you can use the family name followed by the given name.

▶ 30.3

> 田中 (昭) です。
> **Tanaka (Akira) desu.**
> I am (Akira) Tanaka.

> 田中 (昭) と言います。
> **Tanaka (Akira) to iimasu.**
> I am (Akira) Tanaka.

> 田中 (昭) と申します。(VF)
> **Tanaka (Akira) to mooshimasu.**
> I am (Akira) Tanaka.

Mooshimasu is the humble form of **iimasu**, and hence **Tanaka (Akira) to mooshimasu** is the most polite way of giving your name among these three choices. In asking another person's name, the following expressions can be used.

> 失礼ですが、お名前は？ (F)
> **Shitsuree desu ga, o-namae wa?**
> Excuse me, but your name?

> どちら様でしょうか。(VF)
> **Dochira-sama deshoo ka.**
> Your name, please?

> お名前を伺ってもよろしいでしょうか。(VF)
> **O-namae o ukagatte mo yoroshii deshoo ka.**
> May I ask your name?

> 名前なんだっけ？ (I)
> **Namae nan da kke?**
> What's your name (I don't seem to remember)?

34.2 Place of origin

To give one's place of origin or ask someone else's, the noun **shusshin** 'place of origin' can be used.

京都（の）出身です。
Kyooto (no) shusshin desu.
I am from Kyoto.

出身は京都です。
Shusshin wa Kyooto desu.
I am from Kyoto.

ご出身はどちらですか。
Go-shusshin wa dochira desu ka.
Where are you from?

If you are talking about the country, however, **kuni** 'country' should be used.

お国はどちらですか。
O-kuni wa dochira desu ka.
What is your country?

国はアメリカです。
Kuni wa Amerika desu.
(My) country is America.

The expression 'come from' can also be used.

私は京都から来ました。
Watashi wa Kyooto kara kimashita.
I come from Kyoto.

34.3 Age or year at school

You can ask someone's age and give your own using either Japanese or Chinese numbers. Chinese numbers are followed by **-sai** 'age.' In telling age, **-sai** is generally used. Twenty years old, moreover, can be either **nijussai** or **hatachi**.

▶ 16

何歳ですか。
Nansai desu ka.
How old are you?

おいくつですか。
O-ikutsu desu ka.
How old are you?

息子は五歳です。
Musuko wa gosai desu.
My son is five years old.

34.4 Occupation or schooling level, and the area of specialization

34.4.1 Occupation

Words for occupation are **shigoto** 'work' or **shokugyoo** 'occupation.' The most common ways to ask someone's occupation include:

どんなお仕事ですか。(F)
Donna o-shigoto desu ka.
What kind of job (do you have)?

お仕事は何をしていらっしゃるんですか。(F)
O-shigoto wa nani o shite irassharu n desu ka.
What kind of work do you do?

ご職業は？ (F)
Go-shokugyoo wa?
Your occupation?

どんな仕事してるの？ (I)
Donna shigoto shite ru no?
What kind of work do you do?

To give your occupation, you can simply say 'occupation + **desu**' or 'occupation **o shite imasu.**' The noun **kankee no shigoto** 'work related to' can also be used.

弁護士です。
Bengoshi desu.
I am a lawyer.

教師をしています。
Kyooshi o shite imasu.
I am a teacher.

IT関係の仕事をしています。
IT kankee no shigoto o shite imasu.
I am in an IT-related job.

▶ 19.2.1

34.4.2 **Schooling level**

To give one's schooling level or ask someone else's, use **-nensee**. There are no special words like freshman, etc., so regular numbers **ichi**, **ni**, **san**, and **yo** are used. A college senior is **yonensee**.

（大学）何年生ですか。
(Daigaku) nannensee desu ka.
Which year of college are you?

二年生です。
Ninensee desu.
I am a sophomore.

高校三年生です。
Kookoo sannensee desu.
I am a senior in high school.

34.4.3 **Area of specialization**

The word for specialization is **senmon**. For a major in school, **senkoo** can also be used. To refer to someone else's specialization in a formal situation, the polite prefix **go-** is attached. For asking and stating a major, the verb **senkoo suru** can also be used.

ご専門は何ですか。
Go-senmon wa nan desu ka.
What is your area of specialization?

専門は外科です。
Senmon wa geka desu.
My specialty is surgery.

専攻は工学です。
Senkoo wa koogaku desu.
My major is engineering.

工学を専攻しています。
Koogaku o senkoo shite imasu.
I am majoring in engineering.

34.5 Marital status

To state your marital status, words like **kekkon shite iru** 'be married' or **dokushin** 'be single' are used.

結婚しています。
Kekkon shite imasu.
I am married.

独身です。
Dokushin desu.
I am single.

一人です。
Hitori desu.
I am single.

It is generally not polite to inquire about someone else's marital status, but if you must, you can ask by saying **Kekkon shite irasshaimasu ka** or **Dokushin desu ka** or **O-hitori desu ka**. To refer to a person who is married or single, words such as **kikon** 'married,' or **mikon** 'unmarried' can be used.

未婚の男性	**mikon no dansee**	unmarried male
既婚者	**kikonsha**	married person

34.6 Pastimes

To ask or say what one does during one's free time, the following expressions can be used.

暇な時には何をしますか。
Hima na toki ni wa nani o shimasu ka.
What do you do in your free time?

暇な時にはテニスをします。
Hima na toki ni wa tenisu o shimasu.
I play tennis when I have free time.

趣味は何ですか。
Shumi wa nan desu ka.
What is your hobby?

趣味は読書です。
Shumi wa dokusho desu.
My hobby is reading.

趣味は音楽を聞くことです。
Shumi wa ongaku o kiku koto desu.
My hobby is listening to music.

In the **shumi wa X desu** structure, X is a nominal. Hence, a verbal phrase has to be nominalized by **koto**, as in **kiku koto**.

► 18.1

34.7 Family

The word for one's family is **kazoku** and someone else's family is **go-kazoku**. To ask about someone's family, you can say,

何人家族ですか。
Nannin kazoku desu ka.
How many are in your family?

お子さんがいらっしゃいますか。
O-kosan ga irasshaimasu ka,
Do you have children?

Answers might be:

五人家族です。
Gonin kazoku desu.
There are five of us in my family.

二人子供がいます。
Futari kodomo ga imasu.
I have two children.

In Japanese, one has to distinguish between talking about one's own family and someone else's family. The following are some representative terms for each category.

	Own family	*Other's family*
Mother	母 **haha**	お母さん **okaasan**
Father	父 **chichi**	お父さん **otoosan**
Wife	妻 **tsuma** (or 家内 **kanai**)	奥さん **okusan**
Husband	夫 **otto** (or 主人 **shujin**)	ご主人 **go-shujin**
Daughter	娘 **musume**	お嬢さん **ojoosan** (or 娘さん **musumesan**)
Son	息子 **musuko**	息子さん **musukosan** (or 坊ちゃん **botchan**)
Older brother	兄 **ani**	お兄さん **oniisan**
Younger brother	弟 **otooto**	弟さん **otootosan**
Older sister	姉 **ane**	お姉さん **oneesan**
Younger sister	妹 **imooto**	妹さん **imootosan**
Grandmother	祖母 **sobo**	おばあさん **obaasan**
Grandfather	祖父 **sofu**	おじいさん **ojiisan**
Aunt	おば **oba**	おばさん **obasan**
Uncle	おじ **oji**	おじさん **ojisan**
Parents	両親 **ryooshin**	ご両親 **go-ryooshin**

35

Identifying

Identifying oneself and others

In identifying oneself and others the copula **desu** [polite], **iimasu** 'say, call,' and **mooshimasu** 'say [humble]' are used in Japanese. **Desu** is used in place of English 'am, is, are.'

> （私は）山本です。
> **(Watashi wa) Yamamoto desu.** (F)
> I am Yamamoto.

> （私は）山本と言います。
> **(Watashi wa) Yamamoto to iimasu.** (F)
> I am Yamamoto.

> （私は）山本と申します。
> **(Watashi wa) Yamamoto to mooshimasu.** (VF/humble)
> I am Yamamoto.

When indentifying oneself, **watashi** 'I' is often omitted in natural conversations.

In identifying others by referring to them with 'this person', 'that person' and 'that person over there', **kochira**, **sochira** and **achira** are used, respectively. These are polite forms of the demonstratives, **kore**, **sore** and **are**, which are not used to refer to people. **De irasshaimasu**, which is a very polite version of **desu**, can be used to identify someone socially respected.

> こちらは山本さんです。
> **Kochira wa Yamamoto-san desu.**
> This is Mr Yamamoto.

> そちらは山本さんです。
> **Sochira wa Yamamoto-san desu.**
> That person is Mr Yamamoto.

> あちらは山本社長でいらっしゃいます。
> **Achira wa Yamamoto-shachoo de irasshaimasu.**
> That person over there is Mr Yamamoto, the president of the company.

These terms, such as **kochira**, are not appropriate for identifying one's family members. In such cases, simply saying something like **musume desu** 'This is my daughter' is sufficient.

To ask who someone is, use **dare** 'who.'

> あの人はだれですか。
> **Ano hito wa dare desu ka.**
> Who is that person?

In a business situation, if you call a business office, the receptionist might ask who you are by saying,

> どちら様ですか。
> **Dochira-sama desu ka.**
> May I ask who you are? (VF)

35.2 Identifying places

To identify a place, the demonstratives **kore**, **sore**, and **are** are used together with the copula **da/desu**.

領事館はどの建物ですか。
Ryoojikan wa dono tatemono desu ka.
Which one is the Consulate building?

（領事館は）あれです。
(Ryoojikan wa) are desu.
(The consulate) is that one over there.

Sometimes, locative demonstratives **koko**, **soko** and **asoko** can also be used. In showing one's art studio, for example, one can say either **kore** or **koko**.

これが私のアトリエです。
Kore ga watashi no atorie desu.
<u>This</u> is my studio.

ここが私のアトリエです。
Koko ga watashi no atorie desu.
<u>This place</u> is my studio.

35.3 Identifying things

When indentifying things, the demonstratives **kore** 'this thing,' **sore** 'that thing,' **are** 'that thing over there,' and **dore** 'which one' are commonly used.

これは田中さんの傘です。
Kore wa Tanaka-san no kasa desu.
This is Mr/Ms Tanaka's umbrella.

それは中国語の辞書です。
Sore wa Chuugokugo no jisho desu.
That is a Chinese dictionary.

あれは山田さんの車です。
Are wa Yamada-san no kuruma desu.
That thing over there is Mr/Ms Yamada's car.

佐藤さんの辞書はどれですか。
Satoo-san no jisho wa dore desu ka.
Which one is Mr/Ms Sato's dictionary?

36

Telling the time, dates, etc.

Here are counters which are used to tell or ask the time:

Time/duration

Hours: 時間	**jikan**
Minutes: 分	**fun**
Seconds: 秒	**byoo**
Frequency: 回/度	**kai/do**

36.1 Telling and asking the time

The question word for asking the time is 何時 **nan-ji** 'what time'.

今何時ですか。(F)
Ima nanji desu ka.
What time is it now?

今何時？(I)
Ima nanji?
What time is it now?

明日の会議は何時ですか。(F)
Ashita no kaigi wa nanji desu ka.
What time is tomorrow's meeting?

If you want to ask more specifically 'how many minutes,' then you may ask:

今9時何分ですか。(F)
Ima kuji nanpun desu ka.
How many minutes past nine is it now?

今9時何分？(I)
Ima kuji nanpun?
How many minutes past nine is it now?

The current time is expressed by the combination of time and the copula **desu**. The copula **desu** is used when telling the time in formal situations, while it is omitted in informal situations.

今4時50分です。(F)
Ima yoji gojuppun desu.
It is 4.50 now.

今4時50分。(I)
Ima yoji gojuppun.
It is 4.50 now.

今6時10分前です。(F)
Ima, rokuji juppun mae desu.
It is ten to six.

今6時10分前。(I)
Ima, rokuji juppun mae.
It is ten to six.

今6時10分すぎです。(F)
Ima rokuji juppun sugi desu.
It is ten minutes past six.

今6時10分すぎ。(I)
Ima rokuji juppun sugi.
It is ten minutes past six.

36.2 Telling and asking dates

The question words for asking dates are **itsu** 'when' or **nan-gatsu** 'what month,' **nan-nichi** 'what day of the month,' **nan-yoobi** 'what day of the week.' The following are useful temporal expressions.

Months
For the months, **-gatsu** follows the numbers from **ichi** up to **juuni**.

ichi-gatsu 'January,' **ni-gatsu** 'February,' **san-gatsu** 'March,' **shi-gatsu** 'April,' **go-gatsu** 'May,' **roku-gatsu** 'June,' **shichi-gatsu** 'July,' **hachi-gatsu** 'August,' **ku-gatsu** 'September,' **juu-gatsu** 'October,' **juuichi-gatsu** 'November,' and **juuni-gatsu** 'December'.

Note that **ichigatsu** and **ikkagetsu** are different in that the former refers to the month of January whereas the latter indicates duration of 'one month'.

Date of the month

1st	一日	**tsuitachi**
2nd	二日	**futsuka**
3rd	三日	**mikka**
4th	四日	**yokka**
5th	五日	**itsuka**
6th	六日	**muika**
7th	七日	**nanoka**
8th	八日	**yooka**
9th	九日	**kokonoka**
10th	十日	**tooka**
What day	何日	**nannichi**

Beyond 10th: add the number and **nichi**

11th (**juuichi-nichi**)

12th (**juuni-nichi**)

*Exceptional cases are: 14th (**juuyokka**), 20th (**hatsuka**) and 24th (**nijuuyokka**).

Duration of days
For duration of days, except for one day **ichinichi**, the forms for the dates of the month can be used. For the duration of more than one day, **-kan** 'duration' may follow.

1 day	一日	**ichinichi**
2 days	二日	**futsuka(kan)**
3 days	三日	**mikka(kan)**
4 days	四日	**yokka(kan)**
5 days	五日	**itsuka(kan)**
6 days	六日	**muika(kan)**
7 days	七日	**nanoka(kan)**
8 days	八日	**yooka(kan)**
9 days	九日	**kokonoka(kan)**
10 days	十日	**tooka(kan)**
How many days	何日	**nannichi (kan)**

Years

There are two ways of counting years. For the western way of counting years, add **nen** to numbers. For example 1965 is **sen-kyuuhyaku-rokujuu-go-nen**. The traditional system of counting years, which is based on the reigns of emperors, is also commonly used. The current era is **Heesee** (平成), and the year 2012, for example, is **Heesee 24-nen**. The names for eras since 1868 are: **Meeji** (1868–1912), **Taishoo** (1912–late 1926), **Shoowa** (late 1926–early 1989), **Heesee** (1989–).

Duration of years

For duration of years add **nen(kan)** to numbers. For example, ten years is **juu-nen (kan)**. 'How many years' is **nan-nen-(kan)**.

(1) A: 田中さんの誕生日はいつ？ or 田中さんの誕生日は何月何日？ (I)
Tanaka-san no tanjoobi wa itsu or **Tanaka san no tanjoobi wa nan-gatsu nan-nichi?**
When is Mr/Ms Tanaka's birthday?

B: （田中さんの誕生日は）６月３日（だよ）。(I)
(Tanaka san no tanjoobi wa) rokugatsu mikka (da yo).
It is June 3rd.

A: ６月３日は何曜日？ (I)
Rokugatsu mikka wa nan-yoobi?
What day (of the week) is June 3rd?

A: 水曜日。

(2) A: 日本はもうお長いですか。(F)
Nihon wa moo o-nagai desu ka.
Have you been (lived) in Japan for a long time?

B: 私が日本に来たのは１９８０年ですから、もう三十年以上になります。(F)
Watashi ga Nihon ni kita no wa 1980 nen desu kara, moo sanjuunen ijoo ni narimasu.
I came to Japan in 1980, so it has been more than 30 years.

36.3 Telling and asking when something will happen or happened

The question word for 'when' is **itsu**. **Itsu** can be used in reference to day, week, month or year. **Arimasu** 'to be (there), to take place' or **desu** are often used to mean 'something takes place.' **Arimasu** is only used to mean that some event (such as a concert, a party, etc.) takes place. So, it is not possible to say *__tanjoobi wa itsu arimasu ka__ 'when does your birthday take place?'.

A: コンサートはいつありますか。   コンサートはいつですか。
    Konsaato wa itsu arimasu ka.   **Konsaato wa itsu desu ka.**
    When does the concert take place?   When is the concert?

In responding to these questions, either **arimasu** 'to take place' or **desu** can be used.

B1:   土曜日にあります。
    Doyoobi ni arimasu.
    It takes place on Saturday.

B2:   土曜日です。
    Doyoobi desu.
    It's Saturday.

Other verbs such as **okiru** 'to happen, occur' and **okoru** 'to happen', can also be used to mean 'some historical event, natural phenomenon (e.g. typhoon, earthquake, etc.), or something beyond one's control will occur or has occurred.

昨日東北地方で地震が起きました。
Kinoo Toohoku-chihoo de jishin ga okimashita.
There was an earthquake in the Tohoku region yesterday.

A: 明治維新はいつ起きたんですか。
    Meeji-Ishin wa itsu okita n desu ka?
    When did the Meiji Restoration occur?

B1:   1868年に起きました。
    1868 nen ni okimashita.
    It happened in 1868.

B2:   1868年です。
    1868 nen desu.
    It's 1868.

何だか今日はいいことが起きそうな気がする。
Nan da ka kyoo wa ii koto ga okisoo na ki ga suru.
Somehow I feel something good will happen today.

将来またこのような大規模な噴火が起こるかもしれません。
Shoorai mata kono yoona daikibo na funka ga okoru kamo shiremasen.
A large scale eruption like this may happen again in the future.

Both **okoru** 'to happen' and **okiru** 'to get up, arise' can be used in the context where some natural disaster occurs or something out of control happens. However, **okiru** may not replace **okoru** in compound verbs such as **maki-okoru** 'to break out', **waki-okoru** 'to arise'.

In written texts such as newspaper articles or formal contexts such as TV news programs, the Chinese compound **hassee suru** is often used to refer to the occurrence of natural disasters, accidents, or diseases.

この辺では夏になるとよく山火事が発生する。
Kono hen de wa natsu ni naru to yoku yamakaji ga hassee suru.
Forest fires often happen around here in the summer.

36.4 Telling and asking how long something takes

To say how long something takes, the verb **kakaru/kakarimasu** 'to take' or the copula verb **da/desu** is used. In asking how long, the question expression **dono gurai** is used. **Gurai**, or **kurai**, means 'about' and is used to express an approximate number, size, length of time, etc.

Q: ここから駅までどのぐらいかかりますか。
Koko kara eki made dono gurai kakarimasu ka.
How long does it take from here to the station?

Q: ここから駅までどのぐらいですか。
Koko kara eki made dono gurai desu ka.
How long does it take from here to the station?

A: 車で１５分ぐらいかかります。
Kuruma de juugofun gurai kakarimasu.
It takes about 15 minutes by car.

A: 車で１５分くらいです。
Kuruma de juugofun kurai desu.
It's about 15 minutes by car.

Q: 映画はどのぐらいですか。
Eega wa dono gurai desu ka.
How long is the movie?

A: １時間半ぐらいです。
Ichijikan han kurai desu.
It is about an hour and a half.

Q: このプロジェクトはどのくらいかかりますか。
Kono purojekuto wa dono kurai kakarimasu ka.
How long does this project take to complete it?

A: だいたい、１ヶ月くらいでしょう。
Daitai ikkagetsu kurai deshoo.
It will probably be about one month.

37

Describing people, places, states and conditions

37.1 ## Describing people

When describing people (e.g. physical features), X **wa** Y **ga** adjective 'Speaking of X, his Y is . . .' is commonly used. When describing what someone is wearing, verbs of wearing, such as **kiru, haku, kaburu**, are used in **-te iru/imasu** form.

▶ **12.8**

田中さんは目が大きいです。
Tanaka-san wa me ga ookii desu.
Speaking of Mr/Ms Tanaka, he/she has big eyes.

姉は髪が長いです。
Ane wa kami ga nagai desu.
Speaking of my big sister, she has long hair.

山田さんは性格がとてもいいですね。
Yamada-san wa seekaku ga totemo ii desu ne.
Speaking of Mr/Ms Yamada, he/she has a good personality, doesn't he/she?

吉田さんは赤いセーターを着ています。
Yoshida-san wa akai seetaa o kite imasu.
Speaking of Mr/Ms Yoshida, he/she is wearing a red sweater.

佐藤さんはサングラスをかけている人です。
Satoo-san wa sangurasu o kakete iru hito desu.
Mr/Ms Sato is the person who is wearing sunglasses.

37.2 ## Describing places

You can describe a place with an adjective, such as **ookii** 'big,' **kiree na tokoro** 'beautiful place,' or the like. To be more specific, however, the structure X (topic) **wa** Y (subject) **ga** adj. can be used.

A: オーストラリアはどんな所ですか。
   Oosutoraria wa donna tokoro desu ka.
   What kind of place is Australia?

B: オーストラリアは海がきれいです。
   Oosutoraria wa umi ga kiree desu.
   The sea is beautiful there (in Australia).

それから、シドニーオペラハウスが有名です。
Sorekara, Shidonii no Opera Hausu ga yuumee desu.
Also, the Sydney Opera House is famous.

東京は人口が多いです。
Tookyoo wa jinkoo ga ooi desu.
Tokyo has a large population (Lit. The population of Tokyo is large).

あのレストランはパスタがおいしいですよ。
Ano resutoran wa pasuta ga oishii desu yo.
They serve very delicious pasta at that restaurant (Lit. Pasta is delicious at that restaurant).

37.3 Describing the weather

Dictionary form			*-te imasu*		
曇る	**kumoru**	'become cloudy'	曇っている	**kumotte iru**	'be cloudy'
降る	**furu**	'rain/snow'	降っている	**futte iru**	'raining/snowing'
晴れる	**hareru**	'become sunny'	晴れている	**harete iru**	'be sunny'
吹く	**fuku**	'blow'	吹いている	**fuite iru**	'blowing'

東京は今雨が降っています。
Tookyoo wa ima ame ga futte imasu.
It is raining in Tokyo.

北海道は雪が降っています。
Hokkaidoo wa yuki ga futte imasu.
It is snowing in Hokkaido.

今ちょっと曇っています。
Ima chotto kumotte imasu.
It is a little cloudy now.

ニューヨークは今晴れています。
Nyuu Yooku wa ima harete imasu.
It is sunny now in New York.

今風が吹いています。
Ima kaze ga fuite imasu.
It is windy now.

The weather can be described by the use of various adjectives.

今日はちょっと寒いです。
Kyoo wa chotto samui desu.
It is a little cold.

今日は春らしく、暖かいですね。
Kyoo wa haru rashiku, atatakai desu ne.
It is warm today like a spring day, isn't it.

今日は随分暑いですね。
Kyoo wa zuibun atsui desu ne.
It is very hot today, isn't it.

８月にしては涼しいですね。
Hachigatsu ni shite wa suzushii desu ne.
It is cool for August, isn't it.

37.4 Describing the color, size, weight and condition of things

Here are various adjectives describing the color, size, and condition of things. Some colors may be described by a noun phrase (a color term followed by the particle **no**).

Color

-i adjective
赤い **akai** 'red'   青い **aoi** 'blue'   黒い **kuroi** 'black'
黄色い **kiiroi** 'yellow'   茶色い **chairoi** 'brown'   白い **shiroi** 'white'

Noun phrase
緑の **midori no** 'green'   オレンジの **orenji no** 'orange'
紫の **murasaki no** 'purple'   グレーの **guree no** 'gray'

Size and weight
大きい **ookii** 'big'   小さい **chiisai** 'small'
重い **omoi** 'heavy'   軽い **karui** 'light'

Condition
よい/いい **yoi/ii** 'good'   悪い **warui** 'bad'
まあまあ **maamaa** 'so-so'

Here are some examples.

> 私の家はあの白いのです。
> **Watashi no uchi wa ano shiroi no desu.**
> My house is that white one.

Multiple adjectives can be combined with **te**-form to describe the color, size, and condition of things.

> これ、小さくてかわいい鞄ですね。
> **Kore, chiisakute kawaii kaban desu ne.**
> This is a small and cute bag, isn't it.

> 私のラップトップは軽くて便利です。
> **Watashi no rapputoppu wa karukute benri desu.**
> My laptop is light and handy.

> 私のラップトップは重くて不便です。
> **Watashi no rapputoppu wa omokute fuben desu.**
> My laptop is heavy and inconvenient.

37.5 Describing actions and events in progress

In describing actions and events in progress, **-te iru** forms of action verbs are used.

▶ 19.2.1

> ヘンリーは今勉強しています。
> **Henrii wa ima benkyoo shite imasu.**
> Henry is studying now.

> 母は今夕ご飯を食べています。
> **Haha wa ima yuugohan o tabete imasu.**
> My mother is eating dinner now.

まだセールが続いています。
Mada seeru ga tsuzuite imasu.
The sale is still continuing.

留学生の数が増えています。
Ryuugakusee no kazu ga fuete imasu.
The number of study-abroad students is increasing.

Expressions such as **saichuu** 'in the middle of' can be added to emphasize that the event is in progress.

今書いている最中です。
Ima kaite iru saichuu desu.
I am in the middle of writing (it).

37.6 Describing a state or condition

In describing a state or condition, **-te iru** forms of intransitive verbs are often used.

この花、枯れていますよ。
Kono hana, karete imasu yo.
This flower is withered.

水がこぼれていますよ。
Mizu ga koborete imasu yo.
Water is spilt.

The following are some examples of intransitive verbs which can be used to state the condition of an item.

Dictionary form		*Meaning*	*-te iru forms*	
枯れる	**kareru**	wither, become withered	枯れている	**karete iru** be withered
腐る	**kusaru**	rot, become rotten	腐っている	**kusatte iru** be rotten
こぼれる	**koboreru**	spill, get spilled	こぼれている	**koborete iru** be spilled
壊れる	**kowareru**	(something) breaks	壊れている	**kowarete iru** be broken
消える	**kieru**	go off/out	消えている	**kiete iru** be turned off
つく	**tsuku**	come/turn on	付いている	**tsuite iru** be turned on
汚れる	**yogoreru**	get dirty	汚れている	**yogorete iru** be dirty
欠ける	**kakeru**	chip, get chipped	欠けている	**kakete iru** be chipped
割れる	**wareru**	(something) breaks	割れている	**warete iru** be broken
折れる	**oreru**	(something) breaks	折れている	**orete iru** be broken
開く	**aku**	(something) opens	開いている	**aite iru** be open
閉まる	**shimaru**	(something) closes	閉まっている	**shimatte iru** be closed

Additional examples follow.

そのいす、壊れているから気をつけて。(I)
Sono isu, kowarete iru kara ki o tsukete.
That chair is broken, so watch out.

この机、ちょっと曲がって（い）るね。(I)
Kono tsukue, chotto magatte (i)ru ne.
This desk is a bit bent.

そのシャツ、汚れているから洗ってくれない？(I)
Sono shatsu, yogorete iru kara, aratte kurenai?
That shirt is dirty. Can you wash it for me?

あ、人形の腕、折れてる。(I)
A, ningyoo no ude, orete ru.
Ah, one of this doll's arms is broken.

この茶碗、かけて（い）るよ。(I)
Kono chawan, kakete (i)ru yo.
This cup is chipped.

37.7 Describing habitual and future actions and events

Habitual actions and events are described by the expression V-**te iru/imasu** or V-**ru/u/masu**.

Habitual

私は毎日自転車で学校に通っています。
Watashi wa mainichi jitensha de gakkoo ni kayotte imasu.
I commute to school by bicycle every day.

私は健康のために毎朝ビタミンを飲んでいます。
Watashi wa kenkoo no tame ni maiasa bitamin o nonde imasu.
I take vitamins every morning for my health.

私は英語の勉強のために毎朝英語の新聞を読みます。
Watashi wa Eego no benkyoo no tame ni maiasa Eego no shinbun o yomimasu.
I read English newspapers every morning for my English studies.

Future

In describing future actions or events, -**ru/-u/-masu** forms are used. The habitual form and future form can be distinguished by temporal adverbial phrases.

今日の6時頃電話します。   (action)
Kyoo no rokuji goro denwa shimasu.
I will give (you) a call at six o'clock today.

今晩8時から祭りが始まります。   (event)
Konban hachiji kara matsuri ga hajimarimasu.
The festival begins at eight o'clock tonight.

37.8 Describing past actions and events

V-**mashita** (formal) or V-**ta** (informal) is used to describe past actions and events.

昨日田中さんと映画を見に行きました。   (action)
Kinoo Tanaka-san to eega o mi ni ikimashita.
I went to see a movie with Mr/Ms Tanaka yesterday.

コンサートは水曜日にあった。   (event)
Konsaato wa suiyoobi ni atta.
The concert took place on Wednesday.

37.9 ▶ Describing the quantity of things

In describing the quantity of things, the following words can be used.

多い	**ooi**	many, much
少ない	**sukunai**	little, few
たくさん	**takusan**	many
すこし	**sukoshi**	a few

寮に入るより通学する学生の方が多い。
Ryoo ni hairu yori tsuugaku suru gakusee no hoo ga ooi.
There are more students who commute than those who live in dormitories.

今の仕事はやりがいがあるが、給料は少ない。
Ima no shigoto wa yarigai ga aru ga, kyuuryoo wa sukunai.
The present job is rewarding, but the salary is not much.

▶ 13.4

この果物は栄養がたくさんある。
Kono kudamono wa eeyoo ga takusan aru.
This fruit is full of nutrition.

この仕事から期待される利益はほんの少しです。
Kono shigoto kara kitai sareru rieki wa hon no sukoshi desu.
The expected profit from this work is just a little.

37.10 ▶ Describing what something is made out of

Dekite imasu or **tsukurarete imasu** is used to describe what something is made (out) of/from. The particle **kara** is used when the material used is transformed in the process of making something; **de** is chosen when the material does not change during the process.

この机はさくらの木でできています。
Kono tsukue wa sakura no ki de dekite imasu.
This desk is made out of cherry wood.

このカードは和紙で作られています。
Kono kaado wa washi de tsukurarete imasu.
This card is made out of Japanese paper.

豆腐は大豆からできています。
Toofu wa daizu kara dekite imasu.
Tofu is made from soy beans.

37.11 ▶ Describing the current state of something as a result of a past action

V-te imasu is used to describe the current state of something as a result of a past action. Verbs in this category, such as **kekkon suru** 'to get married,' **iku** 'to go,' **shinu** 'to die,' etc., indicate actions which are viewed as occurring instantaneously. In other words, for these actions, one cannot specify a beginning point and an end point.

妹は１０年結婚しています。
Imooto wa juunen kekkon shite imasu.
My younger sister has been married for ten years.

先週から京都に来ています。
Senshuu kara Kyooto ni kite imasu.
I have been in Kyoto since last week.

窓があいていますよ。
Mado ga aite imasu yo.
The window is open.

▶ **19.2.1**

Verbs such as **sumu** 'to live' and **motsu** 'to possess' should also be used in the **-te iru** form to express current state.

去年からニューヨークに住んでいます。
Kyonen kara Nyuu Yooku ni sunde imasu.
She has been living in New York since last year.

最近はみんな携帯電話を持っています。
Saikin wa minna keetai denwa o motte imasu.
These days everyone has cell phones.

38

Comparisons

Comparisons of inequality

Comparisons of inequality, as in 'more expensive than' or 'not as expensive as' are expressed in Japanese with phrases such as **motto** 'more,' X **yori** Y **no hoo ga** 'Y is more . . . than X,' or X **hodo . . . nai** 'not as . . . as X.'

> A: 駅までバスで行こうと思っているんですが . . .
> **Eki made basu de ikoo to omotte iru n desu ga . . .**
> I am thinking of going to the station by bus, but . . . (what do you think?)

> B: 地下鉄の方がバスより便利ですよ。
> **Chikatetsu no hoo ga basu yori benri desu yo.**
> Subway is more convenient than bus.

> A: レストラン藤はおいしいですか。
> **Resutoran Fuji wa oishii desu ka.**
> Is Restaurant Fuji good?

> B: ええ、でもレストラン菊はもっとおいしいですよ。
> **Ee, demo Resutoran Kiku wa motto oishii desu yo.**
> Yes, but Restaurant Kiku is better.

> A: レストラン藤も高いですか。
> **Resutoran Fuji mo takai desu ka.**
> Is Restaurant Fuji expensive too?

> B: いいえ、レストラン藤はこのレストランほど高くありませんよ。
> **Iie, Resutoran Fuji wa kono resutoran hodo takaku arimasen yo.**
> No, Restaurant Fuji is not as expensive as this restaurant.

To ask the addressee to compare two objects, **dochira** (or its colloquial form **dotchi**) is used. If more than three items are compared, **dore** is used.

▶ See **38.3**.

> A: うどんとそばとどちらの方がお好きですか。
> **Udon to soba to dochira no hoo ga o-suki desu ka.**
> Which one would you prefer, udon or soba?

> B: そばの方が（うどんより）好きです。
> **Soba no hoo ga (udon yori) suki desu.**
> I like soba more (than udon).

> A: この四つのレストランの中でどれが一番有名ですか。
> **Kono yottsu no resutoran no naka de dore ga ichiban yuumee desu ka.**
> Which is the most famous among these four restaurants?

B: このイタリアレストランが一番有名です。
Kono Itaria resutoran ga ichiban yuumee desu.
This Italian restaurant is the most famous.

A: 兄弟の中で誰が一番よく食べますか。
Kyoodai no naka de dare ga ichiban yoku tabemasu ka.
Who eats the most among your siblings?

B: 一番下の弟が一番よく食べます。
Ichiban shita no otooto ga ichiban yoku tabemasu.
My youngest brother eats the most.

38.2 Comparisons of equality

Comparisons of equality can be made using the phrase **to onaji kurai** or **gurai** 'the same extent, as . . . as,' or X **wa** Y **to onaji da** 'X is the same as Y.'

東京の物価はニューヨークの物価と同じくらい高い。
Tookyoo no bukka wa Nyuu Yooku no bukka to onaji kurai takai.
The prices in Tokyo are as expensive as in New York.

弟は父と同じくらい背が高いです。
Otooto wa chichi to onaji kurai se ga takai desu.
My younger brother is as tall as my father.

女性の給料は男性の給料と同じですか。
Josee no kyuuryoo wa dansee no kyuuryoo to onaji desu ka.
Are women's salaries the same as men's?

38.3 Comparisons of three or more things

To compare three or more things the expression **x ga ichiban** or **mottomo** is used. Both **ichiban** and **mottomo** mean 'the best' or 'the most' in English. However, **mottomo** is a formal expression and tends to be used in a written context.

すしとてんぷらとさしみの中で、てんぷらが一番好きです。
Sushi to tenpura to sashimi no naka de tenpura ga ichiban suki desu.
Among sushi, tempura, and sashimi, I like tempura the most.

兄弟の中で、兄が一番背が高いです。
Kyoodai no naka de, ani ga ichiban se ga takai desu.
My elder brother is the tallest among the siblings.

日本の山の中で富士山が一番有名です。
Nihon no yama no naka de Fujisan ga ichiban yuumee desu.
Among the mountains in Japan Mt. Fuji is the most famous.

日本三景というのは日本で最も美しいと言われている所です。
Nihon-sankee to yuu no wa Nihon de mottomo utsukushii to iwarete iru tokoro desu.
'Nihon-sankee' refers to three places which are said to be the most beautiful (scenic) places in Japan.

39

Contrast

This chapter covers various words and phrases that are used to express contrast.

39.1 Expressing contrast with conjunctive particles

The conjunctive particle **keredo(mo)** 'but, though' and its more colloquial form **kedo** are most commonly used. Either is placed at the end of the first clause, followed by the second clause. The form of the predicate preceding **keredo(mo)/kedo** can be either plain form or polite form when the second clause is in the polite form.

▶ 22.5

疲れて（い）たけれど（も）宿題をしました。
Tsukarete (i)ta keredo(mo) shukudai o shimashita.
Although I was tired, I did my homework.

皆さんに聞いてみましたけれど（も）よく分かりませんでした。
Minasan ni kiite mimashita keredo(mo) yoku wakarimasen deshita.
Although I asked everyone, I still couldn't figure it out.

The form of the predicate preceding **keredo(mo)/kedo** is usually in the plain form when the second clause is in the plain form.

つまらなかったけれど（も）文句は言わなかった。
Tsumaranakatta keredo(mo) monku wa iwanakatta.
Although it was boring, I didn't complain (about it).

In formal speech or in writing, the conjunctive particle **ga** 'but, though' is more commonly used. The predicate preceding **ga** takes the plain form when the second clause is in the plain form. It takes the polite form when the second clause is in the polite form.

私は日本人ですが、日本語が話せません。
Watashi wa Nihonjin desu ga, Nihon go ga hanasemasen.
I'm Japanese, but I cannot speak Japanese.

父は日本人だが、母はアメリカ人だ。
Chichi wa Nihonjin da ga, haha wa Amerikajin da.
My father is Japanese, but my mother is American.

Using the plain form with **ga** makes the sentence sound rather blunt when speaking, but it is often used in writing.

Another connective particle, **noni** 'although,' is also often used to express contrast when the sentence expresses the speaker's various feelings such as surprise, frustration, irritation, or complaint. See the sections on surprise (**68.2**) and complaints (**81.2**) for examples.

Expressing contrast with connectives

The connective **demo** 'but' is also commonly used in speaking. **Demo** is placed between two sentences that express contrast.

> 田中さんは背が高い。でも佐藤さんは背が低い。
> **Tanaka-san wa se ga takai. Demo Satoo-san wa se ga hikui.**
> Mr/Ms Tanaka is tall. But Mr/Ms Sato is short.

> A: 遊びに行こうよ。
>   **Asobi ni ikoo yo.**
>   Let's go to play.

> B: でも、まだ宿題が終わってない。
>   **Demo, mada shukudai ga owatte nai.**
>   But, I haven't finished my homework.

Other common connectives used to express contrast are:

> だけど　　**dakedo**　　'but' (I)

> 自信はない。だけど、やってみる。
> **Jishin wa nai. Dakedo, yatte miru.**
> I'm not confident. But I will try.

> しかし　　**shikashi**　　'however'

> 可能性はある。しかし、かなり厳しい。
> **Kanoosee wa aru. Shikashi, kanari kibishii.**
> There is a possibility. However, it is very difficult.

> だが　　**daga**　　'however'

> みんな疲れていた。だが、あきらめなかった。
> **Minna tsukarete ita. Daga, akiramenakatta.**
> Everyone was tired. However, nobody gave up.

> ところが　　**tokoroga**　　'nonetheless'

> 誰も期待していなかった。ところが、その商品はよく売れた。
> **Dare mo kitai shite inakatta. Tokoroga, sono shoohin wa yoku ureta.**
> Nobody expected it. Nonetheless, that product sold well.

Connectives used with conjunctive particles

The following connectives also express contrast. They are often used in addition to a conjunctive particle.

> その反面　　**sono hanmen**　　'on the other hand'

> ツアー旅行は安くて便利だが、その反面、団体行動のストレスも多い。
> **Tsuaa ryokoo wa yasukute benri da ga, sono hanmen, dantaikoodoo no sutoresu mo ooi.**
> Escorted tour packages are inexpensive and convenient but, on the other hand, group activities can be stressful.

> 一方　　**ippoo**　　'on the other hand'

> 京都は、夏はひどく暑いけど、一方、冬は寒さが厳しい。
> **Kyooto wa, natsu wa hidoku atsui kedo, ippoo, fuyu wa samusa ga kibishii.**
> In Kyoto, summer is terribly hot, but on the other hand, winter is bitterly cold.

逆に　　　**gyaku ni**　　'on the contrary'

私は好きなものから先に食べるが、逆に、娘は嫌いなものから先に食べる。
Watashi wa suki na mono kara saki ni taberu ga, gyaku ni, musume wa kirai na mono kara saki ni taberu.
I eat things I like first, but, my daughter, on the contrary, eats things she hates first.

In general, conjunctive particles and connectives that express contrast can be used together in a sentence. A conjunctive particle is placed at the end of the first clause, followed first by a connective and then by the second clause.

学校でのいじめ問題は深刻さを増しているが、しかし、解決策はなかなか見つからない。
Gakkoo de no ijime mondai wa shinkokusa o mashite iru ga, shikashi, kaiketsusaku wa nakanaka mitsukaranai.
Though the problem of bullying at school is increasing in seriousness, solutions are not easily found.

よくわからないけど、でも、間違っていると思う。
Yoku wakaranai kedo, demo, machigatte iru to omou.
Though I'm not sure, I think it's wrong.

40

Location and distance

This chapter examines various expressions used in Japanese to state location and distance, including locational nouns such as 'above,' 'below,' 'next to,' etc.

40.1 Expressing location

40.1.1 *aru/arimasu*

To ask and say where something is, Japanese uses the structure of N **wa** location **ni aru/arimasu** 'exist'. The copula **da/desu** is often used instead of the verb **aru**.

> オペラ座という映画館はどこにありますか。
> **Operaza to yuu eegakan wa doko ni arimasu ka.**
> Where is the movie theater called the 'Opera House'?

> オペラ座という映画館はどこですか。
> **Operaza to yuu eegakan wa doko desu ka.**
> Where is the movie theater called the 'Opera House'?

When a copula construction is used, 'location **ni arimasu**' is replaced by 'location **desu**'. Note that the particle **ni** is deleted together with the verb **aru** in the **desu** construction.

The answer to the question also has two versions, one with the verb **aru/arimasu** and the other with the copula **desu**. You can answer the **arimasu ka** question with the copula version and vice versa.

> あそこにあります。　　あそこです。
> **Asoko ni arimasu.**　　**Asoko desu.**
> It's over there.　　It is over there.

40.1.2 *iru/imasu*

To ask and state where someone or some living being is, the verb **iru/imasu** is used.

> スミスさんはどこにいますか。　　スミスさんは教室にいます。
> **Sumisu-san wa doko ni imasu ka.**　　**Sumisu-san wa kyooshitsu ni imasu.**
> Where is Mr/Ms Smith?　　Mr/Ms Smith is in the classroom.

The copula construction is also often used as in the following examples.

> スミスさんはどこ（ですか）。
> **Sumisu-san wa doko (desu ka).**
> Where is Mr/Ms Smith?

> （スミスさんは）教室（です）。
> **(Sumisu-san wa) kyooshitsu (desu).**
> Mr/Ms Smith is in the classroom.

40.2 Indicating precise location

To indicate the precise location, such as 'on top of,' 'under,' 'next to,' etc., Japanese uses nouns expressing a location concept such as **ue** 'top,' **shita** 'below,' **naka** 'inside.' These nouns are modified by nouns indicating what it is on top of, under, inside, etc., as in the following.

> つくえ　の　上
> **tsukue　no　ue**
> desk's top = on top of the desk

> 部屋　　の　中
> **heya　　no　naka**
> room's inside = inside of the room

> 辞書は机の上にあります。
> **Jisho wa tsukue no ue ni arimasu.**
> The dictionary is on top of the desk.

> 喫茶店は駅の隣にあります。　　　　駅の隣です。
> **Kissaten wa eki no tonari ni arimasu.**　　**Eki no tonari desu.**
> The coffee shop is next to the station.

> 学校は家の近くにあります。　　　　家の近くです。
> **Gakkoo wa ie no chikaku ni arimasu.**　　**Ie no chikaku desu.**
> The school is near my house.

> 子供たちは今建物の中にいます。
> **Kodomo-tachi wa ima tatemono no naka ni imasu.**
> The children are inside of the building right now.

Other location nouns include **yoko** 'side,' **mae** 'front,' **ushiro** 'back,' **migi** 'right side,' and **hidari** 'left side.'

Yoko and **tonari** both mean 'beside' and 'next to.' **Tonari** is used when referring to two items belonging to the same category, such as two people, two buildings, two countries, etc., whereas **yoko** can be used when referring to things of different categories.

> コンビニは銀行の隣にあります。
> **Konbini wa ginkoo no tonari ni arimasu.**
> The convenience store is next to the bank.

> タクシー乗り場は銀行の横にあります。
> **Takushii noriba wa ginkoo no yoko ni arimasu.**
> The taxi stand is beside the bank.

The idea of 'between X and Y' is expressed by X **to** Y **no aida**.

> 映画館は銀行とデパートの間にあります。
> **Eegakan wa ginkoo to depaato no aida ni arimasu.**
> The movie theater is between the bank and the department store.

40.3 Indicating distance

To indicate distance from something, Japanese uses X **kara** (distance) **no tokoro ni arimasu** or X **kara** (distance) **desu**.

> 横浜は東京から２７キロメートルです。
> **Yokohama wa Tookyoo kara nijuunana kiromeetoru desu.**
> Yokohama is 27 kilometers from Tokyo.

学校は駅から３００メートルのところにあります。
Gakkoo wa eki kara sanbyaku meetoru no tokoro ni arimasu.
The school is 300 meters from the (train) station.

Distance may also be expressed by the time it takes to get to a place walking, or by bus, train, etc.

郵便局は駅から歩いて５分ぐらいのところにあります。
Yuubinkyoku wa eki kara aruite gofun gurai no tokoro ni arimasu.
The post office is about a five-minute walk from the station.

私の家は駅からバスで１０分です。
Watashi no ie wa eki kara basu de juppun desu.
My house is ten minutes by bus from the station.

To ask how far away a place is you can use expressions such as the following.

空港までどのぐらいかかりますか。
Kuukoo made dono gurai kakarimasu ka.
How long does it take to get to the airport?

タクシーで２０分ぐらいです。
Takushii de nijuppun gurai desu.
It's about 20 minutes by taxi.

京都までどのぐらいですか。
Kyooto made dono gurai desu ka.
How far is it to Kyoto?

新幹線で二時間ぐらいです。
Shinkansen de nijikan gurai desu.
It is about two hours by bullet train.

41

Possession

This chapter covers expressions related to ownership, possession, and belongings.

41.1 Expressing possession of things

To indicate that one has inanimate objects, X **o motte iru/imasu** is commonly used.

> 私は車を持っています。
> **Watashi wa kuruma o motte imasu.**
> I own a car.

> 田中さんは立派なテニスラケットを持っています。
> **Tanaka-san wa rippa na tenisu raketto o motte imasu.**
> Mr/Ms Tanaka has an impressive tennis racket.

X **ga aru/arimasu** can also be used to express possession of things.

▶ 5.3; 12.3

> 私はコンピューターがあります。
> **Watashi wa konpyuutaa ga arimasu.**
> I have a computer.

> 井田さんはお金がたくさんある。
> **Ida-san wa o-kane ga takusan aru.**
> Mr/Ms Ida has a lot of money.

41.2 Expressing possession of animals and pets

To communicate that one has animals or pets, X **o katte iru** is commonly used.

> 私は犬を飼っている。
> **Watashi wa inu o katte imasu.**
> I have a dog.

> この牧場では牛を５０頭飼っています。
> **Kono bokujoo de wa ushi o gojuttoo katte imasu.**
> At this farm, they have/raise 50 cows.

X **ga iru** can also be used to express possession of animals or pets.

▶ 5.3; 12.3

> 私はペットがいます。　　　　うちには猫がいる。
> **Watashi wa petto ga imasu.**　　**Uchi ni wa neko ga iru.**
> I have a pet.　　　　　　　　We have a cat.

41.3 Describing body parts

To indicate that some being has various body parts such as hands, legs, and hair, X **wa** Y **ga aru/arimasu** 'X has Y' is commonly used.

▶ 5.2.3; 12.3

人間は手が二つある。
Ningen wa te ga futatsu aru.
A human has two hands.

蜘蛛は脚が八本あります。
Kumo wa ashi ga happon arimasu.
A spider has eight legs.

When describing characteristics of one's body parts; e.g. one has long legs, short hair, or large hands, possessive expressions such as X **wa** Y **ga aru** or X **wa** Y **o motte iru** are not usually used. Instead, the following structure is used.

▶ 5.2.5; 12.3

■ Person **wa** body part(s) **ga** description (adj.)

小野さんは足が長いです。
Ono-san wa ashi ga nagai desu.
Mr/Ms Ono has long legs.

森さんは髪が短い。
Mori-san wa kami ga mijikai.
Mr/Ms Mori has short hair.

私は手が大きいです。
Watashi wa te ga ookii desu.
I have large hands.

When expressing injuries or illnesses related to one's body parts, the possessive pronoun (X **no**) is not used with one's body part. The subject of the sentence is assumed to be the possessor of the body part.

太郎は足を折りました。
Taroo wa ashi o orimashita.
Taro broke his leg.

私は頭が痛い。
Watashi wa atama ga itai.
My head hurts/I have a headache.

41.4 Other ways of expressing possession

There are many other words that express possession, including the following verbs. They are mainly used in writing or in a professional context.

■ **Shoyuu shite iru** 'to own'

田中さんは多くの株を所有している。
Tanaka-san wa ooku no kabu o shoyuu shite iru.
Mr/Ms Tanaka owns a lot of stocks.

■ **Shoji shite iru** 'to possess, to carry, to have on one'

中学生の6割が携帯電話を所持している。
Chuugakusee no roku wari ga keetai denwa o shoji shite iru.
60 percent of middle school/junior high school students carry a cellphone.

■ **Shozoo shite iru** 'to have in stock, to own'

この美術館は500点を超す美術作品を所蔵している。
Kono bijutsukan wa gohyakuten o kosu bijutsu sakuhin o shozoo shite iru.
This museum has more than 500 art works in its collection.

42

Gifts

42.1 Expressing that someone has given something to the speaker

To express that someone has given something to the speaker, the verb **kureru** is commonly used.

> 井田さんは（私に）マフラーをくれました。
> **Ida-san wa (watashi ni) mafuraa o kuremashita.**
> Mr/Ms Ida gave me a winter scarf.

> 母が（私に）お小遣いをくれた。
> **Haha ga (watashi ni) o-kozukai o kureta.**
> My mother gave me an allowance/pocket money.

When the giver is a social superior of the speaker, **kudasaru** may be used.

► 12.7; 29

> 部長が万年筆をくださった。
> **Buchoo ga mannenhitsu o kudasatta.**
> The department head gave me a fountain pen.

> 先生が手紙をくださいました。
> **Sensee ga tegami o kudasaimashita.**
> My teacher gave me a letter.

The phrase **watashi ni** 'to me' is often omitted when the verbs **kureru/kudasaru** are used because these verbs are mainly used when the recipient is **watashi** 'me,' the speaker.

Another way to convey that someone has given something to the speaker is to use the verb **okuru** 'to give as a gift' in the passive form, **okurareru** 'to be given as a gift.'

> 私は彼から指輪を贈られた。
> **Watashi wa kare kara yubiwa o okurareta.**
> I was given a ring by my boyfriend as a gift.

42.2 Expressing that the speaker has given something to someone

To indicate that the speaker has given something to someone, the verb **ageru** 'to give' is most commonly used.

► 12.7; 29

> 私は妹にワンピースをあげました。
> **Watashi wa imooto ni wanpiisu o agemashita.**
> I gave a dress to my younger sister.

> 友達に誕生日プレゼントをあげた。
> **Tomodachi ni tanjoobi purezento o ageta.**
> I gave a birthday present to my friend.

When the recipient of the gift is a social superior of the speaker, **sashiageru** may be used.

> 私は書道の先生に筆をさし上げました。(VF)
> **Watashi wa shodoo no sensee ni fude o sashiagemashita.**
> I gave a writing brush to my calligraphy teacher.

Another verb, **okuru** 'to give as a gift,' can also be used to convey that the speaker has given a gift to someone.

> 母にカーネーションを贈った。
> **Haha ni kaaneeshon o okutta.**
> I gave carnations to my mother.

It is also common to use **purezento suru** 'to give as a gift.'

> 両親に温泉旅行をプレゼントしました。
> **Ryooshin ni onsen ryokoo o purezento shimashita.**
> I gave a trip to the hot-spring as a gift to my parents.

42.3 Expressing that someone has given something to someone else

The verb **ageru** 'to give' is used to convey that someone has given something to someone else as a gift.

▶ **12.7; 29**

> 小田さんは井野さんに花束をあげた。
> **Oda-san wa Ino-san ni hanataba o ageta.**
> Mr Oda gave a bouquet of flowers to Ms Ino.

> 弟は彼女に指輪をあげました。
> **Otooto wa kanojo ni yubiwa o agemashita.**
> My younger brother gave a ring to his girlfriend.

42.4 Other ways to say that someone has given something to someone else

The verb **okuru** 'to give as a gift' is also used to say that someone has given something to someone else as a gift.

> 森さんは岡さんに映画のチケットを贈りました。
> **Mori-san wa Oka-san ni eega no chiketto o okurimashita.**
> Mr/Ms Mori gave Mr/Ms Oka movie tickets as a gift.

To indicate that someone gives something to someone else but not as a gift, the verb **watasu** may be used.

> 森さんは林さんに傘を渡した。
> **Mori-san wa Hayashi-san ni kasa o watashita.**
> Mr/Ms Mori gave/handed the umbrella to Mr/Ms Hayashi.

43

Kind acts

Expressing that someone does something for the speaker as a favor

To convey that someone does a favor for the speaker, the auxiliary verb **kureru** is used following the **te**-form of the main verb.

▶ **12.7; 19.2.8**

母が洗濯をしてくれた。
Haha ga sentaku o shite kureta.
My mother did the laundry for me.

友達が駅まで車でおくってくれました。
Tomodachi ga eki made kuruma de okutte kuremashita.
My friend gave me a ride/lift to the station.

Even when these events do not involve the speaker's asking for a favor, Japanese speakers tend to use the V-**te kureru** structure to express events in which someone's actions benefit the speaker.

When one's social superior does something for the speaker, **kudasaru** may be used instead of **kureru**.

先生が推薦状を書いてくださった。
Sensee ga suisenjoo o kaite kudasatta.
My teacher wrote a recommendation letter for me.

上司がおやつを持って来てくださいました。
Jooshi ga oyatsu o motte kite kudasaimashita.
My boss brought a snack for me.

Another way to say that someone does something for the speaker is to use the auxiliary verb **morau**.

▶ **19.2.8**

私は友達に新しいソフトの使い方を教えてもらった。
Watashi wa tomodachi ni atarashii sofuto no tsukai kata o oshiete moratta.
My friend taught me how to use new software.
(I had my friend teach me how to use new software.)

When one's social superior does something for the speaker, **itadaku** may be used instead of **morau**.

父の同僚の方に骨董品を見せていただきました。
Chichi no dooryoo no kata ni kottoohin o misete itadakimashita.
My father's colleague showed me an antique object.

43.2 Expressing that the speaker does something for someone as a favor

To convey that the speaker does something for someone as a favor, the auxiliary verb **ageru** is used following the **te**-form of the main verb.

▶ 19.2.8

> 私は友達に教科書を貸してあげた。
> **Watashi wa tomodachi ni kyookasho o kashite ageta.**
> I lent my textbook to my friend.

> いつも妹に英語を教えてあげます。
> **Itsumo imooto ni eego o oshiete agemasu.**
> I always teach English to my younger sister.

When the speaker does something for his/her social superior, **sashiageru** may be used instead of **ageru**.

> 上司を空港まで迎えに行って差し上げました。
> **Jooshi o kuukoo made mukae ni itte sashiagemashita.**
> I went to the airport to pick up my boss.

The use of **-te ageru** and **-te sashiageru** requires caution. Using these structures to express what the speaker does makes it explicit that the speaker's action benefits another person. It could make the recipient of the favor feel indebted to the speaker, a situation which Japanese consider rude and tend to avoid.

V-**te yaru** may be used when the speaker's social status is higher than the recipient's.

> 私は弟に車の運転を教えてやりました。
> **Watashi wa otooto ni kuruma no unten o oshiete yarimashita.**
> I taught my younger brother how to drive.

> 犬を散歩に連れて行ってやった。
> **Inu o sanpo ni tsurete itte yatta.**
> I took my dog for a walk.

43.3 Expressing that someone does something for someone else as a favor

To express that someone does something for another person, the auxiliary verb **ageru** is used.

▶ 19.2.8

> 小野さんは森さんに仕事を紹介してあげた。
> **Ono-san wa Mori-san ni shigoto o shookai shite ageta.**
> Mr/Ms Ono helped Mr/Ms Mori find a job.

> 野田さんは井野さんを手伝ってあげました。
> **Noda-san wa Ino-san o tetsudatte agemashita.**
> Mr/Ms Noda helped Mr/Ms Ino.

When someone does something for someone who is close to the speaker, such as a family member, **kureru** or **kudasaru** should be used.

> 小田さんは弟に本を読んでくださった。
> **Oda-san wa otooto ni hon o yonde kudasatta.**
> Mr/Ms Oda read a book for my little brother.

> 友達が妹を迎えに行ってくれた。
> **Tomodachi ga imooto o mukae ni itte kureta.**
> My friend went to pick up my younger sister.

44

Experience

44.1 ## Expressing one's past experiences

To say that you have done something in the past, use V(past) + **koto ga aru**. **Koto** is a nominalizer and **aru** is the verb indicating existence or possession. The noun **keeken** 'experience' can also be used in a phrase such as V(past) **keeken ga aru**.

▶ 18.1

日本に行ったことがあります。
Nihon ni itta koto ga arimasu.
I have been to Japan.

すしを食べたことがあります。
Sushi o tabeta koto ga arimasu.
I have eaten sushi.

編集をした経験があります。
Henshuu o shita keeken ga arimasu.
I have editing experience.

To indicate how many times you have done something, use number+**do** or number+**kai**. **Nando mo** indicates 'many times,' **nando ka** 'a few times,' and number+**do/kai**+**shika** 'only . . . times.'

▶ 16; 15.4

一度日本に行ったことがあります。
Ichido Nihon ni itta koto ga arimasu.
I have been to Japan once.

「羅生門」という映画は、何度も見たことがあります。
Rashoomon to yuu eega wa nando mo mita koto ga arimasu.
I have seen the movie 'Rashomon' many times.

何度か日本食を食べたことがあります。
Nando ka nihonshoku o tabeta koto ga arimasu.
I have eaten Japanese food a few times.

一度しか日本に行ったことがありません。
Ichido shika Nihon ni itta koto ga arimasen.
I have been to Japan only once.

44.2 ## Expressing how long one has been doing something

To indicate how long one has been doing something or one has been in a certain state, use an expression indicating duration with V-**te** form + **iru**. Duration can be number + **nen** 'year,' number + **ka getsu** 'month,' etc.

五年結婚しています。
Gonen kekkon shite imasu.
I have been married for five years.

日本語は一年ぐらい勉強しています。
Nihongo wa ichinen gurai benkyoo shite imasu.
I have been studying Japanese for about one year.

Another way of expressing how long one has been doing something or one has been in a certain state is to say that a certain number of years (months, etc.) have passed since one did something.

結婚してから一年になります。
Kekkon shite kara ichinen ni narimasu.
It's been one year since I got married.

日本に来てから一ヵ月たちました。
Nihon ni kite kara ikkagetsu tachimashita.
One month has passed since I came to Japan.

日本語の勉強を始めてから三年になります。
Nihongo no benkyoo o hajimete kara sannen ni narimasu.
It has been three years since I began studying Japanese.

44.3 Asking people about their experiences

You can ask someone whether he/she has done something by V(past) **koto ga arimasu ka**, V(past) **keeken ga arimasu ka** or N + **no keeken ga arimasu ka**.

すしを食べたことがありますか。(F)
Sushi o tabeta koto ga arimasu ka.
Have you eaten sushi (before)?

日本に行ったことある？(I)
Nihon ni itta koto aru?
Have you been to Japan?

アルバイトの経験がありますか。(F)
Arubaito no keeken ga arimasu ka.
Do you have part-time work experience?

雑誌の編集した経験ある？(I)
Zasshi no henshuu shita keeken aru?
Do you have magazine editing experience?

▶ 18.1

45

Intentions and plans

Plans and intentions can be expressed with constructions involving nouns such as **tsumori** 'intention,' and **yotee** 'plan.' These are nouns, so the content of the intentions and plans are expressed in the sentence modifying these nouns.

▶ 18.7

45.1 Expressing one's intentions and plans

One's intentions can be expressed by clause **tsumori+da/desu**.

週末はパーティーをするつもりです。
Shuumatsu wa paatii o suru tsumori desu.
I intend to give a party on the weekend.

Note that the verb preceding **tsumori** is always in the nonpast tense form in this construction.

To say that one does not have any intention of doing something, use **tsumori wa nai/arimasen** or **tsumori ja nai/arimasen**.

就職するつもりはありません。
Shuushoku suru tsumori wa arimasen.
I don't have any intention of getting a (regular) job.

One's plans can be expressed by S + **yotee da/desu**.

今日は友達とお茶をする予定です。
Kyoo wa tomodachi to o-cha o suru yotee desu.
I plan to have tea with my friend today.

To say that you do not have any plans to do something, use **yotee wa nai/arimasen**,

今のところ日本に行く予定はありません。
Ima no tokoro Nihon ni iku yotee wa arimasen.
For now, I don't have any plans to go to Japan.

Intentions or plans can also be expressed by a volitional form of verbs (such as **shiyoo**, **ikoo**, **tabeyoo**), as in the following examples.

▶ 12.1

来年留学しようと思っています。
Rainen ryuugaku shiyoo to omotte imasu.
I intend/plan to study abroad next year.

新しい携帯を買おうと思っているんだけど、どれがいいか教えてくれない？
Atarashii keetai o kaoo to omotte iru n da kedo, dore ga ii ka oshiete kurenai?
I intend to buy a new cell phone. Would you tell me which one is good?

45.2 Asking about intentions and plans

To ask about the addressee's intentions and plans, the same **tsumori** and **yotee** constructions can be used in question forms.

今度の夏休みは何をするつもりですか。
Kondo no natsuyasumi wa nani o suru tsumori desu ka.
What do you intend to do next summer vacation?

週末は何か予定がありますか。
Shuumatsu wa nani ka yotee ga arimasu ka.
Do you have any plans this weekend?

何か予定ある？
Nani ka yotee aru?
Do you have any plans?

When asking someone superior about his/her intentions and plans, an honorific prefix should be attached as in **go-yotee**.

週末は何かご予定がおありですか。(VF)
Shuumatsu wa nani ka go-yotee ga o-ari desu ka.
Do you have any plans on the weekend?

45.3 Reporting on others' plans

Statements about someone else's intentions and plans have to be presented as conjectures, inferences, hearsay, or a quote.

▶ 28; 33.2

スミスさんは来年留学するつもりだそうです。
Sumisu-san wa rainen ryuugaku suru tsumori da soo desu.
I hear Mr/Ms Smith plans to study abroad next year.

従業員を首にする予定はないらしい。
Juugyooin o kubi ni suru yotee wa nai rashii.
It seems that they do not plan to cut employees.

46

Temporal relations

46.1 **Expressing sequence**

46.1.1 **Expressing the relationship 'before'**

46.1.1.1 *mae (ni)*

The word **mae** 'before' is used to indicate that one event occurs before another event occurs. The particle **ni** may optionally be dropped. In Japanese, the 'before' clause must come first in the sentence.

> 旅行の前にホテルを探さなくちゃならない。
> **Ryokoo no mae ni hoteru o sagasanakucha naranai.**
> I have to look for a hotel before traveling.

> 仕事に行く前に新聞を読みました。
> **Shigoto ni iku mae ni shinbun o yomimashita.**
> I read a newspaper before going to work.

46.1.1.2 **V(neg.)** *uchi ni*

V(neg.) **uchi ni** also expresses that one event occurs before another event occurs.

> 暗くならないうちに帰りましょう。
> **Kuraku naranai uchi ni kaerimashoo.**
> Let's go home before it gets dark.

> 忘れないうちにメモをしておこう。
> **Wasurenai uchi ni memo o shite okoo.**
> I will make a note before I forget.

Compared with **mae ni**, **-nai uchi ni** carries the connotation that one does something before some unfavorable event happens, with the sense of doing something before it is too late.

46.1.2 **Expressing the relationship 'after' in a single sentence**

46.1.2.1 *ato (de)*

The word(s) **ato (de)** is/are used to indicate that one event occurs after another event occurs. The verb that precedes **ato (de)** has to be in the past tense form.

> あしたは映画を見たあと（で）レストランで食事をします。
> **Ashita wa eega o mita ato (de) resutoran de shokuji o shimasu.**
> Tomorrow after (we) watch a movie, (we) will have dinner at a restaurant.

> 大学を卒業したあとすぐ会社に就職した。
> **Daigaku o sotsugyoo shita ato sugu kaisha ni shuushoku shita.**
> I got a job at a company right after I graduated from college.

A noun phrase that represents an event can be used with **ato (de)** as well. It needs the pre-nominal copula **no** before **ato (de)**.

> 会議の後（で）飲みに行こう。
> **Kaigi no ato (de) nomi ni ikoo.**
> Let's go drinking after the meeting.

46.1.2.2 V-*te* form + *kara*

V-**te** form followed by the particle **kara** also expresses the sense of 'after doing something.'

▶ **22.1**

> 日本に行ってから日本語を勉強する人もいる。
> **Nihon ni itte kara Nihongo o benkyoo suru hito mo iru.**
> There are people who study Japanese after they go to Japan.

> 手を洗ってから食べなさい。
> **Te o aratte kara tabenasai.**
> Wash your hands and then eat.

NOTE | It is important to distinguish this expression from V-**ta kara**, which means 'because.'

46.1.2.3 Expressions that indicate 'as soon as'

Adverbs such as **sugu** 'soon,' **totan ni** 'the minute . . .' and phrases such as V(plain, nonpast) **ya ina ya** 'as soon as' are used to indicate that an event occurs 'as soon as' another event occurs. **Sugu** is the most colloquial expression, while **ya ina ya** has a more literary flavor.

> 家に帰ってすぐ宿題をした。
> **Uchi ni kaette sugu shukudai o shita.**
> I went home and right away I did my homework.

> 「ハリーポッター」は出版されるやいなやベストセラーになった。
> **'Harii Pottaa' wa shuppan sareru ya ina ya besuto seraa ni natta.**
> 'Harry Potter' became a best seller as soon as it was published.

> 娘は私の顔を見たとたんに泣き出した。
> **Musume wa watashi no kao o mita totan ni nakidashita.**
> My daughter started crying the minute she saw me.

46.1.2.4 *-tara* 'when'

When the sequential conditional form **-tara** is used to describe a past event, the consequence clause describes an event that occurred unexpectedly.

▶ **24.3**

> コンサートに行ったら大学時代の同級生に会った。
> **Konsaato ni ittara daigaku jidai no dookyuusee ni atta.**
> I went to a concert, and what do you know? I met a college classmate.

In this sentence, meeting a college classmate was something totally unexpected.

46.1.3 Expressing the relationship 'after' in a separate sentence

Conjunctions such as **soshite** 'and then' and **sorekara** 'and then; afterwards' can be used to indicate that one event occurs after another event.

▶ **22.3**

46.2 Expressing simultaneous actions and situations

46.2.1 Indicating that two actions occur at the same time

To express that one person does two actions at the same time, V_1(stem) **nagara** V_2 is used. V_1 indicates an action which implies a duration. Non-durative verbs such as **kau** 'to buy,' **au** 'to meet,' **tsuku** 'to arrive,' **deru** 'to leave,' **katsu** 'to win,' etc. cannot be combined with **nagara**, because such verbs imply momentary actions, not duration.

> テレビを見ながら勉強してはいけません。
> **Terebi o minagara benkyoo shite wa ikemasen.**
> Do not watch TV while studying.

> 私は音楽を聞きながら散歩するのがすきです。
> **Watashi wa ongaku o kikinagara sanpo suru no ga suki desu.**
> I like listening to music while taking a walk.

> 田中さんは仕事を三つしながら、子供を大学に送った。
> **Tanaka-san wa shigoto o mittsu shinagara, kodomo o daigaku ni okutta.**
> Mr/Mrs Tanaka had three jobs while supporting his/her child going to college.

The person who does the two actions in this construction has to be the same person. Hence, the following sentence is ungrammatical.

> *一郎が掃除しながら、よしこが料理をした。
> *Ichiroo ga sooji shinagara, Yoshiko ga ryoori o shita.
> Ichiro cleaned the room while Yoshiko cooked.

NOTE | In V_1 **nagara**, when V_1 is stative, it means 'although V_1.'

▶ 22.5.8

46.2.2 Expressing that two situations hold during the same time frame

To express that two situations hold simultaneously, CLAUSE1 **aida** CLAUSE2 can be used. Both clauses have to describe a state or continuing situations. The predicate in CLAUSE1 generally takes the nonpast tense form regardless of the tense of CLAUSE2.

> 雪が降っている間一歩も外に出なかった。
> **Yuki ga futte iru aida ippo mo soto ni denakatta.**
> While it was snowing (I) did not step outside.

> 先生が話している間学生は静かに聞いていた。
> **Sensee ga hanashite iru aida gakusee wa shizuka ni kiite ita.**
> While the teacher was talking the students listened quietly.

Since **aida** is a noun, it can be modified by N + **no**.

> 盆休みの間東京は静かだ。
> **Bonyasumi no aida Tookyoo wa shizuka da.**
> Tokyo is quiet during the Bon holiday.

The particle **wa** attached to **aida** indicates contrast.

> 日本語で話している間は静かだが、いったん英語になるとよくしゃべる。
> **Nihongo de hanashite iru aida wa shizuka da ga, ittan eego ni naru to yoku shaberu.**
> (They) are quiet while (they) talk in Japanese, but once the language shifts to English, (they) talk a lot.

Expressing that a situation is the background of an action

To indicate that an action occurs while a situation holds, use **aida ni** 'while' or **uchi ni** 'while.' In CLAUSE1 **aida ni/uchi ni** CLAUSE2, CLAUSE1 provides a time frame during which CLAUSE2 takes place. The predicate in CLAUSE1 is stative or a verb in **-te iru** form. It is also in the nonpast pre-nominal form regardless of the tense of the main clause.

> ルームメイトが寝ている間に、コンピューターを使った。
> **Ruumumeeto ga nete iru aida ni konpyuutaa o tsukatta.**
> I used the computer while my roommate was sleeping.

> 日本にいる間にたくさん旅行をしたいと思っている。
> **Nihon ni iru aida ni takusan ryokoo o shitai to omotte iru.**
> I would like to travel a lot while I am in Japan.

> 休みの間に論文を書き上げてしまいたい。
> **Yasumi no aida ni ronbun o kakiagete shimaitai.**
> I would like to finish writing my paper during the break.

> 暇があるうちに好きなことをやっておくといい。
> **Hima ga aru uchi ni suki na koto o yatte oku to ii.**
> One should do what one likes while one (still) has free time.

> 若いうちにいろいろなことに挑戦するべきだ。
> **Wakai uchi ni iroirona koto ni choosen suru beki da.**
> One should try various things while one is still young.

Compared with **aida ni**, the use of **uchi ni** carries a sense of urgency, the sense of 'let's do it before it is too late, before the situation changes.' In the above sentence, for example, **wakai uchi ni** gives the sense that one is not going to be young forever, so 'while one is still young, challenge oneself.'

This sense of urgency, however, is not felt when the main clause expresses a gradual change, as in the following.

> 毎日少しずつ練習しているうちに上手になった。
> **Mainichi sukoshizutsu renshuu shite iru uchi ni joozu ni natta.**
> (I) became better while practicing a little every day.

In the situation described in this section, the **toki** 'when' clause can also be used.

> ルームメイトが寝ている時（に）、コンピューターを使った。
> **Ruumumeeto ga nete iru toki (ni) konpyuutaa o tsukatta.**
> I used the computer when my roommate was sleeping.

...*mama*

The expression V(past) **mama** indicates that the situation (described in the **mama** clause) continues unchanged.

> 昨日は疲れてしまって、服を着たまま寝てしまった。
> **Kinoo wa tsukarete shimatte, fuku o kita mama nete shimatta.**
> I was so tired yesterday that I ended up sleeping with my clothes on.

In the above sentence, the speaker went to sleep with his/her clothes on. In other words, two situations – having clothes on and sleeping – occurred concurrently. The implication, however, is that one normally changes clothes before going to sleep. This expression is also often used with nouns and demonstrative adjectives such as **sono**, **kono** and **ano**.

靴をはいたまま、入らないでください。
Kutsu o haita mama hairanaide kudasai.
Please do not enter with shoes on.

お金を借りたまま返さないのはよくありません。
O-kane o karita mama kaesanai no wa yoku arimasen.
It is not good to have borrowed money and not return it.

これは、生のまま、食べられます。
Kore wa, nama no mama taberaremasu.
You can eat this raw.

そのままにしておいてください。
Sono mama ni shite oite kudasai.
Please leave it as it is.

NOTE | When V₁ represents a controllable action, **nai mama** is not used. The **-naide** form is the appropriate form.

かぎをかけないで出かけた。（not *かぎをかけないまま出かけた。）
Kagi o kakenaide dekaketa. (not *Kagi o kakenai mama dekaketa.)
(I) went out without locking the door.

▶ **15.3**

47

Explanation, reason and purpose

This chapter covers expressions related to asking and explaining reasons and purposes.

47.1 Asking about and expressing/explaining reasons

To ask about a reason for what has been expressed by your interlocutor, use one of the following questions.

どうしてですか。	**Dooshite desu ka,**	Why (or why not)? (F)
どうして？	**Dooshite?**	Why (or why not)? (I)
なぜですか。	**Naze desu ka.**	Why (or why not)? (F)
なんでですか。	**Nande desu ka.**	Why (or why not)? (F)
なんで？	**Nande?**	Why (or why not)? (I)

To ask for a detailed explanation of the reason, one may say:

どういうわけでしょうか。 (F)
Doo yuu wake deshoo ka.
What may be the reason?

理由は何ですか。 (F)
Riyuu wa nan desu ka.
What is the reason?

理由を説明していただけませんか。 (VF)
Riyuu o setsumee shite itadakemasen ka.
Could you explain the reason?

どうしてか説明してくれませんか。 (F)
Dooshite ka setsumee shite kuremasen ka.
Will you explain why?

▶ 18.6

47.2 *no/n* + copula

When asking for an explanation, it is common to end the sentence with a formal noun **no/n** followed by **desu ka**. The formal noun **no/n** follows the plain form of a predicate.

▶ 18.2.2; 32.2

どうして会社を辞めたんですか。 (F)   なんで来なかったの？ (I)
Dooshite kaisha o yameta n desu ka.   **Nande konakatta no?**
Why did you quit your company?   Why didn't you come?

To express a reason as a response to a why-question in informal speech, use **no**, **n da** or **kara** at the end of the reason statement.

> A: どうして来なかったの？
> **Dooshite konakatta no?**
> Why didn't you come?

> B: 疲れていたの or 疲れていたんだ or 疲れていたから。
> **Tsukarete ita no** or **Tsukarete ita n da** or **Tsukarete ita kara.**
> It's that I was tired. / It's that I was tired. / Because I was tired. The statement with **no** sounds feminine, but **n da** or **kara** are neutral.

In formal speech, **. . . n desu** may be used in place of **no** or **n da** when responding to a why-question.

> 疲れていたんです。
> **Tsukarete ita n desu.**
> It's that I was tired.

> 時間がなかったんです。
> **Jikan ga nakatta n desu.**
> It's that I didn't have time.

Expressions with **. . . n desu/da** are often called explanation modes of speech, as they are often used to either explain something or to seek an explanation. They are also frequently used when asking for a reason or stating a reason. However, **. . . n desu/da** does not really assert the statement as a reason: it merely suggests a reason.

In writing or when asserting a reason, **kara desu** may be used.

> A: どうして怒って（い）るんですか。
> **Dooshite okotte (i)ru n desu ka.**
> Why are you angry?

> B: 約束をやぶったからです。
> **Yakusoku o yabutta kara desu.**
> Because you broke a promise.

To respond to a why-question in formal speech, the formal noun **mono** + **desu kara** can also be used.

▶ **18.3**

> A: どうして京都にいらっしゃったのですか。(VF)
> **Dooshite Kyooto ni irasshatta no desu ka.**
> Why did you go to Kyoto?

> B: 京都の姉が入院したものですから。(F)
> **Kyooto no ane ga nyuuin shita mono desu kara.**
> It's because my older sister in Kyoto was hospitalized.

Mono desu kara is often used when apologizing.

> 三木： どうしていらっしゃらなかったんですか。(VF)
> **Miki:** **Dooshite irassharanakatta n desu ka.**
> Miki: Why didn't you come?

> 杉： すみません、ちょっと体調が良くなかったものですから。(VF)
> **Sugi:** **Sumimasen, chotto taichoo ga yoku nakatta mono desu kara.**
> Sugi: Sorry, I was feeling a bit unwell.

In colloquial speech, the formal noun **mono** is often pronounced as **mon**. It is used to express a reason, as follows.

A: もう食べないの？ (I)
Moo tabenai no?
Aren't you going to eat any more?

B: もうお腹いっぱいだもん。 (I)
Moo onaka ippai da mon.
Because I'm full already.

47.3 Expressing reason and consequence

To express reason and consequence in one sentence, the reason is stated first, followed by the conjunctive particles **kara** or **node**, and finally by the consequence.

具合が悪かったから/ので、会社を休んだ。
Guai ga warukatta kara/node, kaisha o yasunda.
I missed work because I was feeling ill.

時間がなかったから/ので、掃除しなかった。
Jikan ga nakatta kara/node, sooji shinakatta.
I didn't clean because I didn't have time.

Kara and **node** are more or less interchangeable. A subtle difference is that **node** simply states a fact without emphasizing it as a reason, while **kara** emphasizes a statement as a reason. In general, sentences with **node** sound softer and more polite, and therefore it is preferred when asking for a favor.

今日は体調がよくないので、休ませていただきます。
Kyoo wa taichoo ga yokunai node, yasumasete itadakimasu.
I'm not feeling well, and so I would like to take a day off.

一人だと心細いので一緒に行ってくれませんか。
Hitori da to kokorobosoi node issho ni itte kuremasen ka.
I don't feel comfortable alone, so could you go with me?

When adding a reason to one's previous statement, use connectives such as **nazenara** 'to say why,' **dooshite ka to yuu to** 'to state the reason' and **sono riyuu wa** 'the reason is that' and add **kara desu/(da)** at the end of the sentence.

▶ 22.5

私は引っ越ししたくありません。どうしてかというと、今のアパートがすごく気に入っているからです。
Watashi wa hikkoshi shitaku arimasen. Dooshite ka to yuu to, ima no apaato ga sugoku kiniitte iru kara desu.
I don't want to move. The reason is that I really like my current apartment.

このプロジェクトは失敗すると思う。なぜなら、みんな始めからやる気がないから（だ）。
Kono purojekuto wa shippai suru to omoo. Nazenara, minna hajime kara yaruki ga nai kara (da).
I think this project will fail. The reason is that from the beginning no one has been making an effort.

47.4 Asking about and expressing purpose

A question with **dooshite** 'why' is ambiguous between asking for a reason and asking for someone's purpose, so it can be answered with either a reason or a purpose, as in the following example.

A: どうして日本語を勉強しているんですか。
Dooshite Nihongo o benkyoo shite iru n desu ka.
Why are you studying Japanese?

B: おもしろいからです。(Reason)
Omoshiroi kara desu.
Because it's interesting.

C: 日本に留学したいからです。(Reason and purpose)
Nihon ni ryuugaku shitai kara desu.
Because I want to study abroad in Japan.

To ask for someone's purpose specifically, **tameni** 'for' or **mokuteki** 'purpose' may be used.

何のために？	**Nan no tame ni?**	For what?
どういう目的で？	**Doo yuu mokuteki de?**	For what kind of purpose?
何の目的で？	**Nan no mokuteki de?**	For what purpose?

何のために日本語を勉強しているんですか。
Nan no tame ni Nihongo o benkyoo shite iru n desu ka.
For what purpose are you studying Japanese?

どういう目的でインターネットをつかっていますか。
Doo yuu mokuteki de intaanetto o tsukatte imasu ka.
For what kind of purpose have you been using the Internet?

▶ **18.4; 18.9.3**

To state purpose, **tame (ni)** 'in order to' or **yoo ni** 'so that' are commonly used.

A: 何のためにお金を貯めて（い）るんですか。
Nan no tame ni okane o tamete (i)ru n desu ka.
For what purpose are you saving money?

B: 海外旅行をするため（に）です。
Kaigai ryokoo o suru tame (ni) desu.
It is for making oversea trips.

C: 将来困らないようにです。
Shoorai komaranai yoo ni desu.
It is so that I won't have trouble in the future.

▶ See **47.5** on the differences between **tame ni** and **yoo ni**.

With a motion verb like **iku** 'go' and **kuru** 'come,' the purpose of going to or coming to a place is expressed by the verb-stem + **ni**.

コンビニに飲み物を買いに行きました。
Konbini ni nomimono o kai ni ikimashita.
I went to a convenience store to buy drinks.

友達がDVDを借りに来た。
Tomodachi ga DVD o kari ni kita.
My friend came to borrow a DVD.

47.5 | Expressing purpose and consequence

While **tame ni** 'in order to' expresses the purpose of an action, **yoo ni** 'so that' indicates that a certain consequence will be realized as the result of an ation. A **tame ni** clause represents what the speaker thinks he/she can bring about with his/her volition, and hence verbs in **tame ni** clause are action verbs. A **yoo ni** clause, on the other hand, represents a condition, state or events that cannot be controlled by one's will, and the verbs in this construction are usually stative, including potential verbs, negative forms, and **wakaru** 'to understand.'

部屋を暖めるためにヒーターをつけた。
Heya o atatameru tame ni hiitaa o tsuketa.
(I) turned the heater on in order to warm the room.

部屋が暖かくなるようにヒーターをつけた。
Heya ga atatakaku naru yoo ni hiitaa o tsuketa.
(I) turned the heater on so that the room gets warm.

These sentences basically describe the same situation. However, **heya o atatameru** 'to warm up the room' (a transitive verb) is a volitional action and hence it indicates the purpose of an action. On the other hand, **heya ga atatakaku naru** 'the room becomes warm' (an intransitive verb) is a state which obtains as a result of one's action.

The following are some more examples.

風邪が治るように一日中寝ていました。
Kaze ga naoru yoo ni ichinichi-juu nete imashita.
I was sleeping all day long so that my cold would get better.

忘れないようにメモをしておいた。
Wasurenai yoo ni memo o shite oita.
I made a note (for myself) so that I wouldn't forget.

早く起きられるように目覚まし時計をかけて寝た。
Hayaku okirareru yoo ni mezamashi-dokee o kakete neta.
I set my alarm clock before I went to sleep so that I could get up early.

新しい車を買うために貯金しています。
Atarashii kuruma o kau tame ni chokin shite imasu.
I'm saving money in order to buy a new car.

体重を減らすためにダイエットを始めました。
Taijuu o herasu tame ni daietto o hajimemashita.
I went on a diet in order to lose weight.

When the purpose is expressed with a noun phrase, Noun + **no tame ni** is used.

父は家族のために一生懸命はたらいています。
Chichi wa kazoku no tame ni isshookenmee hataraite imasu.
My father is working hard for (the sake of) his family.

世界平和のために働きたいです。
Sekai heewa no tame ni hatarakitai desu.
I want to work for world peace.

47.6 Expressing the means by which to achieve a purpose

To state the means or what is needed to achieve a certain purpose, the formal noun **no** followed by the postposition **ni** 'for' can be used instead of **tame ni**. The **no ni** combination follows the plain form of a verb.

瓶を開けるのに、栓抜きが要りますね。
Bin o akeru no ni, sennuki ga irimasu ne.
You need a bottle opener in order to open the bottle, right?

皮を剥くのに、皮むき器を使った。
Kawa o muku no ni, kawamukiki o tsukatta.
I used a peeler to peel the skin.

47.7 Expressing how to achieve a purpose

To state what one should do or needs to do in order to achieve a goal, the statement which expresses the goal is topicalized using **tame ni wa** or **ni wa**, followed by suggestions, advice, or instructions. Both **tame ni wa** and **ni wa** follow the plain form of a verb.

> 留学するためには、いろいろな準備をしなければいけません。
> **Ryuugaku suru tame ni wa, iroirona junbi o shinakereba ikemasen.**
> In order to study abroad, you must prepare in various ways.

> お金を貯めるには、まず節約から始めるべきだ。
> **O-kane o tameru ni wa, mazu setsuyaku kara hajimeru beki da.**
> To accumulate money, you should start saving first.

48

Cause and effect

48.1 ## Asking about cause

To ask about cause, the noun **gen'in** is used.

原因は何ですか。(F)
Gen'in wa nan desu ka.
As for the cause, what is it?

原因は何？(I)
Gen'in wa nani?
As for the cause, what is it?

何が原因ですか。(F)
Nani ga gen'in desu ka.
What is the cause?

何が原因？(I)
Nani ga gen'in?
What is the cause?

To ask about the cause of an event more specifically, **gen'in** can be modified by the noun modification structure as follows.

▶ 7.2

火事の原因は何ですか。
Kaji no gen'in wa nan desu ka.
As for the cause of fire, what is it?

何が試験に落ちた原因ですか。
Nani ga shiken ni ochita gen'in desu ka.
What caused you to fail the exam?

It is also common to use questions words **naze**, **nande** and **dooshite**, all meaning 'why,' to ask about cause.

▶ 4.3; 18.2; 32.1.2; 32.2

なんで 本棚が倒れたの？
Nande hondana ga taoreta no?
Why did the bookshelf fall down?

どうして橋が落ちたのでしょうか。
Dooshite hashi ga ochita no deshoo ka.
Why did the bridge fall down?

48.2 ## Expressing cause

To express cause, the following sentence structures are commonly used.

X **no gen'in wa** Y **desu.** 'The cause of X is Y.'

火事の原因はたばこです。
Kaji no gen'in wa tabako desu.
The cause of the fire was a cigarette.

X **ga gen'in desu.** 'X is the cause.'

> Q: 何が肥満の原因ですか。
> **Nani ga himan no gen'in desu ka.**
> What is the cause of obesity?

> A: 運動不足が原因です。
> **Undoo busoku ga gen'in desu.**
> Lack of exercise is the cause.

Clause **no/koto ga gen'in desu.** '. . . is the cause.'

> あまり歩かなくなったの/ことが原因です。
> **Amari arukanakunatta no/koto ga gen'in desu.**
> That people walk less is the cause.

Other expressions that are used to express cause are listed below with examples.

> せいだ　　　**see da**　　　'due to'

See da has a negative connotation and is used when the consequence has an adverse effect on the speaker. **See da** is used when the speaker is placing the blame on someone or something rather than stating the cause objectively. Structurally, the cause is expressed as the noun modifier of **see**, i.e. noun **no see** or predicate (plain form) **see**.

▶ 7.2

> 俺が負けたのはおまえのせいだ。
> **Ore ga maketa no wa omae no see da.**
> I lost because of you!

> 朝寝坊したのは、目覚まし時計がならなかったせいだ。
> **Asaneboo shita no wa, mezamashi dokee ga naranakatta see da.**
> That I overslept is due to the alarm clock not ringing.

> 雨にぬれたせいで、風邪をひきました。
> **Ame ni nureta see de, kaze o hikimashita.**
> I caught a cold due to getting wet in the rain.

> おかげだ　　　**okage da**　　　'thanks to'

The cause is expressed as the noun modifier of **okage**, i.e. noun **no okage** or predicate (plain form) **okage**.

▶ 7.2

> 留学できたのは奨学金のおかげだ。
> **Ryuugaku dekita no wa shoogakukin no okage da.**
> That I was able to study abroad is thanks to the scholarship.

> プロジェクトが成功したのはみんなが協力してくれたおかげです。
> **Purojekuto ga seekoo shita no wa minna ga kyooryoku shite kureta okage desu.**
> The success of the project is due to everyone's cooperation.

The verb **motarasu** 'to bring about' is also used to express cause. In this case the cause is stated as the topic or the subject of the sentence.

> その年の台風は大災害をもたらした。
> **Sono toshi no taifuu wa daisaigai o motarashita.**
> The typhoon that year caused severe damage.

> 果物は健康に良い影響をもたらします。
> **Kudamono wa kenkoo ni yoi eekyoo o motarashimasu.**
> Fruits bring about good effects on health.

Expressing relationships of cause and effect

The **te**-form can be used to express cause when two events are closely related as cause and effect.

▶ 22.1

道が混んでいて、遅くなりました。
Michi ga konde ite, osoku narimashita.
The road was congested, and so I was delayed.

番号が分からなくて、連絡できませんでした。
Bangoo ga wakaranakute, renraku dekimasen deshita.
I didn't know the number, and so I couldn't contact you.

The **te**-form can also indicate the cause of one's emotional or physical state.

試験に受かってうれしいです。
Shiken ni ukatte ureshii desu.
I'm glad to have passed the exam.
(Lit. I passed the exam and so I'm glad.)

パーティーに行けなくてがっかりです。
Paatii ni ikenakute gakkari desu.
I'm disappointed that I couldn't go to the party.
(Lit. I couldn't go to the party and so I'm disappointed.)

お腹が空いて目眩がする。
Onaka ga suite memai ga suru.
I feel dizzy from hunger.
(Lit. I'm hungry and so I feel dizzy.)

In formal speech or in writing, instead of **te**-form, the V-stem may be used.

目標を達成でき、感激です。
Mokuhyoo o tassee deki, kangeki desu.
I'm ecstatic to have been able to achieve my goal.

病を患い、入院した。
Yamai o wazurai, nyuuin shita.
I was hospitalized as I developed an illness.

The negative **te**-form **nakute** can be replaced by **zu** in writing or in formal speech.

パーティーに行けず、がっかりです。
Paatii ni ikezu, gakkari desu.
I'm disappointed because I couldn't go to the party.

誰にも会えず、さびしかった。
Dare ni mo aezu, sabishikatta.
I couldn't see anyone, so I was lonely.

When the cause can be expressed by a noun, the particle **de** is used.

地震で本棚が倒れた。
Jishin de hondana ga taoreta.
The bookshelf fell down because of the earthquake.

火事で家が焼けてしまった。
Kaji de ie ga yakete shimatta.
The house burned down due to the fire.

結婚で生活がかわった。
Kekkon de seekatsu ga kawatta.
My lifestyle has changed due to my marriage.

When a consequence is something negative, **see de** is often used to state the cause with a tone of blame.

台風のせいで遠足に行けなかった。
Taifuu no see de ensoku ni ikenakatta.
Because of the typhoon, we couldn't go on the field trip.

ルームメートがうるさかったせいで、全然眠れなかった。
Ruumumeeto ga urusakatta see de, zenzen nemurenakatta.
Because my roommate was noisy, I couldn't sleep at all.

The conditional particle **to** is used to express a natural or logical cause-and-effect relationship.

▶ **24.1**

このボタンを押すと電気がつきます。
Kono botan o osu to denki ga tsukimasu.
When you press this button, the light turns on.

冬になると寒くなります。
Fuyu ni naru to samuku narimasu.
When it becomes winter, it gets cold.

疲れると甘い物がほしくなる。
Tsukareru to amai mono ga hoshiku naru.
When I get tired, I crave something sweet.

49

Describing procedures

Basic phrases used in describing procedures

In describing procedures words such as **mazu** 'first', **hajime ni/saisho ni** 'at the beginning', **tsugi ni** 'next', **soshite** 'then', **sorekara** 'then', **saigo ni** 'finally' or the like can be used. Procedures are usually described using nonpast forms of verbs.

まずお金を入れて、それから欲しいものの番号を押します。
Mazu o-kane o irete, sorekara hoshii mono no bangoo o oshimasu.
First you put in money, and then push the number of the item you want.

まず鍋に油をしき、次に肉を入れて、そして最後に野菜を入れます。
Mazu nabe ni abura o shiki, tsugi ni niku o irete, soshite saigo ni yasai o iremasu.
First you put oil in the pan. Next, you put in meat and then last you put in vegetables.

緑の窓口で切符を買う時は、まず用紙に希望の日にちと電車の時刻を書き入れます。
Midori no madoguchi de kippu o kau toki wa, mazu yooshi ni kiboo no hinichi to densha no jikoku o kakiiremasu.
When you buy a ticket at 'Midori no madoguchi (Japan Railways ticket office),' you first write the date and the time of the train you want on the (request) form.

The conditional expression S **to** S is often used to describe procedures.

▶ **24.1**

まず筆記試験があります。そして、筆記試験にパスすると面接があります。
Mazu hikki shiken ga arimasu. Soshite, hikki shiken ni pasu suru to mensetsu ga arimasu.
First there is a written exam. Then, once/if you pass the written exam, you will be interviewed.

オーブンで一時間ぐらい焼くとおいしいケーキができます。
Oobun de ichijikan gurai yaku to oishii keeki ga dekimasu.
You bake it in the oven for about an hour, and you will have a delicious cake.

50

Changes

While English has many verbs used with adjectives to express changes, such as 'become', 'get', 'turn', 'grow', etc., the most usual way of expressing changes in Japanese involves the verb **naru** 'to become.'

50.1 Talking about changes

The verb **naru** indicates change and it can be used with nouns, adjectives, and verbs. Forms preceding **naru** vary as follows:

Noun:	N **ni naru**
Na-adjective:	**na**-adj.(stem) **ni naru**
I-adjective:	**i**-adj **ku naru**
Verb:	V (plain) **yoo ni naru**

It should be noted that **i**-adjectives are in adverbial form (e.g. **atarashiku**, **yasuku**) and the verb has to be followed by **yoo ni**.

▶ **14.2; 18.4**

弁護士になった。
Bengoshi ni natta.
I became a lawyer.

インターネットで便利になった。
Intaanetto de benri ni natta.
It has become convenient with the Internet.

物価が高くなった。
Bukka ga takaku natta.
The cost of living has become expensive.

漢字が書けるようになった。
Kanji ga kakeru yoo ni natta.
I have become able to write kanji.

大学に入ってよく勉強するようになった。
Daigaku ni haitte yoku benkyoo suru yoo ni natta.
After entering college, (he) came to study hard (i.e. started to study hard).

In general, **naru** constructions can express either a sudden change or a gradual change, but it is more common that these changes are conceived as gradual.

50.2 Change in a negative direction

Negative forms can precede the verb **naru** to indicate that a change has been from an affirmative situation to a negative situation. Since the negative form **-nai** is an adjective, it changes to **-naku (naru)**.

> 卒業して学生じゃなくなった。
> **Sotsugyoo shite gakusee ja naku natta.**
> (I) graduated and so I am not a student any more.

> まわりに建物がたくさん立って、静かじゃなくなった。
> **Mawari ni tatemono ga takusan tatte, shizuka ja naku natta.**
> Many buildings went up around us, and it is no longer quiet (Lit. has become not quiet).

> 壁が汚れて白くなくなった。
> **Kabe ga yogorete shirokunaku natta.**
> The wall got dirty and it is no longer white (Lit. has become not-white).

> 言葉は話していないと、話せなくなる。
> **Kotoba wa hanashite inai to, hanasenaku naru.**
> If you don't keep speaking a language, you become unable to speak it.

With verbs, there is also a **-nai yoo ni naru** 'become not V' in addition to **-naku naru**.

> ご飯が食べられなくなった。
> **Gohan ga taberarenaku natta.**
> It has come to be that I cannot eat food.

> ご飯が食べられないようになった。
> **Gohan ga taberarenai yoo ni natta.**
> It has come to be that I cannot eat food.

These two constructions are similar in meaning. However, the **-nai yoo ni naru** construction might imply that the change occurred gradually over time, while the **-naku naru** construction implies either a gradual change or a sudden change. If the change happened suddenly, therefore, **-naku naru** is the form to be used.

50.3 Verbs of coming and going to express changes

Verbs of coming and going in **te**-form (i.e. **-te kuru** and **-te iku**) can express changes that take place. **-Te kuru** expresses that a certain change has been taking place up to now, and **-te iku** indicates that a change will continue to take place from now on into the future. Both indicate that changes are taking place over some time, whether at a gradual pace or at a rapid pace.

▶ 19.2.6; 19.2.7

> 寒くなってきましたねえ。
> **Samuku natte kimashita nee.**
> It has become cold (don't you think?).

> 日本語がだいぶ話せるようになってきました。
> **Nihongo ga daibu hanaseru yoo ni natte kimashita.**
> I have come to be able to speak Japanese pretty well.

> これから生活はどんどん便利になっていくでしょう。
> **Korekara seekatsu wa dondon benri ni natte iku deshoo.**
> Our daily lives will keep getting more and more convenient (at a rapid pace).

50.4 Other ways of expressing changes

50.4.1 Change caused by evolving events or situations

To indicate that one change causes another change, the **-ba** V(plain nonpast) **hodo** 'the more . . . , the more . . . ; the less . . . , the less . . .' construction can be used. **Ba** is the conditional form.

▶ 24.2

日本語は勉強すればするほど面白くなります。
Nihongo wa benkyoo sureba suru hodo omoshiroku narimasu.
The more you study Japanese, the more interesting it becomes.

考えれば考えるほど分からなくなる。
Kangaereba kangaeru hodo wakaranaku naru.
The more I think about it, the more confusing it becomes.

Other expressions, such as V(plain) **to tomo ni**, V(plain) **ni tsurete** and V(plain) **ni shitagatte**, all meaning 'as V happens,' can also express that a change leads to another change concurrently.

時代が変わるとともに言葉も変わる。
Jidai ga kawaru to tomoni kotoba mo kawaru.
As time changes, language also changes.

電子メールの普及とともに手紙を書くことが少なくなった。
Denshi meeru no fukyuu to tomo ni tegami o kaku koto ga sukunaku natta.
With the spread of email there is less letter writing.

女性の社会進出が進むにつれて経済力のある女性が増えた。
Josee no shakai shinshutsu ga susumu ni tsurete keezairyoku no aru josee ga fueta.
As women's position in society (i.e. workplace) advanced, the number of women with economic power increased.

年を取るにつれて忘れっぽくなるのは普通だ。
Toshi o toru ni tsurete wasureppoku naru no wa futsuu da.
It is natural that one becomes forgetful with age (i.e. as one gets older.)

女性の晩婚化が進むに従って出産率も減っている。
Josee no bankonka ga susumu ni shitagatte shussanritsu mo hette iru.
As women get married later and later, the birth rate is decreasing.

50.4.2 Nouns and verbs that express change

The verb **kawaru** is a general verb that means 'to change.' There are many other verbal nouns which, combined with the verb **suru**, express various types of change. Examples include **henka suru** 'to change,' **henshin suru** 'to transform oneself, metamorphose,' **henkee suru** 'to change form,' **henkan suru** 'switch.'

最近天気がよく変わる。
Saikin tenki ga yoku kawaru.
The weather changes often / is changeable these days.

時代が変わると、人々の考えも変化する。
Jidai ga kawaru to, hitobito no kangae mo henka suru.
When times change, people's ways of thinking change too.

日本の昔話には動物が人に変身する話が多い。
Nihon no mukashi-banashi ni wa doobutsu ga hito ni henshin suru hanashi ga ooi.
There are many Japanese folktales where animals change into people.

日本人の生活は戦後大きく変化した。
Nihonjin no seekatsu wa sengo ookiku henka shita.
The Japanese people's way of life changed a lot after the war.

ワープロではローマ字から日本語に簡単に変換できる。
Waapuro de wa roomaji kara Nihongo ni kantan ni henkan dekiru.
With a word processor you can easily change romanized letters into Japanese characters.

Certain compound verbs can express change. Some examples include V(stem) **dasu** 'to start V-ing,' V(stem) **hajimeru** 'to begin V-ing,' V(stem) **owaru** 'to finish V-ing,' V(stem) **kaeru** 'to change (clothing, shoes, etc.).'

▶ 17.3

急に泣き出した。
Kyuu ni naki-dashita.
(He) started crying all of sudden.

家に帰ったら、すぐ雨が降り出した。
Uchi ni kaettara, sugu ame ga furi-dashita.
When I went home, immediately it started raining.

論文を書き始めてから書き終わるまで二年かかった。
Ronbun o kaki-hajimete kara kaki-owaru made ninen kakatta.
It took two years from the time I started writing a thesis to the time I finished writing it.

寝る前はパジャマに着替えます。
Neru mae wa pajama ni ki-kaemasu.
(I) change into pajamas before I go to sleep.

東京駅で地下鉄に乗り換えてください。
Tookyoo eki de chikatetsu ni nori-kaete kudasai.
Please change to the subway at Tokyo Station.

51

Expressing abilities

There are basically two ways of expressing one's abilities or capabilities. One is to use the verb **dekiru** 'be able to do,' and the other is to use potential forms of verbs. These are explained below.

51.1 **Enquiring and making statements about abilities using *dekiru***

Dekiru is the verb that means 'can do,' and it occurs in the following two constructions.

1. N (often a verbal noun) *ga* (= nominative particle) *dekiru*

料理ができますか。　　　　何語ができますか。
Ryoori ga dekimasu ka.　　**Nanigo ga dekimasu ka.**
Can you cook?　　　　What languages are you proficient in?

英語ができます。
Eego ga dekimasu.
I am good at English.

2. V phrase (in plain nonpast form) *koto ga dekiru*

It should be noted that in this construction, verbs are always in the nonpast tense form, and **koto** nominalizes the verb phrase.

▶ 18.1

日本語を話すことができますか。
Nihongo o hanasu koto ga dekimasu ka.
Can you speak Japanese?

私はピアノをひくことができません。
Watashi wa piano o hiku koto ga dekimasen.
I can't play the piano.

お金があれば、世界中を旅行することができます。
O-kane ga areba, sekai juu o ryokoo suru koto ga dekimasu.
If we have money, we can travel all over the world.

51.2 **Enquiring and making statements about abilities using potential forms**

Potential forms are such forms as **ik-e-ru** 'can go,' **tabe-rare-ru** 'can eat,' **ko-rare-ru** 'can come.' The potential form of **suru** 'to do' is **dekiru** 'can do,' which is the same as the independent verb **dekiru**.

▶ 12.6

A declarative sentence can be changed into a potential sentence by changing **o** to **ga** and by changing the verb into a potential form.

X **ga/wa** Y **o** V	→	X **ga/wa** Y **ga** V(potential)
田中さんが/は漢字を書く。		田中さんが/は漢字が書ける。
Tanaka-san ga/wa kanji o kaku.		**Tanaka-san ga/wa kanji ga kakeru.**
Mr/Ms Tanaka writes **kanji**.		Mr/Ms Tanaka can write **kanji**.

Although **ga** is somewhat preferred in the potential construction, in many cases, the direct object marker **o** can remain as **o** in the potential construction. That is to say, the direct object of a potential verb can be marked either by **ga** or by **o**.

スミスさんは日本語が話せる。
Sumisu-san wa Nihongo ga hanaseru.
Mr/Ms Smith can speak Japanese.

スミスさんは日本語を話せる。
Sumisu-san wa Nihongo o hanaseru.
Mr/Ms Smith can speak Japanese.

スミスさんは日本語の新聞が読めるんでしょうか。
Sumisu-san wa Nihongo no shinbun ga yomeru n deshoo ka.
Can Mr/Ms Smith read Japanese newspapers?

あした何時ごろ来られますか。
Ashita nanji goro koraremasu ka.
When can you come tomorrow?

The question of which particle is used or preferred is not always clear. However, it seems that **o** is preferred when the speaker focuses on the action, and hence as an activity over which the speaker has some control.

(a) 一年間で教育漢字を読めるようにします。
    Ichinenkan de kyooiku kanji o yomeru yoo ni shimasu.
    I will make it so that (the students) can read the **kyooiku kanji**
    (Chinese characters taught in Japanese elementary schools) in a year.

(b) 日本に住んでいたので、自然に日本語が話せるようになりました。
    Nihon ni sunde ita node, shizen ni Nihongo ga hanaseru yoo ni narimashita.
    Since (I) lived in Japan, (as a natural consequence) I came to be able to speak Japanese.

In (a), **o** is preferred since the sentence focuses on the volitional action of bringing about the result, that is, 'being able to read the **kyoiku kanji**.' On the other hand, in (b), **ga** is preferred since the sentence focuses on what naturally occurred.

▶ **10.1**

52

Needs

In Japanese you can express needs or lack of needs with the verb **iru** 'to need,' the nominal adjective **hitsuyoo na** 'necessary' or with an expression such as V-**nakereba naranai** 'need to, have to.'

52.1 Expressing needs with regard to oneself and others

52.1.1 *hitsuyoo*

Hitsuyoo, which means 'need,' can be a noun or a **na**-adjective. As a **na**-adjective, it is **hitsuyoo na** when it modifies a noun, and **hitsuyoo da** when it is used as a predicate.

▶ 13.2

Hitsuyoo as a noun:

> 必要に応じて作ります。
> **Hitsuyoo ni oojite tsukurimasu.**
> (I) will make it depending on needs.

> 健康に注意する必要がある。
> **Kenkoo ni chuui suru hitsuyoo ga aru.**
> There is a need to be careful about one's health. (You need to be careful about your health.)

Hitsuyoo as a **na**-adjective:

> 何か必要なものがあったら、言ってください。
> **Nani ka hitsuyoo na mono ga attara, itte kudasai.**
> If there is anything you need, please tell me.

> 毎日練習することが必要だ。
> **Mainichi renshuu suru koto ga hitsuyoo da.**
> It is necessary to practice every day.

52.1.2 *iru*

The verb **iru** 'to need' can be used to enquire about and state one's needs. The item one needs is marked by the particle **ga**, unless it is a topic.

> お金はいくらぐらいいりますか。 | これ、いる？
> **O-kane wa ikura gurai irimasu ka.** | **Kore, iru?**
> How much money do (we) need? | Do you need this?

> 新しいことを始めるには勇気がいる。
> **Atarashii koto o hajimeru ni wa yuuki ga iru.**
> You need courage to begin a new thing.

V-*nakereba naranai*, V-*nakereba ikenai*

The **ba** conditional form of the negative form (i.e. **-nakereba**) followed by **naranai** or **ikenai** generally expresses obligation. However, in some contexts, it also expresses personal needs, as in the following examples.

▶ **24.2; 80.1**

> お金がないから仕事をしなければならない。
> **O-kane ga nai kara shigoto o shinakereba naranai.**
> Since I don't have money, I need to (have to) work.

> あした朝早いから、早く寝なければいけない。
> **Ashita asa hayai kara, hayaku nenakereba ikenai.**
> Since my day starts early tomorrow, I need to (have to) go to bed early.

Another form that is similar to this is **-nakute wa ikenai/naranai**, and this also expresses one's obligation or needs.

> もっと勉強しなくてはいけません。
> **Motto benkyoo shinakute wa ikemasen.**
> I need to (have to) study more.

▶ For subtle differences between **-naranai** and **-ikenai**, see **80.1.2**.

-Nakereba is often contracted to **-nakya**, and **-nakute wa** to **-nakucha** in conversation.

> 早く寝なきゃ。(I)
> **Hayaku nenakya.**
> I have to (need to) go to bed early.

> もっと勉強しなくちゃ。(I)
> **Motto benkyoo shinakucha.**
> I need to (have to) study more.

52.2 **Expressing lack of needs**

There are various ways of expressing that one does not need anything or one does not need to do something.

■ V(plain, nonpast) **hitsuyoo wa nai**

> 図書館にあるから買う必要はないでしょう。
> **Toshokan ni aru kara kau hitsuyoo wa nai deshoo.**
> Since it is in the library, there is probably no need to buy it.

■ **Iranai** (negative form of **iru**)

> お金はいらない。
> **O-kane wa iranai.**
> I don't need any money.

■ V-**nakute mo ii**

> 忙しかったら、来なくてもいいよ。
> **Isogashikattara, konakute mo ii yo.**
> If you are busy, you don't have to (need to) come.

■ V(plain, nonpast) **made mo nai**

> 勉強しなければ成績が悪くなるのは言うまでもない。
> **Benkyoo shinakereba seeseki ga waruku naru no wa yuu made mo nai.**
> Needless to say, if you don't study, your grade goes down.

■ V(plain, nonpast) **ni wa oyobanai**

悪いことをしたんじゃないんだから、謝るには及ばない。
Warui koto o shita n ja nai n da kara, ayamaru ni wa oyobanai.
Since (I) did not do anything wrong, (I) don't need to apologize.

■ V(plain, nonpast) **koto wa nai**

アクセントの間違いはそんなに気にすることはない。
Akusento no machigai wa sonna ni ki ni suru koto wa nai.
You don't need to be concerned so much about making mistakes in the accent.

52.3 Asking people about their needs

You can enquire about other's needs by saying:

何が必要ですか。
Nani ga hitsuyoo desu ka.
What do you need?

何か必要なものがありますか。
Nani ka hitsuyoo na mono ga arimasu ka.
Is there anything you need?

何がいりますか。
Nani ga irimasu ka.
What do you need?

53

Possibility and probability

53.1 ## Saying whether something is considered possible or impossible

To say that something is considered possible or impossible, Japanese uses a number of expressions, of which the most common are:

53.1.1 ### *kanoo da, fukanoo da, muri da*

kanoo da 'possible,' **fukanoo da** 'impossible,' and **muri da** 'impossible' are all **na**-adjectives.

▶ 13.2

> 奨学金をもらうことは可能でしょうか。
> **Shoogakkin o morau koto wa kanoo deshoo ka.**
> Is it possible to receive a scholarship?

> あしたまでに論文をしあげるのは不可能だ。
> **Ashita made ni ronbun o shiageru no wa fukanoo da.**
> It is impossible to finish the thesis by tomorrow.

> あしたまでにスピーチを覚えるのは無理です。
> **Ashita made ni supiichi o oboeru no wa muri desu.**
> It is impossible to memorize the speech by tomorrow.

Sometimes, the nominal **kanoosee** 'possibility' can be used.

> 試験にパスする可能性はあるでしょうか。
> **Shiken ni pasu suru kanoosee wa aru deshoo ka.**
> Is there a possibility that I will pass the exam?

> 全く可能性がないとは言えない。
> **Mattaku kanoosee ga nai to wa ienai.**
> I can't say that there is no possibility at all.

53.1.2 ### V(stem)-*uru/enai*

A verb (stem) can be combined with **uru** to mean that there is a possibility of the action/state/event expressed by the main verb being realized. The negative form is V(stem)-**enai**. This expression is used with a limited set of verbs, the most frequent of which are **aru** 'to exist' and **okoru** 'to occur.'

> インフレはあり得る。
> **Infure wa ari-uru.**
> Inflation is possible.

世界から戦争がなくなるということはあり得ない。
Sekai kara sensoo ga nakunaru to yuu koto wa ari-enai.
It can't possibly happen that wars will disappear from the world.

V(plain) *kamoshirenai*

V(plain) **kamoshirenai** expresses that something is possible, that it may be true. In colloquial conversation, it is often shortened to **kamo**.

あしたは雪が降るかもしれません。
Ashita wa yuki ga furu kamoshiremasen.
It might snow tomorrow.

景気は回復しないかもしれません。
Keeki wa kaifuku shinai kamoshiremasen.
The economy might not recover.

今度の試験は難しいかなあ。
Kondo no shiken wa muzukashii ka naa.
I wonder if the next test will be difficult.

うん、難しいかも。(I)
Un, muzukashii kamo.
Yes, it might be.

Saying whether something is considered likely or probable

daroo/deshoo

The most common way of expressing that something is likely or probable is to use the sentence-final modal form **daroo** (informal)/**deshoo** (formal). This can follow nouns, **na**-adjectives (stem), **i**-adjectives and verbs (plain form). With **daroo/deshoo**, the speaker is more certain that the statement is true than **kamoshirenai**. This expression is often used with the adverb **tabun** 'probably.'

あの人は多分先生でしょう。
Ano hito wa tabun sensee deshoo.
That person is probably a teacher.

田中さんの住んでいるところはコンビニに近いから便利でしょう。
Tanaka-san no sunde iru tokoro wa konbini ni chikai kara benri deshoo.
Mr/Ms Tanaka's place is close to a convenience store, so it is probably convenient.

セールで買ったら、安いでしょう。
Seeru de kattara, yasui deshoo.
If you buy at a sale, it will be cheap.

あしたは雪が降るでしょう。
Ashita wa yuki ga furu deshoo.
It will probably snow tomorrow.

あの人パーティーに来るかしら。
Ano hito paatii ni kuru kashira.
Do you think he will come to the party?

多分来ないだろう。(I)
Tabun konai daroo.
Probably not.

The degree of certainty expressed by **daroo/deshoo** varies depending on the adverbs used. When it occurs with the adverb **kitto** 'certainly,' the speaker expresses a high degree of certainty. **Daroo/deshoo** is not appropriate when talking about the speaker's own actions. In such a case, **daroo to omoimasu** 'I think I will' should be used.

ピクニックに行きますか。
Pikunikku ni ikimasu ka.
Are you going to the picnic?

多分行かないだろうと思います。
*多分行かないでしょう。
Tabun ikanai daroo to omoimasu.
*Tabun ikanai deshoo.
I probably won't (go).

54

Certainty and uncertainty

54.1 Saying how certain one is of something

The following adverbs and set phrases express the speaker's sense of certainty.

絶対（に）	**zettai (ni)**	'absolutely'
必ず	**kanarazu**	'certainly; necessarily'
きっと	**kitto**	'certainly'
決して	**kesshite** (neg.)	'definitely not'
間違いなく	**machigainaku**	'unmistakably'
まぎれもなく	**magiremonaku**	'no doubt'

明日の試合は絶対に勝てる。
Ashita no shiai wa zettai ni kateru.
We can definitely win tomorrow's match.

田中さんは間違いなく立派なリーダーだと思う。
Tanaka-san wa machigainaku rippa na riidaa da to omou.
I think that Mr/Ms Tanaka is unmistakably a great leader.

Kesshite is used only in negative sentences.

▶ **15.4**

決して嘘はつきません。
Kesshite uso wa tsukimasen.
I definitely don't lie.

The following constructions are also used to state the speaker's certainty. They are often used in combination with an adverb of certainty.

■ Clause (plain) **ni chigainai** 'must be that . . . ,' 'no doubt'

きっと新しい社長は山下さんがなるにちがいない。
Kitto atarashii shachoo wa Yamashita-san ga naru ni chigainai.
It is certain that Mr/Ms Yamashita will be the new company president.

■ Clause (plain) **ni kimatte iru** 'I am sure that . . .'

隆は来ないに決まっている。
Takashi wa konai ni kimatte iru.
I'm sure that Takashi will not come.

54.2 Expressing doubt about something

Various expressions are used to communicate one's doubt, including the following.

■ Clause (plain) **to wa omoenai/masen** 'cannot think that . . .'

あの人が大学生だとは思えない。
Ano hito ga daigakusee da to wa omoenai.
I cannot think that that person is a college student.

うまくいくとは思えません。
Umaku iku to wa omoemasen.
I cannot think that it will go well.

▶ **15.2; 26.2**

■ Clause (plain) **to wa/nante shinjirarenai** 'cannot believe that . . .'

田中さんが正しいとは信じられません。
Tanaka-san ga tadashii to wa shinjiraremasen.
I cannot believe that Mr/Ms Tanaka is right.

そんなことがあるなんて信じられない。
Sonna koto ga aru nante shinjirarenai.
I can't believe that such a thing could/will happen.

▶ **15.2; 26.2**

Another way to express doubt is to use an embedded question with various expressions of doubt.

▶ **26.3**

■ Embedded question + **wakaranai** 'not sure'

それが正しいかどうか分かりません。
Sore ga tadashii ka doo ka wakarimasen.
I'm not sure if that's right or not.

■ Embedded question + **ayashii** 'suspicious'

うまく行くかどうかあやしいと思います。
Umaku iku ka doo ka ayashii to omoimasu.
I suspect that it will not go well.

■ Embedded question + **utagawashii** 'doubtful'

あいつが本当にくるかどうか疑わしいと思います。
Aitsu ga hontoo ni kuru ka doo ka utagawashii to omoimasu.
I think it's doubtful that he will really come.

To express one's general feeling of doubt or uncertainty, the following phrases may be used.

大丈夫かなあ。	**Daijoobu ka naa.**	I wonder if it's okay.
大丈夫ですかねえ。	**Daijoobu desu ka nee.**	I wonder if it's okay.
大丈夫かしら。	**Daijoobu kashira.**	I wonder if it's okay.
うまくいくかなあ。	**Umaku iku ka naa.**	I wonder if it'll go well.
変ですねえ。	**Hen desu nee.**	It's strange, isn't it.
おかしいですねえ。	**Okashii desu nee.**	It's weird, isn't it.

To express one's general sense of doubt toward what one's interlocutor has said, the following phrases may be used.

そうでしょうか。
Soo deshoo ka.
Would that be so?

そうですか。
Soo desu ka.
Is that so?

そうかもしれませんが . . . 。
Soo kamoshiremasen ga . . .
It might be so, but . . .

それはちょっと . . . 。
Sore wa chotto. . . .
That's a little. . . . (implying disagreement)

54.3 Asking people about their level of certainty

To ask how certain people are about what they said, one of the following questions may be used.

本当ですか。(F)	**Hontoo desu ka.**	Is it true? / Are you sure?
ほんと？(I)	**Honto?**	Is it true? / Are you sure?
確かですか。(F)	**Tashika desu ka.**	Are you certain?

絶対そうだって言える？(I)
Zettai soo da tte ieru?
Can you say that for sure?

55

Provisions, conditions, and hypotheses

Expressing open conditions

In open conditions, where conditions may or may not be fulfilled, there are basically four conditionals in Japanese, **tara**, **nara**, **ba** and **to**. All of these express the idea of 'if,' as in the following.

▶ 24

お金があったら、車が買えます。
O-kane ga attara, kuruma ga kaemasu.
If you have money, you can buy a car.

お金があるなら、車が買えます。
O-kane ga aru nara, kuruma ga kaemasu.
If you have money (as you say you do), then you can buy a car.

お金があれば、車が買えます。
O-kane ga areba, kuruma ga kaemasu.
If you have money, you can buy a car. (All you need to buy a car is money.)

お金があると、車が買えます。
O-kane ga aru to, kuruma ga kaemasu.
If you have money, you can buy a car.

The following are some points to remember in using these forms. In the following discussions, S1 refers to the clause preceding the conditionals and S2 to the clause that follows it.

1) *To* vs. *tara*
In both S1 **to** S2 and S1 **tara** S2, S1 is completed before S2 (when two actions are involved). **To** gives the sense that S2 is a natural or logical consequence of S1. Among the four conditional forms, **to** is the least conditional and most temporal in nature and it is more likely used when S1 is certain to happen. Hence, **to** is the most frequently used form in written narratives.

2) *Tara* vs. *nara*
One big difference between **tara** and **nara** is that, while S1 is completed before S2 with **tara**, such is not the case with **nara**. With **nara**, generally, S2 is an event or situation that occurs either concurrently with S1 or before S1 occurs. If S2 is an event which can only be realized after another event in S1 takes place, **nara** is inappropriate.

この本を読むなら、字引がいります。
Kono hon o yomu nara, jibiki ga irimasu.
If you are going to read this book (as you say you are), you will need a dictionary.

*この本を読んだら、字引がいります。
***Kono hon o yondara, jibiki ga irimasu.**
*If you are going to read this book (after you read this book), you will need a dictionary.

Since you need a dictionary while reading the book (i.e. S1 and S2 are concurrent), not after reading the book, **tara** is inappropriate.

> *運動をするなら、やせますよ。
> *Undoo o suru nara, yasemasu yo.
> If you are going to do exercise, you will lose weight.

> 運動をしたら、やせますよ。
> Undoo o shitara, yasemasu yo.
> If you do exercise, you will lose weight.

In this case, since you don't lose weight until after you do exercise, **tara** is appropriate, but not **nara**.

3) *Tara* vs. *ba*

As is indicated above, what is important with the use of **tara** is the temporal sequencing of the two events. **Ba**, on the other hand, gives the necessary and sufficient condition for the realization of S2. So, **ba** often gives the sense of 'all you need to do to realize S2 is S1.'

> 練習したら、上手になりますよ。
> Renshuu shitara, joozu ni narimasu yo.
> If you practice, you (your skill) will improve.

> 練習すれば、上手になりますよ。
> Renshuu sureba, joozu ni narimasu yo.
> If you practice, you (your skill) will improve.

With **tara**, the implication is that S1 precedes S2 – i.e. if you practice, you will get better. With **ba**, on the other hand, the implication is that you need to practice if you want to improve.

The following examples show similarities and differences between these conditionals.

> (a) あなたが行ったら、私も行きます。
>   **Anata ga ittara, watashi mo ikimasu.**
>   If (after) you go, I will go too.

> (b) あなたが行くなら、私も行きます。
>   **Anata ga iku nara, watashi mo ikimasu.**
>   If you go (as you say you will), I will go too.

> (c) あなたが行けば、私も行きます。
>   **Anata ga ikeba, watashi mo ikimasu.**
>   If (provided that) you go, I will go too.

> (d) *あなたが行くと、私も行きます。
>   ***Anata ga iku to, watashi mo ikimasu.**
>   Whenever you go, I go too.

Sentence (a) simply indicates that 'your going' takes place before 'my going.' Sentence (b) with **nara** is used when the interlocutor asserts that he/she is going. In (b), 'my going' can take place before 'your going' or concurrently. Sentence (c) expresses that the only way 'I' will go is if 'you' go. 'Your going' is a necessary condition for 'my going.' Sentence (d) with **to** sounds strange because the sentence implies that 'whenever you go, I always go' as if it is something which automatically happens.

> (e) 日本に行ったら、日本語が上手になるでしょう。
>   **Nihon ni ittara, Nihongo ga joozu ni naru deshoo.**
>   If (after) you go to Japan, your Japanese will improve.

> (f) 日本に行けば、日本語が上手になるでしょう。
>   **Nihon ni ikeba, Nihongo ga joozu ni naru deshoo.**
>   If you go to Japan, your Japanese will improve.
>   All you have to do to improve your Japanese is to go to Japan.

(g)　*日本に行くなら、日本語が上手になるでしょう。
　　*Nihon ni iku nara, Nihongo ga joozu ni naru deshoo.
　　If you go to Japan (as you say you will), your Japanese will improve.

(h)　日本に行くと、日本語が上手になるでしょう。
　　Nihon ni iku to, Nihongo ga joozu ni naru deshoo.
　　If one goes to Japan, one's Japanese will improve.

Again, **tara** focuses on the fact that one's Japanese improves after going to Japan. **Ba** indicates that going to Japan is a necessary condition for improving one's Japanese. **Nara** sounds strange because the sentence indicates that one's Japanese improves even before going to Japan simply upon making an assertion that one is going to Japan. **To** gives the sense that it is a general truth that one's Japanese improves after going to Japan.

55.2　Expressing unfulfilled conditions

A condition which cannot be fulfilled or which is contrary to fact can be expressed by the conditionals **tara** and **ba**. The main sentence generally ends with conjunctions such as **noni** 'although' or **ga** 'but.'

▶ 24; 22.5

もっと勉強したら、パスできたのに。
Motto benkyoo shitara, pasu dekita noni.
If I had studied harder, I could have passed.

お金があれば、行けるんですが。
O-kane ga areba, ikeru n desu ga.
If I had money, I could go (but since I don't have money, I can't).

前もって言ってくれれば手伝ってあげたのに。
Maemotte itte kurereba tetsudatte ageta noni.
If you had told me beforehand, I would have helped you.

日本に留学すればよかったのに。
Nihon ni ryuugaku sureba yokatta noni.
You should have gone to study abroad.

The conditional **nara** sometimes expresses this type of counter-factual condition.

私がばかなら、あなたもばかです。
Watashi ga baka nara, anata mo baka desu.
If I am a fool, so are you.

This sentence might be said when the interlocutor said something like 'you are a fool,' and the speaker strongly denies the interlocutor's assertion.

55.3　Expressing hypotheses

55.3.1　Use of *moshi* and *man'ichi*

Using adverbials such as **moshi** 'if' and **man'ichi** 'if ever' makes it clear that the speaker is presenting a hypothetical situation.

健康保険がないので、もし病気になったら困ります。
Kenkoo hoken ga nai node, moshi byooki ni nattara komarimasu.
Since I don't have health insurance, I will be in trouble in the event (= if) I get sick.

万一問題があったら、連絡します。
Man'ichi mondai ga attara, renraku shimasu.
In the unlikely event that (= if) there are problems, I will let you know.

55.3.2 *(moshi, man'ichi, karini) . . . to shitara*

Another expression which presents hypotheses is predicate (plain) + **to shitara** or **to sureba**, with or without **moshi**, **man'ichi** or **karini**.

もし一億円の宝くじがあたったとしたら、どうしますか。
Moshi ichiokuen no takarakuji ga atatta to shitara, doo shimasu ka.
If you won one hundred million yen on a lottery, what would you do?

パーティーをするとしたら、いつがいいでしょうか。
Paatii o suru to shitara, itsu ga ii deshoo ka.
If we were to have a party, when would be good?

仮にかれの言っていることが正しいとしたら、だれかが嘘をついていることになる。
Karini kare no itte iru koto ga tadashii to shitara, dare ka ga uso o tsuite iru koto ni naru.
If what he is saying is right, then someone else is lying.

間違っているとすれば、どこを直せばいいでしょうか。
Machigatte iru to sureba, doko o naoseba ii deshoo ka.
If I have made mistakes, which (part) should I correct?

55.4 Other conditional expressions

55.4.1 *sae . . . ba* conditional 'if only'

This expression can be used to express a sufficient condition for attaining a desired result. In this sense, it is a stronger statement than the simple **ba** conditional sentence.

The particle **sae** 'only' is most often used with a noun (N **sae** V **ba**) or a verb (V(stem) **sae** **sureba** or V-te **sae ireba**).

▶ 10.3; 24.2

あの人は、暇さえあれば寝ている。
Ano hito wa, hima sae areba nete iru.
He sleeps whenever he has free time.

あの人は、暇がありさえすれば寝ている。
Ano hito wa, hima ga ari sae sureba nete iru.
He sleeps whenever he has free time.

かぜは、薬さえ飲めばなおります。
Kaze wa, kusuri sae nomeba naorimasu.
You will recover from a cold if you just take the medicine. (That's the only thing you need to do.)

かぜは、たくさん寝さえすればなおります。
Kaze wa, takusan ne sae sureba naorimasu.
You will recover from a cold if you just sleep a lot.

When **sae** follows a noun, the focus is on that noun in contrast to other nouns. So, **kusuri sae nomeba** means 'if only you take (drink) medicine, not juice, not milk, etc.' On the other hand, when **sae** follows a verb, it is contrasting with other actions. Hence, **ne sae sureba** means 'if you just sleep, not eat, not go to the doctor, etc.'

毎日クラスに出てさえいれば、そんなに悪い成績はとらないでしょう。
Mainichi kurasu ni dete sae ireba, sonna ni warui seeseki wa toranai deshoo.
If you just attend classes every day, you won't get such bad grades.

55.4.2   N *demo*, -*te mo*

Te-form + **mo** means 'even if' or 'even though.'

子供でもわかります。
Kodomo demo wakarimasu.
Even children will understand.

不便でもかまいません。
Fuben demo kamaimasen.
Even if it is inconvenient, it is fine.

高くても、いいものなら買います。
Takakute mo, ii mono nara kaimasu.
Even if it is expensive, I will buy it if it is a quality product.

雨が降ってもやります。
Ame ga futte mo yarimasu.
Even if it rains, (we) will do it.

辞書を使わなくても読めます。
Jisho o tsukawanakute mo yomemasu.
Even without using a dictionary, (I) can read (it).

This expression can be used with question words such as **ikura** 'how much,' **donna ni** 'how,' **nani** 'what,' **dare** 'who,' and the like. This would mean 'no matter how much, no matter what, no matter who,' etc.

▶ 4.3

どんなに静かでも、図書館では勉強できません。
Donna ni shizuka demo, toshokan de wa benkyoo dekimasen.
No matter how quiet it is, I can't study in the library.

何を食べても太らない人がいるそうです。
Nani o tabete mo futoranai hito ga iru soo desu.
I hear that there are people who do not gain weight, no matter what they eat.

だれに聞いてもわからないことはたくさんあります。
Dare ni kiite mo wakaranai koto wa takusan arimasu.
There are many things that (we) don't know, no matter whom we ask.

Very colloquial forms of these expressions are **datte** and **tatte**.

こんな簡単な漢字、子供だって読めるよ。
Konna kantan na kanji kodomo datte yomeru yo.
Even children can read this kind of easy **kanji**.

日本語を話す時は、少しぐらい間違ったって、気にしない。
Nihongo o hanasu toki wa, sukoshi gurai machigatta tte, ki ni shinai.
When you speak Japanese, you don't have to worry even if you make some mistakes.

幸せは、お金があったって買えない。
Shiawase wa, o-kane ga atta tte kaenai.
You can't buy happiness (even if you have money).

56

Understanding and knowing

Japanese has two verbs which are used to express understanding and knowing but their usages do not always correspond to the ways the English verbs 'understand' and 'know' are used. **Shitte iru**, 'to know,' is generally used to indicate that one has information gained from external sources. **Wakaru**, 'to understand,' expresses the mental state that is achieved through an internal process or by figuring something out.

▶ **19.2.1**

56.1 Spontaneous expression of understanding something

To communicate that one has understood something right there and then, the past tense affirmative form of **wakaru** 'understand' is used.

わかりました。 | わかった。(I)
Wakarimashita. | **Wakatta.**
I understand. | I got it.

56.2 Saying that one understands a subject or a person

To indicate that one understands a subject, the verb **wakaru** is used. The direct object of **wakaru** is marked by **ga**.

日本語がわかります。 | 父は哲学がわかります。
Nihongo ga wakarimasu. | **Chichi wa tetsugaku ga wakarimasu.**
I understand Japanese. | My father understands philosophy.

To denote that one understands a person, the verb **wakaru** is also used. When the direct object of **wakaru** is a person, the particle **no** and the formal noun **koto** is used with the human object as in the following examples.

▶ **7.1; 18.1**

夫のことがよくわかります。
Otto no koto ga yoku wakarimasu.
I understand my husband well.

日記を読んで娘のことがよくわかりました。
Nikki o yonde musume no koto ga yoku wakarimashita.
By reading her diary, I understood my daughter well.

56.3 Saying that one knows a person, place or object

To say that one knows a person or place, use X o **shitte iru/imasu**. In informal speech, **shitte iru** is usually pronounced as **shitte ru**.

私は田中さんを知っています。
Watashi wa Tanaka-san o shitte imasu.
I know Mr/Ms Tanaka.

長野を知ってる。
Nagano o shitteru.
I know Nagano.

To convey that one knows something beyond a superficial level, X **no koto o shitte iru** 'know things about X' is used.

▶ 18.1

僕は彼女のことをよく知っています。
Boku wa kanojo no koto o yoku shitte imasu.
I know my girlfriend well.

パリのことを知っています。
Pari no koto o shitte imasu.
I know Paris.

To ask if someone knows a person or place, **shitte imasu ka** (F) or **shitteru?** (I) is used.

「ガスト」というレストランを知っていますか。
'Gasuto' to yuu resutoran o shitte imasu ka.
Do you know the restaurant called Gusto?

佐藤さん、知ってる？
Satoo-san, shitteru?
Do you know Mr/Ms Sato?

To ask if someone knows an object, X **wa nani ka shitte imasu ka** (F) or **shitteru?** (I) is used.

除湿器は何か知っていますか。
Joshitsuki wa nani ka shitte imasu ka.
Do you know what a dehumidifier is?

You can also use X **tte shitte imasu ka** or **shitteru**.

iPad って知ってる？
iPad tte shitteru?
Do you know what an iPad is?

To convey that one doesn't know a person, place or object, use **shiranai/shirimasen**, not **shitte inai** or **shitte imasen**.

僕は鈴木さんの家族を知らない。
Boku wa Suzuki-san no kazoku o shiranai.
I don't know Mr/Ms Suzuki's family.

私はいいレストランを全然知りません。
Watashi wa ii resutoran o zenzen shirimasen.
I don't know any good restaurants at all.

When one doesn't know one's own plan or idea, **wakaranai/wakarimasen** is used rather than **shiranai/shirimasen**.

まだ今週末は何をするか分かりません。
Mada kon shuumatsu wa nani o suru ka wakarimasen.
I don't know what I will do this weekend yet.

Q:	どう思う？	A:	分からない。
	Doo omou?		**Wakaranai.**
	What do you think?		I don't know.

When asked for information that one does not have, it is possible to respond either with **wakaranai/wakarimasen** 'I can't figure it out' or **shiranai/shirimasen** 'I don't know' depending on the situation.

> A: 田中さんに連絡したいのですが、電話番号を知っていますか。
> **Tanaka-san ni renraku shitai no desu ga, denwabangoo o shitte imasu ka.**
> I want to contact Mr/Ms Tanaka, so do you know his/her phone number?

> B: ちょっとわかりません/知りません。
> **Chotto wakarimasen/shirimasen.**
> I don't really know.

In the above example, speaker A is not merely asking whether B has the information but is also understood to be seeking assistance. In such a case, **wakaranai/wakarimasen** is a more sensible answer. Responding with **shiranai/shirimasen** sounds uncaring when assistance is sought.

56.4 Expressing knowledge of a subject or a skill

Shitte iru/imasu is used to denote that one has some knowledge of a subject or a skill.

> 東洋医学（のこと）を知っています。
> **Tooyoo igaku (no koto) o shitte imasu.**
> I know oriental traditional medicine.

> ケーキの作り方は知ってるよ。
> **Keeki no tsukurikata wa shitteru yo.**
> I know how to make a cake.

> 私は作曲（のこと）を知っています。
> **Watashi wa sakkyoku (no koto) o shitte imasu.**
> I know musical composition.

Ni tsuite may be used in place of the direct object particle **o** with the subject or skill.

> アメリカの法律について知っています。
> **Amerika no hooritsu ni tsuite shitte imasu.**
> I know about American law.

> 東洋医学についてよく知っています。
> **Tooyoo igaku ni tsuite yoku shitte imasu.**
> I know a good deal about (= well) oriental traditional medicine.

Another way to express one's knowledge of a subject is by using the noun **chishiki** 'knowledge.'

> 数学の知識があります。
> **Suugaku no chishiki ga arimasu.**
> I have knowledge of mathematics.

> 応急処置の知識がある。
> **Ookyuushochi no chishiki ga aru.**
> I have knowledge of first aid.

57

Remembering and forgetting

Spontaneous expression of recalling

To indicate that one has just recalled something, the verb **omoidasu** 'to recall' is used in the past affirmative form, i.e. **omoidashita/omoidashimashita**.

> A: 私のこと、覚えてる？　(I)
> **Watashi no koto, oboeteru?**
> Do you remember me?

> B: ええと、ああ、思い出した。
> **Eeto, aa, omoidashita.**
> Um, oh, I remember you now.

ちょっと用事を思い出しましたので、失礼します。
Chotto, yooji o omoidashimashita node, shitsuree shimasu.
I just remembered something I have to do, so I will excuse myself.

Expressing what one remembers

To express what one remembers, use X **o oboete iru/imasu**.

> 一年生の時の先生を覚えています。
> **Ichinensee no toki no sensee o oboete imasu.**
> I remember my first-grade teacher.

> 初めてデートした場所を覚えています。
> **Hajimete deeto shita basho o oboete imasu.**
> I remember the place of my first date.

It is also common to say X **no koto o oboete iru/imasu** to indicate that you remember things about X.

▶ 18.1

> 初めてお酒を飲んだときのことを覚えています。
> **Hajimete osake o nonda toki no koto o oboete imasu.**
> I remember the time when I had alcohol for the first time.

> 幼なじみのことを覚えている。
> **Osananajimi no koto o oboete iru.**
> I remember (things about) my childhood friends.

To say that one remembers a past action, V-**ta koto o oboete iru/imasu** is used.

> よく友達がノートを貸してくれたことを覚えています。
> **Yoku tomodachi ga nooto o kashite kureta koto o oboete imasu.**
> I remember that my friend often lent me his/her notebook.

The word **kioku** 'memory' is also used to denote that one has a memory of a person, place or a thing. **kioku** is mainly used in the following two sentence structures.

■   **kioku ga aru** 'to have the memory of'

What one remembers is expressed by the modifier that precedes **kioku ga aru**.

生まれた時の記憶があります。
Umareta toki no kioku ga arimasu.
I have the memory of when I was born.

ここに財布を置いた記憶があるんだけど . . . 。
Koko ni saifu o oita kioku ga aru n da kedo . . .
I have the memory of putting my wallet here, but . . .

▶ **7.2.3; 25**

■   **kioku shite iru** 'to remember,' 'to have . . . in mind'

When using **kioku shite iru**, what one remembers is expressed in the following ways.

■   **N + o kioku shite iru**

小学校の時の先生の名前をすべて記憶しています。
Shoogakkoo no toki no sensee no namae o subete kioku shite imasu.
I remember the names of all the teachers from my elementary school.

■   Clause + **koto o kioku shite iru**

▶ **18.1**

よく兄弟喧嘩したことを記憶しています。
Yoku kyoodai-genka shita koto o kioku shite imasu.
I remember that we often had sibling fights.

■   Clause + **to kioku shite iru**

▶ **26.2**

母は若い頃パートをしていたと記憶している。
Haha wa wakai koro paato o shite ita to kioku shite iru.
I remember that my mother had a part-time job when she was young.

To say that you remember seeing someone, somewhere, or something, **mioboe ga aru** is used. The word **mioboe** means recognition or familiarity. The object of **mioboe ga aru** is marked by the particle **ni**.

この場所に見覚えがある。
Kono basho ni mioboe ga aru.
I remember seeing this place. (This place looks familiar to me.)

私は田中さんに見覚えがあります。
Watashi wa Tanaka-san ni mioboe ga arimasu.
I remember seeing Mr/Ms Tanaka. (Mr/Ms Tanaka looks familiar to me.)

57.3 Asking people whether they remember a person, place, or thing

To ask people whether they remember a person, place, or thing, you can use any of the sentence structures discussed in **57.2** in the form of a question, but the most commonly used structure is **oboete iru?/oboete imasu ka**.

昔のウォークマンを覚えていますか。
Mukashi no wookuman o oboete imasu ka.
Do you remember the old-fashioned Walkman?

田中さんのこと、覚えてる？
Tanaka-san no koto, oboete ru?
Do you remember Mr/Ms Tanaka?

この車に見覚えがありますか。
Kono kuruma ni mioboe ga arimasu ka.
Do you remember seeing this car?

57.4 Expressing that one has forgotten something or someone

To say that one has forgotten something, use the verb **wasureru** 'to forget' in the past tense form, i.e. **wasureta/wasuremashita**. Because forgetting is something that occurs inadvertently, the verb **wasureru** 'to forget' is also often used with the auxiliary verb **shimau** 'to do . . . , inadvertently/unfortunately.'

▶ **19.2.5**

パスワードを忘れてしまった。
Pasuwaado o wasurete shimatta.
I have forgotten my password.

初めてデートした場所を忘れました。
Hajimete deeto shita basho o wasuremashita.
I have forgotten the place where I had my first date.

To say that one has forgotten someone, **no koto o wasureru** is commonly used.

田中さんのことは忘れました。
Tanaka-san no koto wa wasuremashita.
I have forgotten Mr/Ms Tanaka.

幼なじみのことをすっかり忘れてしまった。
Osananajimi no koto o sukkari wasurete shimatta.
I completely forgot about my childhood friend.

Oboete inai 'not remember' can express more or less the same meaning as 'to have forgotten.'

この人のことを覚えていません。
Kono hito no koto o oboete imasen.
I don't remember this person.

母の出身地を覚えていない。
Haha no shusshinchi o oboete inai.
I don't remember my mother's place of birth.

The verb **dowasure suru** is used to indicate that something has just slipped one's mind.

あの人の名前を度忘れしてしまいました。
Ano hito no namae o dowasure shite shimaimashita.
I have forgotten that person's name just now.

地名を度忘れした。
Chimee o dowasure shita.
The name of the place slipped my mind.

When one wants to sound apologetic about forgetting something, the V-**te shimau** structure needs to be used to make the unintended nature of forgetting explicit.

► **19.2.5**

> 宿題を忘れてしまいました。
> **Shukudai o wasurete shimaimashita.**
> I forgot my homework.

> 顧客の名前を忘れてしまった。
> **Kokyaku no namae o wasurete shimatta.**
> I forgot my client's name.

57.5 Asking people whether they have forgotten something or someone

To ask whether someone has forgotten something or someone, use the following sentence structures.

> **X o wasureta n desu ka.** 'Is it that you forgot X?'
> **X o wasurete shimatta n desu ka.** 'Is it that you inadvertently forgot X?'
> **X no koto o wasurete shimatta n desu ka.** 'Is it that you inadvertently forgot about X?'

> 切符を忘れたんですか。
> **Kippu o wasureta n desu ka.**
> Is it that you forgot the ticket?

> 田中さんのことをわすれてしまったんですか。
> **Tanaka-san no koto o wasurete shimatta n desu ka.**
> Did you forget about Mr/Ms Tanaka?

Another way to ask whether people have forgotten something is to use the negative question **oboete inai no?/n desu ka**.

> この人を覚えていないの？
> **Kono hito o oboete inai no?**
> You don't remember this person?

> さっき言ったことを覚えて（い）ないんですか。
> **Sakki itta koto o oboete (i)nai n desu ka.**
> You don't remember what I just said?

III

Expressing emotions and sensations

58

General comments on the adjectives of emotions and sensations

In Japanese, how speakers express their own feelings, sensations, and desires is distinguished from how someone else's feelings, sensations and desires are expressed. As you can see in many entries in this chapter, one's own emotions, desires and sensations are often expressed by adjectives (e.g. **hoshii** 'want,' **ureshii** 'glad,' **kanashii** 'sad,' etc.) or adjectival phrases (e.g. V-**tai** 'want to V'). These adjectives can be used to express the speaker's own feelings or to inquire about the addressee's feelings, but not to state someone else's feelings. This is because the speaker cannot directly experience someone else's feelings or desires. In order to express someone else's feelings and desires, adjectives are followed by expressions such as **-garu/ -gatte iru** 'to show signs of,' or evidentials such as **yoo da** ('seem'), **rashii** ('seem'), and **soo da** ('I hear; looks like'), or presented as a quote or hearsay.

▶ **28; 13.5**

59

Gratitude

General remarks on expressions of gratitude

The basic expression of gratitude is **arigatoo** 'thanks.' This phrase alone can be used to one's social subordinates and equals, such as one's friends and family members, and to any children. When speaking to one's social superiors, such as one's boss at work and older people and to any adults one does not know well, the formal phrase **gozaimasu** is added to thank them for their kind acts. The past tense form **arigatoo gozaimashita** is used to express thanks for a kind act that the addressee performed in the past. The addition of the adverb **doomo** 'indeed, for some reason' to **arigatoo** phrases make them sound more heartfelt. In casual situations, one may just say (with a bow) **doomo** to express one's appreciation.

The deed or act for which gratitude is expressed appears in a verb phrase preceding **arigatoo (gozaimasu/gozaimashita)**. The verb phrase consists of the main verb in the **te** form followed by one of the giving and receiving verbs functioning as an auxiliary verb, also in the **te**-form; e.g. V-**te** + **kurete, kudasatte, itadaite**. In a very polite situation, the auxiliary appears in the formal (**desu/masu**) style; e.g. verb-**te** + **kudasaimashite, itadakimashite.**

To a friend:

> （手伝ってくれて）ありがとう。
> **(Tetsudatte kurete) arigatoo.**
> Thanks (for your help).

To a colleague who is older:

> A: お宅まで送りましょうか。
> **O-taku made okurimashoo ka.**
> Shall I drive you home?

> B: どうもありがとうございます。とても助かります。
> **Doomo arigatoo gozaimasu. Totemo tasukarimasu.**
> Thank you very much. I would really appreciate it (Lit. I will be rescued).

To a professor:

> 推薦状を書いて下さって（or 下さいまして）ありがとうございました。
> **Suisenjoo o kaite kudasatte (or kudasaimashite) arigatoo gozaimashita.**
> Thank you very much for having written a recommendation letter for me.

In Japanese culture it is important to express one's gratitude to the benefactor multiple times, usually three times. The first time is when the kind act is done (e.g. receiving a gift, being taken out to dinner), the second is when parting with the person on that occasion, and the third is the next time one sees him/her.

先日はどうもありがとうございました。
Senjitsu wa doomo arigatoo gozaimashita.
Thank you very much for the other day.

59.2 Expressions of apology used to express gratitude

Expressions of apology are often used instead of, or in addition to, **arigatoo**, especially to express gratitude for the trouble the addressee went to; e.g. **sumimasen**, **mooshiwake arimasen**. The expression appears in the past tense when thanking (and apologizing) for a kind deed that occurred in the past; e.g. **sumimasen deshita**. As with **arigatoo**, the form varies according to the closeness and the relationship between the speakers, and the significance of the deed. Again, a verb + giving and receiving verbs, both in the **te**-form, may precede the expression of apology; e.g. verb **te** + **itadaite**.

From a sick person to a friend:

お見舞いに来てもらって悪いね。
O-mimai ni kite moratte warui ne.
Thanks for coming to see me; I feel bad/I'm sorry for the trouble you took to come to see me, and I am grateful.

To a neighbor:

昨日はお土産をいただいてありがとうございました。いつもすみません。
Kinoo wa o-miyage o itadaite arigatoo gozaimashita. Itsumo sumimasen.
Thank you for the souvenir yesterday. I always appreciate it (Lit. I'm sorry always).

To a boss:

お招きいただきまして誠に恐れ入ります。
O-maneki itadakimashite makoto ni osore irimasu.
I'm extremely grateful (Lit. I'm extremely sorry) for the invitation.

59.3 Other common expressions

One of the other common expressions of gratitude is **otsukare-sama (deshita)** 'thank you for your hard work (Lit. It must have been tiring).' It was traditionally thought to be appropriate only to one's social subordinates and equals, but its use to one's social superiors is becoming more acceptable recently. Another is **go-kuroo-sama (deshita)** 'thank you for your hard work (Lit. It must have been a lot of work).' This expression is still deemed inappropriate if it is said to one's social superiors. Literally, **tsukareru** means 'get tired,' and **go-kuroo** 'hardship.' The polite ending **deshita** is added to someone with whom one feels social or psychological distance.

To one's social subordinate or equal:

お疲れ様（でした）。
O-tsukare-sama (deshita).
Thank you for your hard work (Lit. It must have been tiring).

To one's social subordinate or equal:

ご苦労様（でした）。
Go-kuroo-sama (deshita).
Thank you for your work (Lit. It must have been a lot of work).

Another type of common expressions of gratitude is one with the phrase **o-sewa** 'care.' **O-sewa ni narimashita** 'thank you for having taken care (of me); Lit. (you) took care of (me)' is appropriate after the kind act is done, especially when parting from the benefactor. **O-sewa ni natte orimasu** 'thank you for (your) care; I am indebted to (you)' expresses appreciation for ongoing care one is receiving. When the benefactor is the addressee, and the beneficiary the speaker, neither is explicitly stated as such. To specify other benefactors (e.g. addressee's family member), the particle **ni** is used. To indicate a beneficiary other than the speaker (e.g. his/her family member), the particle **ga** for subject is used. It is customary in Japan to thank the benefactor on behalf of one's family or other in-group members. These expressions are often combined with **arigatoo gozaimasu/gozaimashita** 'thank you.'

To host family parents:

   大変お世話になりました。
   Taihen o-sewa ni narimashita.
   Thank you very much for having taken such good care of me.

To a boss who helped you with work:

   先日は大変お世話になりまして、ありがとうございました。
   Senjitsu wa taihen o-sewa ni narimashite.
   Thank you very much for your help the other day.

To one's younger sister's co-worker:

   妹がいつもお世話になっております。
   Imooto ga itsumo o-sewa ni natte orimasu.
   Thank you very much for having been kind to my younger sister.

To one's teacher's spouse:

   加藤先生にはいつもお世話になっております。
   Katoo-sensee ni wa itsumo o-sewa ni natte orimasu.
   Prof. Kato has been very kind to me, and I appreciate it.

59.4 Responding to an expression of gratitude

One may respond to an expression of gratitude in various ways depending on the relationship with the other party and the situation. A simple 'no' is an acceptable response in Japanese; **i(i)e** to one's boss or someone one does not know well, and **iya** or **uun** to someone with whom one is close. **Uun** sounds more gentle and feminine than **iya**.

A passerby thanks you for giving him/her directions:

   A: どうもありがとうございます/どうもありがとうございました。
       Doomo arigatoo gozaimasu/doomo arigatoo gozaimashita.
       Thank you very much.

   B: （いえ、）どういたしまして。
       (Ie,) doo itashimashite.
       You're welcome.

A friend thanks you for giving him/her a gift:

   A: プレゼントありがとう。   B: え？ 気に入ってもらえた？
       Purezento arigatoo.   **E? Ki ni itte moraeta?**
       Thanks for the gift.   Did you like it?

A male boss thanks you for fixing a computer problem:

> A:　いや、どうも。直してくれてほんとありがたいよ。
> **Iya, doomo. Naoshite kurete honto arigatai yo.**
> Thanks. I'm really grateful you fixed it.

> B:　あ、いえ、とんでもありません。
> **A, ie, tondemo arimasen.**
> Oh, it's nothing.

60

Apologies and forgiveness

Apologies express one's acknowledgement of failure to fulfil a responsibility or to meet some-one's expectation. An apology expresses one's regret, which then indicates one's humility or consideration for others. Generally, Japanese are more ready to apologize than Americans, seeing it as preferable to take responsibility instead of blaming others. There are a variety of expressions of apology depending on the level of politeness.

60.1 Apologies to a social superior

The following expressions are commonly used when apologizing to a social superior.

> すみません。
> **Sumimasen.**
> I am sorry.

> 申し訳ありません。
> **Mooshiwake arimasen.**
> I am sorry.

> 申し訳ございません。(VF)
> **Mooshiwake gozaimasen.**
> I am sorry.

> 会議に遅れてすみません。
> **Kaigi ni okurete sumimasen.**
> I am sorry for being late for the meeting.

> 会議に遅れまして申し訳ありません。(VF)
> **Kaigi ni okuremashite mooshiwake arimasen.**
> I am very sorry for being late for the meeting.

Sumimasen 'I am sorry' and **mooshiwake arimasen** can be used to express gratitude too. For example, when the host offers tea, **sumimasen** 'I am sorry' and **mooshiwake arimasen** can be used in the sense of 'thank you for your trouble.'

▶ 59.2

60.2 Apologies to an equal or a subordinate

The following formulaic expressions can be used when apologizing to an equal or a subordinate.

ごめんなさい。	ごめん。
Gomennasai.	**Gomen.**
I am sorry.	Sorry.

Both **gomennasai** and **gomen** are used in casual situations and among close friends. **Gomennasai** sounds slightly more polite than **gomen**. **Gomennasai** tends to be used by female speakers. When young children apologize to their parents or teachers, they use **gomennasai**, not **gomen**. **Gomen** is used when the speakers are very close to each other or the speakers feel they are socially equal to each other.

一郎 :	ごめん！電車に遅れちゃって。
Ichiroo:	**Gomen! Densha ni okurechatte.**
Ichiro:	Sorry, sorry to be late.

和雄 :	遅い、遅い！
Kazuo:	**Osoi, osoi!**
	You are late!

Another casual expression used in making an apology is **warui**. **Warui** is an adjective and literally means 'bad.' The expression is never used with **desu**, which marks formal style.

わるい、わるい。
Warui warui!
Sorry, sorry!

60.3 Responding to an apology

Here are some appropriate expressions when responding to an apology.

あ、いいえ。だいじょうぶです。
A, iie. Daijoobu desu.
Oh, no. It is O.K.

どうぞお気になさらないでください。(F)
Doozo o-ki ni nasaranaide kudasai.
That is fine. Don't worry.

気にしないで。(I)
Ki ni shinaide.
That is fine. Don't worry.

60.4 Expressing and responding to forgiveness

Expressions of forgivenenss include **shikata ga nai desu ne** 'it can't be helped,' **kore kara ki o tsukete kudasai** 'Please be careful from now on,' etc. In responding to forgiveness, expressions such as **hontoo ni sumimasen deshita** 'I am truly sorry' or **hontoo ni arigatoo gozaimasu** 'Thank you very much' are commonly used.

61

Empathy

61.1 Saying one is glad about something the other party has just said

The common way to express empathy is **yokatta desu ne** (formal) or **yokatta ne** (informal). **Yokatta** literally means 'was good' and is followed by the sentence final particle **ne**.

▶ 10.4

(1) 学生： お蔭さまで大学院に受かりました！
Gakusee: **O-kagesama de daigakuin ni ukarimashita!**
Student: Thanks to you, I got into graduate school!

先生： ああ、それはよかったですね。
Sensee: **Aa, sore wa yokatta desu ne!** (F)
Teacher: Oh, that's great!

(2) 武： 彼女、明日来てくれるって。
Takeshi: **Kanojo, ashita kite kureru tte.**
Takeshi: My girlfriend says she will be coming tomorrow.

友人： あ、ほんと。よかったね。
Yuujin: **A, honto. Yokatta nee.** (I)
Friend: Really. That's great!

(3) 愛： カラオケコンテストで1位もらっちゃった。
Ai: **Karaoke kontesuto de ichi-i moratchatta.**
Ai: I won the first prize at the karaoke contest!

友人： ええっ、すごいじゃない。よかったねぇ。
Yuujin: **Eee, sugoi ja nai. Yokatta nee.** (I)
Friend: Wow, that's fantastic! I'm glad!

61.2 Saying one is sorry about something the other party has just said

There are some formulaic expressions to say that one is sorry about something the other party has just said.

(1) 課長： 車のキー見つからないんだよ。
Kachoo: **Kuruma no kii ga mitsukaranai n da yo.**
Section Chief: I can't find my car key, you know.

私： そうですか。それは困りましたね。(F)
Watashi: **Soo desu ka. Sore wa komarimashita ne.**
I: Really? That's too bad/upsetting.

285

(2)　渡辺 ：　　昨日は引っ越しでね、さすがに疲れた。
Watanabe:　　**Kinoo wa hikkoshi de ne, sasuga ni tsukareta.**
Watanabe:　　We moved yesterday, and we were exhausted.

同僚 ：　　それは大変でしたね。
Dooryoo:　　**Sore wa taihen deshita ne. (F)**
Colleague:　　It must have been tiring.

(3)　健 ：　　信じられる？ 今週、試験３つ。
Ken:　　**Shinjirareru? Konshuu, shiken mittsu.**
Ken:　　Can you believe it? I've got three exams this week.

友人 ：　　本当。大変だねぇ。
Yuujin:　　**Hontoo. Taihen da nee. (I)**
Friend:　　Is that right? That's a bummer.

(4)　私 ：　　せっかくチケット買ったのに、コンサート、キャンセルに
なっちゃったんですよ。
Watashi:　　**Sekkaku chiketto katta noni, konsaato, kyanseru ni natchatta n desu yo.**
I:　　I went out of my way to buy the ticket, but the concert got canceled.

近所の人 ：　　そうですか。残念ですねぇ。(F)
Kinjo no hito:　　**Soo desu ka. Zannen desu nee.**
Neighbor:　　Is that right? That's too bad.

62

Likes and dislikes

Expressing one's likes and dislikes

The most common way of expressing likes and dislikes is to use the **na**-adjectives **suki** 'like' and **kirai** 'dislike.' These **na**-adjectives usually mark the object with the particle **ga**.

▶ **10.1.1**

私は日本食が好きです。
Watashi wa nihonshoku ga suki desu.
I like Japanese food.

私が好きな日本食は、てんぷらです。
Watashi ga suki na nihonshoku wa tenpura desu.
The Japanese food I like is tempura.

私はアメフットがきらいです。
Watashi wa amefutto ga kirai desu.
I do not like American football.

嫌いなスポーツはありません。
Kirai na supootsu wa arimasen.
There are no sports I don't like.

私は勉強があまり好きではありません。
Watashi wa benkyoo ga amari suki de wa arimasen.
I don't like studying that much.

肉はきらいじゃありませんが、好きでもありません。
Niku wa kirai ja arimasen ga, suki de mo arimasen.
I don't dislike meat, but I don't like it either.

When you want to say 'I like doing something,' use **. . . no ga suki/kirai desu**. **No** nominalizes a verb phrase.

▶ **18.2.1; 10.1**

私は漢字を勉強するのが好きです。
Watashi wa kanji o benkyoo suru no ga suki desu.
I like studying **kanji**.

私は外食するのがきらいです。
Watashi wa gaishoku suru no ga kirai desu.
I don't like eating out.

Suki/kirai can also be used for people. **Hanako ga suki desu** or **Hanako no koto ga suki desu** can mean either 'I like Hanako' or 'I love Hanako.' The verb meaning 'to love' – **ai suru/ ai shite iru** – is generally reserved for professing one's love for a person.

Strong likes/dislikes can be expressed by a prefix **dai-** as in **daisuki/daikirai**.

> 日本食が大好きです。
> **Nihonshoku ga dai-suki desu.**
> I like Japanese food very much.

> 人の前で話すのが大きらいです。
> **Hito no mae de hanasu no ga dai-kirai desu.**
> I very much dislike speaking in public.

Another way of expressing one's likes/dislikes is to use a phrase **. . . ga ki ni itta/itte iru** '. . . suits my taste' or **. . . ga ki ni iranai** '. . . does not suit my taste.'

> 新しいアパートが気に入りました。/ 気に入っています。
> **Atarashii apaato ga ki ni irimashita. / ki ni itte imasu.**
> I like my new apartment. (My new apartment suits my taste.)

> 教科書が気に入らない。
> **Kyookasho ga ki ni iranai.**
> I don't like the textbook.

62.2 Asking about likes and dislikes

Simply convert the statements in **62.1** into question form.

> 日本食はお好きですか。
> **Nihonshoku wa o-suki desu ka.**
> Do you like Japanese food?

> どんな映画が好きですか。
> **Donna eega ga suki desu ka.**
> What kind of movies do you like?

> 何をするのが好きですか。
> **Nani o suru no ga suki desu ka.**
> What do you like doing?

> 何かきらいな食べ物ある？ (I)
> **Nanika kirai na tabemono aru?**
> Is there some food you don't like?

62.3 Reporting on others' likes and dislikes

If you are sure of someone else's likes and dislikes, you can use direct statements like **suki desu/kirai desu**, but preferably in **. . . n desu** or in the **te**-form.

▶ 18.2.2; 22.1

> 主人はゴルフが好きなんです。
> **Shujin wa gorufu ga suki na n desu.**
> (It's that) my husband likes golf.

> 子供はビデオゲームが好きで . . .
> **Kodomo wa bideogeemu ga suki de . . .**
> My child likes video games, and . . .

Usually, however, you use a reportive style or evidentials in talking about someone else's likes/dislikes.

▶ 28

先生はクラシック音楽がお好きだそうです。
Sensee wa kurasshikku ongaku ga o-suki da soo desu.
I hear that the Professor likes classical music.

田中さんは猫より犬の方が好きなようです。
Tanaka-san wa neko yori inu no hoo ga suki na yoo desu.
It seems that Mr/Ms Tanaka likes dogs more than cats.

ジョンは日本食が好きみたいだね。
Jon wa nihonshoku ga suki mitai da ne.
John seems to like Japanese food.

63

Desires and preferences

63.1 Expressing one's desires

The most common expressions for stating desires involve the adjectives **hoshii** and **-tai**, both meaning 'want.' Since desires are internal feelings that are accessible only to the person feeling the desire, the Japanese language distinguishes between the speaker's own feelings of desire and the desires of others, which the speaker cannot directly feel.

▶ 58

63.1.1 *hoshii*

The adjective **hoshii** is used when the object of desire is a noun (a thing or a living thing). The target of desire is marked by the particle **ga**, and the subject is always the first person unless it is a question.

▶ 10.1.1

お金がほしい。
O-kane ga hoshii.
I want money.

いい友達がほしいです。
Ii tomodachi ga hoshii desu.
I want good friends.

おみやげは別にほしくない。
O-miyage wa betsuni hoshikunai.
I don't particularly want any souvenirs.

63.1.2 V-*tai*

When the object of desire is an action, the suffix **tai** is attached to the stem of a verb (e.g. **yomi-tai**, **tabe-tai**, etc.) The object of a verb is marked either by **ga** or **o**, and the subject is always the first person, unless it is a question.

日本に行きたい。   日本食が/を食べたいと思います。
Nihon ni iki-tai.   **Nihonshoku ga/o tabe-tai to omoimasu.**
I want to go to Japan.   I would like to eat Japanese food.

Verbal nouns such as **ryokoo** 'travel,' **kenkyuu** 'research,' etc. are always used with **-tai**, not **hoshii**, since they denote actions.

ヨーロッパに旅行がしたい。
Yooroppa ni ryokoo ga shi-tai.
I want to travel to Europe.

63.1.3 V-*te hoshii*

Hoshii 'want' can be combined with the **-te** form of verbs with the meaning of 'I want (you/someone) to do something.' This is the same meaning expressed by **-te morai-tai** Lit. 'want to receive the favor of someone doing something.'

先生にパーティーに来てほしい。
Sensee ni paatii ni kite hoshii.
I would like my teacher to come to my party.

天ぷらの作り方を教えてほしいんですが . . .
Tenpura no tsukuri kata o oshiete hoshii n desu ga . . .
I would like you to teach me how to make tempura.

63.2 Asking about the addressee's desires

Hoshii and V-**tai** can be used in question form.

今何が一番ほしいですか。
Ima nani ga ichiban hoshii desu ka.
What do you want most right now?

どこへ行きたいですか。
Doko e iki-tai desu ka.
Where do you want to go?

田中さん、大学院に行きたいと思う？
Tanaka-san, daigakuin ni iki-tai to omou?
Mr/Ms Tanaka, do you want to go to graduate school?

In English, 'Do you want to V?' can be an invitation, but in Japanese, the expression V-**tai desu ka** cannot be used as an invitation. Instead, **-masen ka** (e.g. **ikimasen ka**) is the correct way of inviting someone to go. (see **74.3**) Also, asking a superior's desires by using **hoshii desu ka** or V-**tai desu ka** is too direct and is inappropriate. For example, if you are asking your superior if he/she wants to have tea, you do not say, 'Do you want tea?'. Rather, **O-cha ikaga desu ka** 'how about some tea' is the appropriate expression. If you want to ask your teacher if he/she wants to see the DVD you have, you do not say **kono eega o goran ni nari-tai desu ka**. Rather you would say **Kono eega o goran ni narimasu ka**.

63.3 Reporting and asking about others' desires

In talking about someone else's desires, you need to add **-garu/-gatte iru** 'to show signs of' to the stems of **hoshii** and V-**tai**.

▶ 58

スミスさんは日本に行きたがっています。
Sumisu-san wa Nihon ni iki-ta-gatte imasu.
Mr/Ms Smith wants to go to Japan.

クリスマスには子供がほしがっているおもちゃを買ってやろうと思っています。
Kurisumasu ni wa kodomo ga hoshi-gatte iru omocha o katte yaroo to omotte imasu.
For Christmas I am thinking of buying the toy that my child wants.

Of course another's desires can also be talked about using **hoshii** and **-tai** if they are accompanied by evidential markers or as a report or a quote.

▶ 26.2; 33; 28

田中さんはいつも暇な時間がほしいと言っています。
Tanaka-san wa itsumo hima-na jikan ga hoshii to itte imasu.
Mr/Ms Tanaka always says he/she wants free time.

母は温泉に行きたいようです。
Haha wa onsen ni iki-tai yoo desu.
My mother seems to want to go to a hot spring.

あの人、車がほしいんだって。
Ano hito, kuruma ga hoshii n datte.
He wants a car, I hear.

63.4 Expressing one's preferences and asking about someone else's

To express one's own preferences and ask about someone else's, you can use expressions such as X **ga ii** 'I prefer X,' X **de ii** 'X will suffice,' X **no hoo ga ii** 'X is better,' or the like.

日本に行くんだったら、春か秋がいい。
Nihon ni iku n dattara, haru ka aki ga ii.
If (I) am going to Japan, I prefer spring or fall.

Q: コーヒーとお茶とあるんですが、どちらにしますか。
Koohii to o-cha to aru n desu ga, dochira ni shimasu ka.
We have coffee and tea. Which do you prefer?

A(1):   私はお茶でいいです。
Watashi wa o-cha de ii desu.
Tea is fine.

A(2):   私はお茶の方がいいです。
Watashi wa ocha no hoo ga ii desu.
I prefer tea.

Q: アニメの中でどれが好き？ (I)
Anime no naka de dore ga suki?
Which anime do you like?

A: トトロが好き。
Totoro ga suki.
I like Totoro.

Q: ご希望の時間がありますでしょうか。(F)
Go-kiboo no jikan ga arimasu deshoo ka.
Do you have a time preference?

A: 午後三時ごろが都合がいいんですが . . . 。
Gogo sanji goro ga tsugoo ga ii n desu ga. . . .
Three o'clock in the afternoon is convenient for me, but. . . .

64

Hopes and wishes

Expressing one's hopes and wishes

To express one's hopes and wishes, expressions such as **. . . to/-ba/-tara ii** 'it would be good if' can be used. This expression is often followed by **n desu ga/n da kedo** 'it is the case but' or **naa** (particle expressing exclamation).

> 日本で就職できるといいんですが。
> **Nihon de shuushoku dekiru to ii n desu ga.**
> I hope I can get a job in Japan.

> かぜがはやく治るといいですね。
> **Kaze ga hayaku naoru to ii desu ne.**
> I hope your cold gets better soon.

> 戦争がなくなるといいなあ。
> **Sensoo ga nakunaru to ii naa.**
> It would be so nice if there were no wars!

> あまり間違いがなければいいんですが。
> **Amari machigai ga nakereba ii n desu ga.**
> I hope I did not make too many mistakes.

When the expression contains the past tense form **yokatta** or the conjunction **noni** 'although,' it expresses wishes/hopes that are contrary to what happened or the current situation. With this counterfactual connotation, **to yokatta** is usually not used.

▶ 24.2

> 日本に行けばよかった。
> **Nihon ni ikeba yokatta.**
> I wish I had gone to Japan. (Lit. it would have been good if I went to Japan.)

> 言わなければよかった。
> **Iwanakereba yokatta.**
> I wish I did not say/had not said that.

Noni, moreover, cannot express a wish or regret about the speaker's own action – it is always a comment about someone else's action.

> 大学院に行けばいいのに。
> **Daigakuin ni ikeba ii noni.**
> I wish you/he/she would attend graduate school.

> もっと早く寝たらいいのにねえ。
> **Motto hayaku netara ii noni nee.**
> It would be good if you/he/she went to bed earlier.

Other ways of expressing hopes and wishes

Nouns such as **kiboo** 'hope,' **nozomi** 'hope,' **mikomi** 'prospect' can be used to express hopes and wishes, although such expressions sound a little more formal.

日本で仕事をするのが私の望みです。
Nihon de shigoto o suru no ga watashi no nozomi desu.
It's my hope/wish to work in Japan.

留学を希望しています。
Ryuugaku o kiboo shite imasu.
I wish to study abroad.

まだ助かる見込みはある。
Mada tasukaru mikomi wa aru.
There is still hope that he/she will survive.

65

Joy and sorrow

Expressing one's joy and sorrow

One's joy and sorrow may be expressed in a number of ways including the following.

65.1.1 Joy

やったあ！	**Yattaa!**	I did it!
最高！	**Saikoo!**	The best!
感激！／感激です。	**Kangeki! / desu!**	I'm ecstatic!
幸せ！／幸せです。	**Shiawase! / desu.**	I feel deep happiness.
うれしい！／うれしいです。	**Ureshii! / desu.**	I'm glad.

喜びで胸がいっぱいです。
Yorokobi de mune ga ippai desu.
My heart is filled with joy.

うれしくてどうしたらいいかわかりません。
Ureshikute doo shitara ii ka wakarimasen.
I'm so happy I don't know what to do.

65.1.2 Sorrow

悲しいです。	**Kanashii desu.**	I'm sad.
残念です。	**Zannen desu.**	It's regrettable.
がっかりです。	**Gakkari desu.**	I'm disappointed.
つらいです。	**Tsurai desu.**	It's painful.
切ないです。	**Setsunai desu.**	It's heartrending.
胸が痛みます。	**Mune ga itamimasu.**	My heart aches.

悲しみで胸がいっぱいです。
Kanashimi de mune ga ippai desu.
My heart is filled with sorrow.

悲しくてどうしたらいいか分かりません。
Kanashikute doo shitara ii ka wakarimasen.
I'm so sad I don't know what to do.

65.2 Reporting on others' joy and sorrow

To state other people's joy and sorrow, the adjectives used in the previous section must be used with such evidential markers as **soo**, **rashii** and **yoo**.

► 28; 58

花嫁は幸せそうです。
Hanayome wa shiawase soo desu.
The bride seems happy.

妹は悲しそうです。
Imooto wa kanashi soo desu.
My younger sister seems sad.

鈴木さんはとてもつらいようです。
Suzuki-san wa totemo tsurai yoo desu.
Mr/Ms Suzuki appears to be really suffering.

花嫁の父親は切ないらしいよ。
Hanayome no chichioya wa setsunai rashii yo.
I gather that the bride's father is heartbroken.

You can also report on other people's joy or sorrow by attaching **garu/gatte iru** 'to show signs of . . . ,' thereby turning an adjective into a verb form.

負けたチームは残念がっています。
Maketa chiimu wa zannen gatte imasu.
The team that lost is disappointed.

妹は寂しがっていました。
Imooto wa sabishigatte imashita.
My younger sister was lonely.

Alternatively, you can express other people's joy or sorrow as a quote or hearsay.

田中さんはうれしいと言っていました。
Tanaka-san wa ureshii to itte imashita.
Mr/Ms Tanaka said that he/she was happy.

息子さんが留学してご両親はとてもさびしいそうです。
Musuko-san ga ryuugaku shite go-ryooshin wa totemo sabishii soo desu.
I hear that their son is studying abroad and the parents are very lonely.

Verbs that express emotion, such as **yorokobu** 'to rejoice' and **kanashimu** 'to grieve,' are used in the V-**te iru** form to express other people's joy or sorrow. They can be used without evidential markers.

同僚は喜んでいます。
Dooryoo wa yorokonde imasu.
My colleague is rejoicing.

家族は悲しんでいます。
Kazoku wa kanashinde imasu.
The family is grieving.

両親は嘆いています。
Ryooshin wa nageite imasu.
My parents are lamenting.

66

Fear or worry

Expressing one's own fear

To express one's fear of something, the adjective **kowai** 'to be afraid of; scary' is most commonly used.

私は犬がこわいです。
Watashi wa inu ga kowai desu.
I'm afraid of dogs.

僕は暗闇がこわい。
Boku wa kurayami ga kowai.
I'm afraid of the dark.

The adjective **osoroshii** 'terrifying' may also be used.

私は天災が恐ろしいです。
Watashi wa tensai ga osoroshii desu.
I'm terrified of natural disasters.

The verb **osoreru** 'to fear' can also be used in **te iru** form to express one's fear.

私は失敗を恐れていました。
Watashi wa shippai o osorete imashita.
I feared failure.

Reporting on others' fear

To report on others' fear, adjectives that express fear are used with evidential markers such as **yoo** and **rashii**, or by verbalizing the adjective using **-gatte iru** 'showing signs of . . . ,' which attaches to the stem of the adjective.

▶ 28; 58

佐藤さんは鼠をこわがっています。
Satoo-san wa nezumi o kowa-gatte imasu.
Mr/Ms Sato is afraid of mice.

Verbs that express fear are used in the V-**te iru** form to express other people's fear.

同僚たちは社長のお説教を恐れています。
Dooryoo-tachi wa shachoo no o-sekkyoo o osorete imasu.
My colleagues are afraid of the company president lecturing them.

It is also common to express other people's fear as a quote or hearsay.

山田さんは蜘蛛がこわいそうです。
Yamada-san wa kumo ga kowai soo desu.
I hear that Mr/Ms Yamada is afraid of spiders.

山下さんは奥さんが恐ろしいと言っていました。
Yamashita-san wa okusan ga osoroshii to itte imashita.
Mr Yamashita said that he was afraid of his wife.

66.3 | Expressing one's own worry

To express one's own worry, the following expressions are commonly used.

心配です。	**Shinpai desu.**	I'm worried.
心配しています。	**Shinpai shite imasu.**	I'm worried.
不安です。	**Fuan desu.**	I'm feeling anxious.
悩んでいます。	**Nayande imasu.**	I'm troubled.

To express what one is worried about, different sentence structures are used depending on which expression is used.

■ **N ga shinpai da/desu** or **fuan da/desu**

自分の将来が心配です。
Jibun no shoorai ga shinpai desu.
I'm worried about my future.

両親の老後が不安だ。
Ryooshin no roogo ga fuan da.
I'm anxious about my parents' old age.

■ **N o** or **-ni tsuite shinpai shite imasu**

娘の健康を心配しています。
Musume no kenkoo o shinpai shite imasu.
I'm concerned for my daughter's health.

環境問題について心配しています。
Kankyoo mondai ni tsuite shinpai shite imasu.
I'm worried about environmental problems.

■ **N ni** or **ni tsuite nayande imasu**

転職について悩んでいます。
Tenshoku ni tsuite nayande imasu.
I have been worried about changing my job.

ペットのしつけに悩んでいます。
Petto no shitsuke ni nayande imasu.
I'm having trouble with training my pet.

The noun phrase that expresses what one is worried about is often followed by the particle **no** and the formal noun **koto**, as in these examples.

► 18.1

将来のことが心配です。
Shoorai no koto ga shinpai desu.
I'm worried about my future.

娘の健康のことを心配しています。
Musume no kenkoo no koto o shinpai shite imasu.
I'm concerned about my daughter's health.

What one is worried about can also be expressed using an embedded question.

► 26.3

すぐに就職できるかどうか心配だ。
Suguni shuushoku dekiru ka doo ka shinpai da.
I'm worried about whether I can get a job soon.

いつ両親に本当のことを言ったらいいのか悩んでいます。
Itsu ryooshin ni hontoo no koto o ittara ii no ka nayande imasu.
I have been worrying about when to tell my parents the truth.

友達ができるかどうか不安です。
Tomodachi ga dekiru ka doo ka fuan desu.
I'm feeling anxious about whether I can make friends.

父の会社がつぶれないかどうか心配しています。
Chichi no kaisha ga tsuburenai ka doo ka shinpai shite imasu.
I'm worried about whether my father's company will go bankrupt.

Reporting on others' worry

To report on others' worry, adjectives that express worry are used with evidential markers such as **yoo** and **rashii**, or by verbalizing the adjective using **-gatte iru** 'showing signs of . . . ,' which attaches to the stem of the adjective.

► 28; 58

山田さんはプロジェクトがうまく行くかどうか心配なようだ。
Yamada-san wa purojekuto ga umaku iku ka doo ka shinpai na yoo da.
Mr/Ms Yamada is worried about whether the project will go well.

同僚は会社の将来について不安がっています。
Dooryoo wa kaisha no shoorai ni tsuite fuan gatte imasu.
My colleague is anxious about our company's future.

Verbs that express worry, such as **nayamu** and **shinpai suru,** are used in the V-**te iru** form to express other people's worry. They can be used without evidential markers.

友達は大学に行くべきかどうか悩んでいる。
Tomodachi wa daigaku ni iku beki ka doo ka nayande iru.
My friend is worrying about whether he should go to college.

田中さんは鈴木さんのことを心配しています。
Tanaka-san wa Suzuki-san no koto o shinpai shite imasu.
Mr/Ms Tanaka is worried about Mr/Ms Suzuki.

67

Distress and regret

67.1 ## Spontaneous expressions of distress and regret

To express spontaneous feelings using a verb, the past tense form is used even though what is being expressed is a current state. Adjectives are used in the nonpast form when expressing spontaneous feelings.

困りました。(F)	**Komarimashita.**	I'm troubled.
閉口した。(I)	**Heekoo shita.**	I'm dumbfounded.
途方に暮れた。(I)	**Tohoo ni kureta.**	I'm at my wits' end.
がっかりした。(I)	**Gakkari shita.**	I'm disappointed.
苦しいです。(F)	**Kurushii desu.**	I'm suffering.
残念です。(F)	**Zannen desu.**	It's regrettable.
がっかりだ。(I)	**Gakkari da.**	It's disappointing.
うんざりだ。(I)	**Unzari da.**	I'm sick and tired.

Short sounds and phrases like the following are sometimes used in a distressing situation.

ああ！	**Aa!**	Ugh!
もう！	**Moo!**	Ugh!
やだ！	**Yada!**	No!
最悪！	**Saiaku!**	The worst!
最低！	**Saitee!**	The lowest!
困ったなあ。	**Komatta naa.**	That's too bad/upsetting.
どうしよう。	**Doo shiyoo.**	What should I do?
あ〜あ。	**Aaa.** (high-low-high pitch)	Good grief!
いけない！/しまった！	**Ikenai! / Shimatta!**	Oops!

67.2 ## Describing one's own distress and regret

One's own distress and regret may be communicated by expressions including the following. The V-**te iru** form is used to describe one's internal state more objectively while the past tense form is used to express an immediate, spontaneous reaction of distress and regret.

困っています。	**Komatte imasu.**	I'm in trouble.
途方に暮れて（い）る。	**Tohoo ni kurete (i)masu.**	I'm at my wits' end.
落ち込んで（い）る。	**Ochikonde (i)masu.**	I'm feeling depressed.
がっかりして（い）る。	**Gakkari shite (i)masu.**	I'm disappointed.
後悔しています。	**Kookai shite imasu.**	I'm regretting it.
苦しいです。	**Kurushii desu.**	I'm suffering.
残念です。	**Zannen desu.**	It's regrettable.

To express the cause or reason of the distress or regret, **te**-form is used.

▶ 22.1; 48.3

一緒に行けなくて、残念だよ。(I)
Issho ni ikenakute, zannen da yo.
I'm sorry for not being able to go with (you).

彼女が来なくて、がっかりです。
Kanojo ga konakute, gakkari desu.
It's disappointing that she did not come.

試験に落ちて、落ち込んでるんだ。(I)
Shiken ni ochite, ochikonde ru n da.
I'm feeling depressed because I failed the exam.

両親に嘘をついて、後悔しています。
Ryooshin ni uso o tsuite, kookai shite imasu.
I regret that I lied to my parents.

Another way to express what one regrets is by using the formal nouns **no** or **koto**.

■　　Clause + **no/koto wa zannen/gakkari da**.

このチームが負けたの/ことは残念だ。(I)
Kono chiimu ga maketa no/koto wa zannen da.
It's a shame that this team lost.

すぐに引っ越しできないの/ことは残念ですね。(F)
Sugu ni hikkoshi dekinai no/koto wa zannen desu ne.
It is regrettable that you cannot move right away.

■　　Clause + **no/koto o kookai shite iru**.

学生時代に留学しなかったの/ことを後悔しています。
Gakusee jidai ni ryuugaku shinakatta no/koto o kookai shite imasu.
I regret that I didn't study abroad when I was a student.

One's regret can also be expressed using the predicate in **ba**-form followed by **yokatta**.

▶ **24.2**

留学すればよかった。
Ryuugaku sureba yokatta.
I wish I had studied abroad.

嘘をつかなければよかったです。
Uso o tsukanakereba yokatta desu.
I wish I hadn't lied.

In addition, the V-**te shimau** structure is used to express the speaker's feeling that what happened was unfortunate or regrettable.

▶ **19.2.5**

宿題を忘れてしまいました。
Shukudai o wasurete shimaimashita.
I forgot my homework.

財布をなくしてしまいました。
Saifu o nakushite shimaimashita.
I lost my wallet.

風邪をひいてしまった。
Kaze o hiite shimatta.
I caught a cold.

67.3 Reporting on others' distress and regret

To report on others' distress or regret, adjectives that express distress or regret are used with evidential markers such as **yoo** and **rashii**, or by verbalizing the adjective using **-gatte iru** 'showing signs of . . . ,' which attaches to the stem of the adjective.

▶ 28; 58

息子は友達ができなくてとてもつらそうです。
Musuko wa tomodachi ga dekinakute totemo tsura soo desu.
Our son seems to be suffering because he has not made friends.

子供たちは試合に負けたことを残念がっています。
Kodomo-tachi wa shiai ni maketa koto o zannen gatte imasu.
The children are regretting that they (have) lost (in) the game.

Verbs that express distress or regret are used in the V-**te iru** form to express others' distress or regret. They can be used without evidential markers.

先生はがっかりしています。
Sensee wa gakkari shite imasu.
The teacher is disappointed.

田中さんは落ち込んでいます。
Tanaka-san wa ochikonde imasu.
Mr/Ms Tanaka is feeling depressed.

兄は後悔しています。
Ani wa kookai shite imasu.
My older brother is feeling regret.

弟は試合に負けて、くよくよしています。
Otooto wa shiai ni makete, kuyokuyo shite imasu.
My younger brother is whining because he lost the game.

被害者は苦しんでいます。
Higaisha wa kurushinde imasu.
The victims are suffering.

森さんは借金に苦悩しています。
Mori-san wa shakkin ni kunoo shite imasu.
Mr/Ms Mori is tormented by his/her debts.

68

Surprise

68.1 ## Spontaneous expressions of surprise

One's spontaneous feelings of surprise can be communicated by expressions including the following. These expressions are in the past tense form of a verb, even though what is being expressed is a current state. Also, when one is in the state of surprise, one often forgets the consideration of formality; therefore the plain form is used more often than the polite form.

びっくりしたあ！	**Bikkuri shitaa!**	I'm surprised!
おどろいたあ！	**Odoroitaa!**	I'm shocked!
たまげたあ！	**Tamagetaa!**	I'm flabbergasted!
びっくりしました！	**Bikkuri shimashita!**	I'm surprised!
驚きました！	**Odorokimashita!**	I'm shocked!
わあ！	**Waa!**	Wow!
うわ！	**Uwa!**	Ugh!
へえ？	**Hee?**	Really?
え？	**E?**	Huh?
うそ！	**Uso!**	You're kidding!
まさか！	**Masaka!**	That's impossible!
信じられない！	**Shinjirarenai!**	I can't believe it!
ほんと？	**Honto?**	Is it true?

▶ 31.11

68.2 ## Expressing surprise with regard to someone or something

To express what surprises one, various sentence structures may be used, including:

68.2.1 ### N *ni (wa)* or V (plain)/Adj. (pre-nominal) *no* or *koto ni (wa) bikkuri suru/bikkuri da/odoroku*

子供たちの成長の早さに（は）びっくりしています。
Kodomo-tachi no seechoo no hayasa ni (wa) bikkuri shite imasu.
I'm surprised how quickly the children grow.

今時の小学生に（は）びっくりする。
Ima doki no shoogakusee ni (wa) bikkuri suru.
I'm surprised by today's elementary school children.

田中さんが急に退職したのに（は）驚きました。
Tanaka-san ga kyuu ni taishoku shita no ni (wa) odorokimashita.
I'm astonished that Mr/Ms Tanaka has resigned so suddenly.

子供たちが静かなことに（は）驚いた。
Kodomo-tachi ga shizukana koto ni (wa) odoroita.
I was amazed how quiet the children were.

68.2.2   *te*-form + *bikkuri suru/odoroku*

ケーキが大きくてびっくりしました。
Keeki ga ookikute bikkuri shimashita.
The cake was big and so I was surprised.

優勝できて、驚いています。
Yuushoo dekite, odoroite imasu.
We were able to win, and I'm astonished.

68.2.3   Expressing surprise with the connective *noni* 'although'

The connective **noni** 'although, in spite of,' which is used to express contrast, is often employed when the speaker is surprised by the event expressed by the clause following **noni**.

雪があんなに降ったのに、すぐに融けてしまった。
Yuki ga anna ni futta noni, sugu ni tokete shimatta.
Although it snowed so much, it melted right away.

ワインを三本も飲んだのに、酔っぱらいませんでした。
Wain o sanbon mo nonda noni, yopparaimasen deshita.
Despite the fact that I drank three bottles of wine, I didn't get drunk.

69

Hunger, thirst, and fatigue

Spontaneous expressions of hunger, thirst, and fatigue

To express spontaneous feelings of hunger, thirst, and fatigue, the predicate takes the past tense form, even though what is being expressed is the current state of being hungry, thirsty, or tired.

> お腹がすいた/すきました。
> **Onaka ga suita/sukimashita.**
> I'm hungry.

> はらがへった/はらが減りました。 (masculine)
> **Hara ga hetta/hara ga herimashita.**
> I'm hungry.

> 喉が渇いた/渇きました。
> **Nodo ga kawaita/kawakimashita.**
> I'm thirsty.

> 疲れた/疲れました。
> **Tsukareta/tsukaremashita.**
> I'm tired.

Onomatopoetic expressions that express hunger, thirst, and fatigue are listed below.

> お腹がペコペコ（だ）/です。
> **Onaka ga pekopeko (da)/desu.**
> I'm starving.

> 喉がカラカラ（だ）/です。
> **Nodo ga karakara (da)/desu.**
> I'm thirsty.

> くたくた（だ）/です。
> **Kutakuta (da)/desu.**
> I'm exhausted.

Asking about the addressee's condition with regard to hunger, thirst, and fatigue

To ask whether your addressee is hungry, thirsty, or tired, the following questions are commonly used. The expressions that use the **te(i)ru** form have a more objective and indirect tone.

> お腹、すいた/すいてる？
> **Onaka, suita/suite ru?**
> Are you hungry?

お腹がすきましたか/すいていますか。
Onaka ga sukimashita ka / suite imasu ka.
Are you hungry?

喉が渇きましたか/渇いていますか。
Nodo ga kawakimashita ka / kawaite imasu ka.
Are you thirsty?

疲れましたか/疲れていますか。
Tsukaremashita ka / Tsukarete imasu ka.
Are you tired?

69.3 Reporting on others' hunger, thirst, and fatigue

To report on other people's hunger, thirst, and fatigue, evidential markers such as **mitai**, **rashii** and **yoo** are used. They can also be expressed as a quote or hearsay.

▶ 28; 58

妹はお腹がすいたようだ。
Imooto wa onaka ga suita yoo da.
My little sister seems hungry.

田中さんは喉が渇いたみたいです。
Tanaka-san wa nodo ga kawaita mitai desu.
Mr/Ms Tanaka looks thirsty.

道子さんは疲れたと言っていました。
Michiko-san wa tsukareta to itte imashita.
Michiko said that she was tired.

To ask if someone other than your addressee is hungry, thirsty, or tired, form the question using **n ja nai** or its formal variations **n ja nai desu ka** and **n ja arimasen ka / no dewa arimasen ka**. The predicate before **n** or **no** takes the pre-nominal form.

ゆみちゃんはお腹がすいて（い）るんじゃない？ (I)
Yumi-chan wa onaka ga suite (i)ru n ja nai?
Isn't Yumi hungry?

お兄さんは喉が渇いているんじゃないですか。 (F)
Oniisan wa nodo ga kawaite iru n ja nai desu ka.
Isn't your older brother thirsty?

お父さんは疲れているのではありませんか。 (F)
Otoosan wa tsukarete iru no dewa arimasen ka.
Isn't your father tired?

70

Pain or discomfort

Expressing one's pain or discomfort

One's pain is generally expressed by the adjective **itai** 'painful' or the verb **itamu** 'something hurts.' The adjective **itai** takes the form of (person) **ga/wa** (body parts) **ga itai**. Since **itai** is an emotive adjective, in its bare form it always indicates the feeling/pain of the first person.

頭が痛いんです。 歯が痛むんです。
Atama ga itai n desu. **Ha ga itamu n desu.**
I have a headache. I have a toothache.

Note that **itai** is also used as an interjection meaning 'Ouch!'.

General physical discomfort can be expressed by such expressions as the following.

体がだるいんです。
Karada ga darui n desu.
I feel listless.

ちょっと気持ちが悪いんです。
Chotto kimochi ga warui n desu.
I don't feel well.

今日は気分が悪くて . . . 。
Kyoo wa kibun ga warukute . . .
I don't feel good today . . .

今日はあまり調子がよくなくて . . . 。
Kyoo wa amari chooshi ga yokunakute . . .
I don't feel good today, so . . .

70.2 **Use of mimetic words to describe pain and discomfort**

▶ 4.2

The use of mimetic words is crucial in describing pain since they can convey the degree and type of pain in an immediate and vivid manner. Some of the mimetic words that are often used to describe pain include:

ずきずき ： 頭/歯がずきずき痛んで、眠れなかった。
Zukizuki: **Atama/ha ga zukizuki itande, nemurenakatta.**
Throbbing pain: I had a throbbing headache/toothache, and could not sleep.

きりきり ： 頭/胃がきりきり痛い。
Kirikiri: **Atama/i ga kirikiri itai.**
Piercing pain: I have a piercing headache/stomachache.

がんがん：　　　　　頭ががんがん痛い。
Gangan:　　　　　**Atama ga gangan itai.**
Splitting pain:　　　I have a splitting headache.

しくしく：　　　　　おなかがしくしく痛い。
Shikushiku:　　　**Onaka ga shikushiku itai.**
Dull persistent pain:　I have a dull pain in the stomach.

70.3　Asking about and reporting on others' pain or discomfort

70.3.1　Reporting on others' pain or discomfort

In describing another's pain or discomfort, one has to add expressions such as **-garu** or other evidential markers including **rashii**, **soo da**, **yoo da**, or the like.

▶ 28; 58

子供が痛がって泣くので、困りました。
Kodomo ga itagatte naku node, komarimashita.
My child cried because (he/she) was in pain, and I did not know what to do.

田中さんは頭が痛いようです。
Tanaka-san wa atama ga itai yoo desu.
It seems that Mr/Ms Tanaka has a headache.

真弓さんは今日はちょっと元気がなさそうです。
Mayumi-san wa kyoo wa chotto genki ga nasa-soo desu.
Mayumi does not seem to be so cheerful today.

70.3.2　Asking about another's pain or discomfort

In asking about another's pain or discomfort, it is better to ask more general questions such as 'Is anything wrong?' or 'What's the matter?' or the like.

どうしましたか。
Doo shimashita ka.
What's wrong?

どうしたの？
Doo shita no?
What's wrong?

ちょっと元気がないようだけど、どこか悪いんですか。
Chotto genki ga nai yoo da kedo, doko ka warui n desu ka.
You don't look so cheerful. Is anything wrong?

If you want to ask a more specific question, you can ask:

どこが痛いんですか。
Doko ga itai n desu ka.
Which part hurts?

どう痛むんですか。
Doo itamu n desu ka.
How does it hurt?

▶ 18.2.2

70.4 Expressions for common medical problems

The following are some of the expressions which can be used to describe common medical problems.

かぜをひく	**kaze o hiku**	to catch a cold
熱が出る	**netsu ga deru**	to have a fever
熱がある	**netsu ga aru**	to have a fever
寒気がする	**samuke ga suru**	to have a chill/the chills
吐き気がする	**hakike ga suru**	to be nauseated
せきが出る	**seki ga deru**	to cough
下痢だ	**geri da**	to have diarrhea
めまいがする	**memai ga suru**	to feel dizzy
くしゃみが出る	**kushami ga deru**	to sneeze
けがをする	**kega o suru**	to be injured
（足を）折る	**(ashi o) oru**	to break (one's leg)
呼吸が苦しい	**kokyuu ga kurushii**	to have difficulty breathing
（のどが）はれる	**(nodo ga) hareru**	to have a swollen (throat)

70.5 Expressions for common dental problems

歯が痛い	**ha ga itai**	to have a toothache
歯茎がはれる	**haguki ga hareru**	to have a swollen gum
親知らずをぬく	**oyashirazu o nuku**	to pull out a wisdom tooth
虫歯	**mushiba**	tooth decay

71

Satisfaction and dissatisfaction

Expressing one's own satisfaction

How one expresses satisfaction sometimes depends on what one is talking about. For example one might say **Totemo yokatta desu** 'it was very good' in talking about a trip, concert, hotel, or the like, but if one is talking about food or books/movies, one would probably say **Totemo oishikatta desu** 'it was delicious' or **Totemo omoshirokatta desu** 'it was interesting,' respectively. The following are some common ways of expressing one's satisfaction.

すばらしい（です）。	すばらしかった（です）。
Subarashii (desu).	**Subarashikatta (desu).**
It's wonderful.	It was wonderful.
最高（です）。	最高だった/でした。
Saikoo (desu).	**Saikoo datta/deshita.**
Great! The best!	It was the best.
すごい！	
Sugoi!	
Great!	
すごくいい（です）。	すごくよかった（です）。
Sugoku ii (desu).	**Sugoku yokatta (desu).**
It is really good.	It was really good.
とてもいい（です）。	とてもよかった（です）。
Totemo ii (desu).	**Totemo yokatta (desu).**
It's very good.	It was very good.
大変いい（です）。	大変よかった（です）。
Taihen ii (desu).	**Taihen yokatta (desu).**
It's very good.	It was very good.
すてき（です）。	すてきでした。
Suteki (desu).	**Suteki deshita.**
It's nice/wonderful.	It was nice/wonderful.
満足しています。	
Manzoku shite imasu.	
I am satisfied.	
文句なし（です）。	
Monku nashi (desu).	
No complaints.	
気に入っています。	気に入りました。
Ki ni itte imasu.	**Ki ni irimashita.**
I like it. (I am fond of it).	I liked it.

けっこうおいしい（です）。   けっこうおいしかった（です）。
Kekkoo oishii (desu).   **Kekkoo oishikatta (desu).**
It tastes pretty good.   It tasted pretty good.

まあまあ（です）。   まあまあでした。
Maa maa (desu).   **Maa maa deshita.**
So-so.   It was so-so.

71.2 Expressing one's own dissatisfaction

Dissatisfaction can be indicated by expressions including the following.

ぜんぜんよくない／よくありません／よくないです。
Zenzen yokunai/yokuarimasen/yoku nai desu.
It's not good at all.

ひどい（です）。
Hidoi (desu).
It's terrible.

最低（です）。
Saitee (desu).
It's the worst.

だめ（です）。
Dame (desu).
No good.

ひどすぎる／ひどすぎます。
Hido sugiru/hido sugimasu.
It's too terrible.

あまりよくない／よくありません／よくないです。
Amari yokunai/yokuarimasen/yoku nai desu.
It's not too good.

ちょっと物足りないと思います／思いました。
Chotto monotarinai to omoimasu/omoimashita.
I am/was not completely happy with it. (i.e. I think it is lacking somewhat.)

今いちです。
Imaichi desu.
It leaves a little to be desired.

71.3 Ways of mitigating dissatisfaction

When one is not completely satisfied but does not want to sound so negative, the following expressions can be used.

► 18.1; 15.2; 18.6

■ Adj. ことは adj. が

この間のパーティーはどうでしたか。
Kono aida no paatii wa doo deshita ka.
How was the party the other day?

おもしろいことはおもしろかったんですが...。
Omoshiroi koto wa omoshirokatta n desu ga, . . .
It was interesting, but . . .

■ Adj. はない

あのホテルはどうでしたか。
Ano hoteru wa doo deshita ka.
How was the hotel?

悪くはないけど、...。
Waruku wa nai kedo, ...
It wasn't bad, but ...

■ Adj. ないわけではないが、

今の仕事はどうですか。
Ima no shigoto wa doo desu ka.
How is your current job?

おもしろくないわけではないんですが、ちょっと仕事量が多すぎます。
Omoshirokunai wake de wa nai n desu ga, chotto shigoto ryoo ga oo sugimasu.
It's not that it is uninteresting, but there is too much work.

71.4 Asking about and reporting on others' satisfaction or dissatisfaction

71.4.1 Asking about others' satisfaction or dissatisfaction

The following expressions can be used to ask whether the addressee is satisfied or not.

これでいいですか。
Kore de ii desu ka.
Is this OK (with you)?

これでよろしいでしょうか。(VF)
Kore de yoroshii deshoo ka.
Is this OK (with you)?

これでだいじょうぶですか。
Kore de daijoobu desu ka.
Will this do?

気に入った？(I)
Ki ni itta?
Do you find (it) to your liking? (Do you like it?)

お気に入りましたでしょうか。(VF)
O-ki ni irimashita deshoo ka.
Do you find (it) to your liking? (Do you like it?)

71.4.2 Reporting on others' satisfaction or dissatisfaction

Many of the expressions introduced in the previous section can be used to report another's satisfaction or dissatisfaction. However, just like another's emotions, one cannot directly experience another's feelings of satisfaction or dissatisfaction, so they have to be framed in a quotation or with evidentials such as **yoo da** or **rashii**.

▶ 28; 58

学生は満足しているようです。
Gakusee wa manzoku shite iru yoo desu.
It seems that the students are satisfied.

これでいいみたい。

Kore de ii mitai.

It seems that (he/she) is OK with this.

だいじょうぶのようです。

Daijoobu no yoo desu.

(He/she) is OK with this, it seems.

プレゼントが気に入ったみたいですよ。

Purezento ga ki ni itta mitai desu yo.

It looks like (he/she) likes the present.

不満らしいです。

Fuman rashii desu.

It seems that (he/she) is dissatisfied.

いろいろ文句があるみたいです。

Iroiro monku ga aru mitai desu.

(He/she) seems to have many complaints.

IV

Speaking as performing acts

72

Advice and suggestions

Seeking advice or suggestions

There are various ways to ask for advice or suggestions, including the following.

> どうすればいいでしょうか。
> **Doo sureba ii deshoo ka.**
> What should I do?

> どうしたらいいと思う？
> **Doo shitara ii to omou?**
> What do you think I should do?

> 何かいい方法はないかな。
> **Nani ka ii hoohoo wa nai ka na.**
> Do you know any good way to do it?

> ちょっと相談にのってもらえませんか。
> **Chotto soodan ni notte moraemasen ka.**
> Could I consult you about something?

> アドバイスをお願いします。
> **Adobaisu o onegai shimasu.**
> Please advise me.

The issue on which one is seeking advice is often introduced by the phrase **n desu ga/kedo** or **n da kedo**.

> 何度ダイエットをしてもやせられないんですが、どうすればいいでしょうか。(F)
> **Nando daietto o shite mo yaserarenai n desu ga, doo sureba ii deshoo ka.**
> No matter how many times I go on a diet, I can never lose weight, so what should I do?

> ５年間もつきあって（い）る彼がプロポーズしてくれないんだけど、
> どうしたらいいと思う？(I)
> **Gonenkan mo tsukiatte (i)ru kare ga puropoozu shite kurenai n dakedo, doo shitara ii to omou?**
> My boyfriend, whom I have been dating for five years, has not proposed to me, so what do you think I should do?

When the addressee already knows about the issue, the speaker can bring up the topic by saying X **no koto na n desu ga/kedo**.

> 推薦状のことなんですけど、誰にお願いすればいいでしょうか。
> **Suisenjoo no koto na n desu kedo, dare ni onegai sureba ii deshoo ka.**
> About the letter of recommendation, who(m) should I ask?

Giving affirmative advice or suggestions

To express affirmative advice or suggestions, the V-**tara** (conditional structure) + **doo desu ka** 'why don't you . . . , how about . . .' is commonly used. **Ta** in **tara** is the plain past affirmative form of the verb.

▶ 12.1; 24.3

専門家に相談したらどうですか。(F)
Senmonka ni soodan shitara doo desu ka.
Why don't you talk with a specialist?

V-**tara doo desu ka** is shortened to V-**tara doo** or V-**tara** in casual speech.

医者に行ったらどう？(I)
Isha ni ittara doo?
How about going to the doctor?

もう少し待ってみたら？(I)
Moo sukoshi matte mitara?
Why don't you wait a little longer and see?

Another phrase often used to give affirmative advice is V-**ta hoo ga ii** 'you had better do. . . .' While the expression V-**tara doo desu ka** is phrased as a question, the expression using **hoo ga ii** is in the form of a statement. Therefore the expression with **hoo ga ii** sounds more assertive. The plain past affirmative form of verbs is used before **hoo ga ii**.

よく考えたほうがいいですよ。
Yoku kangaeta hoo ga ii desu yo.
You had better think carefully.

毎日運動したほうがいいですよ。
Mainichi undoo shita hoo ga ii desu yo.
You had better exercise every day.

薬を飲んだほうがいいよ。
Kusuri o nonda hoo ga ii yo.
You had better take the medicine.

You can use **n ja nai**, **n ja nai desu ka** or **n ja arimasen ka** following **hoo ga ii** to make it sound less assertive.

本当のことを言ったほうがいいんじゃない？(I)
Hontoo no koto o itta hoo ga ii n ja nai?
Wouldn't it be better if you told the truth?

別の店で買ったほうがいいんじゃないですか。(F)
Betsu no mise de katta hoo ga ii n ja nai desu ka.
Wouldn't it be better if you bought it at another store?

早く帰ったほうがいいんじゃありませんか。(F)
Hayaku kaetta hoo ga ii n ja arimasen ka.
Wouldn't it be better if you went home early?

Another commonly used expression is V-**ba ii/daijoobu desu yo**.

▶ 24.2

新しいのを買えばいいですよ。
Atarashii no o kaeba ii desu yo.
All you have to do is buy a new one.
(Lit. It'll be fine if you buy a new one.)

知って（い）る人に聞けば大丈夫だよ。
Shitte (i)ru hito ni kikeba daijoobu da yo.
All you have to do is ask someone who knows.
(Lit. It'll be fine if you ask someone who knows.)

V-**ba ii/daijoobu** is used to present what seems to be an easy solution to the issue at hand. Therefore this expression is often used to give reassurance.

72.3 Giving negative advice or suggestions

To give negative advice, V(plain, nonpast, neg.) **hoo ga ii** 'You had better not do . . .' is commonly used.

あのレストランには行かないほうがいいですよ。
Ano resutoran ni wa ikanai hoo ga ii desu yo.
You'd better not go to that restaurant.

嘘をつかないほうがいいよ。
Uso o tsukanai hoo ga ii yo.
You'd better not lie.

Advice given with **hoo ga ii** sounds assertive. You can use **n ja nai**, **n ja nai desu ka** or **n ja arimasen ka** following **hoo ga ii** to make it sound less assertive.

あせらないほうがいいんじゃない？ (I)
Aseranai hoo ga ii n ja nai?
Wouldn't it be better if you didn't hurry so much?

気にしないほうがいいんじゃないですか。 (F)
Ki ni shinai hoo ga ii n ja nai desu ka.
Wouldn't it be better if you didn't worry?

今は引っ越さないほうがいいんじゃありませんか。 (F)
Ima wa hikkosanai hoo ga ii n ja arimasen ka.
Wouldn't it be better if you didn't move house right now?

Another commonly used negative advice phrase is V (plain, nonpast, neg.) **kereba ii/daijoobu desu yo**.

▶ 24.2

誰にも言わなければいいですよ。
Dare ni mo iwanakereba ii desu yo.
All you have to do is not tell anyone.
(Lit. It'll be fine if you don't tell anyone.)

写真（を）見せなければ大丈夫だよ。
Shashin (o) misenakereba daijoobu da yo.
All you have to do is not show the photos.
(Lit. It'll be fine if you don't show the photos.)

V(plain, nonpast, neg.)-**kereba ii/daijoobu** is used to present what seems to be an easy solution to the issue at hand. Therefore advice given in this form sounds reassuring.

72.4 Responding to advice or suggestions

How one responds to advice or suggestions will depend on the content of the advice or suggestions. However, regardless of the content, in polite conversation, Japanese speakers tend to avoid totally rejecting an addressee's advice or suggestions. The following phrases may be used in one's initial response. The **te**-form of verbs and the auxiliary verb **miru** 'to try, to see' are frequently used when responding to advice or suggestions to express 'I will (V) and see what happens.'

▶ 19.2.3

そうですね。もう少し考えてみます。
Soo desu ne. Moo sukoshi kangaete mimasu.
That's right, isn't it. I will think about it a bit more.

そうかもしれませんね。
Soo kamoshiremasen ne.
That may be right, isn't it.

分かりました。よく検討してみます。
Wakarimashita. Yoku kentoo shite mimasu.
All right. I will consider that carefully.

そうかもしれないね。とりあえず、やってみるよ。(I)
Soo kamoshirenai ne. Toriaezu, yatte miru yo.
That may be right. For now, I will try that.

To mildly express one's rejection or doubt toward a given piece of advice, the following phrases may be used.

え－、でもなあ . . . 。(I)
Ee, demo naa . . .
Um, but . . .

うーん、そうですかねえ . . . 。(F)
Uun, soo desu ka nee . . .
Hmm, I wonder if that would work . . .

そうは言ってもねえ . . . 。(I)
Soo wa itte mo nee . . .
You say so, but . . .

73

Requests

Which expression you use in making a request depends on many factors, including the social status of the person of whom you are asking a favor, the formality of the situation, the gender of the speaker and of the addressee, and the type of relationship. In a work situation, for example, colleagues (equals in status) might use very formal or polite request forms, and a superior might also use polite requests in talking to his/her younger colleagues. On the other hand, family members or close friends will make a request in informal ways. One also uses more polite requests in asking for a more difficult favor. In general, requests are made with the verbs of giving and receiving in Japanese. The following are some typical expressions in making requests.

73.1 Making requests in more formal situations

73.1.1 V-*te itadakemasen ka*, V-*te itadakemasu ka*

Using the verb **itadaku** (the humble form of **morau** 'receive') in its potential question form is the most polite way of asking a favor. It is used as in V-**te itadakenai deshoo ka** 'Is it not possible for me to receive the favor of your doing . . . ?,' V-**te itadakemasen ka** 'May I not receive the favor of your doing . . . ?,' or V-**te itadakemasu ka** 'May I receive the favor of your doing . . . ?' V-**te itadakenai deshoo ka** form is the most polite, and thus, is normally used in making a request of social superiors. It is also common to make some introductory remark, such as **chotto onegai ga aru n desu ga** 'I have a favor to ask you,' or **sumimasen ga** 'I am sorry to bother you.'

▶ 19.2.8

ちょっとお願いがあるんですが。推薦状を書いていただけないでしょうか。
Chotto o-negai ga aru n desu ga. Suisenjoo o kaite itadakenai deshoo ka.
I have a request. Would you be able to write a recommendation letter for me?

すみません、ちょっとこの書類に目を通していただけないでしょうか。
Sumimasen, chotto kono shorui ni me o tooshite itadakenai deshoo ka.
I am sorry, but would you be able to look through this document?

すみません、この仕事ちょっと手伝っていただけませんか。
Sumimasen, kono shigoto chotto tetsudatte itadakemasen ka.
I am sorry, but would you be able to help me with this work?

あしたまで待っていただけますか。
Ashita made matte itadakemasu ka.
Will you please wait until tomorrow?

One can also make a request by simply saying that one would like the addressee to do something.

▶ 63.1.2

すみません。あしたまで待っていただきたいんですが。
Sumimasen. Ashita made matte itadakitai n desu ga.
Sorry, but I would like you to wait until tomorrow.

Instead of V-**te** form, **o**-V(stem) **itadaku** can also be used, although this expression sounds rather business-like.

すみませんが、今日中にお送りいただけますか。
Sumimasen ga, kyoo-juu ni o-okuri itadakemasu ka.
I am sorry, but will you send (it) out some time today?

お調べいただけますか。
O-shirabe itadakemasu ka.
Will you check (this)?

If you are asking a very difficult favor, use the expression V-**te itadaku wake ni wa ikanai deshoo ka** 'Is it at all possible for you to do me the favor of V-ing?.'

今日中に送っていただくわけにはいかないでしょうか。
Kyoo-juu ni okutte itadaku wake ni wa ikanai deshoo ka.
Is it at all possible for you to send it out some time today?

会議の時間を変えていただくわけにはいかないでしょうか。
Kaigi no jikan o kaete itadaku wake ni wa ikanai deshoo ka.
Is it at all possible for you to change the meeting time?

▶ 18.6

73.1.2 V-*te moraemasen ka*, V-*te moraemasu ka*

V-**te morau** (neutral form meaning 'receive') can be used in making requests in similar forms as V-**te itadaku**. It is, however, not as polite as V-**te itadaku**. V-**te moraemasen ka** can be said, for example, to workplace colleagues or by superiors to subordinates.

▶ 19.2.8

手伝ってもらえませんか。
Tetsudatte moraemasen ka.
Can I ask you to help me?

これ、直してもらえますか。
Kore naoshite moraemasu ka.
Can I ask you to correct (it)?

73.1.3 V-*te kuremasen ka*

Requests can be made by using the verb **kureru**. However, it is not as polite as requests made by -**itadaku** and -**morau**, and hence it is not used in making requests to superiors.

▶ 19.2.8

あとでオフィスに来てくれませんか。
Ato de ofisu ni kite kuremasen ka.
Will you come to my office later?

飲み物を買ってきてくれませんか。
Nomimono o katte kite kuremasen ka.
Will you buy me something to drink?

o-negai 'request'

The noun **negai** meaning 'wish, desire, hope' with an honorific prefix **o-** is often used in making requests.

► 63.1.2; 18.2.2

推薦状をお願いしたいんですが。
Suisenjoo o onegai shitai n desu ga.
I would like to ask for (your) recommendation letter.

予約をお願いしたいんですが。
Yoyaku o onegai shitai n desu ga.
I would like to make a reservation.

一つお願いがあるんですが。
Hitotsu onegai ga aru n desu ga.
I have a favor to ask you.

すみません。もう一度お願いできますか。
Sumimasen. Moo ichido onegai dekimasu ka.
Sorry, but can you (do it, repeat it) one more time?

73.2 Making requests in informal situations

In making requests among family members and close friends, plain forms of the verbs **kureru** and **morau** are used. It can be preceded by a phrase such as **warui kedo** 'I feel bad, but. . . .'

► 19.2.8

ペン貸してくれない？
Pen kashite kurenai?
Will you lend me a pen?

悪いけど、パソコン貸してもらえない？
Warui kedo, pasokon kashite moraenai?
Sorry, but can I borrow your computer?

あとで電話してくれる？
Ato de denwa shite kureru?
Will you call me later?

あとで電話してもらえる？
Ato de denwa shite moraeru?
Can you call me later?

In very informal situations, such as among close friends, V-**te** would be sufficient.

ペン貸して！	ちょっと待って！
Pen kashite!	**Chotto matte!**
Lend me a pen!	Wait!

73.3 V-*te* *kudasai* 'please V'

V-**te kudasai** can be used to make a request. However, it has the connotation of ordering someone to do something rather than asking someone to do something, and thus it is more appropriate when a superior uses it toward his/her subordinates. This form is also used in giving instructions.

じゃ、あとで電話してください。　　　ここにサインをしてください。
Ja, ato de denwa shite kudasai.　　**Koko ni sain o shite kudasai.**
Please call me later.　　　　　　　　Please sign here.

73.4 Responding to a request

73.4.1 Giving an affirmative response

In responding to a request, an affirmative response can be given by saying:

はい／ああ、いいですよ。(higher status → lower status)
Hai/aa, ii desu yo.
Yes, sure.

はい。(lower status → higher status; between equals) (F)
Hai.

はい、わかりました。(lower status → higher status; between equals) (F)
Hai, wakarimashita.
Yes, I understand.

はい、承知しました。(lower status → higher status) (F)
Hai, shoochi shimashita.
Yes, certainly.

うん、いいよ。(between equals) (I)
Un, ii yo.
Sure, OK.

73.4.2 Giving a negative response

If the request has to be refused, it is important to be tactful in doing so and not hurt the other person's feeling or face. Normally, there is some hesitation when one is going to give a negative response. This could be a short pause or an expression such as **soo desu nee** 'well' or **uun** 'well.' A reason for noncompliance is usually given, such as not having time, not having enough knowledge, etc. The following are some typical negative responses.

うーん、今ちょっと忙しいんですが。
Uun, ima chotto isogashii n desu ga.
Well, I am a little busy right now.

すみませんが、今ちょっと暇がなくて。
Sumimasen ga, ima chotto hima ga nakute.
I am sorry, but I don't have time right now, and . . .

そう言われても、ちょっと困るんですが。
Soo iwarete mo, chotto komaru n desu ga.
Well, you say that, but I am in a difficult spot.

今ちょっと都合がわるいんですが。
Ima chotto tsugoo ga warui n desu ga.
It is a little inconvenient for me right now.

Pleading for time to think about it can often be a polite refusal.

じゃ、ちょっと考えておきます。
Ja, chotto kangaete okimasu.
Well, I will think about it.

じゃ、ちょっと考えさせてください。
Ja, chotto kangaesasete kudasai.
Then, let me think about it.

A more direct refusal can be given among intimate friends or family members.

ペン貸してくれない？	だめだよ。今使ってるから。
Pen kashite kurenai?	**Dame da yo. Ima tsukatte ru kara.**
Will you lend me a pen?	No. I am using it now.
それ見せて？	いやだよ。まだ読んでるんだから。
Sore misete?	**Iya da yo. Mada yonde ru n da kara.**
Let me see it.	No. I am still reading it.

▶ 18.2.2; 22.4

74

Offers and invitations

74.1 **Making an offer of something or to do something**

When you are offering or suggesting specific items, expressions such as **ikaga desu ka** (formal) or its more informal variants **doo desu ka** and **doo**? are useful. Sometimes a suggested item is followed by the particle **demo** 'or something,' which suggests that there are other alternatives and hence the offer sounds less imposing (and more polite.)

> お茶でもいかがですか。
> **O-cha demo ikaga desu ka.**
> How about some tea?

> 一杯どう？
> **Ippai doo?**
> How about a drink?

When you want to offer to do something for an interlocutor, V-**mashoo ka** 'shall I do . . .' or more informal V(volitional form) **ka** can be used.

► 12.1

> お手伝いしましょうか。/お手伝いいたしましょうか。(VF)
> **O-tetsudai shimashoo ka. / O-tetsudai itashimashoo ka.**
> May I help?

> 手伝いましょうか。(F)
> **Tetsudaimashoo ka.**
> May I help?

> 手伝おうか。(I)
> **Tetsudaoo ka.**
> May I help?

In very formal situations, the humble expression **o-**V(stem) **suru** is used to refer to your own action that pertains to someone superior to you.

► 29.4

74.2 **Accepting or declining an offer**

In accepting an offer, the following expressions can be used.

お茶でもいかがですか。	あ/ええ、いただきます。
O-cha demo ikaga desu ka.	**A/Ee, itadakimasu.**
	Yes, thank you. I will.

手伝いましょうか。/お手伝いしましょうか。
Tetsudaimashoo ka. / O-tetsudai shimashoo ka.
May I help?

あ/ええ、お願いします。
A/Ee, o-negai shimasu.
Yes, please.

あ、すみません。
A, sumimasen.
Thank you. (I am sorry.)

手伝おうか。
Tetsudaoo ka.
May I help?

うん、ありがとう。
Un, arigatoo.
Yes, thank you.

In turning down an offer, you have to be careful not to hurt the other person's feelings. It is generally better to express some appreciation for the offer first and then give the reason why the offer is not accepted.

▶ **22.4; 39.2**

お茶でもいかがですか。
O-cha demo ikaga desu ka.
How about some tea?

あ、ありがとうございます。でも、今日はちょっと用事がありますので。
A, arigatoo gozaimasu. Demo, kyoo wa chotto yooji ga arimasu node.
Yes, thank you, but I have some things I have to do today, so . . .

荷物、持ちましょうか。/お持ちしましょうか。
Nimotsu, mochimashoo ka / o-mochi shimashoo ka.
May I help you with your luggage?

あ、だいじょうぶです。軽いですから。
A, daijoobu desu. Karui desu kara.
I am fine – it's not heavy (Lit. because it is light).

一杯どう？
Ippai doo?
How about a drink?

うん、ありがとう。でも、今日は仕事がたくさんあるから、ちょっと遠慮しとく。
Un, arigatoo. Demo, kyoo wa shigoto ga takusan aru kara, chotto enryo shitoku.
Yes, thank you, but I have a lot of work today, so I will pass on it today.

手伝おうか。
Tetsudaoo ka.
May I help?

うん、でも、大丈夫だよ。もうほとんど終わったから。
Un, demo, daijoobu da yo. Moo hotondo owatta kara.
Yeah, thanks, but I am OK, because the work is almost finished.

74.3 ## Inviting someone to a place or an event

The most common way of inviting someone to a place or an event is to use the nonpast negative form of verbs followed by the question marker **ka** (formal style) or followed by a question intonation (informal style.) Using the exalting form of verbs makes it more polite, and this is the form used in inviting someone superior to you.

▶ **29.3**

今週末遊びにいらっしゃいませんか。(VF)
Konshuumatsu asobi ni irasshaimasen ka.
Won't you come visit me this weekend?

一度遊びに来ませんか。(F)
Ichido asobi ni kimasen ka.
Won't you come visit me sometime?

一度遊びに来ない？(I)
Ichido asobi ni konai?
Come visit me sometime.

Another way of inviting someone is to first introduce your plan and ask if the interlocutor would like to join you. This is probably the most polite way of inviting someone superior to you.

今週末日本食のレストランに行こうと思っているんですけど、
先生もいかがですか。(VF)
**Konshuumatsu nihonshoku no resutoran ni ikoo to omotte iru n desu kedo,
sensee mo ikaga desu ka.**
We are thinking of going to a Japanese restaurant this weekend, and how about you joining us, Professor X?

みんなで野球の試合を見に行こうと思っているんだけど、ジョンもどう？(I)
Minna de yakyuu no shiai o mi ni ikoo to omotte iru n da kedo, Jon mo doo?
We are thinking of going to a baseball game. Why don't you join us, John?

74.4 Accepting or declining an invitation

74.4.1 Accepting an invitation

The following responses can be given to accept an invitation to a place or an event.

是非お願いします。
Zehi o-negai shimasu.
Yes, I'd love to.

是非ご一緒させてください。
Zehi go-issho sasete kudasai.
Certainly, please let me join you.

喜んで。
Yorokonde.
Gladly.

遠慮なくお邪魔します。(when invited to someone's home.)
Enryo naku o-jama shimasu.
I will gladly accept your invitation.

ぜったい行く。(I)
Zettai iku.
I will definitely go/come.

うん、もちろん。ありがとう。(I)
Un, mochiron. Arigatoo.
Yes, of course. Thank you.

74.4.2 Declining an invitation

Japanese people prefer not to be too direct in declining invitations, since a refusal could hurt the other person's feelings. Therefore, when they cannot accept an invitation, they tend to do it indirectly. The expression such as **chotto** 'a little' with or without a reason is a standard way of declining invitations. When the speaker says **chotto**, it is understood that it means 'a little inconvenient.'

その日はちょっと ... 。
Sono hi wa chotto...
That day is kind of ...

私はちょっと ... 。
Watashi wa chotto...
I am a bit ...

すみません。その日はちょっと。別の用事があって。
Sumimasen. Sono hi wa chotto. Betsu no yooji ga atte.
I am sorry. I have other business to take care of on that day, so ...

These phrases can be preceded by remarks of regret such as **mooshiwake nai n desu ga** 'I am sorry but,' **zannen desu ga** 'regretfully,' or **warui kedo** 'I am sorry but,' or the like.

残念ですが、その日はちょっと ... 。
Zannen desu ga, sono hi wa chotto...
I am sorry but that day is a little ...

悪いけど、先約があって。(I)
Warui kedo, sen'yaku ga atte.
Too bad, I have a previous engagement, so ...

Thus, in declining an invitation, the Japanese speaker takes great care not to hurt the other person's feelings. At the same time, the person who does the invitation also shows concern for the feelings of the person who has to refuse the invitation. One does this by displaying under-standing for the person's refusal, thereby making it easier for the person to refuse the invitation. The following is an example of such an interchange.

A: 今度の週末にみんなで野球の試合を見に行くんだけど、行かない？
Kondo no shuumatsu ni minna de yakyuu no shiai o mi ni iku n da kedo, ikanai?
We are going to watch a baseball game this coming weekend. Would you like to come?

B: 今週の週末はちょっと ... 。
Konshuu no shuumatsu wa chotto...
This weekend is a little ...

A: 何かほかに予定があるの？
Nani ka hoka ni yotee ga aru no?
You have some other plans?

B: うん、ちょっとね。
Un, chotto ne.
Yes, kind of.

A: じゃあ、仕方ないね。
Jaa, shikata nai ne.
Then, it can't be helped.

B: ごめんね。また今度誘ってね。
Gomen ne. Mata kondo sasotte ne.
Sorry. Please ask me again.

75

Orders (commands)

Giving affirmative orders

To give a command in the affirmative form, the V(stem) **nasai** structure is commonly used. This is the command form most commonly used when parents reprimand their children or when bosses lecture their subordinates. It is also used in written instructions.

> 宿題をしなさい。
> **Shukudai o shi nasai.**
> Do your homework.

> よく考えなさい。
> **Yoku kangae nasai.**
> Think hard.

> 括弧に適当な言葉を書きなさい。
> **Kakko ni tekitoona kotoba o kaki nasai.**
> Write an appropriate word in the parentheses.

Command expressions with the V(stem) **na** structure are sometimes used in casual speech.

> 食べな。
> **Tabena.**
> Eat.

> やめな。
> **Yamena.**
> Quit it.

The following rude command form may be used in masculine style speech. Command forms are obtained as follows:

- Irregular verbs: **suru** 'to do' changes to **shiro**; **kuru** 'to come' to **koi**.

> 掃除しろ。
> **Sooji shiro.**
> Clean (it)!

> ビールをもってこい。
> **Biiru o motte koi.**
> Bring beer!

- **ru**-verbs: final **-ru** of the dictionary form changes to **ro**.

> ゆっくり食べろ。
> **Yukkuri tabero.**
> Eat slowly!

よく見ろ。
Yoku miro.
Look carefully!

■ **u**-verbs: final **-u** vowel of the dictionary form changes to **e**.

早く帰れ。
Hayaku kaere.
Go home soon!

もっと飲め。
Motto nome.
Drink more!

75.2 Giving negative orders

To command others not to do something, **na** is attached to the dictionary form of verbs. This negative command form is masculine and sounds very rough.

動くな。
Ugoku na.
Don't move.

何も言うな。
Nani mo yuu na.
Don't say anything.

Another form of negative command takes the same form as the plain nonpast negative form.

ぐずぐずしない！
Guzu guzu shinai.
Don't dilly-dally!

文句言わない！
Monku iwanai!
Don't complain!

やすまない！
Yasumanai!
Don't take a break!

In the negative command form associated with women's speech, **no** is attached at the end of the plain nonpast negative form. This form is often used by mothers scolding children.

喧嘩しないの！
Kenka shinai no!
Don't quarrel!

泣かないの！
Nakanai no!
Don't cry!

うるさくしないの！
Urusaku shinai no!
Don't be noisy!

▶ 12

76

Directions and instructions

Seeking and giving directions

Some simple ways to ask directions are:

道を教えてくれませんか。/いただけませんか。(F/VF)
Michi o oshiete kuremasen ka / itadakemasen ka.
Would you please give me directions?

道をお尋ねしたいんですが。(VF)
Michi o o-tazune shitai n desu ga.
I would like to ask you for directions.

There are also various ways to ask for directions to a specific place, including the following. Replace X with the name of the place to which you need to get directions.

X（まで）の行き方を教えてほしいんですが。(F)
X (made) no iki kata o oshiete hoshii n desu ga.
I would like you to show me how to get to X.

X はどう行けばいいか教えていただけませんか。(VF)
X wa doo ikeba ii ka oshiete itadakemasen ka.
Could you please tell me how I can get to X?

X までの道をお尋ねしたいんですが。(VF)
X made no michi o o-tazune shitai n desu ga.
I would like to ask you directions to X.

X（まで）はどう行けばいいですか。(F)
X (made) wa doo ikeba ii desu ka.
How can I get to X?

X（まで）の行き方を教えてくれない？(I)
X (made) no iki kata o oshiete kurenai?
Can you tell me how to get to X?

The following words and phrases are often used to give directions to a place.

まっすぐ行く	**massugu iku**	to go straight
右に曲がる	**migi ni magaru**	to turn right
左に曲がる	**hidari ni magaru**	to turn left
角を曲がる	**kado o magaru**	to turn at the corner
まがる	**magaru**	to turn
わたる	**wataru**	to cross
すぎる	**sugiru**	to pass
信号	**shingoo**	traffic light
橋	**hashi**	bridge

踏切	**fumikiri**	railroad crossing
前	**mae**	front
十字路	**juujiro**	crossroads, intersection
交差点	**koosaten**	crossroads, intersection
丁字路	**teejiro**	T junction
後ろ	**ushiro**	behind
一つ目の〜	**hitotsume no ...**	first ...
二つ目の〜	**futatsume no ...**	second ...
三つ目の〜	**mittsume no ...**	third ...
右に見える	**migi ni mieru**	to be visible on one's right
左に見える	**hidari ni mieru**	to be visible on one's left

The following dialogue exemplifies asking and giving directions.

A: すみません、善光寺はどう行けばいいか教えていただけませんか。
Sumimasen, Zenkooji wa doo ikeba ii ka oshiete itadakemasen ka.
Excuse me, could you please tell me how to get to the Zenkoji temple?

B: この道をまっすぐ行って、２つ目の信号を右に曲がってください。
少し行ったら丁字路になっていますから、そこを左にまがって、
１０分ぐらい行ったら右に見えると思います。
**Kono michi o massugu itte, futatsume no shingoo o migi ni magatte kudasai.
Sukoshi ittara teejiro ni natte imasu kara, soko o hidari ni magatte, juppun
gurai ittara migi ni mieru to omoimasu.**
Go straight ahead on this street and turn right at the second traffic light. If you
continue a little more, you will get to a T-junction, so turn left there, and if you
go ten more minutes or so, I think you will see it on your right.

76.2 Seeking and giving instructions

To express 'how to do X' in Japanese, the verb stem + **kata** 'way, method' is used.

▶ **17.2**

作り方	使い方
tsukuri kata	**tsukai kata**
how to make	how to use

The particles **o** and **ni** are replaced by **no** when the V(stem) + **kata** phrase is used, as in the examples below.

寿司を作る	→	寿司の作り方
sushi o tsukuru		**sushi no tsukuri kata**
to make sushi		how to make sushi

自転車に乗る	→	自転車の乗り方
jitensha ni noru		**jitensha no nori kata**
to ride a bicycle		how to ride a bicycle

Particles other than **o** and **ni** are followed by the particle **no** when the V-stem + **kata** phrase is used.

面接で話す	→	面接での話し方
mensetsu de hanasu		**mensetsu de no hanashi kata**
to talk at an interview		how to talk at an interview

子供と接する	→	子供との接し方
kodomo to sessuru		**kodomo to no sesshi kata**
to deal with children		how to deal with children

When using verbs that contain **suru**, such as **benkyoo suru** 'to study,' **sooji suru** 'to clean,' **ryoori suru** 'to cook,' among many others, the particle **no** needs to be inserted before **shi kata**.

勉強する   →   勉強の仕方
benkyoo suru   **benkyoo no shi kata**
to study   how to study

料理する   →   料理の仕方
ryoori suru   **ryoori no shi kata**
to cook   how to cook

The expression with V(stem) + **kata** can be used to seek instructions on how to do something, as exemplified below.

切符の買い方を教えていただけませんか。(VF)
Kippu no kai kata o oshiete itadakemasen ka.
Would you mind showing me how to buy a ticket?

コピー機の使い方を教えてほしいんですが。(F)
Kopiiki no tsukai kata o oshiete hoshii n desu ga.
I would like you to show me how to use the copy machine.

このゲームのやり方を教えてくれない？(I)
Kono geemu no yari kata o oshiete kurenai?
Will you teach me how to play this game?

Other phrases that may be used to seek instruction are **doo** 'how,' **dono yoo ni** 'in what manner,' **doo yatte** 'how,' and **dono yoo ni shite** 'by doing what.'

このゲームはどうやって遊びますか。(F)
Kono geemu wa doo yatte asobimasu ka.
How do you play this game?

このコピー機はどのように使いますか。(F)
Kono kopiiki wa dono yoo ni tsukaimasu ka.
How do you use this copy machine?

ソーセージはどうやって作るの？(I)
Sooseeji wa doo yatte tsukuru no?
How do you make sausages?

着物はどのようにしてたためばいいですか。(F)
Kimono wa dono yoo ni shite tatameba ii desu ka.
How should I fold a kimono?

A sequence of instructions, such as how to make something, can be given in much the same way as procedures.

▶ 49

The following instructions are on how to make a sunny-side-up egg.

まず、中火でフライパンを熱しサラダ油を敷きます。次に卵を割り入れて、ふたをします。白身が固まったら蓋を取って火を止めます。最後に塩をふって、皿にのせます。
Mazu, chuubi de furaipan o nesshi sarada abura o shikimasu. Tsugi ni tamago o wari irete, futa o shimasu. Shiromi ga katamattara futa o totte hi o tomemasu. Saigo ni shio o futte, sara ni nosemasu.
First, heat a skillet/frying pan on medium high and coat the bottom with vegetable oil. Next, break an egg, put it in and put a lid on the skillet. When the white becomes firm, take the lid off and turn the stove off. Lastly, sprinkle on some salt and serve on a plate.

Instructions are also often given with the V-**te kudasai** form.

使用後は早めに水気を拭き取ってください。
Shiyoogo wa hayame ni mizuke o fukitotte kudasai.
After use, please wipe away moisture as soon as possible.

用途以外には使用しないでください。
Yooto igai ni wa shiyoo shinaide kudasai.
Please do not use it for purposes not specified.

77

Confirmation

77.1 ## Confirming what the other party has just said

To confirm what the other person has just said, relevant information + **desu ne** is often used.

▶ 10.4

田中 : パーティーは来週の日曜日の<u>六時から</u>ですので、
是非いらしてください。

Tanaka: **Paatii wa raishuu no nichiyoobi no rokuji kara desu node, zehi irashite kudasai.**
The party starts at six next Sunday, so please come.

山中 : 来週の日曜日<u>六時から</u>ですね。楽しみにしています。

Yamanaka: **Raishuu no nichiyoobi rokuji kara desu ne. Tanoshimi ni shite imasu.**
Six o'clock next Sunday, right? I am looking forward to it.

At a restaurant

田中 : 私は天丼お願いします。

Tanaka: **Watashi wa tendon o-negai shimasu.**
I will have tendon (tempura on rice).

山中 : 私はちらしにします。

Yamanaka: **Watashi wa chirashi ni shimasu.**
I will have chirashi.

店員 : 天丼一つとちらし一つですね。少々お待ちください。

Ten'in: **Tendon hitotsu to chirashi hitotsu desu ne. Shooshoo o-machi kudasai.**
Server: One tendon and one chirashi, right? Please wait a little.

77.2 ## Requesting confirmation

Sentence-final particle **ne** is the most frequently used way to request confirmation from the addressee.

新幹線の乗り場はここですね。
Shinkansen no noriba wa koko desu ne.
This is where we get on the bullet train, right?

高橋さんですね。
Takahashi-san desu ne.
You are Mr/Ms Takahashi, right?

Daroo/deshoo can also be used in requesting confirmation from the addressee. The use of **n desu** as in the first two examples below indicates that the speaker makes certain assumptions and asks the addressee to confirm those assumptions. Without **n(o) desu**, the speaker has a strong conviction and asks the addressee to confirm or agree.

▶ 18.2.2

あの人のこと好きなんでしょう？
Ano hito no koto suki na n deshoo?
You like him/her, right?

留学するんでしょう？
Ryuugaku suru n deshoo?
You are going to study abroad, right?

この本面白いだろう？
Kono hon omoshiroi daroo?
This book is interesting, don't you think?

私の気持ちわかるでしょう？
Watashi no kimochi wakaru deshoo?
You understand my feeling, right?

The sentence-final particle combination **yo ne** can also be used to request confirmation from the addressee.

▶ 10.4.4

借りていた本返したよね。
Karite ita hon kaeshita yo ne.
I returned to you the book I borrowed, right?

パーティーにいらっしゃいますよね。
Paatii ni irasshaimasu yo ne.
You are coming to the party, right?

喧嘩する時は日本語より英語の方がしゃべりやすいよね。
Kenka suru toki wa Nihongo yori Eego no hoo ga shaberi yasui yo ne.
It's easier to speak English than Japanese when we quarrel, don't you think?

77.3 Confirming a fact

Daroo/deshoo can also be used to confirm knowledge or understanding on the part of the addressee, which leads to further comment on the item or topic of the conversation.

▶ 53.2.1

あそこに赤いレンガの建物がある<u>でしょう</u>？あの建物は明治の初めの建物なんですよ。
Asoko ni akai renga no tatemono ga aru <u>deshoo</u>? Ano tatemono wa Meeji hajime no tatemono na n desu yo.
You see the red brick building over there, right? That was built at the beginning of the Meiji era.

インターネットのサイトがある<u>でしょ</u>？あそこに登録して何でも屋をみつけたんだって。
Intaanetto no saito ga aru <u>desho</u>? Asoko ni tooroku shite nandemoya o mitsuketa n datte.
There is an Internet site, right? (He/she) registered on that site and found a handyman.

A similar function can be seen with the rhetorical expression **ja nai desu ka** (and its more colloquial variants **ja nai/jan**).

アメリカの大学だと宿題とかレポートとかいろいろある<u>じゃないですか</u>。
でも、日本の大学ではそういうものもあまりないので、あまり勉強になり
ませんでした。

**Amerika no daigaku da to shukudai toka repooto toka iroiro aru <u>ja nai desu ka</u>.
Demo, Nihon no daigaku de wa soo yuu mono mo amari nai node, amari benkyoo
ni narimasen deshita.**

At American universities students have to do homework and write reports and things
like that. But, at Japanese universities they don't have such things, so (we) did not
learn much.

XXハウスっていう寮がある<u>じゃん</u>。あそこに住んでたんだけど、隣の人がうるさ
くて大変だった。

**XX Hausu tte yuu ryoo ga aru <u>ja n</u>. Asoko ni sunde ta n da kedo, tonari no hito
ga urusakute taihen datta.**

There is a dorm called XX House, right? I lived there, but the people in the next room
were noisy, and it was terrible.

In the last utterance, the speaker introduces the item **ryoo** 'dorm' by confirming that the addressee
shares the knowledge, thereby establishing a reference for **asoko** 'that place' in the second
utterance.

78

Permission

78.1 **Seeking permission**

To seek permission, as in 'May I come in?,' 'Is it OK to come in?,' 'Do you mind if I come in?,' or 'Let me come in,' Japanese uses a number of expressions. There are also varying degrees of politeness associated with these expressions. The most common and neutral way of seeking permission is to use V-**te mo ii desu ka** and its stylistic variations.

78.1.1 **V-*te mo ii desu ka* and its stylistic variants**

This expression literally means 'is it all right if I do . . . ?' Changing **ii desu ka** to **yoroshii desu ka** or **yoroshii deshoo ka** makes it more polite, while **ii?** is very casual. The words **kamaimasen ka** or **kamawanai?** can be substituted for **ii desu ka**.

> この部屋を使ってもいいですか。
> **Kono heya o tsukatte mo ii desu ka.**
> Is it all right to use this room? (May I use this room?)

> この部屋を使ってもよろしいでしょうか。(VF)
> **Kono heya o tsukatte mo yoroshii deshoo ka.**
> Is it all right to use this room? (May I use this room?)

> ペン借りてもいい？(I)
> **Pen karite mo ii?**
> May I borrow your pen?

> お金はあとで払ってもかまいませんか。(F)
> **O-kane wa ato de haratte mo kamaimasen ka.**
> Is it all right to pay the money later?

> たばこすってもかまわない？(I)
> **Tabako sutte mo kamawanai?**
> Is it OK if I smoke?

It is good practice to provide a reason for seeking permission, using expressions such as . . . **n da/desu kedo**, . . . **n desu ga**.

▶ 18.2.2; 22.5

> ちょっと買い物に行きたいんですけど、自転車使ってもいいでしょうか。
> **Chotto kaimono ni ikitai n desu kedo, jitensha tsukatte mo ii deshoo ka.**
> I would like to go shopping. May I use your bicycle?

78.1.2 Causative form + verbs of receiving *itadaku/morau*

The use of the causative form of verbs with verbs of receiving is also very common in seeking permission. The literal sense of this expression is that the speaker receives the benefit of someone letting him/her do something. There are basically five ways to use this construction.

▶ 20.4.3

78.1.2.1 *-(s)asete itadakemasen ka/-(s)asete moraemasen ka*

In this construction, the verbs **itadaku/morau** are in the potential form, meaning 'is it possible?; may I?'

> コンピューターを使わせていただけませんか。(VF)
> **Konpyuutaa o tsukawasete itadakemasen ka.**
> Would you let me use your computer?

> その本ちょっとコピーさせてもらえませんか。
> **Sono hon chotto kopii sasete moraemasen ka.**
> Would you let me copy the book? (May I copy the book?)

> ちょっと待たせてもらえないかな。(I)
> **Chotto matasete moraenai ka na.**
> I wonder if you would let me wait a little. (Please let me wait a little.)

> 荷物おかせてもらえる？ (I)
> **Nimotsu okasete moraeru?**
> Can you let me keep my luggage here?

78.1.2.2 *-(s)asete itadakitai n desu ga/-(s)asete moraitai n desu ga*

Here the desiderative form of **itadaku/morau** is used.

▶ 63.1.2

> 用紙に先生のお名前を書かせていただきたいんですが、よろしいでしょうか。(VF)
> **Yooshi ni sensee no o-namae o kakasete itadakitai n desu ga, yoroshii deshoo ka.**
> I would like to ask you to let me put your name on the (application) form. Is it all right, Professor?

> 写真をとらせてもらいたいんですが、いいですか。
> **Shashin o torasete moraitai n desu ga, ii desu ka.**
> I would like you to let me take pictures. Is it OK?

> そのペン使わせてもらいたいんだけど、いい？ (I)
> **Sono pen tsukawasete moraitai n da kedo, ii?**
> I want to ask you to let me use the pen. OK?

78.1.2.3 *-(s)asete itadaite mo ii desu ka/-(s)asete moratte mo ii desu ka*

Here, the standard **-te mo ii desu ka** is used with V(causative) **itadaku/morau**.

> もう少し考えさせていただいてもよろしいでしょうか。（VF)
> **Moo sukoshi kangaesasete itadaite mo yoroshii deshoo ka.**
> Would you let me think (about it) a little more?

> ちょっと言わせてもらってもいいですか。
> **Chotto iwasete moratte mo ii desu ka.**
> Would you let me say something?

> ちょっとここにおかせてもらってもいい？ (I)
> **Chotto koko ni okasete moratte mo ii?**
> Will you let me keep my (luggage) here?

78.1.2.4 **...** *dekiru* **'can'**

-(S)asete itadaku/-(s)asete morau can be embedded in the **koto (ga) dekiru** phrase.

> ここで待たせていただくこと、できますか。(F)
> **Koko de matasete itadaku koto, dekimasu ka.**
> Can you let me wait here?

> ちょっと考えさせてもらうこと、できる？(I)
> **Chotto kangaesasete morau koto, dekiru?**
> Can you let me think (about it) a little?

▶ **51.1**

78.1.2.5 **-(s)asete itadaku wake ni wa ikanai deshoo ka**

This is a very polite way of asking permission, which is most appropriate if you think it will be rather difficult to obtain permission or if you think what you are asking is somewhat beyond a reasonable request.

> 試験を一日早く受けさせていただくわけにはいかないでしょうか。(VF)
> **Shiken o ichinichi hayaku ukesasete itadaku wake ni wa ikanai deshoo ka.**
> Is it not possible for you to allow me to take the exam one day early?

> 一週間休暇をとらせていただくわけにはいかないでしょうか。(VF)
> **Isshuukan kyuuka o torasete itadaku wake ni wa ikanai deshoo ka.**
> Is it at all possible for you to let me take a one-week vacation?

> 車を使わせてもらうわけにはいかないかなあ。(I)
> **Kuruma o tsukawasete morau wake ni wa ikanai ka naa.**
> I wonder if it is at all possible for you to let me use your car.

▶ **18.6**

78.1.3 **Causative form + verbs of giving** *kudasaru/kureru*

You can also use the causative form of verbs followed by **kudasai** or **kureru**. This expression, however, is not as polite as the one with the verbs of receiving (cf. **78.1.2**).

> ちょっと休ませてください。
> **Chotto yasumasete kudasai.**
> Please let me rest a little.

> ちょっと考えさせてくれる？
> **Chotto kangaesasete kureru?**
> Will you let me think (about it) a little?

78.2 **Giving permission**

The form V-**te mo ii desu** and its stylistic variants can be used to give permission.

> ひらがなで書いてもいいです。
> **Hiragana de kaite mo ii desu.**
> You may write (it) in **hiragana**.

In responding to someone asking for permission, the following expressions can be used.

> ええ、いいですよ。
> **Ee, ii desu yo.**
> Yes, it's fine. (= Yes, certainly.)

うん、いいよ。
Un, ii yo.
Yes, it's fine. (= Yeah, sure.)

どうぞ。（どうぞ。）
Doozo. (Doozo.)
Please, (go ahead). (Certainly.)

どうぞV- てください。
Doozo V-te kudasai.
Please do. . . .

どうぞおV(stem)ください。
Doozo o-V(stem) kudasai.
Please do. . . .

ええ、かまいませんよ。
Ee, kamaimasen yo.
Yes, it's all right.

ええ、もちろん、どうぞ。
Ee, mochiron, doozo.
Yes, of course. Please (certainly).

The following are some sample ways of responding to specific requests.

(1) この部屋を使ってもよろしいでしょうか。(VF)
     Kono heya o tsukatte mo yoroshii deshoo ka.
     May I use this room?

     ええ、どうぞ、お使いください。/ええ、どうぞ。どうぞ。
     Ee, doozo, o-tsukai kudasai.   **Ee, doozo. Doozo.**
     Yes, please go ahead and use it.   Yes, please, please. (Yes, sure, sure.)

(2) ペン借りてもいい？(I)
     Pen karite mo ii?
     May I borrow your pen?

     うん、いいよ。
     Un, ii yo.
     Yes, it's OK. (Yeah, sure.)

(3) 写真をとらせてもらいたいんですが、いいですか。
     Shashin o torasete moraitai n desu ga, ii desu ka.
     I would like you to let me take pictures. Is it all right?

     ええ、どうぞ、どうぞ。
     Ee, doozo, doozo.
     Yes, please, please. (= Yes, certainly.)

78.3 Denying permission

To withhold permission, you can use expressions such as **sumimasen ga chotto** 'I am sorry, but,' **warui kedo** 'I feel bad, but,' **mooshiwake arimasen ga** 'I am very sorry, but,' and **dame** 'no good.'

この部屋を使ってもよろしいでしょうか。
Kono heya o tsukatte mo yoroshii deshoo ka.
May I use this room?

(i) 申し訳ありませんが、先約がありますので。
Mooshiwake arimasen ga, sen'yaku ga arimasu node.
I am very sorry, but others have already reserved it.

(ii) すみませんが、今ほかの人が使っていますので。
Sumimasen ga, ima hoka no hito ga tsukatte imasu node.
I am sorry, but someone else is using it right now.

写真をとらせてもらいたいんですが、いいですか。
Shashin o torasete morai-tai n desu ga, ii desu ka.
I would like you to let me take pictures. Is it all right?

(i) あのう、ちょっと今都合が悪いんですが。
Anoo, chotto ima tsugoo ga warui n desu ga.
Well, it's a little inconvenient right now.

(ii) 悪いけど、今ちょっと忙しいので...。
Warui kedo, ima chotto isogashii node ...
I am sorry, but I am a little busy right now, so ...

ペン借りてもいい？
Pen karite mo ii?
May I borrow your pen?

(i) 悪いけど、今使ってるんだ。
Warui kedo, ima tsukatte ru n da.
I am sorry, but I am using it right now.

(ii) だめだよ。今使ってるんだから。
Dame da yo. Ima tsukatte ru n da kara.
No way. I am using it right now.

In responding to a request such as V-**te mo ii desu ka**, one can answer with V-**te wa ikemasen**, which means 'you may not/you must not.' However, this sounds very authoritative, and should be used only by superiors or people who have authority.

▶ 79

79

Prohibition

Forbidding someone to do something

V-*te wa ikemasen* and its variants

The most standard way to express prohibition is to say V-**te wa ikenai/ikemasen**, which literally means 'it is wrong to V.' Other variations of this expression such as V-**te wa komaru** 'it is problematic' or V **te wa dame da** 'it is bad' are also available. This expression conveys a strong tone of command, so this is not used toward superiors. You should use negative requests rather than prohibition toward superiors or strangers, such as **-naide itadakenai deshoo ka** 'May I ask you not to do V?'.

▶ 72

何も言わないで休んではいけません。
Nani mo iwanaide yasunde wa ikemasen.
You must not be absent without saying anything (i.e. without giving notice).

寝坊しては困ります。
Neboo shite wa komarimasu.
You should not oversleep (in the morning) / It is problematic if you oversleep in the morning.

予習しないで授業に来てはだめです。
Yoshuu shinaide jugyoo ni kite wa dame desu.
It is not OK for you to come to class without having done the preparation.

In casual conversations, **-te wa** and **-de wa** are contracted to **-cha** and **-ja**, respectively.

何も言わないで休んじゃいけない。
Nani mo iwanaide yasunja ikenai.
You should not be absent without saying anything.

寝坊しちゃ困る。
Neboo shicha komaru.
It is not good if you oversleep (in the morning).

予習しないで授業に来ちゃだめ。
Yoshuu shinaide jugyoo ni kicha dame.
You should not come to class without preparing for it.

These colloquial expressions can be used among close friends or family members without an authoritative commanding tone.

V-*nai koto ni natte imasu*

When something is prohibited by a rule, **-nai koto ni natte imasu** 'it is a rule that one does not do . . .' can be used.

建物の中ではたばこをすってはいけないことになっています。
Tatemono no naka de wa tabako o sutte wa ikenai koto ni natte imasu.
It is a rule that you must not smoke inside the buildings.

雑誌は貸し出しできないことになっています。
Zasshi wa kashi-dashi dekinai koto ni natte imasu.
As a rule, you cannot check the magazines out.

79.1.3 Verbs denoting prohibition

The verbs **kinshi suru** 'to prohibit' and **yurusanai** 'not permit' can be used to express that something is not permitted by law or regulation.

アメリカでは２１歳以下の若者が酒を飲むことは禁止されています。
Amerika de wa nijuuissai ika no wakamono ga sake o nomu koto wa kinshi sarete imasu.
In America, young people under 21 years old are prohibited from drinking.

関係者以外の出入りは許されていない。
Kankeesha igai no de-iri wa yurusarete inai.
Unauthorized persons are prohibited from entering (this building).

80

Obligation and duty

Expressing obligation and duty with regard to oneself and others

There are basically three ways of expressing obligation and duty in Japanese.

-nakereba naranai and *-nakute wa naranai*

-nakereba is the negative conditional form and **-nakute** is the negative **-te** form, and the expressions literally mean 'it is not good if you don't do (it).'

> 日本では家にあがる時、靴を脱がなければなりません。
> **Nihon de wa ie ni agaru toki, kutsu o nuganakereba narimasen.**
> In Japan, when (before) you enter the house, you have to take off your shoes.

> 間違いは直さなければなりません。
> **Machigai wa naosanakereba narimasen.**
> You must correct your mistakes.

> 宿題は予定日に出さなくてはなりません。
> **Shukudai wa yoteebi ni dasanakute wa narimasen.**
> You must hand in homework on the due dates.

> 家賃は毎月払わなくてはならない。
> **Yachin wa maigetsu harawanakute wa naranai.**
> We must pay rent every month.

This expression is generally used to express that one has to do something because of social, legal, or personal expectations. Hence, the obligation expressed here generally holds true for people in general.

Note that the negave obligation (i.e. the sense of 'should not') is conveyed by **-te wa ikenai**, which is discussed in chapter **79**.

-nakereba ikenai and *-nakute wa ikenai*

Here, the word **ikenai** 'it is not good' is used instead of **naranai** (see **80.1.1**).

> もう少し漢字を覚えなければいけませんね。
> **Moo sukoshi kanji o oboenakereba ikemasen ne.**
> You should memorize more **kanji**, you know.

> 今日はパーティーに行けません。来週試験があるから、勉強しなくてはいけないんです。
> **Kyoo wa paatii ni ikemasen. Raishuu shiken ga aru kara, benkyoo shinakute wa ikenai n desu.**
> I can't go to the party today. I have an exam next week, so I have to study.

While the **-naranai** version speaks of obligation that is generally true for everyone, the **-ikenai** version expresses obligation that is based on individual circumstance, needs and expectations. Therefore, it is often directly aimed at the addressee, giving strong advice, a command, a strong request, or the like.

80.1.3 *beki*

This form follows the plain nonpast tense form of verbs and carries the sense of 'one should do . . .' When the verb is **suru** 'to do,' both **suru beki** and **su beki** are possible. Compared with **-nakereba naranai/ikenai** and **-nakute wa naranai/ikenai**, **beki** expresses a stronger sense of obligation, which is almost a personal conviction that one ought to do it.

> 政治家は国民の意見を聞くべきだ。
> **Seejika wa kokumin no iken o kiku beki da.**
> The politicians ought to listen to the opinions of the people.

> 留学生は日本に行ったら、ホームステイをすべきだ。
> **Ryuugakusee wa Nihon ni ittara, hoomusutee o su beki da.**
> Students should participate in a homestay program when they go to Japan.

> A: 日本語で書こうか、英語で書こうか、迷っているんです。
>   **Nihongo de kakoo ka, Eego de kakoo ka, mayotte iru n desu.**
>   I am wondering whether to write it in Japanese or in English.

> B: そりゃあ、日本語で書くべきだよ。
>   **Soryaa, Nihongo de kaku beki da yo.**
>   Of course, you should write it in Japanese.

The negative version of this construction is V **beki de wa nai**.

> いったん結婚したら離婚するべきではないと言う人がいる。
> **Ittan kekkon shitara rikon suru beki de wa nai to yuu hito ga iru.**
> There are people who say that once one gets married, one should not get divorced.

> 私は、女性は子供が生まれても、仕事をやめるべきではないと思う。
> **Watashi wa, josee wa kodomo ga umarete mo, shigoto o yameru beki de wa nai to omou.**
> I think women should not quit their jobs even after having children.

Since **beki da** imparts a sense of strong personal conviction, this expression is inappropriate for stating what one has to do as part of social custom. Consider the custom in Japan where one has to take off one's shoes before entering the house.

> 日本では家にあがる時、靴を脱がなければなりません。
> **Nihon de wa ie ni agaru toki, kutsu o nuganakereba narimasen.**
> In Japan, when (before) you enter the house, you have to take off your shoes.

> ？日本では家にあがる時、靴を脱ぐべきだ。
> **?Nihon de wa ie ni agaru toki, kutsu o nugu beki da.**
> In Japan, when (before) you enter the house, you ought to take off your shoes.

Here, if **beki da** is used, it sounds as if the speaker is indignant that someone did not take off his/her shoes. In an ordinary situation, **nakereba naranai** 'have to' is an appropriate expression.

80.2 Other ways of expressing obligation and duty

80.2.1 With the word *gimu* 'obligation'

> 国民は税金を払う義務がある。
> **Kokumin wa zeekin o harau gimu ga aru.**
> People have an obligation to pay taxes.

> 子供は小学校と中学校に行くことを義務づけられている。
> **Kodomo wa shoogakkoo to chuugakkoo ni iku koto o gimu-zukerarete iru.**
> It is obligatory that children attend elementary and junior high schools.

80.2.2 *-neba naranai*

-neba is the written form of **-nakereba**.

> 借りたお金は返さねばならない。
> **Karita okane wa kaesaneba naranai.**
> One has to repay the money one borrows.

80.2.3 *-nai to ikenai*

To here is a conditional form, and **-nai to ikenai** literally means 'it's not OK if (you) don't.'

> 贈り物をもらったら、お返しをしないといけない。
> **Okurimono o morattara, okaeshi o shinai to ikenai.**
> If one receives a gift, one has to give a return gift.

80.2.4 V-*nai wake ni wa ikanai*

This expression is used when one feels obliged to do it although one does not really want to do it. It has the connotation that one has no choice but to do it. The sense of obligation is based on social, moral, or situational reasons.

> 上司に頼まれたらやらないわけにはいかない。
> **Jooshi ni tanomaretara yaranai wake ni wa ikanai.**
> When I am asked by my superior (to do something), I am obliged to do it.

> パーティーには部長もいらっしゃるので行かないわけにはいかない。
> **Paatii ni wa buchoo mo irassharu node ikanai wake ni wa ikanai.**
> Since the head of the department is coming, I have no choice but (am obligated) to attend the party.

NOTE | When the verb is affirmative in this construction, the sentence means 'can't very well do (something).'

> 上司が帰る前に帰るわけにはいかない。
> **Jooshi ga kaeru mae ni kaeru wake ni wa ikanai.**
> I can't very well go home before my superior goes home.

80.2.5 V-*zaru o enai*

This construction is similar in meaning to V-**nai wake ni wa ikanai**, but it is more literary in flavor. It is, however, used in colloquial speech. **Zaru** is a classical negative form. For verbs, **nai** can be simply replaced by **zaru**, as in **ikanai** 'not go' to **ikazaru**, **tabenai** 'not eat' to **tabezaru**. For **suru** 'to do,' however, **sezaru** is the appropriate form. This construction has the connotation that one does not really want to do something, but is forced to do it because of social, personal or moral reasons.

自分の間違いを認めざるを得ないでしょう。
Jibun no machigai o mitomezaru o enai deshoo.
(He/she) would probably have to admit his/her mistake.

悪天候のため会議をキャンセルせざるを得なかった。
Aku tenkoo no tame kaigi o kyanseru sezaru o enakatta.
We were forced to cancel our meeting due to bad weather.

81

Complaints

81.1 Complaints directed to the addressee

The choice of words and sentence structures for expressing complaints depends on various factors: what the complaint is about, how upset one is, how diplomatic one needs or wants to be, and one's personality. Some expressions of complaint directed to the addressee are exemplified in this section. (See 87.5 about complaining about a purchase afterwards.)

(a) Phrases that precede a complaint
It is common to introduce one's complaint with some phrase that softens the harshness of the complaint.

たいへん言いにくいのですが、... (F)
Taihen iinikui no desu ga,...
This is difficult to say, but...

あまり言いたくないのですが、... (F)
Amari iitakunai no desu ga,...
I don't really want to say this but...

すみませんが、... (F)
Sumimasen ga,...
Excuse me but...

申し訳ありませんが、... (F)
Mooshiwake arimasen ga,...
I'm sorry but...

恐縮ですが、... (F)
Kyooshuku desu ga,...
I'm terribly sorry but...

悪いんだけど、... (I)
Warui n da kedo,...
I feel bad saying this but...

The following are some examples of complaints commonly made.

(b) Complaints regarding noise

隣の部屋の者ですけど、申し訳ないんですが、もう少しだけ静かにしていただけるとありがたいんですけど...。
Tonari no heya no mono desu kedo, mooshiwake nai n desu ga, moo sukoshi dake shizuka ni shite itadakeru to arigatai n desu kedo...
I'm your neighbor, but, I'm sorry, but, I would appreciate it if you could be just a little quieter...

349

音がちょっとうるさいんですが、少し静かにしていただけないでしょうか。
Oto ga chotto urusai n desu ga, sukoshi shizuka ni shite itadakenai deshoo ka.
The noise is bothering me, so would it be possible to quiet down a little?

(c) Complaints regarding trash/littering

言いにくいんですが、ここにお宅のゴミがずっとおきっぱなしだと思うんですけど、片付けていただけないでしょうか。
Iinikui n desu ga, koko ni o-taku no gomi ga zutto okippanashi da to omou n desu kedo, katazukete itadakenai deshoo ka.
I feel awkward saying this, but, I think you have left your trash here for a long time, could you please clear it away?

恐縮ですが、皆が迷惑するので、ゴミは決まった日に出すようにしていただけないでしょうか。
Kyooshuku desu ga, minna ga meewaku suru node, gomi wa kimatta hi ni dasu yoo ni shite itadakenai deshoo ka.
I'm sorry, but, everyone will be inconvenienced, so, would it be possible to try to take out the trash on the set pick-up day?

(d) Other complaints that may occur in daily life

The following types of complaints can be expressed toward people close to you.

貧乏揺すりやめてくれない？ (I)
Binboo yusuri yamete kurenai?
Would you stop your fidgeting?

私のものを勝手に食べないでくれる？ (I)
Watashi no mono o katte ni tabenaide kureru?
Would you stop eating my stuff without asking me?

私物には触って欲しくないんだけど。 (I)
Shibutsu ni wa sawatte hoshikunai n da kedo.
I don't want you to touch my personal stuff, though.

夜遅く電話をかけてこないでくれない？ (I)
Yoru osoku denwa o kakete konaide kurenai?
Would you not call me late at night?

何も知らないくせに、そんなこと言わないでよ。 (I)
Nani mo shiranai kuseni, sonna koto iwanaide yo.
You don't know anything, so don't say things like that.

▶ 18.2.2; 22.6; 73

81.2 Complaining about someone else

When one wants to complain about someone else, the following constructions can be used.

- (a) V-te kurenai (see 19.2.8)

    先輩たちは僕の実力を認めてくれないんです。 (F)
    Senpai-tachi wa boku no jitsuryoku o mitomete kurenai n desu.
    The seniors don't recognize my true ability.

    道子さんが、本を返してくれないんです。 (F)
    Michiko-san ga, hon o kaeshite kurenai n desu.
    Michiko wouldn't return my book to me.

- (b) Passive (see 21.4)

    田中さんに日記を読まれてしまったんです。 (F)
    Tanaka-san ni nikki o yomarete shimatta n desu.
    Mr/Ms Tanaka read my diary.

となりのアパートの人に一晩中騒がれた！ (I)
Tonari no apaato no hito ni hitoban-juu sawagareta!
My next door neighbor was noisy all night long!

■ (c) Causative Passive (see **21.5**)

上司に遅くまで飲まされて、たいへんだったよ。 (I)
Jooshi ni osoku made nomasarete, taihen datta yo.
I was made to drink till late at night by my boss; it was difficult.

カラオケを何時間も聞かされました。 (F)
Karaoke o nan jikan mo kikasaremashita.
I was made to listen to karaoke for hours.

■ (d) **Bakari/bakkari** (see **18.9.1**)

鈴木さんは寝てばかりいます。 (F)
Suzuki-san wa nete bakari imasu.
Mr/Ms Suzuki is always sleeping.

佐藤さんは嘘ばっかりつくから、信用できない。 (I)
Satoo-san wa uso bakkari tsuku kara, shin'yoo dekinai.
Mr/Ms Sato is all lies, so I can't trust him/her.

■ (e) **Noni** 'although' (see **22.5.3**)

手伝ってあげたのに、お礼の言葉もなかったんです。 (F)
Tetsudatte ageta noni, oree no kotoba mo nakatta n desu.
Even though I helped them, there wasn't even a word of thanks.

約束したのに、森さんは来なかった。 (I)
Yakusoku shita noni, Mori-san wa konakatta.
Mr/Ms Mori didn't come even though he/she promised me.

■ (f) **Kuse ni** 'although' (see **22.5.6**)

兄は自分が悪いくせに、いつも人のせいにする。
Ani wa jibun ga warui kuseni, itsumo hito no see ni suru.
My older brother always blames others even though it's his own fault.

81.3 Complaints about a hotel/inn room

To raise complaints regarding a hotel or inn room, the issue is addressed to a receptionist, front desk clerk, or whoever is in charge of the guest room. One's complaint is often expressed in a sentence that ends with . . . **n desu ga/kedo**, which should prompt some response from the other person.

► **18.2.2**

部屋の臭いが気になるんですが。 (F)
Heya no nioi ga ki ni naru n desu ga . . .
The smell of the room bothers me so . . .

禁煙の部屋を予約していたはずなんですけど。 (F)
Kin'en no heya o yoyaku shite ita hazu na n desu kedo . . .
I was supposed to have reserved a non-smoking room so . . .

部屋が汚れているんですが。 (F)
Heya ga yogorete iru n desu ga . . .
The room is dirty so . . .

A specific request to resolve the issue could be added after . . . **n desu ga/kedo**.

部屋がちょっとカビ臭いんですが、別の部屋にかえていただけませんか。(F)
Heya ga chotto kabi kusai n desu ga, betsu no heya ni kaete itadakemasen ka.
My room smells a bit moldy, so could you give me another room?

となりの部屋がうるさくて眠れないんですけど、注意していただけないでしょうか。(F)
Tonari no heya ga urusakute nemurenai n desu kedo, chuui shite itadakenai deshoo ka.
The room next door is noisy and I can't sleep, so would it be possible for you to talk to them?

81.4 Responding to complaints directed to oneself

If a complaint is directed to you and if it is a reasonable complaint that can be resolved right away, you may say a word of apology and proceed to do what is necessary. You may add a small excuse for causing the problem, but it is not necessary.

▶ **60**

A: すみません、隣の部屋の者ですけど、ちょっと音を小さくしてもらえますか。(F)
Sumimasen, tonari no heya no mono desu kedo, chotto oto o chiisaku shite moraemasu ka.
Excuse me, I'm your neighbor, but, can you please lower the volume a little?

B: あ、すみません。すぐ小さくします。お皿を洗いながら聞いていたので、つい大きくしすぎちゃったみたいです。ご迷惑をおかけしました。(F)
A, sumimasen. Sugu chiisaku shimau. O-sara o arainagara kiite ita node, tsui ookiku shisugichatta mitai desu. Go-meewaku o o-kake shimashita.
Oh, I'm sorry. I'll turn it down right away. I was listening to it while doing the dishes, so I inadvertently made it too loud. I'm sorry to have inconvenienced you.

智子： ちょっと、貧乏揺すりやめてくれる？(I)
Tomoko: Chotto, binboo yusuri yamete kureru?
Tomoko: Hey, can you stop fidgeting?

武史： あ、ごめん。ついくせで。(I)
Takeshi: A, gomen. Tsui kuse de.
Takeshi: Oh, sorry. It's just my habit.

If the complaint directed to you does not seem reasonable, you may respond with one of the following remarks, but it may aggravate the situation.

そんなこと言われても、困ります。(F)
Sonna koto iwarete mo, komarimasu.
Even though you say that, there's nothing I can do about it.

そんなこと言われても、どうにもならないんです。(F)
Sonna koto iwarete mo, doo ni mo naranai n desu.
Even though you say that, I can't do anything about it.

そう言われても、こまったなあ。(I)
Soo iwarete mo, komatta naa.
Even though you say that, there's nothing I can do about it.

▶ **55.4.2**

81.5 Responding to other types of complaints

When someone complains about someone else or something, people often respond with appropriate **aizuchi** phrases (see **31.11**) and express their empathy. Some may also offer suggestions or advice about the complaints when it seems appropriate.

孝子： 会社の先輩に遅くまでつきあわされちゃって、最低。(I)
Takako: Kaisha no senpai ni osoku made tsukiawasarechatte, saitee.
Takako: My senior colleague made me accompany her until late, it was horrible.

翠： そうかあ、たいへんだったね。(I)
Midori: Soo kaa, taihen datta ne.
Midori: Is that so? That was tough, wasn't it?

孝子： もうくたくただよ。(I)
Takako: Moo kutakuta da yo.
Takako: I'm exhausted, I'm telling you.

翠： 分かる、分かる。今夜はもう、ビデオでも見て、のんびりしよう。
Midori: Wakaru, wakaru. Kon'ya wa moo, bideo demo mite, nonbiri shiyoo.
Midori: Sure, sure. Let's relax the rest of the night by watching videos or something.

Another way to respond to complaints directed to someone or something is to chime in with your own similar complaints.

太郎： 彼女がさ、毎日電話しろって、うるさいんだよね。(I)
Toroo: Kanojo ga sa, mainichi denwa shiro tte, urusai n da yo ne.
Toro: My girlfriend, you know, tells me to call her every day, it's too much.

次郎： えー、そうなんだ。まあ、俺の彼女もいろいろうるさいよ。
 毎日メールしないと怒るし。(I)
Jiroo: Ee, soo na n da. Maa, ore no kanojo mo iroiro urusai yo.
 Mainichi meeru shinai to okoru shi.
Jiro: Oh, I see. Well, my girlfriend is annoying in various ways too.
 Like she gets mad if I don't e-mail her every day.

82

Compliments

Complimenting one's equal or social subordinate

In Japanese, the way a compliment is phrased can vary greatly depending on the relationship between the speaker and the addressee as well as what the compliment is about. Unlike English, **ii** 'good' does not always work as a compliment. You may use either the formal or informal styles of speech with your equal or subordinate, depending on the situation and your relationship with them.

Complimenting one's equal or social subordinate about what he/she did

> すごくよかったですよ。(F)
> **Sugoku yokatta desu yo.**
> It was very good!

> すばらしかったですよ。(F)
> **Subarashikatta desu yo.**
> It was excellent!

> すごく面白かったですよ。(F)
> **Sugoku omoshirokatta desu yo.**
> It was very interesting!

> よくやったね。(I)
> **Yoku yatta ne.**
> You did well, didn't you?

> よくがんばったね。(I)
> **Yoku ganbatta ne.**
> You worked hard, didn't you?

> すごくうまいね。(I)
> **Sugoku umai ne.**
> You are very skillful, aren't you?

> さすがだね。(I)
> **Sasuga da ne.**
> Just what we expect from you, isn't it?

To point out a specific part to praise, the **te**-form is often used.

> プロジェクトの進め方がすごくスムーズで、よかったよ。(I)
> **Purojekuto no susumekata ga sugoku sumuuzu de, yokatta yo.**
> Really, the way you carried out the project was very smooth and that was good.

> 要点が分かりやすくて、うまく書けていましたよ。(F)
> **Yooten ga wakariyasukute, umaku kakete imashita yo.**
> The main points were easy to understand and so it was well written, you know.

When complimenting someone on food/cooking, expressions other than **ii** 'good' are used.

おいしい！
Oishii!
Delicious!

美味い！
Umai! (male/rough)
Tasty!

盛りつけもきれいですね。(F)
Moritsuke mo kiree desu ne.
The presentation is also beautiful.

作るの、難しそうですね。(F)
Tsukuru no, muzukashi soo desu ne.
It looks hard to make.

これってどうやって作るの？(I)
Kore tte doo yatte tsukuru no?
How do you make this?

作り方、教えてくれる？(I)
Tsukuri kata, oshiete kureru?
Will you tell me how to make it?

82.1.2 **Complimenting one's equal or social subordinate about his/her personality or ability**

やさしいですね。(F)
Yasashii desu ne.
You are kind, aren't you?

たよりになるね。(I)
Tayori ni naru ne.
You are dependable, aren't you?

頭いいね。(I)
Atama ii ne.
You are smart, aren't you?

これ、よく書けていますね。(F)
Kore, yoku kakete imasu ne.
This is well written, isn't it?

To compliment someone's ability, X **ga joozu** or **umai** 'skillful' are commonly used.

字が上手ですね。(F)
Ji ga joozu desu ne.
Your handwriting is good, isn't it?

説明の仕方がうまいね。(I)
Setsumee no shikata ga umai ne.
You are skilled at explaining things?

82.1.3 **Complimenting one's equal or social subordinate on possessions**

かっこいいですね。/ かっこいいXですね。(F)
Kakkoii desu ne. / Kakkoii X desu ne.
That's cool. / That's a cool X.

きれいだね。/ きれいなXだね。(I)
Kiree da ne. / Kiree na X da ne.
That's pretty. / That's a pretty X.

すてきだね。/ すてきなXだね。(I)
Suteki da ne. / Suteki na X da ne.
That's fabulous. / That's a fabulous X.

82.2 Complimenting one's social superior

Much caution needs to be taken when one decides to compliment one's social superior in Japanese. Japanese people tend to be very conscious about hierarchical relations, and a 'compliment' is generally viewed as something a superior gives to a subordinate based on his/her evaluation of the subordinate. A subordinate is not considered to be in a position to evaluate a superior, and hence complimenting his/her superior is usually not appropriate. Therefore, a direct translation of compliments used in English does not work when one wants to compliment one's superior in Japanese.

82.2.1 Complimenting one's social superior about what he/she did

When complimenting what one's social superior did, it is inappropriate to use words that sound evaluative such as **yokatta desu** 'it was good.' Instead, it is common to express your thanks for the benefits you gained because of what the superior did.

とても勉強になりました。ありがとうございました。
Totemo benkyoo ni narimashita. Arigatoo gozaimashita.
I learned a lot from you. Thank you.

とても興味深いお話を聞かせていただいて、ありがとうございました。
Totemo kyoomi bukai o-hanashi o kikasete itadaite, arigatoo gozaimashita.
Thank you for letting me hear a very interesting talk.

感動しました。ありがとうございます。
Kandoo shimashita. Arigatoo gozaimasu.
I was moved. Thank you.

とても感銘を受けました。ありがとうございます。
Totemo kanmee o ukemashita. Arigatoo gozaimasu.
It made a great impression on me. / I was deeply impressed. Thank you.

とても参考になるご意見をうかがい、ありがとうございました。
Totemo sankoo ni naru go-iken o ukagai, arigatoo gozaimashita.
Thank you for letting me listen to your very useful opinions.

82.2.2 Complimenting one's social superior about his/her personality or ability

To compliment one's superior's personality or ability, the compliment is embedded in an expression of gratitude. It is not appropriate to use expressions that sound evaluative such as **shinsetsu desu ne** 'you are kind' or **ii hito desu ne** 'you are a nice person.'

いつも親切にしていただいて、感謝しております。
Itsumo shinsetsu ni shite itadaite, kansha shite orimasu.
I'm thankful for your continuous kindness.
(Instead of 'You are so kind.')

いつも助けていただいてばかりで、申し訳ありません。
Itsumo tasukete itadaite bakari de, mooshiwake arimasen.
Thank you for always helping me.
(Instead of 'You are so helpful.')

82.2.3 Complimenting one's social superior's possessions

Although you are not directly commenting on your superior when you compliment your superior's possessions, it is best to avoid using words like **ii** 'good,' which may sound judgmental. More emotive expressions like **suteki** 'fantastic' and **subarashii** 'wonderful' are commonly used. In the examples below, replace X with the item you are praising.

素敵ですね。/ 素敵なXですね。
Suteki desu ne. / Suteki na X desu ne.
That's fantastic. / That's a fantastic X.

素晴らしいですね。/ 素晴らしいXですね。
Subarashii desu ne. / Subarashii X desu ne.
That's splendid. / That is a splendid X.

82.3 Responding to compliments directed at oneself

How you respond to compliments may depend on various factors such as what the compliment was about, who complimented you, and what impression you wish to make. You may say **arigatoo** 'thank you (informal)' or **arigatoo gozaimasu** 'thank you (formal)' when someone compliments you. However, it is common to say something else in addition to or instead of 'thank you.' Various cases and examples are given below.

82.3.1 Responding to compliments received from one's equal or social subordinate

(a) Responding to compliments about one's work

Compliment from one's subordinate

今回のプロジェクト、大成功でしたね。(F)
Konkai no purojekuto, daiseekoo deshita ne.
This project was a huge success.

Response examples

皆が協力してくれたおかげですよ。(F)
Minna ga kyooryoku shite kureta okage desu yo.
Really, it's thanks to everyone's cooperation.

頑張った甲斐があったよ。(I)
Ganbatta kai ga atta yo.
I'm glad that I did my best.

Xさんのおかげだよ。(I)
X-san no okage da yo.
I owe it to Mr/Ms X.

そんなふうにほめられると恥ずかしいけど、うれしいよ。(I)
Sonna fuu ni homerareru to hazukashii kedo, ureshii yo.
I feel embarrassed to be praised like that, but I feel pleased.

(b) Responding to compliments about one's physical appearance.

Compliment from one's equal

田中さんの髪の毛、すごくきれい。(I)
Tanaka-san no kaminoke, sugoku kiree.
Your hair is so beautiful.

Response examples

そんなこと言われたのはじめてだよ。(I)
Sonna koto iwareta no hajimete da yo.
This is the first time anyone has said such a thing.

そうかな。ありがとう。(I)
Soo ka na. Arigatoo.
You think? Thanks.

そんなこといわれると、はずかしいよ。(I)
Sonna koto iwareru to, hazukashii yo.
I'm embarrassed to be told such a thing.

(c) Responding to compliments about one's personality or ability.

Compliment from one's subordinate

田中さんは優しいんですね。(F)
Tanaka-san wa yasashii n desu ne.
Mr/Ms Tanaka, you are kind.

Response examples

優しいんじゃなくて、おせっかいなだけだよ。(I)
Yasashii n ja nakute, osekkai na dake da yo.
I'm not kind, I'm just meddlesome.

そんなことないよ。(I)
Sonna koto nai yo.
Not really.

Compliment from one's equal

料理、上手だねえ。(I)
Ryoori, joozu da nee.
You are good at cooking.

Response examples

ほんと？ありがとう。(I)
Honto? Arigatoo.
Really? Thank you.

いや、そんな、ほめられるほどじゃないけど。(I)
Iya, sonna, homerareru hodo ja nai kedo.
No, it's nothing to be praised for, though.

(d) Responding to compliments about one's possessions.

One may respond to a compliment about one's possessions by:

(i) Providing information about the object in question:

Compliment from one's subordinate

その時計かっこいいですね。(F)
Sono tokee kakkoii desu ne.
That watch is cool.

Response examples

えー、そうかなあ？去年の誕生日にもらったんだけどね。(I)
Ee, soo ka naa? Kyonen no tanjoobi ni moratta n da kedo ne.
You think so? I got it for my birthday last year.

たいした物じゃないけどね。ありがとう。(I)
Taishita mono ja nai kedo ne. Arigatoo.
It's nothing special, but thanks.

(ii) Pointing out something negative about the object in question:

Compliment from one's equal

その鞄、かわいい！(I)
Sono kaban, kawaii!
That bag is cute!

Response examples

そうかな？ありがとう。けっこう安かったんだけどね。(I)
Soo ka na? Arigatoo. Kekkoo yasukatta n dakedo ne.
Really? Thank you. It was pretty cheap though.

そう？もっと小さいのがよかったんだけど。(I)
Soo? Motto chiisai no ga yokatta n dakedo.
Really? I wanted a smaller one though.

(iii) Returning a compliment:

Compliment from one's subordinate

すごく素敵なスカートですね。(F)
Sugoku suteki na sukaato desu ne.
It's such a nice skirt.

Response examples

そうですか。Xさんの靴もかわいいですよね。(F)
Soo desu ka. X-san no kutsu mo kawaii desu yo ne.
You think so? Your shoes are cute too, aren't they?

そう？ Xさんのジャケットも素敵だね。(I)
Soo? X-san no jaketto mo suteki da ne.
You think so? Your jacket is fabulous too.

82.3.2 ## Responding to compliments received from one's superior

(a) Responding to compliments about one's work

> Compliment from one's superior
>
> 今日の発表、とてもよくできていましたよ。
> **Kyoo no happyoo, totemo yoku dekite imashita yo.**
> Your presentation today was really well done.
>
> Response examples
>
> 皆さんが協力してくれたおかげなんです。
> **Minasan ga kyooryoku shite kureta okage na n desu.**
> That's because everyone gave me their cooperation.
>
> Xさんのおかげです。ありがとうございました。
> **X-san no okage desu. Arigatoo gozaimashita.**
> I owe it to you. Thank you.
>
> まだまだ力不足ですが、ご親切なお言葉、ありがとうございます。
> **Mada mada chikara busoku desu ga, go-shinsetsu na o-kotoba, arigatoo gozaimasu.**
> I still have a lot to improve, but thank you for your kind words.

(b) Responding to compliments about one's physical appearance

> Compliment from one's superior
>
> 背が高くてかっこいいね。
> **Se ga takakute kakkoii ne.**
> You are tall and good looking.
>
> Response examples
>
> そんなふうに言ってくださるのはXさんだけです。
> **Sonna fuu ni itte kudasaru no wa X-san dake desu.**
> You are the only person to say such a thing.
>
> 僕なんかよりYさんの方がずっとかっこいいです。
> **Boku nanka yori Y-san no hoo ga zutto kakkoii desu.**
> Mr Y is much better-looking than me.

(c) Responding to compliments about one's personality or ability

> Compliment from one's superior
>
> 君は本当に努力家だねえ。
> **Kimi wa hontoo ni doryokuka da nee.**
> You are really diligent.
>
> Response examples
>
> 努力家というよりしつこいだけなんです。
> **Doryokuka to yuu yori shitsukoi dake na n desu.**
> Rather than diligent, I'm persistent.
>
> 私なんかより優秀な方がたくさんいるおかげで、いつも助かっているんです。
> **Watashi nanka yori yuushuu na kata ga takusan iru okage de, itsumo tasukatte iru n desu.**
> Thanks to people who have a lot more talent than I do, I'm always supported.

Compliment from one's superior

> いつも仕事がはやいね。
> **Itsumo shigoto ga hayai ne.**
> You always get your work done promptly.

Response example

> いいえ、これからもがんばります。
> **Iie, korekara mo ganbarimasu.**
> No, I will continue to do my best.

(d) Responding to compliments about one's possessions.

One may respond to a compliment about one's possessions by:

(i) Pointing out something negative about the object in question:

Compliment from one's superior

> きれいなスカーフですね。
> **Kiree na sukaafu desu ne.**
> It's a beautiful scarf, isn't it.

Response example

> え、そうですか。ありがとうございます。ほんの安物なんですけど。
> **E, soo desu ka. Arigatoo gozaimasu. Honno yasumono na n desu kedo.**
> Oh, you think so? Thank you. It's only a cheap one.

(ii) Providing information about the object in question:

Compliment from one's superior

> いいスーツだね。
> **Ii suutsu da ne.**
> It's a nice suit.

Response examples

> え、ほんとですか。入社式のために思い切って買ったんです。
> **E, honto desu ka. Nyuushashiki no tame ni omoikitte katta n desu.**
> Oh, really? I bought it for the new employee welcome ceremony.

> ありがとうございます。母が卒業祝いに買ってくれたものなんです。
> **Arigatoo gozaimasu. Haha ga sotsugyoo iwai ni katte kureta mono na n desu.**
> My mother bought it for me as a graduation gift.

► 18.2.2; 29; 59

83

Promises and warnings

83.1 ## Expressing promises

To state a promise, use the nonpast tense. Promises are often accompanied by adverbs such as **zettai (ni)** 'definitely' and **kanarazu** 'surely, certainly, without fail.'

> 絶対に誰にも言いません。
> **Zettai ni dare ni mo iimasen.**
> I will never tell anyone.

> 何かあったら、必ず連絡します。
> **Nani ka attara, kanarazu renraku shimasu.**
> I will surely contact you if anything happens.

> もう絶対うそをつきません。
> **Moo zettai uso o tsukimasen.**
> I will never lie any more.

> 約束します。
> **Yakusoku shimasu.**
> I promise.

To explicitly say 'I promise to do . . . ,' use V(plain) **yakusoku o suru** or V(plain) **to yakusoku suru**.

> タバコをすわない約束をします。
> **Tabako o suwanai yakusoku o shimasu.**
> I promise not to smoke.

> もう嘘をつかないと約束するよ。
> **Moo uso o tsukanai to yakusoku suru yo.**
> I promise that I won't lie any more.

► 7.2.3; 26.2

83.2 ## Warning someone to do (or not to do) something

To warn people to do or not to do something, various sentence structures may be used, depending on the seriousness of the warning. Some take the form of a command; others take the form of a suggestion or request.

- (a) Command (see **75**)

> 早く行きなさい。遅刻するよ。
> **Hayaku ikinasai. Chikoku suru yo.**
> Go quickly. You'll be late.

もう寝なさい。明日の朝、起きられないよ。
Moo nenasai. Ashita no asa, okirarenai yo.
Go to bed already or you won't be able to get up tomorrow morning.

■ (b) V(plain, nonpast negative form) + **hoo ga ii** (see **72.3**)

あのレストランは行かないほうがいいよ。
Ano resutoran wa ikanai hoo ga ii yo.
You'd better not to go to that restaurant.

■ (c) V(plain, past affirmative form) + **hoo ga ii**

お母さんに怒られるから、早く帰ったほうがいいですよ。
Okaasan ni okorareru kara, hayaku kaetta hoo ga ii desu yo.
You'd better go home early because you'll be scolded by your mother.

■ (d) Prohibition (see **79.1**)

ここに車をとめてはいけません。
Koko ni kuruma o tomete wa ikemasen.
You must not park a car here.

■ (e) V-**te** form + **kudasai** (see **73.3**)

皆が気持ちよく過ごせるように規則を守ってください。
Minna ga kimochi yoku sugoseru yoo ni kisoku o mamotte kudasai.
Please follow the rules so that everyone can stay comfortably.

やけどをする恐れがあるので、子供には使わせないでください。
Yakedo o suru osore ga aru node, kodomo ni wa tsukawasenaide kudasai.
There is a possibility of getting burned, so please don't let children use it.

落とさないように気をつけてください。
Otosanai yoo ni ki o tsukete kudasai.
Be careful not to drop it.

■ (f) Polite request: **o-/go-**verb **kudasai** (see **29.3**)

火気の取り扱いにご注意下さい。
Kaki no toriatsukai ni go-chuui kudasai.
Please be careful handling fire.

お早めにお召し上がり下さい。
O-hayame ni o-meshiagari kudasai.
Please eat soon.

おたばこはご遠慮下さい。
O-tabako wa go-enryo kudasai.
Please refrain from smoking.

Another way to warn people is to state what will happen if he/she doesn't do what is expected, using the conditional structure.

▶ **24.1**

早く行かないと、遅刻するよ。
Hayaku ikanai to, chikoku suru yo.
If you don't leave soon, you'll be late.

よく聞いていないと、分からなくなりますよ。
Yoku kiite inai to, wakaranaku narimasu yo.
If you are not listening well, you will become lost (Lit. You will stop being able to understand).

The verb **keekoku suru** 'to warn' is used to state a serious warning. The content of the warning is expressed using **yoo (ni)**.

> 危険地域には入らないよう（に）警告します。
> **Kiken chiiki ni wa hairanai yoo (ni) keekoku shimasu.**
> We warn you not to enter hazardous areas.

> 一週間以内に避難するよう（に）警告します。
> **Isshuukan inai ni hinan suru yoo (ni) keekoku shimasu.**
> We warn you to evacuate within one week.

84

Opinions

84.1 Expressing one's opinion

84.1.1 *omou* and *kangaeru*

The verbs **omou** 'to think/feel' and **kangaeru** 'to think' are commonly used to express one's opinion. **Kangaeru** expresses opinions resulting from active thinking; e.g. analysis and logical reasoning, and therefore sentences with **kangaeru** sound more objective. On the other hand, **omou** expresses opinions that are more intuitive, emotional or subjective.

> 他の人の迷惑になることはしてはいけないと思う。
> **Hoka no hito no meewaku ni naru koto wa shite wa ikenai to omou.**
> I think that we should not do things that cause trouble to others.

> 社会福祉は重要だと考えます。
> **Shakai fukushi wa juuyoo da to kangaemasu.**
> I think that social welfare is important.

> その考えは単純すぎるように思います。
> **Sono kangae wa tanjun sugiru yoo ni omoimasu.**
> I feel that that idea seems too simplistic.

84.1.2 *beki da*

To express stronger opinions, **beki da** 'should, ought to' may be used. It is often used with **omou** 'to feel' or **kangaeru** 'to think.'

> ▶ 80.1.3

> すべての子供が教育を受けるべきです。
> **Subete no kodomo ga kyooiku o ukeru beki desu.**
> All children should receive education.

> やれることは全てやるべきだと思う。
> **Yareru koto wa subete yaru beki da to omou.**
> I think that we should do everything we can.

84.1.3 Indirect ways to express one's opinion

The following structures are used to express one's opinion less directly.

■ Pre-nominal form + **yoo na ki ga suru**: 'I feel that . . .'

> この計画はうまくいかないような気がします。
> **Kono keekaku wa umaku ikanai yoo na ki ga shimasu.**
> I feel that this plan will not work out.

- Pre-nominal form + **yoo ni kanjiru**: 'I feel that . . .'

  この規則は不公平なように感じます。
  Kono kisoku wa fukoohee na yoo ni kanjimasu.
  I feel that this rule is unfair.

- Pre-nominal form + **no de wa nai deshoo ka**
  or
  Pre-nominal form + **n ja nai deshoo ka**: 'I wonder . . . ; Wouldn't it be . . .'

▶ 32.3.2

もう少し話し合ったほうがいいのではないでしょうか。
Moo sukoshi hanashiatta hoo ga ii no de wa nai deshoo ka.
I wonder if it would be better to discuss this a little longer.

まだ間に合うんじゃないでしょうか。
Mada maniau n ja nai deshoo ka.
Wouldn't it be that we'd still be on time?

In casual speech, **n ja nai deshoo ka** is shortened to **n ja nai?**

あきらめたほうがいいんじゃない？
Akirameta hoo ga ii n ja nai?
Wouldn't it be better to give up?

When expressing one's opinion in Japanese, it is common to preface the opinion with phrases like 'I may be wrong,' 'it may be too extreme to say it this way' or 'I feel bad to say it this way,' as in the following examples.

間違っているかもしれないけど、田中さんは本当は佐藤さんのことが好きなんじゃないでしょうか。
Machigatte iru kamoshirenai kedo, Tanaka-san wa hontoo wa Satoo-san no koto ga suki na n ja nai deshoo ka.
I may be wrong but I wonder if the truth is that Mr Tanaka likes Ms Sato.

言い過ぎかもしれないけど、この計画はすでに破綻していると思います。
Iisugi kamoshirenai kedo, kono keekaku wa sudeni hatan shite iru to omoimasu.
I may be saying too much, but I think this plan has already failed.

言っちゃ悪いけど、あの人変だと思う。
Itcha warui kedo, ano hito hen da to omou.
I feel bad saying this, but I think that person is strange.

84.2 Asking for other people's opinions

To ask for other people's opinions, use one of the following questions.

どう思う？ (I)
Doo omou?
What do you think?

どう考えますか。 (F)
Doo kangaemasu ka.
What do you think?

どうお考えですか。 (VF)
Doo o-kangae desu ka.
What do you think?

何か意見がありますか。 (F)
Nani ka iken ga arimasu ka.
Do you have any opinion?

To ask for others' opinions about a specific topic, **ni tsuite** 'about' or **ni kanshite** 'regarding' is used to state the topic.

> 環境問題についてどうお考えですか。(VF)
> **Kankyoo mondai ni tsuite doo o-kangae desu ka.**
> What do you think about environmental problems?

> 小学校で英語を教えることに関して、何か意見がありますか。(F)
> **Shoogakkoo de Eego o oshieru koto ni kanshite, nani ka iken ga arimasu ka.**
> Do you have any opinion about teaching English in elementary schools?

84.3 Reporting on other people's opinions

The opinion of another person is commonly reported as a quotation or in the form of hearsay.

> 田中さんは外国語を勉強する必要はないと考えているそうです。
> **Tanaka-san wa gaikokugo o benkyoo suru hitsuyoo wa nai to kangaete iru soo desu.**
> I hear that Mr/Ms Tanaka thinks that one does not need to study a foreign language.

> 父は高校も義務教育にするべきだと言っています。
> **Chichi wa kookoo mo gimu kyooiku ni suru beki da to itte imasu.**
> My father says that we should make high school education mandatory.

> 母は「人を傷つけることをしてはいけない」と言っていました。
> **Haha wa 'Hito o kizutsukeru koto o shite wa ikenai' to itte imashita.**
> My mother said 'We must not do things that hurt people.'

The noun **iken** 'opinion' can also be used to express other people's opinions. The content of the opinion is stated in an appositive clause that modifies the noun **iken**.

▶ 7.2.5

> 田中さんは外国語を勉強する必要はないという意見です。
> **Tanaka-san wa gaikokugo o benkyoo suru hitsuyoo wa nai to yuu iken desu.**
> Mr/Ms Tanaka is of the opinion that one does not need to study a foreign language.

The verbs **omou** and **kangaeru** are used in **te**-form + **iru/imasu** to express other people's opinion.

> 鈴木さんはインターネットは人間の生活を豊かにすると考えています。
> **Suzuki-san wa intaanetto wa ningen no seekatsu o yutaka ni suru to kangaete imasu.**
> Mr/Ms Suzuki thinks that the Internet enriches human life.

> 母はテレビは子供の教育によくないと思っています。
> **Haha wa terebi wa kodomo no kyooiku ni yokunai to omotte imasu.**
> My mother thinks that TV is not good for children's education.

85

Agreement, disagreement, and indifference

85.1 Expressing agreement and disagreement

There are various ways to express your agreement or disagreement depending on how clearly or openly you want to express it. Since 'disagreeing' may be confrontational and potentially create an embarrassing moment, the speaker often expresses his/her disagreement in an indirect, mitigated manner.

85.1.1 Expressing agreement with the prior speaker's comment

A: これ、高いですね。　　　　　B: そうですね。
Kore, takai desu ne.　　　　　　**Soo desu ne.**
This is expensive, isn't it.　　　　It is, isn't it.

A: これ、高いね。　　　　　　　B: そうだね。
Kore, takai ne.　　　　　　　　**Soo da ne.**
This is expensive, isn't it.　　　　Yeah, right.

In these examples speaker B agrees with speaker A's comment. The use of the sentence final particle **ne** by both speakers indicates that they share the same opinion. This style of conversation creates rapport between the speakers. The following expressions can be used when the speaker agrees with the prior speaker's opinion or idea.

85.1.2 Expressing agreement with the prior speaker's opinion, idea, or suggestion

（それは）いい考えですね。(F)
(Sore wa) ii kangae desu ne
(That) is a good idea.

（それ）いい考えだね。/ 考えね。(I)　(Feminine)
(Sore) ii kangae da ne. / kangae ne.
(That) is a good idea.

私もそう思います。(F)
Watashi mo soo omoimasu
I think so too.

私もそう思う。(I)
Watashi mo soo omou.
I think so too.

私も同感です。(F)
Watashi mo dookan desu.
I agree.

なるほどね。
Naruhodo ne.
I see. (Indeed.)

私も賛成です。(F)
Watashi mo sansee desu.
I agree too.

私も賛成。(I)
Watashi mo sansee.
I agree too.

よろしいんじゃないでしょうか。(VF)
Yoroshii n ja nai deshoo ka.
I think it is good.

いいんじゃない。(I)
Ii n ja nai.
I think it's good.

(それは) いいですね。(F)
(Sore wa) ii desu ne
(That) sounds good.

(それ) いいね。(I)
(Sore) ii ne.
(That) sounds good.

Expressing disagreement with the prior speaker's comment

In expressing disagreement with the prior speaker's comment, expressions such as **soo desu ka? soo?** or **soo ka na?** can be used.

A: これ、きれいですね。(F)　　　B: そうですか。
 Kore kiree desu ne.　　　　　　**Soo desu ka.**
 This is pretty, isn't it.　　　　　　Is that so?

A: これ、きれいだね。(I)　　　　B: そう？ or そうかな？
 Kore kiree da ne.　　　　　　　**Soo?** or **Soo ka na?**
 This is pretty, isn't it.　　　　　　Is that so?

When the speaker disagrees with the prior speaker's comment, moreover, he/she usually delays his/her response by a pause and/or uttering fillers such as **uun** 'uhm,' or **maa** 'well,' or the like.

Also, it is generally good to first acknowledge the prior speaker's comment or opinion and then disagree, using contrastive connectives or conjunctions.

A: 日本の大学生はアルバイトばかりしていて、ちっとも勉強しないみたい。
 Nihon no daigakusee wa arubaito bakari shite ite, chittomo benkyoo shinai mitai.
 It seems that Japanese college students spend their time doing part-time jobs and don't study at all.

B: うん、でも勉強する人はちゃんとやってるんだよ。
 Un, demo benkyoo suru hito wa chanto yatte ru n da yo.
 Yeah, but there are students who do study.

A: 日本では仕事のあと飲みに行くのも仕事の一つなんだよ。
Nihon de wa shigoto no ato nomi ni iku no mo shigoto no hitotsu na n da yo.
In Japan it is part of one's job to go out for a drink after work, you know.

B: うーん、それはそうかもしれませんが。でも、早く家に帰りたくても、誘わ
れたら断れないし。
**Uun, sore wa soo kamo shiremasen ga. Demo, hayaku uchi ni kaeritakute mo
sasowaretara kotowarenai shi.**
Yeah, that might be true. But, even if you want to go home early, it is difficult to
say no if you are invited.

The following expressions can also be used in expressing 'disagreement' in an indirect manner.

さあ、どうでしょうかね。(F)
Saa doo deshoo ka ne.
Well, I don't know.

さあ、どうかな。(I)
Saa doo ka na.
Well, I don't know.

それはそうだと思いますが . . .。(F)
Sore wa soo da to omoimasu ga . . .
I think that's right, but . . .

確かにそれもそうなんですが . . .。
Tashika ni sore mo soo na n desu ga . . .
That's indeed true, but . . .

In the following examples, disagreement is more openly expressed.

私はそうは思いませんが . . .。(F)
Watashi wa soo wa omoimasen ga . . .
I don't think so but . . .

私はそうは思わないけど . . .。(I)
Watashi wa soo wa omowanai kedo . . .
I don't think so but . . .

それは違うんじゃないでしょうか。(F)
Sore wa chigau n ja nai deshoo ka.
I think it might not be so.

それは違うんじゃない？(I)
Sore wa chigau n ja nai?
Isn't that wrong?

私は反対です or 反対します。(F)
Watashi wa hantai desu or **hantai shimasu.**
I disagree with it.

私は反対。(I)
Watashi wa hantai.
I disagree.

85.2 Asking about agreement and disagreement

It is not very common in Japanese society to ask directly about agreement and disagreement.
Instead, the speaker may ask what the addressee thinks.

田中さんのアイデアの方がいいと思うんですが、どう思いますか。(F)
Tanaka-san no aidea no hoo ga ii to omou n desu ga, doo omoimasu ka.
I think Tanaka's idea is better, but what do you think?

こっちの方がいいと思うけど、どう思う？ (I)
Kotchi no hoo ga ii to omou kedo, doo omou?
I think this one is better, but what do you think?

田中さんにお願いしようと思うんですが、どうでしょうか。(F)
Tanaka-san ni o-negai shiyoo to omou n desu ga, doo deshoo ka.
I am thinking of asking Mr/Ms Tanaka to do it, but what do you think?

田中さんにお願いしようと思うんだけど、どうかな。(I)
Tanaka-san ni o-negai shiyoo to omou n da kedo, doo ka na.
I am thinking of asking Mr/Ms Tanaka to do it, but what do you think?

In some cases such as meetings, conferences, debating, etc., it is appropriate to directly ask about agreement and disagreement.

今の意見に賛成しますか、反対しますか。Or 賛成ですか、反対ですか。
Ima no iken ni sansee shimasu ka, hantai shimasu ka. Or Sansee desuka, hantai desu ka.
Do you agree or disagree with this opinion?

85.3 Expressing indifference

To express that you do not either agree or disagree, the following expressions can be used.

どちらでもけっこうです。(VF)
Dochira demo kekkoo desu.
Either one would be fine.

どちらでもいいですよ。(F)
Dochira demo ii desu yo.
Either one is fine.

どっちでもいいよ。(I)
Dotchi demo ii yo.
Either one is fine.

どっちでもかまわないよ。(I)
Dotchi demo kamawanai yo.
Whichever is fine.

どうでもいいよ！(I)
Doo demo ii yo!
I don't care!

86

Choosing and deciding

Asking about and expressing choice

The most common expression to ask about choice is X **to** Y **to, dochira (no hoo) ga ii desu ka** (formal) 'Which is better, A or B?' or X **to** Y **to, dotchi ga ii?** (informal). **Dotchi** is an informal form of **dochira** 'which.' The second **to** 'and' is often dropped in informal conversation, while it is kept in formal contexts.

> A: 冷たい飲み物と温かい飲み物とどちら（の方）がいいですか。
> **Tsumetai nomimono to atatakai nomimono to dochira (no hoo) ga ii desu ka.**
> Which would you prefer, a hot drink or a cold drink?

> B: 今日はちょっと寒いから、温かい飲み物の方がいいです。
> **Kyoo wa chotto samui kara, atatakai nominono no hoo ga ii desu.**
> Since it is a bit chilly today, I prefer a hot drink.

> B: 今日はちょっと寒いから、温かい飲み物をお願いします。
> **Kyoo wa chotto samui kara, atatakai nominono o onegai shimasu.**
> Since it is a bit chilly today, something warm please.

> A: コーヒーと紅茶（と）どっちがいい？ (I)
> **Koohii to koocha (to) dotchi ga ii?**
> Which do you want, coffee or tea?

> B: コーヒー、お願い。
> **Koohii, o-negai.**
> Coffee, please.

The other common expression **. . . ni shimasu** (formal), **. . . ni suru** (informal) can also be used in asking about or giving a choice.

> 赤と白（と）どちらにしますか。
> **Aka to shiro (to) dochira ni shimasu ka.**
> Would you like red (wine) or white?

> 赤と白とどちらになさいますか。(VF)
> **Aka to shiro to dochira ni nasaimasu ka.**
> Would you like red (wine) or white?

> ホットとアイスとどちらにしますか。/ なさいますか。
> **Hotto to aisu to dochira ni shimasu ka. / nasaimasu ka.**
> Would you like hot or iced (coffee)?

> 和食と中華とどっちにする？ (I)
> **Washoku to chuuka to dotchi ni suru?**
> Japanese or Chinese food, which would you like?

Asking about and expressing decisions

In expressing decisions, V(plain nonpast) **koto ni shimashita** and V(plain nonpast) **koto ni kettee shimashita (or kimemashita)** are commonly used. V **koto ni kettee shimashita** expresses a formal rather than a personal decision.

▶ **18.1**

来年日本に留学することにしました。
Rainen Nihon ni ryuugaku suru koto ni shimashita.
I have decided to study in Japan next year.

いろいろ考えて、日本の大学院に行くことに決めました。
Iroiro kangaete, Nihon no daigakuin ni iku koto ni kimemashita.
After much thought, I've decided to go to a graduate school in Japan.

就職するか、大学院に行くか, 迷った、んですが、大学院に行くことにしました。
Shuushoku suru ka, daigakuin ni iku ka, mayotta n desu ga, daigakuin ni iku koto ni shimashita.
I was not sure whether I should go to graduate school or get a job, but I have decided to go to graduate school.

会議の結果、来年から税率を５％引き上げることに決定した。
Kaigi no kekka, rainen kara zeeritsu o gopaasento hikiageru koto ni kettee shita.
At the conference, it was decided to increase the tax rate by 5 percent.

国会は消費税の引き上げを決定した。
Kokkai wa shoohizee no hikiage o kettee shita.
The National Diet decided to increase the sales tax.

議会は軍を引き上げることを決定した。
Gikai wa gun o hikiageru koto o kettee shita.
Congress/Parliament decided to withdraw the military.

Koto ni shimashita is similar to **koto ni narimashita** in that both indicate a decision. When one decides to study abroad, one can state this with either of the following sentences.

(a)   日本に留学することにしました。
      Nihon ni ryuugaku suru koto ni shimashita.
      I have decided to study in Japan.

(b)   日本に留学することになりました。
      Nihon ni ryuugaku suru koto ni narimashita.
      It has been arranged that I will study in Japan.

Sentence (a) indicates the speaker's volitional decision making, and hence indicates that whether he/she studies in Japan or not dependeds only on his personal decision. Sentence (b), on the other hand, implies that the decision was made by someone else or by circumstances, and seems to imply that the speaker did not have control over the decision. Even in cases where the speaker did make a personal decision, using **-ni naru** gives the impression that the speaker recognizes that other forces were at work, and hence sounds more indirect and humble.

▶ **21.6.3**

86.3 ## Changing one's mind

V **koto ni shimashita** or V(neg.) **koto ni shimashita** can be used to indicate that you have changed your mind. The expression is often preceded by a clause which explains the situation.

よく考えて、来年は留学しないことにしました。
Yoku kangaete, rainen wa ryuugaku shinai koto ni shimashita.
After thinking carefully, I have decided not to study abroad.

大学院に行こうと思ったんですが、やっぱり就職する事にしました。
Daigakuin ni ikoo to omotta n desu ga, yappari shuushoku suru koto ni shimashita.
I thought I would go to graduate school, but I have decided to get a job after all.

Other expressions such as **yamemashita** 'have given up' or **ki ga kawarimashita** 'I changed my mind' may also be often used to indicate that one has changed one's mind.

今年新しい車を買おうって思ったんですが、やっぱりやめました。
Kotoshi atarashii kuruma o kaoo tte omotta n desu ga, yappari yamemashita.
I thought of buying a new car, but I gave up the idea.

最初はスペインに行こうかなって思ったんですが、気が変わりました。
Saisho wa Supein ni ikoo ka na tte omotta n desu ga, ki ga kawarimashita.
Initially I thought I would go to Spain, but I changed my mind.

87

Shopping

87.1 ## Asking whether something is in the store

X wa arimasu ka or **X wa arimasen ka** is commonly used in asking whether an item is in the store. The difference between **X wa arimasu ka** or **X wa arimasen ka** is that the latter (the negative question) sounds less direct and therefore more polite.

▶ 5.3

87.2 ## Asking the price of something

The price of something can be asked by **X wa ikura desu ka** 'regarding X how much is it?'.

これはいくらですか。
Kore wa ikura desu ka.
How much is this?

このカードは一枚いくらですか。
Kono kaado wa ichimai ikura desu ka.
How much is one of these cards?

87.3 ## Purchasing something

When purchasing something, **X o kudasai** is commonly used. The particle **o** is often omitted in natural conversations.

これ（を）ください。	これ（を）おねがいします。
Kore (o) kudasai.	**Kore (o) o-negai shimasu.**
I will take this.	May I take this?

Kore o onegai shimasu sounds more polite and indirect than **kore o kudasai**.

87.4 ## Asking how long the store is open

To ask how long the store is open, use the expression **aite imasu** 'be open' or the copula **desu**.

日曜日は何時から何時まで開いていますか。
Nichiyoobi wa nanji kara nanji made aite imasu ka.
From what time to what time is (the store) open on Sunday?

日曜日は何時から何時までですか。
Nichiyoobi wa nanji kara nanji made desu ka.
From what time to what time is (the store) open on Sunday?

Complaining about a purchase

If you need to complain after making a purchase, explain the reason for the complaint by
. . . n desu + kedo/ga . . .

▶ 81

At a shop/department store

> すみません、この皿、昨日買って、家で開けてみたら、2枚、ふちのところがか
> けてたんですけど。
> **Sumimasen, kono sara kinoo katte ie de akete mitara, ni mai fuchi no tokoro ga
> kakete ta n desu kedo . . .**
> Excuse me, I bought these plates yesterday. When I opened the box at home, I found
> that two plates were chipped on the edge . . .

> このみかん、腐ってるんですけど . . .。換えてもらえますか。
> **Kono mikan, kusatte ru n desu kedo . . . Kaete moraemasu ka.**
> This orange is rotten . . . Can I exchange it?

> これ、きのう買ったんですけど、賞味期限すぎてるようなんですけど . . .。
> **Kore, kinoo katta n desu kedo, shoomi kigen sugite ru yoo na n desu kedo . . .**
> I bought this yesterday, but it looks like the expiration date/sell-by date has already past . . .

88

Ordering

There are two major formulaic expressions used in ordering food or other items such as books: **onegai shimasu** and **kudasai**. **O-negai shimasu** means 'I would like to make a request' and is used in making a request for the addressee's services or actions. The other expression is **kudasai**, which means 'please give me X.' This expression is normally used when making a request for specific items or objects rather than for the addressee's services.

88.1 Ordering food in a restaurant

In ordering food at a restaurant, either **o-negai shimasu** or **kudasai** can be used because the speaker is requesting the addressee's service or action (i.e. preparing and bringing food) as well as specific food. In response to the waiter or waitress taking the order, X **ni shimasu** 'I will have X' may also be used.

> てんぷらをお願いします。
> **Tenpura o o-negai shimasu.**
> Can I order tempura?

> てんぷらをください。
> **Tenpura o kudasai.**
> Tempura, please.

> 私はてんぷらにします。
> **Watashi wa tenpura ni shimasu.**
> I will have tempura.

In natural conversations the particle **o** tends to be omitted.

> てんぷら、お願いします。
> **Tenpura, o-negai shimasu.**
> May I order tempura?

> てんぷら、ください。
> **Tenpura, kudasai.**
> Tempura, please.

Counters can be added to indicate the number of orders. Again, the particle **o** tends to be omitted in natural conversation.

> てんぷら1つと、そば1つ、おねがいします。
> **Tenpura hitotsu to, soba hitotsu, o-negai shimasu.**
> May I have one order of tempura and one order of soba?

> てんぷら1つと、そば2つ、ください。
> **Tenpura hitotsu to, soba futatsu, kudasai.**
> Please give me one order of tempura and two orders of soba.

88.2 Ordering food for delivery over the telephone

When ordering food for delivery over the phone **o-negai shimasu** should be used instead of **kudasai**, because the speaker is making a request for delivery service rather than for specific items. To make the request less assertive and more polite, the sentence pattern V-**tai n desu ga/kedo** 'I would like to order' is often used. Again the particle **o** tends to be omitted. There are multiple ways of ordering food over the phone. For delivery, words such as **demae** and **haitatsu** are used. In addition to the use of the expression **o-negai shimasu**, the V-**te morau** structure is also often used in making a request.

> もしもし、すし3人前、お願いしたいんですが。
> **Moshi moshi, sushi sannin mae, o-negai shitai n desu ga.**
> Hello. I would like three orders of sushi.

> もしもし、出前、お願いしたいんですが。
> **Moshi moshi, demae, o-negai shitai n desu ga.**
> Hello. I would like to have a delivery.

> もしもし、ピザ、配達してもらえますか。
> **Moshi moshi, piza, haitatsu shite moraemasu ka.**
> Hello, can I have pizza delivered?

> もしもし、ピザ、配達してもらいたいんですが。
> **Moshi moshi, piza, haitatsu shite moraitai n desu ga.**
> Hello, I would like to have pizza delivered.

▶ **19.2.8; 63.1.3; 73.1**

88.3 Ordering other things

The phrase **o-negai shimasu**, as well as the V-**tai** structure and the combination of **onegai shimasu** and V-**tai**, can be used to order other things. To make the request sound less blunt, V-**tai** can be followed by the expression **n desu ga**.

> 本の注文、お願いします。
> **Hon no chuumon, o-negai shimasu.**
> An order for a book, please.

> 本の注文、お願いしたいんですが。
> **Hon no chuumon, o-negai shitai n desu ga.**
> I would like to put in an order for a book.

> 本を注文したいんですが。
> **Hon o chuumon shitai n desu ga.**
> I would like to order a book, please.

> 注文したい本があるんですが。
> **Chuumon shitai hon ga aru n desu ga.**
> There is a book that I would like to order.

89

Reservations

In making a reservation expressions such as **yoyaku o onegai shimasu** 'I request to make a reservation' or **yoyaku shitai n desu ga** 'I would like to reserve X' are used. Sentences often end with the connective particles **ga** or **kedo** 'but,' which makes the request sound milder.

89.1 Reserving a ticket for an event or transportation

In reserving a ticket for an event or transportation, **X no yoyaku o onegai shimasu** is commonly used. The particle **o** is often omitted in natural conversations.

> 成田まで、切符の予約、お願いします。
> **Narita made, kippu no yoyaku, onegai shimasu.**
> I would like to reserve a ticket for Narita, please.

> 成田まで、切符2枚、予約お願いします。
> **Narita made, kippu ni-mai, yoyaku onegai shimasu.**
> I would like to reserve two tickets for Narita, please.

> 10日のコンサートのチケット2枚、予約、お願いします。
> **Tooka no konsaato no chiketto nimai, yoyaku onegai shimasu.**
> I would like to reserve two tickets for the concert on the 10th.

> 10日のコンサートのチケット、2枚、予約したいんですが。
> **Tooka no konsaato no chiketto, nimai, yoyaku shitai n desu ga.**
> I would like to reserve two tickets for the concert on the 10th.

89.2 Reserving a place to stay

In reserving a place to stay (e.g. hotel) the combination of **onegai shimasu** 'I request' and V-**tai** 'want to do' is primarily used. Sentences ending with **n desu ga/kedo** make the request less assertive and more polite.

> 予約、お願いしたいんですが。
> **Yoyaku, onegai shitai n desu ga.**
> I would like to make a reservation.

> 6月10日から2泊で、予約、お願いしたいんですが。
> **Rokugatsu tooka kara nihaku de, yoyaku, onegai shitai n desu ga.**
> I would like to reserve a room from June 10th for two nights.

> 6月10日から2泊、部屋を予約したいんですが。
> **Rokugatsu tooka kara nihaku, heya o yoyaku shitai n desu ga.**
> I would like to reserve a room from June 10th for two nights.

６月１０日から２泊、泊まりたいんですが。
Rokugatsu tooka kara nihaku, tomaritai n desu ga.
I would like to stay from June 10th for two nights.

６月１０日から２泊、シングルの/ツインの部屋を予約したいんですけど。
Rokugatsu tooka kara nihaku, shinguru no/tsuin no heya o yoyaku shitai n desu kedo.
I would like to reserve a single/twin room from June 10th for two nights.

▶ **18.2.2; 63.1.2**

89.3 ## Canceling a reservation

When canceling a reservation, sentences often end with **ga** or **kedo** to make the request sound milder. Sentences with **ga** may sound slightly more formal than sentences with **kedo**. To make the request sound less assertive and more polite, the phrase **sumimasen (ga)** 'excuse me (but)' may precede the expressions of request.

すみませんが、キャンセル、お願いしたいんですが/けど。
Sumimasen ga, kyanseru, onegai shitai n desu ga/kedo.
Excuse me/I am sorry, but I would like to cancel my reservation.

すみませんが、予約、キャンセルしたいんですが/けど。
Sumimasen ga, yoyaku, kyanseru shitai n desu ga/kedo.
Excuse me/I am sorry, but I would like to cancel my reservation.

Sometimes the speaker, by using the **nakereba ikenai** 'have to' pattern, may avoid an embarrassing situation by indicating that he was obliged by circumstances to cancel the reservation. Sentences may end with **kedo** or the V-**te shimau** structure in order to express the speaker's feeling of regret.

すみません、予約、キャンセルしなければいけないんですけど。
Sumimasen, yoyaku, kyanseru shinakereba ikenai n desu kedo.
I am sorry, but I need to cancel my reservation.

すみません、予約、キャンセルしなければいけなくなってしまって。
Sumimasen, yoyaku, kyanseru shinakereba ikenaku natte shimatte.
I am sorry, but I need to cancel my reservation.

To give a reason for the cancellation, use V-**te** form or reason clauses such as **. . . node** 'because.'

ちょっと都合が悪くなって、予約、キャンセルしたいんですけど。
Chotto tsugoo ga waruku natte, yoyaku, kyanseru shitai n desu kedo.
I'd like to cancel my reservation, as something came/has come up.

急な仕事が入って、予約、キャンセルしなければいけないんですが。
Kyuuna shigoto ga haitte, yoyaku, kyanseru shinakereba ikenai n desu ga.
Some urgent business just came up, and I need to cancel my reservation.

急な用事が入ってしまったので、予約キャンセルしたいんですが。
Kyuu na yooji ga haitte shimatta node, yoyaku, kyanseru shitai n desu ga.
Some urgent matter came/has come up, so I would like to cancel my reservation.

ちょっと予定が変わってしまって、予約、キャンセルしたいんですが。
Chotto yotee ga kawatte shimatte, yoyaku, kyanseru shitai n desu ga.
My schedule has changed, so I would like to cancel my reservation.

Appendix I

Hiragana charts

A. Basic **hiragan**a symbols

あ a	い i	う u	え e	お o
か ka	き ki	く ku	け ke	こ ko
さ sa	し shi	す su	せ se	そ so
た ta	ち chi	つ tsu	て te	と to
な na	に ni	ぬ nu	ね ne	の no
は ha	ひ hi	ふ fu	へ he	ほ ho
ま ma	み mi	む mu	め me	も mo
や ya		ゆ yu		よ yo
ら ra	り ri	る ru	れ re	ろ ro
わ wa				を o
ん n				

B. **Hiragana** with small **ya**, **yu**, and **yo**

きゃ kya	きゅ kyu	きょ kyo
しゃ sha	しゅ shu	しょ sho
ちゃ cha	ちゅ chu	ちょ cho
にゃ nya	にゅ nyu	にょ nyo
ひゃ hya	ひゅ hyu	ひょ hyo
みゃ mya	みゅ myu	みょ myo

りゃ rya	りゅ ryu	りょ ryo

C. **Hiragana** with diacritical marks

が ga	ぎ gi	ぐ gu	げ ge	ご go
ざ za	じ ji	ず zu	ぜ ze	ぞ zo
だ da	ぢ ji	づ zu	で de	ど do
ば ba	び bi	ぶ bu	べ be	ぼ bo
ぱ pa	ぴ pi	ぷ pu	ぺ pe	ぽ po

ぎゃ gya	ぎゅ gyu	ぎょ gyo
じゃ ja	じゅ ju	じょ jo

びゃ bya	びゅ byu	びょ byo
ぴゃ pya	ぴゅ pyu	ぴょ pyo

Appendix II

Katakana charts

A. Basic **katakana** symbols

ア a	イ i	ウ u	エ e	オ o
カ ka	キ ki	ク ku	ケ ke	コ ko
サ sa	シ shi	ス su	セ se	ソ so
タ ta	チ chi	ツ tsu	テ te	ト to
ナ na	ニ ni	ヌ nu	ネ ne	ノ no
ハ ha	ヒ hi	フ fu	ヘ he	ホ ho
マ ma	ミ mi	ム mu	メ me	モ mo
ヤ ya		ユ yu		ヨ yo
ラ ra	リ ri	ル ru	レ re	ロ ro
ワ wa				ヲ o
ン n				

B. **Katakana** with small **ya**, **yu** and **yo**

キャ kya	キュ kyu	キョ kyo
シャ sha	シュ shu	ショ sho
チャ cha	チュ chu	チョ cho
ニャ nya	ニュ nyu	ニョ nyo
ヒャ hya	ヒュ hyu	ヒョ hyo
ミャ mya	ミュ myu	ミョ myo

リャ rya	リュ ryu	リョ ryo

C. **Katakana** with diacritical marks

ガ ga	ギ gi	グ gu	ゲ ge	ゴ go
ザ za	ジ ji	ズ zu	ゼ ze	ゾ zo
ダ da	ヂ ji	ヅ zu	デ de	ド do
バ ba	ビ bi	ブ bu	ベ be	ボ bo
パ pa	ピ pi	プ pu	ペ pe	ポ po

ギャ gya	ギュ gyu	ギョ gyo
ジャ ja	ジュ ju	ジョ jo

ビャ bya	ビュ byu	ビョ byo
ピャ pya	ピュ pyu	ピョ pyo

D. Additional **katakana** symbols and combinations

			シェ she	
			ジェ je	
			チェ che	
ツァ tsa	ツィ tsi		ツェ tse	ツォ tso
	ティ ti	テュ tyu		
	ディ di	デュ dyu		
ファ fa	フィ fi		フェ fe	フォ fo
ヴァ va	ヴィ vi	ヴ vu	ヴェ ve	ヴォ vo
	ウィ wi		ウェ we	ウォ wo

Appendix III

Verb basic conjugation table

	Dictionary form	Meaning		Nonpast		Past	
				Plain form	Polite form	Plain form	Polite form
irregular verbs	suru	to do	Affirmative	suru	shimasu	shita	shimashita
			Negative	shinai	[1]shimasen	shinakatta	[1]shimasen deshita
	kuru	to come	Affirmative	kuru	kimasu	kita	kimashita
			Negative	konai	[1]kimasen	konakatta	[1]kimasen deshita
-u verbs	nomu	to drink	Affirmative	nomu	nomimasu	nonda	nomimashita
			Negative	nomanai	[1]nomimasen	nomanakatta	[1]nomimasen deshita
	kau	to buy	Affirmative	kau	kaimasu	katta	kaimashita
			Negative	kawanai	[1]kaimasen	kawanakatta	[1]kaimasen deshita
	kaeru	to return	Affirmative	kaeru	kaerimasu	kaetta	kaerimashita
			Negative	kaeranai	[1]kaerimasen	kaeranakatta	[1]kaerimasen deshita
	iku	to go	Affirmative	iku	ikimasu	itta	ikimashita
			Negative	ikanai	[1]ikimasen	ikanakatta	[1]ikimasen deshita
-ru verbs	taberu	to eat	Affirmative	taberu	tabemasu	tabeta	tabemashita
			Negative	tabenai	[1]tabemasen	tabenakatta	[1]tabemasen deshita

[1] For the polite negative form in both the nonpast and past tenses, an alternative form derived by attaching **desu** to the plain negative form is also commonly used; e.g., **shinai desu** (nonpast polite negative form of **suru**) and **shinakatta desu** (past tense polite negative form **suru**).

Appendix IV

Copula and adjective basic conjugation table

	Dictionary form	Meaning		Nonpast		Past	
				Plain form	Polite form	Plain form	Polite form
copula	da	to be	Affirmative	da	desu	datta	deshita
			Negative	ja nai	[1]ja arimasen	ja nakatta	[1]ja arimasen deshita
	de aru	to be	Affirmative	de aru	de arimasu	de atta	de arimashita
			Negative	de nai	[1]de arimasen	de nakatta	[1]de arimasen deshita
i-adjectives	takai	high	Affirmative	takai	takaidesu	takakatta	takakattadesu
			Negative	takakunai	[1]takaku arimasen	takakunakatta	[1]takaku arimasen deshita
	atsui	hot	Affirmative	atsui	atsuidesu	atsukatta	atsukattadesu
			Negative	atsukunai	[1]atsuku arimasen	atsukunakatta	[1]atsuku arimasen deshita
	ii	good	Affirmative	ii	ii desu	yokatta	yokatta desu
			Negative	yokunai	[1]yoku arimasen	yokunakatta	[1]yoku arimasen deshita
na-adjectives	shizuka	quiet	Affirmative	shizuka da	shizuka desu	shizuka datta	shizuka deshita
			Negative	shizuka ja nai	[1]shizuka ja arimasen	shizuka ja nakatta	[1]shizuka ja arimasen deshita
	kiree	pretty	Affirmative	kiree da	kiree desu	kiree datta	kiree deshita
			Negative	kiree ja nai	[1]kiree ja arimasen	kiree ja nakatta	[1]kiree ja arimasen deshita

[1] For the polite negative form in both the nonpast and past tenses, an alternative form derived by attaching **desu** to the plain negative form is also commonly used; e.g., **ja nai desu** (nonpast tense polite negative form of **da**) and **ja nakatta desu** (past tense polite negative form **da**).

Bibliography

Davies, R. J. and Ikeno, O. (2002) *The Japanese Mind*, Boston: Tuttle.

Horiguchi, S. (1997) *Nihongo kyoiku to kaiwa bunseki* (Japanese language teaching and conversation analysis,) Tokyo: Kuroshio.

Hudson, M. E. (1994) *English Grammar for Students of Japanese*, Ann Arbor: Olivia and Hill Press.

Kuno, S. (1973) *The Structure of the Japanese Language*, Cambridge, Mass: MIT Press.

Makino, S. and Tsutsui, M. (1986) *A Dictionary of Basic Japanese Grammar*, Tokyo: The Japan Times.

Makino, S. and Tsutsui, M. (1995) *A Dictionary of Intermediate Japanese Grammar*, Tokyo: The Japan Times.

Makino, S. and Tsutsui, M. (2008) *A Dictionary of Advanced Japanese Grammar*, Tokyo: The Japan Times.

Martin, S. (1975) *A Reference Grammar of Japanese*, New Haven and London: Yale University Press.

Maynard, S. K. (2009) *An Introduction to Japanese Grammar and Communication Strategies* (2nd ed.), Tokyo: The Japan Times.

McGloin, N. H. (1989) *A Student's Guide to Japanese Grammar*, Tokyo: Taishukan.

Shibatani, M. (1990) *The Languages of Japan*, Cambridge: Cambridge University Press.

Tsujimura, N. (2007) *An Introduction to Japanese Linguistics*, Malden, MA/Oxford, UK: Blackwell Publishing.

Index

INDEX

INDEX